Journalism Ethics at th

This book provides journalism students with an easy-to-read yet theoretically rich guide to the dialectics, contradictions, problems, and promises encapsulated in the term 'journalism ethics'.

Offering an overview of a series of crises that have shaken global journalism to its foundations in the last decade, including the coronavirus pandemic, the Black Lives Matter movement, and the 2020 US presidential election, the book explores the structural and ethical problems that shape the journalism industry today. The authors discuss the three principle existential crises that continue to plague the news industry: a failing business model, technological disruption, and growing public mistrust of journalism. Other topics covered include social media ethics, privacy concerns, chequebook journalism, as well as a new analysis of journalism theory that critiques the well-worn tropes of objectivity, the Fourth Estate, freedom of the press, and the marketplace of ideas to develop a sophisticated materialist reimagining of journalism ethics.

This is a key text for students of journalism, mass communication, and media ethics, as well as for academics, researchers, and communications professionals interested in contemporary journalism ethics.

Roger Patching has spent more than half a century as a journalist and a journalism educator. He worked for nearly 20 years in daily journalism for a newspaper, radio station, and TV station in Adelaide, South Australia, before moving to Sydney to work for the international media wire service Australian Associated Press, followed by a decade with the national broadcaster ABC in Brisbane. Then followed more than 30 years at various Australian universities, teaching broadcast journalism, sports reporting, and ethics. He is a life member of the national journalism educators' association JERAA. Roger has co-authored nine journalism texts. This is his fourth collaboration with Dr Hirst.

Martin Hirst is a founding director of the Centre for Journalism, Media and Democracy at AUT University in Auckland, NZ, and co-editor of the journal *Political Economy of Communication*, published by the International Association for Media and Communication Research. Martin is the author of *News 2.0* (Allen & Unwin 2011) and *Navigating Social Journalism* (Routledge 2018). He has collaborated with other writers on *From Broadcast to Narrowcast: Communication and New Media* (Oxford 2007), *Scooped: The Politics and Power of Journalism in Aotearoa New Zealand* (AUT Press 2012), and *So You Want to Be a Journalist* (Cambridge 2012). Martin spent 20 years in journalism and a similar number of years in academia. He now writes and paints from his studio in Melbourne.

Journalism Ethics at the Crossroads

Democracy, Fake News, and the News Crisis

Roger Patching and Martin Hirst

Routledge
Taylor & Francis Group

LONDON AND NEW YORK

First published 2022
by Routledge
2 Park Square, Milton Park, Abingdon, Oxon OX14 4RN

and by Routledge
605 Third Avenue, New York, NY 10158

Routledge is an imprint of the Taylor & Francis Group, an informa business

British Library Cataloguing-in-Publication Data
A catalogue record for this book is available from the British Library

Library of Congress Cataloging-in-Publication Data
Names: Patching, Roger, 1944- author. | Hirst, Martin, author.
Title: Journalism ethics at the crossroads : democracy, fake news, and the
news crisis / Roger Patching, Martin Hirst.
Description: London ; New York : Routledge, 2021. | Includes
bibliographical references and index.
Identifiers: LCCN 2021007139 | ISBN 9780367197278 (hardback) |
ISBN 9780367197285 (paperback) | ISBN 9780429242892 (ebook)
Subjects: LCSH: Journalistic ethics. | Journalism--Objectivity. | Fake
news. | Journalism--History--21st century.
Classification: LCC PN4756 .P38 2021 | DDC 174/.907--dc23
LC record available at https://lccn.loc.gov/2021007139

ISBN: 978-0-367-19727-8 (hbk)
ISBN: 978-0-367-19728-5 (pbk)
ISBN: 978-0-429-24289-2 (ebk)

DOI: 10.4324/9780429242892

Typeset in Bembo
by Taylor & Francis Books

Contents

Preface: Not the book we thought we were writing

Melbourne/Gold Coast 20 January 2021

This is not the book we intended to write. At the beginning of 2020 we were half-way through the writing process when the world was turned upside down. We all started talking about 'the 'rona' and a new medical term entered our conversations: COVID-19. Life would never be the same again. The issues we had been writing about—the changes in the state of mainstream media world-wide and the impact that was having on journalistic ethics—expanded exponentially. The major crises facing journalism in 2019—falling trust in the media, the failing economics of the industry, the effects of digital technologies, and the fight against fake news—were swamped by the tsunami of the cor-onavirus pandemic. Then, in October 2020, President Donald Trump announced he too was infected with SARS-CoV-2 as the coronavirus is offi-cially known (Wu et al. 2020). This truly was the 'October Surprise' of the 2020 US presidential election race that, once again, upended any certainties and conventions surrounding the campaign. The campaign, the 3 November election, and the aftermath kept the entire world on the edge of its seat: Trump refused to concede and made outrageous false claims about the election being 'stolen' from him. The media environment had become so toxic by this time that tens of millions of Americans believed Trump's lies. America was plunged into political turmoil.

Earlier in 2020, as the number of COVID-19 cases raced into the millions across the globe and the death toll climbed into the hundreds of thousands, another event that would shake the news media to its foundations took place in the United States. A policeman killed an unarmed black man, George Floyd, by crushing his neck with his knee for more than nine minutes. The death may have passed un-noticed globally had it not been for the ubiquitous 'passer-by' recording the tragic event on a mobile phone. Mr Floyd's death saw the rebirth of the 'Black Lives Matter' movement in the US, and—virus-like, it too quickly spread worldwide. In the ensuing months of protests that continued across America—and in some other Western countries—journalists too became targets of police violence. A disturbing trend seemingly encouraged and applauded by President Trump (Spocchia 2020).

No return to the 'old normal'

The surprises kept coming in 2021. The year opened with a mob of angry and confused Trump supporters storming into the Capitol building in Washington DC in the last desperate act of trying to overturn the results of the 3 November ballot. One woman was killed near the Congressional chamber when security guards opened fire. Outside in Freedom Plaza, Trump supporters took the former President's constant cries of 'fake media' to their logical conclusion and smashed thousands of dollars of television equipment belonging to Associated Press.

Earlier that morning Trump appeared at a 'Stop the Steal' rally and incited the crowd to march through Washington streets. Many people—finally including a few of his own supporters—condemned Trump's inflammatory and senseless goading of the crowd. After the MAGA true believers, Proud Boy fascists, and assorted conspiracy theorists stormed into the Capitol building, Trump refused to condemn them. Instead, he issued an 'I love you' video and

Figure 0.1 Capital Riots—Ellie Hall

several tweets applauding the actions of the deluded 'patriots'. In response, Twitter suspended the President's personal account for 12 hours and threatened to make the ban permanent unless he deleted the inflammatory tweets. Inevitably, Trump refused and was kicked off Twitter and most other social media platforms.

Despite the turmoil of the previous year, Joe Biden was sworn in as the 46th President of the United States of America on 20 January 2021, as per the constitutional schedule but with Washington DC under an unprecedented military lockdown. We had to stop writing at this point as Routledge was patiently waiting for us to deliver the manuscript. We presume that Donald J. Trump has not 'miraculously' disappeared as he once said the coronavirus would. What we can say, with some certainty, is that the crisis we mention in the title of this book has not gone away and that the opportunity it presents for us to reimagine, re-invent, and re-purpose journalism is still before us.

It became obvious to us—as we are sure it has to you too—that the world has significantly changed over the course of 2020. In some ways we are reminded of the advice we gave to our journalism students when Princess Diana died on 31 August 1997, and when commercial jetliners ploughed into the World Trade Center towers on 11 September 2001: sometimes events are life-changing, and they will shape the consciousness of a generation. 2020 is one of those years. Any one of the key events would mark it as such, but to have a triple-header of such magnitude ensure it will be remembered and talked about for years to come.

Journalism ethics at the crossroads

We finally settled on a title for this book towards the end of 2020 and after we had assessed the impact of each of the contingent crises of that year. We always intended to talk about digital disruption, the collapsing business model, and the trust deficit but adding the coronavirus, Donald Trump, and Black Lives Matter to the equation convinced us that their impact on journalism would also be game-changing. Why? Because the more we examined the news media's responses to COVID, to Trump, and to BLM, the more we realised that the old paradigm—the 'old normal'—of journalistic practice was no longer fit for purpose. Whichever way we tried to slice and dice the evidence, the same answer was staring back at us from the page: at crucial moments the news media failed to live up to its own purported ideals to inform the public and serve the public interest. Not every day, not on every story, and certainly not every journalist. But we could not ignore the fact that the media in general was struggling to come to terms with the scale of the crisis, the depth of public distrust, suspicion and anger, and the mendacity of the political elite. Further, we argue that the decline in public trust in journalism is intrinsically linked to the economic crisis—the issue of how journalism is funded. We make no apology for this focus as we see it as a crucial element of journalism ethics. Reporters and editors are always trumpeting the mantra 'Follow the money!' when they're on the trail of a juicy exclusive about corruption and underhanded dealing. Well, we believe that following the money trail in the news industry will lead to useful explanations for the crisis in trust and the decline in ethical accountability that has contributed to it. This thesis is discussed at length in Chapters 5 and 14 using a materialist, political economy perspective.

This is the broad background to our crossroads metaphor. In folklore and in Greek mythology, a crossroads is associated with making a difficult choice between two paths 'between worlds', one leading to salvation, the other to ruin (Mibba 2012). As a profession—if that is what it is—journalism is facing a difficult choice at a crossroads where one path is to continue as if it is 'business as usual', and where the other path takes a turn into the unknown. We are sure you won't be surprised to learn that our inclination is to take the more difficult route into a future where there is no 'business as usual'. The old certainties, the old routines, and the old modes of thinking about journalism have been found wanting. The definition of insanity has always been repeating the same actions while expecting a different outcome. It is time for change. In the wake of the life-changing events outlined here, and because of their impact on both news institutions and on journalists, we decided to restructure the book, effectively upending our original plan. The book now begins with the crisis and ends, hopefully, with some useful insights and suggestions about saving journalism's reputation as an important element of democratic public life.

Throughout this book we talk often of 'crisis and opportunity' because, first, we don't want to come across as being completely negative and, second, every cloud has a silver lining. A crisis is also an opportunity. In this case, the choice of future paths does present journalism with an opportunity to reflect on the past, come to terms with mistakes and chart a new course for the future.

A personal note

We know some people will be curious about this, but our responsibility for the contents of this book are equally shared. In case it's important: Roger drafted Chapters 1 and 2 and Chapters 7–11 in the second section, while Martin drafted Chapters 4–6 and the final theoretical section (Chapters 12–17). We both contributed substantially to the Preface, the Introduction and Chapter 3. In previous editions we have paid various media organisations hundreds of pounds sterling for permission to reproduce some of their ethically suspect front pages to illustrate our discussions. We have taken the conscious decision this time not to 'reward' those groups by paying the considerable amounts they charge for reproduction rights. Most of the front pages mentioned later and in the bibliography can be accessed through a simple online search.

Acknowledgements

We continue to value and appreciate the support and encouragement of our wives, Jenny Patching and Tiffany White, and in Roger's case his children, during the longer-than-usual writing stage of this book.

In the past we have been able to meet in person irregularly either in Melbourne or on the Gold Coast to discuss progress on the text. Like everything else in 2020 the pandemic meant Martin was in lockdown in Melbourne for months and we were limited to emails and the odd Zoom meeting. Our friendship survived and our collaboration was fruitful.

This book would not have been possible without the help and support—and ready acceptance of our mid-stream change in focus—of the staff at Routledge in London. A special thanks to the long-suffering Priscille Biehlmann for her unwavering support and assistance. Our copy editor, Sandra Stafford, was a pleasure to work with and corrected our numerous errors. Production editor Fiona Hudson Gabuya steered the book through the final hurdles and to the finish line. Also thanks to Margaret Farrelly who originally approached us to rework our previous efforts and steered our proposal through the editorial machinery.

Finally, Roger wants you to know that if you find the new theory chapters heavy going, direct your complaints to Martin.

Roger Patching, Gold Coast
Martin Hirst, Melbourne
May 2021

List of abbreviations

ABC	Australian Broadcasting Corporation (Australia's national broadcaster)
AEJMC	Association for Education in Journalism and Mass Communication
AFP	Australian Federal Police
AI	Artificial intelligence
ALRC	Australian Law Reform Commission
AP	Associated Press (international news service)
APC	Australian Press Council
ASIO	Australian Security Intelligence Organisation
ASJMC	Association of Schools of Journalism and Mass Communication
BBC	British Broadcasting Corporation. British national broadcaster
BLM	Black Lives Matter
CBC	Canadian Broadcasting Corporation
CBS	Columbia Broadcasting System (US TV network)
CNN	American cable news network
CEO	Chief Executive Officer
CIA	Central Intelligence Agency (America's spy agency)
CPJ	Committee to Protect Journalists
IPSO	Independent Press Standards Organisation
ICIJ	International Consortium of Investigative Journalists
IFEX	International Freedom of Expression Exchange (formerly); now global network of NGOs
IFJ	International Federation of Journalists
IWMF	International Women's Media Foundation
JMC	Journalism and Mass Communication (students)
MBA	Master of Business Administration
MEAA	Media Entertainment and Arts Alliance (the journalists' union in Australia)
MSM	Mainstream media
MSNBC	American news network
NGO	Non-government organisation

NORCAL-SPJ	Northern California chapter of Society of Professional Journalists
NPR	National public radio (US public radio network)
NUJ	National Union of Journalists (UK)
NRA	National Rifle Association (US)
NYT	The New York Times
OANN	One America News Network (right-wing news network)
PIJI	Public Interest Journalism Initiative (Australia)
PPE	Personal Protective Equipment
PTSD	Post-Traumatic Stress Disorder
RSF	Reporters Without Borders
SBS	Special Broadcasting Service (Australia's multicultural national broadcaster)
SMH	The Sydney Morning Herald
SPJ	Society of Professional Journalists (US journalists' association)
UAV	Unmanned aerial vehicles (drones)
UNESCO	United National Educational, Scientific and Cultural Organisation
WHO	World Health Organization
WMD	Weapons of Mass Destruction
WNIP	What's new in publishing

Introduction

Ethics, trust, and the crisis of journalism

The importance of ethics

Ethics in journalism is important. It always has been. Without a commitment to ethical practice journalism is not reliable, and it cannot be trusted. Perhaps today, the struggle to define and practise ethical journalism is harder than it has ever been. In some ways, the idea that doing journalism ethically is a struggle is intimately linked to the perception that doing journalism has never been more dangerous than it is today. These two themes are brought together throughout this book as symptoms of the critical condition in which both journalism and the news industry are currently languishing.

Everything about journalism involves ethical considerations. Media workers decide what is news. Reporters decide what angle(s) they will chase on a particular story; who they will interview; what questions they will ask; what answers they will include in their story (and what they will leave out); how they will frame the story and how it will be presented. The answers to all these questions are subjective and will reflect the ideological perspectives of the various people in the news production process, and therefore contain the potential for bias. That's why ethics is important.

The underlying theme of the text as a whole is that only by addressing head on the issues outlined and understanding both the causes, and where answers might emerge from, can current and future journalists hope to be part of the solution, rather than part of the problem. Our starting point is 'fake news' because it is topical (we heard about it almost daily from the ex-leader of the Western world), and because it provides a window into the undersea chaos we're about to enter.

Fake news is a symptom, not the disease

Fake news is an important topic that gathers up a number of threads relating to journalism ethics, but in our view, it is a symptom, not the disease itself. If fake news is a symptom, what is the underlying pathology, and what has brought on the deterioration in the patient? The illness that debilitates the news ecosystem has been caused by the collapse of the old certainties and a withering away of

DOI: 10.4324/9780429242892-1

the fundamental foundations that propped up journalism for most of the past 200 years. Age, a lack of exercise, and mental complacency are the disease vectors attacking the vital organs of the news industry. In this book we explore the sickness in the news industry through first, a diagnosis, then suggesting a treatment plan, and finally offering a prognosis about the health of the industry if it is able to recover. Our diagnosis is that the news industry—and therefore journalism, as well—is facing an unprecedented series of interlocking crises that have weakened its immune system and now threaten its very existence. Our treatment plan involves rethinking and re-emphasising the importance of ethical thinking and ethical practice across all aspects of journalism, both inside and outside the newsroom. Our prognosis is that without such radical intervention, journalism will soon be on life support, unable to function on its own. If this comes to pass, the news industry is in danger of a slow and painful death as more and more citizen-consumers withdraw their financial support for its products. The importance of economics—what we call the political economy of news—is explored in Chapters 4 and 14.

The political economy of ethics

Ethics is often considered to be a branch of philosophy and therefore somehow above the realm of the economy, but that is too simplistic. Philosophy does not exist in a vacuum. It has deep roots in social structures and in historical circumstances too. Journalism is the same. While it is considered to be an intellectual pursuit and socially regarded as a profession, the practice of journalism has, for at least 300 years, been intrinsically tied to the economy. News organisations have historically made money by accepting advertising, or more theoretically correct, packaging audiences and selling them to companies who want to advertise (Fuchs 2009).

This is why we argue that ethical considerations in journalism are also tied—for better, or worse—to the economic form that news takes. Current research suggests that, while some news outlets are experiencing a growth in subscriptions, overall the industry has been in steady decline—in terms of both circulation and advertising revenues—for nearly a decade (Barthel 2017). The consequences of doing nothing—just hoping that a 'business as usual' approach will be sufficient—is like ignoring the early signs of a potentially fatal illness and thinking the patient will recover on their own.

Does journalism have a future?

We are 'doctors of journalism', not magicians, so we cannot pretend that we have the answers at our fingertips when it comes to making a prognosis about the future of journalism and the news industry. We think our examination of the patient might provide some clues, but we are not miracle workers and the scale of the problem—particularly the economic malaise—may not respond even if we apply all of the available treatments. Having said that, our medical knowledge is such that we know injecting 'antibodies' into a diseased patient—in this case a new generation of journalists armed with the right kind of knowledge—may well help the body's natural defences fight off the infection. We also have some thoughts to offer about how the media might go about rebuilding trust in traditional journalism. We won't give away too much here—read the final chapter.

Is an ethical overhaul the cure?

We have been thinking about this question for a long time—most of the last 30 years—and the best we can say is 'Yes'. We have taken the view that strong, ethical journalism, with a commitment to the public interest as its starting point, is the lifeblood of any system of government that makes the claim to being democratic. Without the critical information that journalism provides, a citizen of any nation—or indeed the global citizen—has little or no means of knowing how and why they are being governed the way they are from day to day. For nearly 200 years journalists have played the much heralded, but little understood, role of the 'Fourth Estate'. In this role, as the eyes and ears of citizens, journalists are said to hold those in power—elected officials and the 'captains' of industry—to standards of public accountability. When journalistic standards slip, the reporter's ability to carry out their Fourth Estate mission is diminished. How can journalists who are willing to cut ethical corners to chase down a story be expected to hold public officials to account 'without fear or favour'? We hope to answer this along with other practical and philosophical questions of ethical practice throughout the text.

How to use this book

You will notice the reference to 'fault lines' in varying contexts here and in other chapters. This is our way of describing the various contradictory approaches to ethical issues as they arise during everyday activities in newsrooms around the world. Fault lines also represent the clash of dynamic social forces that pressurise journalistic activity and 'push' reporters towards certain ways of thinking. Fault lines are discussed at length in the chapters on dialectical thinking and philosophy (Chapters 12–14). In a departure from our past volumes on the same topic, we deliberately choose to articulate the headline-grabbing issues about the challenges facing the media first, followed by our 'cases' approach, where we take stories, mostly from 'yesterday's headlines', to illustrate the practical problems that emerge in newsrooms the world over. This approach, we believe, makes the book readable—it deals with the exciting material first—and it is also logical. If we want to solve the problems, we need a good understanding of what they are and how they have become so urgent. By placing the more theoretical material in the final third of the book we can build on the empirical knowledge and the case studies explored in the first two sections. We think this also mirrors our belief that the path to becoming a better journalist is a process of lifelong learning. This is how we all gain new knowledge and insights, relying on a combination of theory and practice, and the application of one to the other. In the final section—the theoretical area—you are invited to ponder questions raised by the issues covered. We hope this will help you formulate your own deeper thinking about journalism, ethics and democracy.

The first section (Chapters 1–6) is an exploration of the ethical implications of the news 'crisis'—digital disruption, the economic collapse, falling trust and the rise of fake news—and new chapters on the impact of the coronavirus on journalism and another on the media's response to the latest 'Black Lives Matter' protests. This section details where we think journalists did a good job and where the news media failed. It offers evidence for our 'crossroads' thesis.

The second section (Chapters 7–11) is where we discuss contemporary responses to long-standing ethical dilemmas such as journalists using social media, privacy, dubious methods, sources and whistleblowers, and the new dangers facing reporters working in foreign 'hot spots' that are now being replicated closer to home. There is no doubt that digital disruption and the financial woes of the news industry are revealing new fault lines right across the spectrum of these more 'traditional' areas of ethical concern. These new dilemmas need to be addressed as we choose a new path to leave our crossroads.

The final section (Chapters 12–17) sets out our responses to the problem of restoring trust in a news ecosystem in the midst of unstoppable digital disruption and in an industry beset with economic and ethical crises. Here is where we make the arguments in favour of resisting the temptation to return to business as usual. In this concluding section we explain why our ethical framework relies heavily on the philosophical and historical foundations of ethical decision-making, drawing strongly on the work of the late American journalistic ethicist, John Merrill. We've included a discussion of some key issues, such as the marketplace of ideas, objectivity, the Fourth Estate and freedom of the press, and the closing chapter presents our argument for a reimagining of ethical thinking in a more collective fashion as a way to begin rebuilding public trust in the institution of journalism.

The purpose of this book is to position the arguments about the various issues and the philosophical traditions in which ethics are usually discussed within an overall theoretical framework that we hope will help you both as a student and as a working journalist. It will hopefully give you the analytical skills and sound arguments for making ethical decisions.

There's one thing you can be sure about with journalism ethics: there will always be something to talk about. Be prepared.

How do you make an ethical decision?

There is no set of ten commandments for journalists; codes of ethics can never be more than a guide to action because circumstances will always vary. The best approach is to adopt a reasoning and decision-making process that can help under most circumstances. There are no simple solutions to ethical dilemmas in journalism. Editors, reporters, sub-editors and producers need to be aware at all times of both the practical and philosophical issues. We believe a familiarity with both approaches is necessary in preparing for the privilege and responsibility that comes with ethical editorial decision-making. You should have developed an ethical framework for how you will conduct yourself as a journalist before you do too many journalism assignments as part of your degree, and before you enter the media workforce. You certainly will have developed at least a draft version of your 'worldview'—your way of understanding the world—long before you reach university. Hopefully, further education will help you deepen and refine your understanding.

Once you are in the media you will need to make ethical decisions quickly. Realise, though, that you are not what we call an 'ethical orphan'. There are other reporters in the newsroom you can consult. The senior staff at your media organisation should be made aware as early as possible of any ethical dilemma you are facing. They may take the decision out of your hands. Many of the examples and case studies in following chapters do not show some reporters in the best light, and we need to balance that by saying that the vast majority of journalists make simple, and sometimes complex, ethical decisions on a daily basis that go unnoticed because they don't create a ripple of attention. As you will see time and time again, there are very few black and white answers to ethical dilemmas. If there were, they wouldn't be dilemmas. There are mostly varying shades of grey. In each instance you needed to weigh up the pros and cons—using the methods we're about to discuss—and reach a decision on the information before you, much as you will have to do once you join the media workforce.

The big questions: The who, what, where, when, why, and how of an ethical decision

So how do you go about making an ethical decision, given there are often so many conflicting ideas or positions? If you're discussing an ethical dilemma in a university assignment or tutorial there are a number of aspects to consider—including the following.

- What factors will have the most bearing on the decision—personal, social, economic, legal, or political? What affects are they likely to have on your decision—major or minor? Which is the most important if several are involved? How do you balance conflicting factors?
- Who are the various parties involved? Do you have any obligation to any of them (for example, respecting their confidence, or loyalty to a source)? What about the other obligations—to the public, your employer, your workmates or your colleagues in the profession?
- What are the relative merits of the various people involved?
- Will justice be served for all by your action?

- Will you be helping someone who deserves assistance?
- Is the action prompted by a wrong you have committed and need to make amends for?
- What outcome would satisfy each of the parties involved? How will your chosen course of action affect each of them? (And that includes your boss.)
- What are the 'power dynamics' of the situation? Who might have power over you, or others involved in the issue, and what's your relationship with them? This could be colleagues, your employer, the sources you're using, or even someone close to you, like a partner, family member, or close friend.
- What courses of action are open to you? What are the best and worst possible outcomes for the various scenarios?
- Will anyone be harmed by your preferred choice of action? By how much? Is the 'good' brought about by your action outweighed by the potential harm?
- How can you minimise unnecessary harm to all concerned?
- Are you just using a person as a means to an end without considering the effect your action will have on them?
- Would honouring any ideal or value you hold invalidate your chosen course of action?
- Are there any rules or principles—like Codes of Ethics or Charters of Editorial Independence—that would automatically invalidate your proposed course of action?
- Which of the alternative courses of action would generate the greatest benefit or the least harm for the greatest number?
- Are any of the alternative courses of action based on your or your organisation's best interests?
- And after reviewing all that, what would you do?

We believe this guide for ethical decision-making was first developed by the journalism staff at the University of Oregon in the United States and has been adapted by many others, including by the authors in ethics subjects they have taught over the years. These notes on ethical decision-making are unashamedly adapted from a previous edition where there's also a more detailed approach to decision-making designed by Martin (Patching and Hirst 2014, 221–31).

Questions for discussion

1   How much news do you consume on a daily or weekly basis?
2   Where do you source your news nowadays?
3   Do newspapers have a future? What about radio or free-to-air television?
4   We've made much of the 'trust deficit' in mainstream media nowadays, how much trust do you place, for instance, is your local tabloid newspaper?

5 What changes have you noticed in your local newspaper in recent years? Can they all be put down to financial woes?
6 How do you discern truth from 'fake news'? Discuss your method.
7 What role does ethics play in modern mainstream media?
8 What are the arguments for (and against?) a code of ethics for Google, Facebook, and Twitter?
9 What can be done about the crisis of trust?

1 News in crisis

Responding to the pandemic

Change comes at you quickly

Most of us were forced to change our way of life significantly in 2020 as the coronavirus (SARS-CoV-2) swept across the globe. The pandemic upended our daily routines, and it is likely to be some time before any kind of 'new normal' is achieved. We are certain it will be nothing like the 'old normal'; it will involve living with future pandemics (WHO 2020). The SARS-CoV-2 virus is likely to be the biggest story in the world so far this century, and it will dominate the news for some time. Few stories, aside from an international financial crisis or a world war, can affect as many people as a virulent global pandemic. Such was the impact of COVID-19 that by the end of September 2020, infections had passed 33 million and deaths totalled more than a million (Tonkin, Briggs, and Hepburn 2020). With a surge in the numbers of cases and deaths in Europe, India and United States, that by July 2021 cases globally had topped 40 million and deaths 4 million, according to the World Health Organization. Responses to the pandemic varied from country to country as researchers toiled to find a vaccine and governments grappled with the massive health and economic impacts. Countries experienced huge pressure on their health sector and introduced economic shutdowns to varying degrees and for varying periods. Millions of people were temporarily or permanently out of work.

For the mass media, covering COVID-19 presented its own set of ethical challenges—many of which we discuss in general in later chapters—but which were there during the darkest days of the pandemic. On the day in mid-December 2020 that the US Electoral College confirmed that Democrat candidate Joe Biden had won the presidential election 306 votes to President Trump's 232, America passed a grim milestone—more than 300,000 deaths from the coronavirus (Marsh 2020). The daily death rate was regularly exceeding 3,000—more than the US lost on D-Day in the Second World War or the terrorist attacks of 9/11 (Hollingsworth and Renault 2020). As Christmas approached, *The Washington Post* reported someone in the US was dying from COVID-19 every 33 seconds—five in the time it took to listen to Bing Crosby's 'White Christmas' (Bump 2020b). A report in late December 2020 noted that more than 500 journalists and media workers in more than 57

DOI: 10.4324/9780429242892-2

countries had died from COVID-19, about ten times the numbers killed worldwide while doing their job or in retribution for that work (Hare 2020).

One of those issues involved editors and reporters deciding when and how to hold governments to account for their tardy or botched responses to the developing crisis. Just as the media is there to hold the powerful—in this case mostly governments and their leaders—to account for their decisions, the media also needs to be accountable for its coverage. While they were quick to call those in power to account, journalists were not so quick to accept responsibility for some of their dubious and dangerous coverage. The former editor of *The Guardian*, Alan Rusbridger, summed up the seriousness of the media's role in the early months of the pandemic:

> The penny seems to be dropping in some quarters that journalism can be a matter of life and death. How many of our friends and loved ones die in this pandemic is to a great extent reliant on what people believe to be the truth about its seriousness.
>
> (Rusbridger 2020b)

The 'truth about its seriousness' should have come from governments through the media, but in too many cases both governments and media chose to politicise the virus rather than work together to overcome it. We will discuss the 'myth of objectivity' later but put bluntly it is obvious in times like these that journalists are not simple observers of what's happening. They are active 'players' in the unfolding tragedy—they decide what is news, how it will be covered and what issues will be given prominence (Jericho 2019). Journalists bear a huge responsibility to get it right. While the *exceptional*, the *novel* or the *horrific* have been criteria for deciding what constitutes news for decades (Masterton and Patching 1986, 12), some of the stories widely reported during the pandemic were dangerously wrong. There were myriad conspiracy theories swirling around social media, but some of the most dangerous were those given credibility by being amplified and repeated by the mainstream media.

At times of international crisis, like a world war or global financial crisis, the media is supposed to play a vital role in getting the latest, accurate information to their audiences. For the best part of 2020, coronavirus-related news dominated our newspapers, TV screens, radio and online sites and all too often that 'accurate information' was, sadly, pessimistic, rather than optimistic. But what value was accurate news to an audience that in large part was moving away from trusting the mainstream media to report accurately (Park et al. 2020) and that was receiving mixed messages from their political leaders? How can there be a shared trust when leaders, like former US President Donald J. Trump, are playing down the impact of the pandemic, or when commentary from those chasing a 'clickbait' headline gives oxygen to conspiracy theories, or suggests the virus is not *that* serious or claims there was no scientific evidence to support medical advice like social distancing or wearing a mask in public. 2020 was a year of rapid change and uncertainty: every facet of life has been affected, and the media has not been excepted from the chaos.

The impact of Donald Trump

The leader of the free world at the time had plenty to say during the height of the pandemic, and much of it did little to alleviate the anxiety of most of the American public. In the early days, leaders the world over realised that to inform their citizens about the severity of the pandemic, they needed the support of the media. That posed a dilemma for President Trump. How does he manage a huge health and economic crisis when he has been consistently telling people for years not to trust the media? The President and the media were the main sources of the latest information about the pandemic and state of the economy. President Trump was widely criticised for his handling of the pandemic. Initially the criticism centred on his early downplaying of the risks of the virus and suggesting at one stage that it would simply disappear like a 'miracle' come the (Northern) spring (The New York Times 2020). Then came other mistakes like the lack of testing at ports of entry, the bungled quarantine operation for infected cruise ship passengers, and a shortage of testing kits (Bell 2020). Research has since shown that President Trump was the 'single largest driver' of misinformation about the pandemic in the US (Stolberg and Weiland 2020). As the number of cases and the death toll mounted to where the United States had more fatalities than any other country, the President started having daily press briefings at the White House, which began as an opportunity for the Coronavirus Task Force to report to the American public, but soon took on the usual adversarial role of the President taking exception to anyone from the assembled media suggesting he might be at least partly responsible for the spread of the pandemic because of his early inaction, or questioning some of his more outlandish suggestions of cures, like injecting bleach. In June, Trump blamed the media for reporting the large number of cases being disclosed by widespread testing and even suggested he might stop the testing (Sheth 2020). Critics said the daily news briefings became little more than election-year campaign rallies with the President dominating the podium and self-praising his own handling of the pandemic. The criticism came to a head in mid-June when the major networks dropped their live coverage of one briefing when the President played a 'propaganda' video criticising the media's coverage and showing prominent figures praising his handling of the crisis (Knott 2020). At the time debate was raging in US media circles about how much of the 'briefings' the TV networks should broadcast live. Did the media carry some blame for the President's spreading of suspect Coronavirus information by giving him a regular platform (Jones 2020b)? A member of *The New York Times'* editorial board, Michelle Cottle, was in no doubt: '[I]t falls to the media to serve the public interest by no longer airing his briefings live,' she wrote (Cottle 2020). When members of the White House press corps did question the President's actions (or lack of them) he reverted to his 'fake news' media-bashing mantra and attacked the journalists' integrity. What the President failed to see—or purposely chose to ignore—was that it was the media's job to ask pertinent questions at such critical times. They were not there to undermine the President, but to inform the public. In other words, to do their job (Jones 2020c).

The story so far: How coverage of the pandemic played out across the globe

We will detail in later chapters how mainstream media across the globe has been on life support for most of the 21st century. But at a time when the public the world over was clamouring for reliable information on the impact of the coronavirus on their everyday lives, the worldwide decline of mainstream media was further exacerbated by pandemic-fuelled recessions. In many countries, media advertising revenues dried up, and many newspapers, magazines and broadcast news outlets were forced to either cut their output, drastically reduce staff or close down temporarily or permanently. Ironically, at a time when the world needed journalists the most, the biggest story in the world this century was costing thousands of those journalists—the recorders of the first draft to history—their jobs (G. Smith 2020; Flynn 2020).

From the early days of the pandemic the predictions for mainstream media were dire. In the United States newspapers were said to be facing an 'extinction-level' crisis (Gabbatt 2020) while there was a similar prediction for mass media in developing countries (Ahmed 2020); for example, an extensive report by the Reuters Institute on journalism in what it termed 'emerging economies and the Global South' was released in early 2021 (Radcliffe 2021). In the United Kingdom, media commentator Roy Greenslade suggested the pandemic would 'finish off' many titles (Greenslade 2020). By July 2020, more than 36,000 journalists in the United States had either been sacked, furloughed (temporarily laid-off), or had their pay cut (Radcliffe 2020). A month later came the news that more than 2,000 had lost their jobs in the UK (Mayhew and Tobitt 2020) and a further 1,000 in Australia (Meade 2020b). Organisation after organisation announced plans to cut production costs by various combinations of publication suspensions, pay cuts, staff lay-offs or furloughs. In Australia, the pandemic accelerated the already developing trend of print closures. In mid-May 2020, The Public Interest Journalism Initiative reported that more than 200 Australian newsrooms had closed temporarily or permanently since early 2019 (PIJI 2020). While the lay-offs were biggest in the newspaper sector, there were also major cuts in magazines with many printing their last editions, and big staff cuts—including some high-profile presenters—in the broadcast sector. Many of those who survived the massive cuts worldwide found themselves under added pressures, working from their loungerooms, studies or kitchen tables. The public wanted the latest information, and although the overall trend in the past decade had been for online to overtake television as the most frequently used source of news, the coronavirus temporarily reversed that trend (Newman 2020). Major news organisations in the UK, US and Australia also reported a temporary surge in digital subscriptions (Mayhew 2020a; Turvill 2020; Warren 2020b).

Challenges to press freedom

The gravity of the situation for the mainstream media wasn't helped by governments around the globe using the crisis to clamp down on press freedom under the guise of combating misinformation and 'fake news' (Simon 2020; IFJ/IFEX 2020a). According to a survey of more than 1,300 journalists in 77 countries released by the International Federation of Journalists to coincide with World Press Freedom Day in April 2020, 75 per cent said they had faced official restrictions, obstruction or intimidation while trying to report on the pandemic. Dozens reported being arrested, facing lawsuits or being assaulted while trying to cover the pandemic: 'From Greece to Indonesia and from Chad to Peru journalists used words such as precarious, problematic, terrible, worse, declining and restricted to assess the media freedom environment' (IFJ/IFEX 2020b).

The countries that usually end up at the bottom of the Reporters Without Borders annual Media Freedom Index that we refer to in the chapter 'Journalism under threat' as 'the usual suspects' were using the pandemic to further stifle press freedom. Stories about media oppression highlighted Egypt (Press Gazette 2020), the Philippines (ABC 2020d), Ecuador (Constante 2020), Hungary (Walker 2020), China (Birtles 2020), and parts of the Pacific, notably Fiji and Papua New Guinea (Anthony 2020; Robie 2020). One of *Time* magazine's 2018 Persons of the Year, Philippine journalist Maria Ressa (2020), in an article titled 'We can't let the virus infect democracy' added a few more—India, Brazil, Jordan, and Thailand—in her wrap-up of those countries that were using the pandemic to further cut press freedom and freedom of expression in general.

Aside from the challenges thrown up by governments trying to control the release of information about the pandemic, there were other more personal issues for journalists—like the danger of catching COVID-19 during their 'frontline' reporting and maintaining their mental health. Journalists had to quickly adapt to new ways of reporting, adopt varying safety protocols, lockdown measures and travel bans. Like so many other workers worldwide, they had to adapt to working from home, often in lockdown. For those reporting 'in the field', PPE (personal protective equipment) became part of their tools of trade, along with hand sanitiser and learning to 'social distance'. The requirement for social distancing meant that usually bustling newsrooms were largely empty for most of the year. At the height of the pandemic newspapers (and some TV and radio programs) were being produced with almost no one in the office except for skeleton production crews. A majority of the 1,628 respondents to a *Press Gazette* survey released in early August 2020 said they did not expect to return to their offices either at all or before the end of the year

(Mayhew 2020b). Proprietors with an eye to saving on costly rental space or building occupancy could see merit in having their staff largely working from home on a permanent basis. For many journalists, the job of reporting will never be the same again.

A couple of ethical lessons from the pandemic

To better understand how members of the media were handling the many facets of covering the pandemic, the International Center for Journalists and the Tow Center for Digital Journalism at Columbia University (both in the US) undertook a major survey involving more than 1,400 English-speaking journalists and media workers in 125 countries (Posetti, Bell, and Brown 2020). The initial findings back up much of what we have been saying—when the public is relying on credible journalism to stay safe and informed 'journalists and news organisations are grappling with a mental health crisis, financial peril, physical safety threats, and press freedom attacks, while simultaneously battling pandemic levels of disinformation' (Journalism and the Pandemic Survey 2020). Nieman Lab's Sarah Scire put another way, saying journalists were struggling with mental health, financial hardship and disinformation in what she labelled a 'startling and disturbing' survey (Scire 2020). The 30-page initial report is a sobering read.

The 'Journalism and the Pandemic Survey' found that many journalists were reacting proactively to counter the tsunami or disinformation around the pandemic (Posetti, Bell, and Brown 2020, 22). Some news organisations had set up specific COVID-19 disinformation rounds; others were using more fact-checking and digital verification tools to expose false videos, images, and memes connected to the pandemic. They were also collaborating with other news organisations, non-government organisations, and academics to isolate disinformation. Some have even engaged their audiences in fact-checking to combat the spread of false information (Posetti, Bell, and Brown 2020, 22).

The impact on journalists' mental health

> When journalists cover crises, tragedies, and disasters, and interview people affected by them, they face a complicated task: to not cause additional harm to the victims, while at the same time taking care of their own mental health.
>
> (Simanovych 2020)

The sheer magnitude of the pandemic, and the myriad tragedies it threw up, meant that journalists needed to be prepared mentally, as well as physically, to cover it. The mental health of journalists has become an important topic in recent years as more research uncovers the links between frontline reporting and PTSD (Seely 2019). The quote from Olga Simanovych began a story about the resources available to those covering the pandemic in the early days from her organisation, the Global Investigative Journalism Network, and also discussed the trauma-related resources available from the Dart Center for Journalism and Trauma (Simanovych 2020). In summary, the advice was straightforward: prepare for covering what will be a traumatic story and have a plan for handling the trauma associated with it. The early results from a mental health survey of 73 journalists from international news organisations mid-2020 showed that 70 per cent said they were suffering from psychological distress from covering the pandemic (Selva and Feinstein 2020).

Misinformation, disinformation, and an 'infodemic'

Considering the huge amount of information available about COVID-19 when it first came to public attention in early 2020, news coverage and social media were bound to be infected by misinformation and disinformation in what some called an 'infodemic'—an epidemic of both accurate and inaccurate information. Often it was difficult to tell the difference. We all make mistakes leading to our unwittingly circulating misinformation, but during the pandemic 'misinformation' and 'disinformation' were used at times interchangeably, and there is a distinct difference. Disinformation takes incorrect information a step further, circulating deliberately misleading, biased information or propaganda for a particular purpose ('Misinformation' vs. 'Disinformation': Get informed on the difference n.d.). There was plenty of highly dubious information and conspiracy theories circulating on COVID-19, not only on the Internet, but also in the mainstream media. You probably heard much of it: *The virus came from a research facility in Wuhan, China. Wasn't it the American military that sent it to China? No, it was circulated on the 5G phone network.* More dangerous, though, was the medical misinformation. One survey, released in August 2020, said at least 800 people worldwide had died in the first three months of the year, and thousands more were hospitalised, from following unfounded medical cure claims found on the Internet (Satariano 2020). At times misinformation was spreading on the Internet as fast as the virus and all-too-often making the mainstream media. We mention often in other chapters the importance of fact-checking. You have an ethical responsibility to ensure that what you are writing is accurate—not some scatterbrain theory that might give your audience some light relief from a deadly pandemic. If it involves a potential cure, it could be life-threatening.

When do you demand accountability?

In times of international crisis, the media tends to suspend its traditional sceptical view of government actions in favour of supporting and publicising the government's latest moves to alleviate the impact. But that 'truce' didn't last long in some countries as the pandemic dragged on for months with no vaccine in sight. In Australia, *The Guardian*'s Lenore Taylor (2020) put the dilemma this way: 'How... should we balance legitimate questioning of government decisions with the danger of further undermining public faith in expert advice and institutions?'

In the US, reporters started challenging the President after he was shown to be dismissive and slow to realise the gravity of the pandemic. In Australia, Daniel Andrews, the Premier of the country's worst-hit state, Victoria, held press conferences for more than 100 days straight that ran for up to two hours outlining the latest news on the 'war on COVID-19'. On the day the Premier was outlining specific details of the Stage 4 (strictest) lockdown, which included an overnight curfew, some in the media were more interested in pursuing him over who was responsible for the botched hotel quarantine scheme for returning travellers. Twitter exploded with angry Victorians saying they wanted more detail on the restrictions, not continuous questioning in a 'blame game' of journalists seeking a 'gotcha' moment. The questions needed to be asked, but not while the public needed practical advice on the impact of the unprecedented restrictions. Martin and his wife were caught in the middle of those restrictions, and Queensland-based Roger spent a fortnight in hotel quarantine after a few days in South Australia. Melbourne-based media ethicist Denis Muller (2020) was highly critical of the coverage by Australia's largest media group: 'Rupert Murdoch's News Corporation, in significant parts of its coverage of the coronavirus pandemic, has become a clear and present danger to the welfare of Australian society,' he wrote. It's a valuable ethical lesson to be learned: by all means ask the questions about accountability but pick the appropriate time.

Were those girls really 'Enemies of the State'?

Chapter 8 is devoted to a lengthy discussion of an individual's right to privacy or, put another way, the media's penchant for invading people's privacy. There is also mention of the right to a fair trial. Both these major ethical and legal issues were ignored by the Murdoch media in Australia—notably Brisbane's *Courier Mail*—when two young women of South Sudanese heritage, and who subsequently tested positive to COVID-19, allegedly lied on their paperwork on returning to Queensland from a brief holiday Melbourne. The *Courier Mail*'s front page headline echoed President Trump's anti-media sentiment labelling the girls 'Enemies of the State' (Marszalek 2020). The paper took photos of the girls from their Facebook pages. Murdoch papers interstate (and most of the media) followed the *Courier Mail*'s lead in 'naming and shaming' the two young women. Twitter again went into overdrive criticising the paper's racist vilification and pointing out that a number of more high-profile Australians had not been 'named and shamed' when they avoided quarantine requirements on their return from overseas. The Queensland Human Rights Commission said some members of Brisbane's African communities reported abusive texts and social media harassment while others worried their children would be harassed on their way to and from school (Smee and Meade 2020). The story deserved to be told, but why the front-page splash when others, caught for similar offences and far more prominent in the community, were not given anything like the same treatment? Unfortunately, the answer is a deep layer of institutional racism in some sectors of the news media that they feel gives them a licence to dox and defame people of colour (Richards 2020)—a topic we will return to in the next chapter.

Case study: Could Bob Woodward have saved lives?

American journalists Bob Woodward and Carl Bernstein are among the best-known reporters in the world for their part in the downfall of US President Richard Nixon in 1974. Their tireless reporting of the 'Watergate' scandal is seen as a watershed in journalism worldwide and as inspiring a new generation of journalists the world over (Hirst and Patching 2005). Since that ground-breaking reporting nearly half a century ago, Woodward has become an 'elder statesman' of American journalism, known more for his books on US presidents than any reporting for his long-time employer, *The Washington Post*. His latest book—*Rage*—is his second on President Trump, and the pre-publicity for its release in September 2020 contained bombshells from the President and created a major ethical dilemma. Trump told Woodward that he knew early in 2020 that the virus was deadly, he often publicly said the opposite, insisting it would go away. However, Woodward did not reveal this bombshell news at the time the interviews were recorded. Putting aside the actions of the President in deliberately misleading the public, we are focusing here on the actions of the revered journalist in not reporting the President's stance before the pandemic death toll reached into the thousands. Could Woodward's earlier reporting of his interviews with the President have saved lives?

On one side of the dilemma are those who say that Woodward had an obligation to his public to inform them of the President's position. Some could see no ethical or moral defence for Woodward not publishing the material as soon as he had it (Levin 2020). Others simply said he made the wrong choice of when to publish (Bailey 2020). In their view he should not have held onto his scoop until his book was about to be published. Some of the criticism of the country's most famous celebrity journalist was quite brutal—'he decided not to tell anyone, and nearly 200,000 people have since died' (Perez and Sirota 2020). Woodward spoke to the *Post*'s media columnist Margaret Sullivan about the rationale behind holding on to the scoop until mid-September, but after weighing up the evidence she came to the conclusion: 'Still, the chance—even if it's a slim chance—that those revelations could have saved lives is a powerful argument against waiting this long' (Sullivan 2020a).

So how did the famous journalist defend that he knew the President was lying to the American public about 'a matter of life and death' and not reveal it immediately?

For Woodward, the President's revelations posed two major problems: he didn't know the source of Trump's information, and 'the biggest problem I had, which is always a problem with Trump, is I didn't know if it was true' (quoted in Sullivan 2020). To be fair to Woodward, given Trump's track record, why should the President ever have been trusted without thorough fact-checking? It took three months to confirm that what Trump said was true and by then the country already knew, or should have known, the truth about the deadly nature of the virus, and that the President had been down-playing its severity (Jones 2020a). Woodward doesn't see himself as a day-to-day reporter. He sees his role as needing to provide more complete context than a news story would provide. Also, he wanted to publish closer to US election day, so that the President's actions would be remembered on the first Tuesday in November 2020.

Questions for discussion

Should Woodward have reported the President's comments or not? Could it have saved lives?

We see some merit in both sides of this argument—a true ethical dilemma and an important one. There is almost no simple answer to this dilemma, so we suggest you debate the issue in your class or tutorial. What side would you take?

There's an additional element to this discussion for you to consider too: Woodward claimed he held back the interview material because he thought it would have more impact closer to the 3 November presidential election. Was he right to do this?

This question opens up one of the key fault lines that we think animate debates about the future of journalism and journalism ethics today: Where is the line to be drawn between neutral reporting and journalism as political activism?

2 News in crisis

Responding to Black Lives Matter

An explosion of anger

'It was the most beautiful thing,' said President Trump. 'Wasn't it really a beautiful sight? It's called law and order,' he added. The former President was describing Minneapolis police felling Canadian MSNBC reporter Ali Velshi while he was covering a Black Lives Matter demonstration in the wake of the police killing of George Floyd in May 2020. Depending on which report you read of the President's remarks, made at a rally in Pennsylvania four months after Floyd's death, Velshi was either struck in the knee by multiple rubber bullets (Spocchia 2020) or a single projectile (Visser 2020). Regardless of how many rubber bullets struck the reporter, the President's remarks were typical of his long-standing attitude towards the mainstream media that is discussed in numerous contexts in this book. Openly lauding police violence against journalists should have no place in public discourse, let alone from the then leader of the free world. As a spokesman for MSNBC stated at the time: 'When the President mocks a journalist for the injury he sustained while putting himself in harm's way to inform the public, he endangers thousands of other journalists and undermines our freedoms' (quoted in Spocchia 2020).

The death of 46-year-old George Floyd at the hands of the Minneapolis police was a crossroads moment for the Black Lives Matter movement, and also for the mass media. Not only for American journalists covering the BLM protests, but for overseas journalists covering the story as well. Between January 2020 and 4 January 2021, US police killed 994 people. Black Americans are disproportionally represented in the figures—50 per cent of deaths but only 13.5 per cent of the population, according to a *Washington Post* database tracking the killings (Washington Post 2021). BLM also spread to other Western countries in 2020, including France, the UK, and Australia. There was a global explosion of anger against police aggression following George Floyd's murder and it was highly political, infused with a sense of anti-capitalist politics (Çetinkaya 2020). As we shall see, this political flavour was not easy to understand or report on for many journalists. In later chapters we will attempt to explain this in terms of journalistic ideologies.

The Black Lives Matter movement began in the US in mid-2013 after George Zimmerman was acquitted of the shooting death of Black teenager

DOI: 10.4324/9780429242892-3

Trayvon Martin 17 months earlier. As the death toll among Black (mainly) men continued to rise, the movement organised street demonstrations in protest. But it was 'reborn' in a major way with the death of Floyd at police hands. George's final moments, captured on a mobile phone, crying out 'I can't breathe' and calling for his mother, galvanised public opinion and lead to widespread protests across America, and in other countries, including the United Kingdom and Australia. In the US, the demonstrations continued for months in numerous cities. Some of those demonstrations degenerated into attacks on buildings and looting, playing into President Trump's 'Law and Order' campaign in the election year. The police response to the protests was also violent. In many instances tear gas, rubber bullets, and baton charges were used against largely peaceful crowds.

George Floyd's death was one in the all-too-frequent killings of Black Americans by police. A few months earlier, Louisville police raided the apartment of 26-year-old Black woman Breonna Taylor during a flawed drug investigation. Taylor and her boyfriend were roused from bed and the boyfriend fired once at police thinking they were intruders. Police returned fire, killing Taylor (McCarthy and Bryant 2020). In a civil suit that followed, the city of Louisville agreed to pay Taylor's family US$12 million, described at the time as one of the highest such payments in a police shooting in years (McCarthy and Bryant 2020). A grand jury would later decline to file homicide charges against the officers involved, leading to further protests across the nation (Blackburn and Lovan 2020). August 2020 saw another police shooting—of Jacob Blake—in Kenosha, Wisconsin followed by more demonstrations and rioting. This time the shooting—seven shots in the back—was not fatal but relatives reported Blake was paralysed. The local protests that followed saw a 17-year-old White youth, Kyle Rittenhouse, armed with military-style semi-automatic rifle fatally shoot two protesters and injure another while 'patrolling' the city with a gang of heavily armed self-styled 'vigilantes' (Thebault and Armus 2020). At the time of writing—January 2021—the protests were continuing in major cities across the United States as racial tensions continued to tear at the country's social fabric. In April 2021, disgraced police officer Derek Chauvin was convicted for Floyd's murder, but in the same week, police in Columbus, Ohio, shot and killed Ma'Khia Bryant, a 16-year-old Black girl.

On the day that the US Congress and Senate were confirming Joe Biden's victory in the 2020 presidential election, large groups of overwhelmingly White Trump supporters rioted in Washington DC. It was a day that reminded many Black Americans of the racial divide in how America is policed. The protestors in DC—many of them members of openly fascist street gangs like the Proud Boys—were not tear-gassed or met with rubber bullets. On the contrary, video emerged of law enforcement officers removing barriers so that the mob could gain access to the Capitol building. It seemed that some police were willing to pose for selfies with the thugs who broke into the literal home of American democracy. The high-profile Black correspondent for MSNBC, Joy-Ann Reid, was scathingly critical of the mob violence and the hypocritical police response, saying it proved that White Americans 'are not afraid of the cops' and act as if they 'own the place'. Reid also noted that if the protestors had been Black, 'there would already be people, shackled, arrested *en masse*, or dead' (cited in Gramenz 2021).

Covering the protests is dangerous for the media

Covering the widespread BLM demonstrations and counter-protests by White supremacists, who are often heavily armed, made covering politics in America a dangerous assignment for journalists in 2020. The numbers are updated almost daily by the US Press Freedom Tracker group but from the 25 May killing of George Floyd to 29 October the near-900 attacks on media covering the protests included at least 120 arrests, 222 assaults (160 by law enforcement agencies) and a total of 544 other press freedom violations (Press Freedom Tracker 2020b). The police attacks included assaults with rubber bullets, tear gas, and pepper spray. By comparison, Press Freedom Tracker put total violations against the media in 2019 at 152, in 2018 it was 132 and in 2017, 144 (Douglas 2020). The police assaults on journalists were not limited to the American media. Channel 7 Australia reporter Amelia Brace and her cameraman Tim Myers were attacked by police in Washington while reporting live on a protest outside the White House (Jackson and Easton 2020). Myers was bashed with a police shield, and Brace was hit with a rubber bullet. At its height, there were demonstrations in 30 American cities. Journalists attacked while covering other demonstrations included a freelance photojournalist, Linda Tirado, who was hit in the face with a foam bullet that left her blind in one eye while others were tear-gassed or hit with rubber bullets (Douglas 2020; Noor 2020b). Journalists were routinely arrested while covering the protests, including one Black CNN reporter, who was handcuffed and taken into custody while live on air (Noor 2020b). So frequent and serious were the police attacks on journalists covering protests in Portland, Oregon, that reporters and legal observers filed legal actions challenging police and federal agents over their frequent use of tear gas, rubber bullets, 'flash bangs' (a blinding flash of light followed by an intensely loud bang), and what were termed other 'less lethal' weapons (Brown 2020). In mid-October, the Ninth Circuit judges restrained federal agents from targeting journalists and legal observers for assault and arrest during protests while they considered a government appeal over an earlier injunction granted against the agents (Brown 2020). Usually, the media use the police as their authoritative sources for information about crimes, in this context about protest marches, riots, and looting. They are usually seen as reliable and 'official'. For decades our television screens have been filled with police dramas and more recently police-based reality TV programmes where they are invariably portrayed as 'the good guys'. But their open hostility towards journalists doing their job in reporting on Black Lives Matter protests has fractured that long-standing relationship, at least in the United States. One young reporter, Lewis Raven Wallace, issued a *mea culpa* of sorts and recounts the moment he realised that too many White reporters were missing the story because they didn't understand: 'I am White: mostly White newsrooms typically weren't sufficiently attentive to police killings or any racial justice issue' (Wallace 2019, 29). We will return to Lewis in later chapters, but it is worth noting now that his observation is right. White journalists need to move out of their privilege, and news organisations need to start hiring more people of colour and giving them the freedom to report from the bottom up; from the street, not just the view from the newsroom and the boardroom.

There was widespread criticism of the police action against journalists, with political leaders in Germany, Australia, and rather hypocritically, Turkey, calling on the United States (and the then President) to respect press freedom (Specia 2020). They were joined by journalism academics across the America (ASJMC & AEJMC 2020) and UNESCO (Scaffidi 2020). CNN's chief international anchor and a senior adviser to the Committee to Protect Journalists (CPJ), Christine Amanpour, summed up the dangers of covering both the BLM movement and the pandemic in the US:

> Covering civil unrest is already a challenge for journalists and, when coupled with the COVID-19 pandemic, journalists are presented with an extraordinarily risky situation in trying to protect both their health and safety.
>
> (quoted in Santa-Wood 2020)

When it became obvious that media workers were in danger of physical harm covering protests in 'the land of the free', both the Committee for the Protection of journalists (CPJ 2020a) and the Poynter Institute issued advice on how to stay safe (Tompkins 2020).

Objects of hate

'How journalists became objects of hate' is the title of an opinion piece for CNN by historian and cultural commentator, Ruth Ben-Ghiat (2020), which refers at length to the 'unprecedented level of hostility to the press'. Such hostility is nothing new, but President Trump 'upped the ante' to turn journalists into objects of hate in the eyes of many police officers and White supremacists. With so many journalists assaulted and arrested, Ben-Ghiat (2020) suggests, 'they look to the public like the criminals Trump suggests they are'. Soon after George Floyd's death, the President blamed what he called the 'lamestream media' for the nationwide protests, also calling journalists 'truly bad people with a sick agenda' (quoted in Tracy and Abrams 2020). The Poynter Institute's senior media writer, Tom Jones, said protesters who harassed the media were simply following the President's lead (Jones 2020e). Earlier he had noted in his daily newsletter that, given the President's rhetoric, 'it should come as no surprise that the media was a target for violence and attack all over the nation during its coverage of the protests' (Jones 2020a). Given the figures already quoted, it is obvious that journalists remained the objects of hate in the eyes of many law enforcement officers and, of course, Trump supporters well past the November 2020 election day.

Ethics lessons from reporting the BLM movement

Unexpected by-products of the renewed Black Lives Matter movement in 2020 were questions surrounding the reporting of racial issues and the diversity debate triggered in newsrooms across America and also in the United Kingdom and Australia. It exploded when *The New York Times* published an opinion piece by Republican senator Tom Cotton entitled 'Send in the troops' (Singh 2020). The decision to publish the opinion piece, which advocated deploying troops against Black Lives Matter protesters, drew widespread criticism. Dozens of journalists from the *Times* joined the criticism pointing out that inciting a heavy-handed response to the protests put Black journalists, and people of colour more broadly, in danger (Singh 2020). *Times* executives scrambled to allay the anger of staff and readers, issuing a statement saying the politician's essay did not meet the newspaper's editorial standards (Tracy, Abrams, and Lee 2020). The editor in charge of that section of the paper, James Bennet, told staff he had not read the op-ed before it was published and resigned a couple of days later (Luscombe 2020). That high-profile resignation was followed by another—that of the *Philadelphia Inquirer*'s executive editor Stan Wischnowski. In both cases the editors had lost the support of their newsroom staff. Wischnowski walked after staff staged a 'sick and tired' walkout over the tasteless headline 'Buildings matter, too' (Jones 2020f). Protests quickly spread to other major newsrooms across the nation including *The Washington Post, The Los Angeles Times,* and News Corp's *Wall Street Journal.* It broadened into what commentators characterised as a 'raging debate' (Stelter 2020) that saw 'revolts erupting in America's Big Newsrooms' (Smith 2020b). *The New York Times*' Ben Smith dates the timeline for newsroom change back to lessons learned by Black Americans covering the demonstrations in Ferguson, Missouri, in 2014 that followed the death of 18-year-old Black man Michael Brown Jr., again at the hands of a White policeman. Then came the election of Donald Trump and his bigoted language towards protesters and his denouncing of journalists in general (Smith 2020b). The concern, bubbling for so long under the surface, came to a head with Senator Cotton's op-ed. Mainstream journalists were asking questions like:

> What should news outlets do differently when leaders spread 'enemy of the people' lies? How should opinion sections adapt in the age of information wars? When are 'both sides' equally valid and when are they not? Who decides?
>
> (Stelter 2020)

Research from Syracuse University showed reporters who favoured impartiality and those who favoured empathy shared a desire to re-focus journalism onto how they report on marginalised groups (Munno and Craig 2020).

Can journalism be both impartial and empathetic?

From in-house arguments to very public disagreements on social media, journalists were debating how to reshape their profession under the new and expanded pressures in which reporters—and Black American journalists in particular—found themselves working. Basically, the debate centred on whether objectivity was still relevant. According to the Syracuse University research already cited, on one side of the debate were those traditionalists who believed in remaining neutral and dispassionate, while on the other side of the debate were those who wanted to report while 'situating themselves as allies of protesters' (Munno and Craig 2020). This is another issue that places journalism ethics firmly at a crossroads where difficult choices about future directions must be made. For us, objectivity has always been problematic and in recent years it has become the focus of more sustained scrutiny from both journalists and journalism scholars (Maras 2013).

Objectivity has always been an aspiration of journalists the world over. It has come to mean giving both sides of an issue an airing from a position of neutrality, and letting the readers make up their minds (Gessen 2020). But not all arguments have two sides. Some have more, particularly in debates around political decisions, and some statements don't need to be the subject of debate, like whether disinfectant should be taken seriously as a treatment for COVID-19, or the devastating impacts of climate change. The notion of 'moral clarity', a concept defined by *The New Yorker*'s columnist Masha Gessen (2020) as 'a quest, guided by clear values and informed by facts and context, and clearly aligned with the original concept of journalistic objectivity' is one suggestion for a replacement. In response to BLM and an awakening of consciousness among reporters, the shape of journalism in the US might be slowly changing 'driven by a journalism that is more personal, and reporters more willing to speak what they see as the truth without worrying about alienating conservatives' (Smith 2020b). The debate continues and it is an issue we re-visit in the later theory chapters.

The other major debate raised by the BLM movement was the lack of diversity in American newsrooms, and to a lesser extent in British and Australian news organisations. At the height of the debate it was being suggested that in America 'journalism has a race problem' (Merrefield 2020). About three-quarters of US newsroom employees are non-Hispanic White, compared with about two-thirds of all workers, and about half newsroom staff are White men. Racial and ethnic minorities make up about 40 per cent of the US population (Merrefield 2020), but their numbers in American newsrooms do not reflect that diversity. The long-standing result of this lack of diversity has led, in the eyes of Pulitzer Prize-winning Black journalist Wesley Lowery, to a situation where 'the mainstream has allowed what it considers objective truth to be decided almost exclusively by White reporters and their mostly White bosses' (Lowery 2020). About the same time in Australia, *The Saturday Paper*'s Madeline Hayman-Reber was pointing out that her country was 'in the midst of a realisation…how deeply ingrained what could be called "unconscious" racism is in this country' (Hayman-Reber 2020). The lack of cultural diversity and sensitivity in Australian media workplaces, and the problems that people of colour and Indigenous reporters had in reporting BLM issues was raised by journalists and commentators alike (Clure 2020; Zhou 2020; Rogers 2020). Similar arguments were being aired in the United Kingdom (Tobitt 2020b, 2020c). Probably Australia's best-known indigenous journalist, Stan Grant, presented an edition of the ABC's prestigious *Four Corners* current affairs TV programme at the height of the BLM demonstrations in the US, and commented in a piece to camera that:

> *Four Corners* has been on air more years than I have been alive and I am the first indigenous person ever to report for it. And when we do break through that colour line we are expected to be grateful and humble.
>
> (Grant 2020)

An analysis by Media Diversity Australia researchers, released in August 2020, said Australian news and current affairs programmes across all TV channels were overwhelmingly curated, framed, and presented by journalists and commentators from an Anglo-Celtic background (Rodrigues 2020). But the methodology for establishing the central finding—that 75 per cent of faces on Australian television were Anglo-Celtic, while they made up only 58 per cent of the population—was challenged (Palmer 2020). The Black Lives Matter demonstrations in several Australian capital cities in mid-2020 centred mainly on protests over the rising number of Aboriginal deaths in custody. Writer and long-time leader of the journalists' union in Australia, the MEAA, Chris Warren, believes that the reliance on police sources and an exclusion of Indigenous voices has created journalism in Australia that is 'incomplete and unbalanced' (Warren 2020c). At the core of the problem, Warren says, is the lack of diversity in Australian newsrooms.

Covering BLM also became a mental health issue for journalists

Just as was the case for journalists covering the pandemic at a time of staff and production cutbacks (discussed in the previous chapter), the stress associated with covering the Black Lives Matter demonstrations, and protests that at times turned into riots and looting, affected media workers' mental health in 2020. How to navigate between their personal feelings about the issues and those involved and their professional duty to report what was happening to the wider community posed its own problems. In the authors' early newsroom days most potential mental health issues were 'solved' at an after-work drinking session, rather than in a therapist's office. Thankfully, that's no longer the case. Journalists nowadays show a greater willingness to talk about their mental struggles and are no longer reticent in seeking help. In the context of covering traumatic events like the BLM protests and the unwarranted increase in police violence towards them, media personnel quickly realised that mental health was as important as physical health (Morell 2020). Reporters who had been dealing with the relentless nature of covering a global pandemic that may have affected them or their family, were faced with the added stress of covering protests at which they risked being injured and arrested for doing their job. Major news organisations around the globe realised decades ago that they owed a duty of care to their staff regarding mental health issues like Post-Traumatic Stress Disorder (PTSD) and set up systems for journalists needing help to cope with their everyday assignments. Other frontline or 'first responder' workers, like police, firefighters and ambulance personnel realised long before the media that theirs was a mentally challenging environment in which to work. But the combination of the state of the media industry, the pandemic, and the BLM protests and riots, brought mental health into sharper focus in 2020.

Another ethics lesson from BLM: 'Framing' stories

The way the general public views protests, and social movements—like Black Lives Matter—is formed in large part by what they read or see in the media (Kilgo 2020). Journalism has long emphasised the drama, inconvenience, and disruption caused by protesters clogging the streets, without devoting much attention to their grievances or demands. The ongoing BLM demonstrations across America give ample evidence of this 'framing' of the news agenda by journalists. Researcher Danielle Kilgo looked at stories on the demonstrations in Minneapolis following the death of George Floyd and found consistent reference to four recognised 'frames' of protest—riot (emphasising disruptive behaviour), confrontation (describing demonstrations as combative), spectacle (focussing on the dramatic and emotional behaviour of protesters) and debate (mentioning protesters' demands, agendas, goals and grievances) (Kilgo 2020), what social scientists call the 'protest paradigm'. The tight deadlines associated with covering such stories leads journalists to rely all-too-often—as we noted earlier—on authorities, like the police, as their sources. The way they usually centre their protest stories around the impact on traffic, local businesses and property is one way that the 'protest-as-nuisance' frame is widely seen in print and broadcast media (Pierre-Louis 2020). It is an ethical decision how a story is framed. The media has an important job in deciding how demonstrations like those organised by the BLM movement are 'framed': Is it a law-and-order issue that needs suppression to maintain the status quo, or is it a legitimate social justice movement way overdue for less-biased coverage? Journalists also have to make a difficult ethical choice about how they will manage relationships with the police in light of the criticisms they are facing for racialised policing, violence against protestors, and seeming to align themselves with openly racist activists.

Case study: The role of the cartoonist

Cartoonists live on the edge of controversy. Theirs is the task of summarising complex issues, usually in a single frame of art. The limited number of brushstrokes required to make a humorous, political or social justice point often leads to their 'crossing the line' of what the public considers acceptable or in good taste. But cartoonists have an important role to play in mainstream media—a cartoon can change the direction of a political debate or galvanise opposition to an issue or an individual. There have been several cartoons in Rupert Murdoch's News Corp papers in Australia in recent years that have drawn international attention to issues of race. In our opinion all three that we have chosen here (after they had received widespread international condemnation) are 'racist', but as author Roger discovered when he discussed two of them in university journalism ethics classes, not all students agree. So, we're suggesting you debate the pros and cons of each and reach your own conclusions. In each case we will outline what the cartoon showed. The authors have no intention of paying News Corp for the rights to reproduce any of them. They are easily found with a simple online search.

The first was a cartoon by the late Bill Leak, cartoonist for *The Australian*, published in August 2016. It showed an Australian Indigenous man with an open beer can in one hand who could not remember his son's name when the boy was returned to him by a truncheon-carrying White policeman. Indigenous leaders in Australia saw the cartoon as reinforcing stereotypes of Aborigines as 'second-class citizens' and 'not knowing about their children or having any role in raising' them (ABC 2016). Leak defended the cartoon as an honest depiction of the truth (Meade 2016). Seven months after the cartoon was published, Bill Leak died suddenly (Thorpe 2017).

The second cartoon emerged during the US Open tennis titles in September 2018. By *Herald Sun* cartoonist Mark Knight, the cartoon depicted Black American tennis champion Serena Williams throwing a tantrum during the women's final. It was the cartoonist's take on the controversial game in which Williams lost to Japan's Naomi Osaka after being given three code violations, including one for breaking her racquet and another for verbal abuse of the chair umpire. The cartoon shows a 'large' Williams stomping on her racquet with a dummy on the ground and the umpire asking Osaka, 'Can you just let her win?' (ABC 2018). It was widely criticised around the world as 'recycling centuries-old stereotypes' of Black Americans and publishing it showed 'an extraordinary lack of judgment' (Younge 2018). Surprisingly to us, the Australian print media's regulatory body, The Australian Press Council, decided the cartoon did not breach its standards (APC 2019).

The third cartoon was published during the 2020 US election campaign and was the work of Bill Leak's son, Johannes, again for *The Australian*. The cartoon had then US Presidential candidate Joe Biden referring to his newly announced running mate, Democrat senator Kamala Harris, as a 'little brown girl'. While the newspaper's editor-in-chief, Chris Dore defended the cartoon saying Leak was only quoting Biden's words, critics pointed out that Biden was referring to children who might be inspired by Harris's candidacy, not to Harris herself (Meade 2020a). Some thought the cartoon was as sexist as it was racist (Warren 2020a).

The debate

When you Google the cartoons mentioned (or their creators), you will be taken to any number of URLs that will give you further points for debate on the respective cartoons. Then consider some of the following questions.

1   What is the role of the cartoonist? Are they legitimately there sometimes to offend?
2   Take a vote in class. Who thinks the cartoons are racist? The Aboriginal father? Serena Williams' tantrum? The 'little brown girl'? All of them? None of them? Why?
3   Where would you draw the line in such social commentary?
4   Is it to be expected that sometimes cartoonists will 'cross the line'?
5   Are there any budding cartoonists among the group? Can you come up with an alternative take on any of the cited cartoons?

Questions for discussion

The very idea of 'race' is controversial. While some important genetic markers—for certain diseases, for example—exist alongside variations in skin colour and physiological features, there is also a convincing argument that 'race' as we understand it today is a socially constructed category and that the real problem is 'racism', not racial differences. This is a big topic beyond the scope of this book, but it is not something that reporters from any ethnic background can afford to ignore or be ignorant about. Given this controversy, we think it's important to have some discussion around both general issues and specific reportorial dilemmas.

1   What is race and is it important?
2   What is racism and how should it be reported?
3   How can stories that focus on rioting, looting and clashes with police be reframed to highlight important social issues that lie behind the actions of disenfranchised communities?
4   How can journalists help to overcome their over-reliance on official sources—such as police officers and government officials—when reporting social justice issues?

5   When sourcing commentary on social issues, how should journalists address the power imbalance between community groups and activists and well-funded government or private agencies?

6   How would you cover a Black Lives Matter (or similar) protest in your city or town?

7   Should White supremacists be considered as credible sources?

8   Look around, how diverse is your social group or the group of colleagues you work or study with?

3 News in crisis

The fake news crisis

Fake news, ideology, and truth

In this chapter, our main aim is to describe and discuss what we see as the important and distinct categories of fake news. This requires us to examine our deeply held concepts of truth. We make the argument that some forms of fake or false news are inherent in the practices of journalism and in the business models of the news industry. This chapter also discusses fake news in relation to ideology and major concepts explored in other chapters. For example, fake news cannot be objective in any sense of how we use it in this book. On one hand, fake news is obviously very subjective in that it represents a conscious decision to deceive. On the other hand, it is a false representation of facts, so it cannot be said to represent objective reality either. The concept of 'fake news' is not new. It dates back to Roman times when Octavian waged a false propaganda campaign against Antony designed to smear his reputation, according to Posetti and Matthews (2018) in their review of 'fake news' and disinformation 'through the ages' (1). The modern history of 'fake news'—in most cases propaganda to push a cause or individual—can be traced through the major developments in communication, from the invention of the printing press by Gutenberg in the 15th century to the creation of the Internet and through any number of national conflicts and two World Wars. There's a strong argument that propaganda—'fake news' if you prefer—is necessary in times of major conflict, like the World Wars or the two Gulf Wars, in order to ensure support for the troops 'over there' from 'the folks back home', a topic we take up again in Chapter 11. That form of fakery might be accepted as 'propaganda for a purpose', but 'fake news' by another name—fabrication, or simply made up—is another thing altogether.

Fabrication is by no means only the province of working journalists—it abounds on the Internet. However, long before smart phones and tablets brought the Internet to everyone's fingertips, newspapers were being regularly hoaxed. Our favourite was the infamous 'Hitler Diaries' hoax of 1983. Put simply, the diaries were forged, fabricated, made up, and the prestigious Murdoch UK newspaper, *The Sunday Times*, fell for the ruse and published six pages of excerpts. Murdoch joined with *Newsweek* to secure the serial rights to the fictitious diaries for £600,000 (Greenslade 2008).

DOI: 10.4324/9780429242892-4

Hoaxing a newspaper with fake diaries is one thing, but in the past few years 'fake news' has become far more insidious. Ex-President Trump 'popularised' and, for some 'weaponised', the concept. In countries where press freedom is constantly under threat—like China, Turkey, Hungary, Russia, Libya, Hong Kong, Poland, and Somalia—political leaders regularly invoke the mantra of 'fake news' to justify repressive actions against their media (Erlanger 2017). They use it as an excuse for legislation aimed at silencing their political and media critics. In 2019, Singapore—not known for its endorsement of the principles of freedom of the press—introduced its version of laws aimed at curtailing 'fake news'. They gave government ministers the power to decide what is true and what is false (IFJ/IFEX 2019). The law allows government ministers to order the removal or modification of online content they consider to be false or against the public interest. The Bill carries maximum penalties of ten years in jail and a fine of SG$1 million (Walden 2019). A politician in Singapore first used it over a social media post in late 2019 that questioned the independence of state investment firms (The Guardian 2019). Neighbouring Malaysia had introduced a similar law the previous year under disgraced former Prime Minister Najib Razak, but it was repealed soon after his successor, Mahathir Mohamad, came to office (Walden 2019).

In Australia, the term 'fake news' has been used by politicians to discredit the media (Carson and Farhall 2019). Carson and Farhall researched media reports, Australia's Parliamentary proceedings (known as Hansard), and politicians' websites, media releases, and Facebook and Twitter communications for references to 'fake news'. Their key findings were consistent with overseas research in that conservative politicians were the most likely to use 'fake news' language and were usually either fringe politicians seeking media attention, or senior politicians trying to discredit the media or political opponents. Use of the term peaked when Parliament was sitting, and journalists working for the Australian national broadcaster, the ABC, were the most likely targets (Carson and Farhall 2019). More concerning for the authors was the finding that when the media were accused of generating 'fake news', they reported it but seldom contested the accusation, giving their audiences no reason to doubt it (Carson and Farhall 2019). Senior Australian conservative members of parliament also promoted Donald Trump's ridiculous conspiracy theories about the 2020 presidential election, including claims that Trump actually won. On the same day that pro-Trump thugs stormed the Capitol building in Washington DC, Australia's Prime Minister refused to criticise his Liberal-National Party coalition colleagues for continuing to spread disinformation about a Trump 'victory', instead hiding behind the cheap 'freedom of speech' excuse (Galloway 2021). It's not 'freedom of speech' when you are deliberately spreading information you know to be false for the purpose of inciting violence.

'Fake news' emerges in many different settings, which means it is difficult to pin down. How to define fake news is not an easy question to answer because in the clamour and noise that has exploded around the term in recent years simple definitions have tended to become lost. We really hadn't heard much about fake news until ex-President Trump started accusing any reporting that he didn't like as being 'fake', but since then pundits, academics, and pretty much anyone with an opinion, has weighed in to give us several competing definitions and a few that we can actually use to begin making sense of the issue. We will canvas a few definitions because we think it is useful to break down 'fake news' into distinct categories. It is important to do this because the problem of fake news is now much bigger than just Trump's Twitter tantrums and rallying calls. We will start with the former US President because he is at the epicentre of the 'fake news' fault lines.

Donald Trump's definition of 'fake news'

According to the Trump Twitter Archive, the first captured use of the term 'fake news' by the President on Twitter was 10 December 2016, just after his election victory:

> Reports by @CNN that I will be working on The Apprentice during my Presidency, even part time, are ridiculous & untrue - FAKE NEWS!
>
> (Trump 2016, 10 December)

True to form, on the day we first began drafting this chapter—15 December 2019—the President tweeted about 'fake news' at least four times in a three-hour period in which he tweeted more than ten times. However, Trump wasn't finished yet: over the course of that one day he fired off more than 25 tweets before we stopped counting. The President was an obsessive tweeter and he tweeted obsessively about 'fake news'—more than 650 times between December 2016 and December 2019, on average about five times a week according the archived numbers (Brown 2019). Trump is quite proud of the term 'fake news' and even claimed—modestly of course—to have been the one to have popularised the epithet:

> 'I do notice that people are declaring more and more fake news, where they go, "Fake news!"' the president said during an Oval Office interview with *The New York Times*. 'I even see it in other countries. *I don't necessarily attribute that to me. I think I can attribute the term to me.* I think I was the one that started using it, I would say.'
>
> (Gruynbaum 2019, emphasis added by authors)

The rule-of-thumb for Trump appears to be that if an item of news upsets him, makes him angry or does not accord with his view of the world, then it becomes, in his eyes, 'fake news'. In that rare Oval Office interview with the *NYT*, Trump explained that he saw himself as a 'victim' of unfair coverage by many news outlets. 'I do think it's very bad for a country when the news is not accurately portrayed,' he said. 'I really do. And I do believe I'm a victim of that, honestly' (Gruynbaum 2019). It was this sense of victimhood, repeated often (Wehner 2020) that drove his definition of 'fake news'.

We saw the President's disgruntled attacks on the media intensify in number and in tone over his term of office. He moved from 'fake news' to calling the American news media—even, eventually, his once-favourite network, Fox News—'enemies of the people', or a variant on that dangerous term. The United States, and indeed the world, had never seen anything quite like the tsunami of tweets from the President. More than 56,000 tweets had been logged from mid-2014 to the time his account was suspended on 6 January 2021 (Trump Twitter Archive V2 2021). Reading through the tweets, when they are all aggregated, is an astonishing glimpse into Donald Trump's mood, motivations, and hatreds. The bulk of original tweets (as opposed to retweets) are almost child-like in their simplicity and in their repetition of the President's favourite themes: attacking his enemies (whether real or not); touting his own greatness and achievements (real and mostly imagined); denouncing the media when it criticises him; and praising the Fox News network whenever it defends him. However, there was a good reason to pay close attention to Trump's tweets because—like most of his re-election rallies and public statements—they often contained their own version of 'fake news'. Which brings us to our second definition—the parallel universe of unreality in which Donald Trump operated and projected onto the world around him.

Trump's disinformation campaigns

> 'They know in a debate centred on facts, truth and reality, they lose. Their only mechanism to survive is to muddy the waters, distort, distract and hope if they repeat lies often enough, they become real.'
>
> (Kurt Bardella, cited in Smith 2019)

Kurt Bardella knows what he's talking about. A former Republican staffer who became a Democrat when Donald Trump became President, he had a unique insider's view of the President's motivation for spreading 'fake news' of his own. Bardella was quoted from an interview he gave to *The Observer* for an article published online with the headline 'The lies have it: Republicans abandon truth in Trump impeachment defence'. *The Observer*'s David Smith wrote:

> 'A bewildering array of fake news, warped facts and conspiracy theories have been propagated' in an attempt to blunt the Congressional probe that at the time was moving slowly but surely towards impeaching the President for abuses of power and obstructing Congress.
>
> (Smith 2019)

The object of the disinformation campaign was two-fold: first, Trump's fans didn't care if he lied; they loved it because it represented the 'outsider' status that Trump claimed. Second, for anybody trying to make sense of the claims and counter-claims in the impeachment story, the disinformation coming from Trump loyalists created confusion and doubt. It is clear, as Juliane Lischka notes, Trump was operating strategically when he raised accusations of 'fake news'. It is both 'a systematic approach to delegitimize the news as an institution' and 'a means [for Trump] to retain direct authority' over the new narrative (Lishka 2019, 288).

The President certainly ramped up the tweeting and the rallies and disinformation campaign throughout 2019 as the impeachment scandal deepened and as he geared up for his ultimately unsuccessful re-election campaign in 2020. It saw an increase in frequency and audacity in sowing mistruths and distrust, but it was not new. Trump's presidency began with the lies issued from the White House about the size of his inauguration crowds in January 2017 and from that point they mushroomed, ballooned, intensified, and multiplied on a daily basis. According to a count by *The Washington Post*, Trump had made more than 22,000 false or misleading claims by late August 2020, and the paper's Trump fact-checkers predicted he would exceed 25,000 by election day (Kessler, Rizzo, and Kelly 2020). In fact, *The Washington Post* fact-checking team found 30,573 false or misleading claims had been made by the President during his four years in office (Kessler, Rizzo, and Kelly 2021). In President Trump's first 100 days in office the team catalogued 492 suspect claims but on 2 November 2020—the day before the election—they counted 503 false or misleading claims by the former President (Kessler, Rizzo, and Kelly 2021). The one unifying factor in all of Trump's falsehoods was that they were designed to make him look good and his enemies look bad, or weak. Outside of that logic there was no rhyme or reason to the President's misinformation. He lied about anything and everything; the size of the lie or its consequences seemed irrelevant. Here's a sample tweet from late 2019:

> Today I opened a major Apple Manufacturing plant in Texas that will bring high paying jobs back to America. Today Nancy Pelosi closed Congress because she doesn't care about American Workers!
>
> (Trump 2019)

Trump did visit an Apple manufacturing plant in Texas on 21 November 2019, but it had been open and operating since 2013. Congress was operating on that day, passing legislation and holding impeachment inquiries (Mekelburg 2019).

The 'fake news' mantra spreads and the media reacts

The 45th President of the United States is on the public record as saying he attacked the news media constantly 'to discredit you all and demean you all, so when you write negative stories about me, no one will believe you' (CBS News 2018). The former President has never confirmed these remarks, allegedly made to CBS journalist Lesley Stahl in 2016. In fact, it is more likely that he would deny making such a comment and call it 'fake news'. That one of the most powerful national leaders in the world was comfortable deliberately inciting distrust and hatred of the news media is shocking enough. Even more shocking—or at least it was until the world got used to it, as it did for his propensity for bending the truth past breaking point—was that the US President would use Twitter as a platform to constantly criticise his perceived enemies personally and the news media generally. In August 2018 more than 300 American newspapers united to publish separate editorials on what they saw as the dangers of the Trump administration's never-ending assault on the American mainstream media but it had no effect (Doubek 2018). The President lashed out at the papers that denounced his constant attacks labelling them in yet another tweet as 'the opposition party' (Durkin and Agencies 2018).

The really bad news, according to *The New York Times*, was that by the close of 2018, President Trump's almost daily attacks on the news media, and his constant praise for Fox News—until it stopped touting for him during the 2020 election season—were working to solidify his base among conservative Republicans: 'The president has succeeded in casting journalists as the prime foils on his never-ending reality show, much to the delight of those who cheer him on at rallies' (Rutenberg 2018). At a rally in Pennsylvania, Trump complained his previously favourite TV network was 'putting more Democrats on than Republicans', prompting the crowd to boo the almost-always Pro-Trump channel (Mujezinovic 2019). As *NYT* columnist Charles Blow had commented two weeks earlier: 'The presidential bully pit is as powerful, or possibly more powerful, than any media outlet, in part because it is often propagated by those same outlets' (2019).

Trump ratcheted up the rhetoric another notch the following month when he accused *The New York Times* of 'a virtual act of treason' after it published a story that the US was increasing cyber attacks on Russia (Pompeo 2019). While the paper had not been backward in defending itself and other media that had raised the ire of the President, *The Times'* publisher, A.G. Sulzberger, penned an op-ed following the 'treason' attack taking the highly unusual step of submitting it to an opposition paper, Rupert Murdoch's *Wall Street Journal*, for publication (Sulzberger 2019). Among the 'fighting words' in the piece, Sulzberger warned the American people about their President:

> He's gone from misrepresenting our business, to assaulting our integrity, to demonizing our journalists with a phrase that's been used by generations of demagogues. Now the president has escalated his attacks even further, accusing the *Times* of a crime so grave it is punishable by death.
>
> (Sulzberger 2019)

A few months later, the *NYT*'s executive editor, Dean Baquet, accused the President of putting his reporters' lives at risk by subjecting them to such frequent personal abuse (quoted in Waterson 2019b).

The former President's performance (or lack of it) in the early days of the 2020 coronavirus pandemic was widely criticised at home and abroad, leading to some amazing scenes at his regular briefings about the spread of the virus. Reporters in the White House press corps, most often the subject of his abusive tirades, started demanding answers for the President's inaction, and he reverted to his standard practice of attacking the integrity and performance of the reporters asking the questions. While we devoted the first chapter to a discussion of the issues for the media raised by the pandemic, one comment is more relevant here, offering a considered opinion of the reasoning behind the President's penchant for declaring something 'fake news'. The respected *Washington Post* media columnist Margaret Sullivan, under the headline 'What it really means when Trump calls a story "fake news"', suggested:

> [T]he history of the Trump administration has shown that the loudest cries of 'fake news' accompany the most damning journalism. Coming from him, the phrase now dependably has another meaning: 'all-too-accurate reporting that damages my reputation'.
>
> (Sullivan 2020b)

A notable milestone was reached at the height of the pandemic as the President tweeted his 2000th attack on the 'lamestream media' (Press Freedom Tracker 2020a). While the rants of the President make it difficult for honest journalists to do their job in America, his 'fake news' mantra made it even more difficult—and dangerous—for reporters around the world (Dickey 2018). As we mentioned in the introductory chapter, and will pursue further in Chapter 11, across the globe authoritarian leaders seized on the phrase 'fake news'—and the legitimacy conferred on it by a US President—as a tool with which to attack their critics and push back on media scrutiny. *The Washington Post* labelled the spread of the 'fake news' mantra around the world as one of the President's 'dubious achievements' (The Washington Post 2019).

How does so much 'fake news' make it into the mainstream media?

Everyone has their favourite 'fake news' story, from basketball great Michael Jordan threatening to move his team from North Carolina over that State's law banning transgender people from using the bathroom of their choice (Murtha 2016) to the story that the founder of Corona beer had left millions of dollars in his will to everyone in his small town (Andrew Griffin 2016). These stories circulated first on the Internet but were quickly picked up by mainstream media and published widely. We picked those two examples arbitrarily because 2016 was the year that 'fake' news stories (as they were called then before President Trump invoked his version of the phrase) had an effect on that year's US presidential election. While the Internet has been a 'happy hunting ground' for conspiracy theorists since it began, one of many fake news stories aimed at discrediting the 2016 Democrat presidential candidate Hillary Clinton would have dangerous results, even as late as 2019. Initially the fictitious 'pizzagate' conspiracy story was that the Comet Ping Pong pizza restaurant in Washington was where Mrs Clinton, and other Democrat leaders, took kidnapped children to be molested and trafficked (Kang 2016). After the election, an armed man 'raided' the pizza restaurant with an assault rifle and fired several shots, planning to free children he believed were trapped in a slave ring, only to send frightened patrons and staff dashing in all directions. He was jailed for four years (Haag and Salam 2017). Two years later the restaurant was the target of an arson attack (Sommer 2019). Once the fake 'story' involved a presidential candidate it jumped from the domain of the conspiracy theorists to mainstream media. Mrs Clinton made one of her rare post-election appearances a few days after the first attack to warn against what she called the 'epidemic of fake news' and to call on lawmakers to make sure such stories don't put lives at risk (Edelman 2016).

How does such obvious rubbish make it into credible mainstream media outlets? Roger remembers the early advice of one of his mentors: 'If it sounds too good to be true, it probably is'. It's still good advice. But the reasons for fake or false news reports making the mainstream are many. One obvious reason, as we suggest in Chapters 1 and 5, is the current parlous financial state of the mainstream media worldwide with job losses leading to more pressure on fewer journalists to produce more stories (Rawlinson 2016). Staff numbers haven't improved since Kevin Rawlinson offered his commentary. He referred to those pressures leading to 'dodgy stories' being reported uncritically and dubious stories being tolerated 'because a click is a click' (Rawlinson 2016). He quoted a former editor of the debunking website Snopes, Brooke Binkowski, who pointed to a 'whole cottage industry of people who put out fake news', something that became obvious in the wake of the 2016 US presidential campaign.

Fake news and ideology

It is important to consider the issue of fake news in relation to the concept of ideology because fake news is itself often operationalised in the service of what we commonly call ideology. What we mean by this is that fake news is 'weaponised' in political discourse with the aim of promoting one (ideological) perspective and degrading its opposite, or opposing, ideology. So how do we define ideology? This is a complex area and it is fair to say that several complementary and contradictory definitions of ideology are in play at any one time. An ideology can be defined in simple terms as a 'worldview'; that is, the way that a person, or social grouping (class, social strata or other cohort of like-minded people) might choose to understand the world around them and how it works. This is a good, working and fairly neutral definition of ideology, but ideology can also have both positive and pejorative associations. Fake news is one category of ideology that can be inscribed with negative and pejorative connotations in that its function is the 'propping up of an oppressive form of power' through 'distorting and dissimulating social reality' (Eagleton 2007, 43).

The idea that ideology is just false consciousness—not an accurate representation of the world—has been largely debunked (McCarney 2005). Instead, we can refer to ideology as a partially true account of the world—see our discussion of common sense in Chapter 16—but one that hides the true essence of class, exploitation, and alienation, as social relations that structure the reality of capitalist society. Thus, ideology is useful to the ruling class because it disguises the true class nature of their power: 'Ideology gives to the social formation a false unity, a false coherence' (Costello 1979, 4). Control of the news media contributes to control over the ways in which people think, and what they think about and ultimately, this contributes to the ideological 'hegemony' of the ruling class (Ramos Jr. 1982). As former steelworker turned professor of media studies, Lee Artz (2006) puts it: 'Media and communication both reflect and reproduce the practices and values of the society in which they function… always in the context of relations of power…at discrete, yet ongoing, historical moments' (13). As we detail in Chapters 13–15, our position is that the news media and journalism play a role in normalising the distorted—ideological— view of the world because of the economic and political role they play within the culture industries of capitalism.

If we discount the fringe media such as Breitbart and One America News Network (OANN), the most obvious examples of mainstream media circulating fake news for political purposes is of course the Fox network and other media assets owned by Rupert Murdoch. There is no doubt that Fox and media pundits who circulate in its orbit enabled the worst of Donald Trump by amplifying his lies and creating some of their own which the ex-President then recirculated via his Twitter feed. However, there is a wider and deeper explanation of fake news that circulates via mainstream media under cover of being general, genuine and straightforward reporting. Edward Herman and Noam Chomsky (1988) called this 'manufacturing consent' and Robert McChesney (2000) called it 'rich media, poor democracy' to reflect the impact of the media's role. Mike Wayne (2003, 134) explains the news media's role as the outcome of a very important fault line, the tension between the media as a site of capital accumulation and as an information provider. We pick up this theme in Chapters 5 and 14 where our concept of the 'duality' of news as a commodity in a market economy (capitalism) is explained. The ideological power of the news media is evident in the coverage of business news which amplifies claims about the fair and equitable nature of the market and demonises workers in trade unions, particularly when they withdraw their labour—the source of capitalists' profits—by going on strike (ibid., 174). Thus, there is, for us, a sense in which all news has some 'fake' elements in it. This is not a conscious practice; we don't think journalists are evil propagandists, it is a function of what we describe as a flawed philosophical outlook on the world (ontology) and a flawed method of thinking about the world (epistemology). If you want to know more about this right now, skip ahead to Chapter 13.

How to identify fake news

As Heather Bryant (2018) wrote: 'The universe of people trying to deceive journalists keeps expanding.' What can individual journalists do to identify false news? Arm yourself with the latest verification tools. Here are some simple aspects to consider: Who wrote the story? (Do a quick online search on them.). Who is the source of the story? (Have you ever heard of them before?) Read beyond the 'clickbait' headline (they can be outrageous) to see if the story justifies the treatment. Consider consulting a fact-checking site. If the story seems totally 'over the top' it might be an attempt at satire. Research the site and the author. And search online for how to spot 'fake news'!

Questions for discussion

1   What have you read lately that you would classify as 'fake news'? Why?
2   What verification tools do you use?
3   How else do you spot 'fake news'?
4   How would you suggest the media stopped ex-President Trump's tirades against it?
5   Was there an argument for the media to ignore the President's election rallies in 2020?
6   Why didn't the White House press corps just refuse to attend Trump's COVID-19 briefings until he treated them with more respect?
7   What have you read or learned about the concept of 'ideology' in social studies or political science? Do you agree or disagree with the idea that the news media is ideological in the sense that it—in Herman and Chomsky's phrase—is 'manufacturing consent'.

4 News in crisis

Digital disruption

Does technology drive the future of journalism?

What is the next big technological disruptor that will alter the course of journalism in the future? It is probably going to be artificial intelligence (AI), a technology that the head of search engine giant Google has described as 'more profound than fire or electricity'. The then CEO of Google, Sundar Pichai, continued his remarks by saying that we need to be 'thoughtful about AI, and that it's "fair to be worried" about it too' (Schleifer 2018). Artificial intelligence is already a multi-billion-dollar industry, and AI is used in a range of products and services, particularly in what has become known as the 'Internet of Things', but also in data analysis, driverless vehicles and journalism. That's right, smart machines are now compiling news stories and many people claim that AI-generated news is indistinguishable from copy written by humans (Parsons 2020). Artificial intelligence forces us to confront what we have called the 'techno-legal' and 'techno-ethical' 'time-gap' (Hirst and Patching 2007; Patching and Hirst 2014). We define these terms quite simply as referring to the time delay between a new technology being deployed or marketed as a new commodity and the catch up of legal and ethical regulation. The gap occurs because new technologies are often put to work well before any ethical or legal issues are resolved, or even come to public attention. Artificial intelligence is a good illustration of this problem. This chapter explains our conceptual framework of the 'techno-legal' and 'techno-ethical' 'time-gap' that we use to approach many of the 'cases' in contemporary journalism practice. They are examples of the paradox created by the digital dialectic. This chapter explains the impact of recent and rapid technological change on ethical journalism practice, for example AI and the use of drones. A key discussion in this chapter is around the current—and as yet unresolved—question: Can artificial intelligence and machine learning solve the 'fake news' problem? This chapter explores the nature of news algorithms and the motivations of their human creators. Alongside an easily comprehended discussion of the emerging literature on this topic, we will illustrate our argument with prominent case studies and an exploration of recent attempts to implement AI in the service of authenticating news. This chapter will be careful to avoid the trap of

DOI: 10.4324/9780429242892-5

'technological determinism' that often accompanies discussions of social media, and new digital platforms.

Journalism and artificial intelligence

> In a bleak scenario, automation may increase already-existing pressures on productivity at the expense of journalistic quality.
>
> (Slaček Brlek, Smrke, and Vobič 2017)

Journalists are already facing a bleak economic future as we shall see in the next chapter. The news industry is shedding jobs, wages are stagnant, and news workers are facing the same general problems of precarious employment, part-time work, and a shrinking market for freelancers. Automation of news writing is yet another source of pressure that is a manifestation of the collapsing profitability of the news industry.

Today, there are robots writing the news. Automated journalism—converting raw data into a news 'text' via algorithms—is here (Carlson 2015). At the moment 'robot reporters' are mainly producing copy on stock markets or sports results, but global news agencies such as Associated Press, Bloomberg, and Reuters are trialling new algorithms to deliver content across other news genres; *The Guardian, Forbes* magazine, *The Washington Post*, and many of the world's biggest news outlets are also using machine-made copy (Peiser 2019). Whether you see this as a threat to journalists or an opportunity probably depends on whether you profit from this new technology or feel that it might threaten your job. From the business side of news, automation is a cost-saver but also might help drive new subscriptions by generating copy on labour-intensive beats like real estate that appeal to local readers. To soften the blow, supporters of AI news often argue that it frees up reporters to do more interesting work, such as investigative reporting or feature writing (WNIP 2018). To be honest, we are not convinced by this argument. Actuarial studies show that within the next decade—by the early 2030s—30 per cent of the global workforce (800 million people) will be displaced by AI or robots (McClelland 2020). On the upside, new industries may emerge creating new jobs, but this is perhaps an overly optimistic view given the current parlous state of the global capitalist economy.

Where we are today is the result of about a decade of innovation, but the next generation of AI is expected within five years (using 2020 as a baseline). Technologists are predicting that AI will be capable of 'unsupervised learning' in which algorithms learn without any human intervention (Toews 2020). If this seems like the stuff of nightmares, it's because it is. Science fiction has long had an interest in the idea of intelligent machines coming to the conclusion that human life forms are holding them back. In these dystopian scenarios, the ultra-smart machines turn on humans and wipe them out. When you think about it, what's to stop this from happening? At the moment governments and international agencies like the European Union are developing non-enforceable guidelines that leave it up to designers and programmers to achieve 'trustworthy AI'

(Ritchie and Clarke 2019), which still leaves plenty of room for unscrupulous 'mad scientists' to build killer machines. Outside of Isaac Asimov's famous—but fictional—three laws of robotics[1] there is no legal impediment at the moment to the exponential growth in machine learning and ever more powerful artificial intelligence. Many researchers also argue that Asimov's maxims are not failsafe and could cause a robot to harm humans under some circumstances (Salge 2017). It's clear more work needs to be done in this area. However, we don't even have to look that far ahead to see ethical problems arising with AI. There is bias built in to many of the algorithms that currently manage artificial intelligence; these are the biases of the programmers and some of them are subconscious. In recent research an implicit racial bias has been detected in some AI applications across facial-recognition software, health services, human resources, and scholarship selection processes. The problem is that the learning set data used to train these machine brains is itself structurally biased against the representation of minority groups and so they can only reproduce results that confirm or reinforce these biases (Better Programming 2020).

The problem here is an ethical fault line that we will encounter often in the rest of this book: the development of new technologies is driven by the profit motive and this does not necessarily align with what's best for us. This is an example of the commercial imperatives that energise an unrestrained market economy, taking precedence over public interest issues. It is perhaps the biggest fault line in journalism and certainly, in our view, drives a lot of unethical practices. It is a deep and active contradiction between the aims and objectives of the news industry and journalism as a public service with a democratic purpose. As we will discuss in the next chapter, the market is not democratic and, at the end of the day, does not care about democracy, it only cares about profits. This is illustrated in the current global impasse around how best to manage and regulate artificial intelligence and the application of machine learning. Key players in the United States, Europe, and China—where AI development is concentrated—do not want too much regulation because (they argue) it places limits on innovation. The giant global technology companies want 'light touch' regulation as this is most favourable to their commercial interests (Grossman 2020), but the plotlines in the 1987 sci-fi film *RoboCop* are a salient reminder that corporate interests and the public interest are often worlds apart. Communications scholar John Keane (2018, 221) has written a prophetic warning about the political, legal and ethical paradox that thinking machines bring to the fore:

> If some humans manage in the near future to monopolise the design and application of artificial intelligence and robots, then that privileged class of humans will exercise an unfair hand in deciding our future…
>
> (Keane 2018, 221)

The bottom line in discussions about the seemingly unstoppable spread of AI in the news industry is the questions it raises about the future of journalism as work. However, as Matt Carlson notes in his article 'The robotic reporter', the issue has to be seen as one of political economy, not just technology: 'ongoing reductions in news staffing due to difficulties in generating both online and offline revenues from news content' (Carlson 2015, 423) is the actual threat to journalists' jobs; the technology is just the means by which news industry bosses and investors hope to reconnect to profitability.

The many problems that arise with fake news, particularly on social media, have led many commentators and technology experts to suggest that algorithms might be best situated to control and police instances of fake news. However, algorithms create their own problems. Algorithms are basically mathematical formulae, set by human programmers to do specific jobs in response to pre-determined stimuli. When coupled to the relatively new science of 'machine learning', algorithms are designed to adjust their responses to stimuli based on what they are able to 'learn' from previous interactions. The issue remains though, algorithms are only as good as their human programmers make them and they can be subject to the inbuilt bias of their creators, whether conscious or not. Are humans better at ethical decision-making? Probably. Investing in the ability of machines to solve problems created by humans is tempting because it seems like an easy fix, but it is actually a denial of responsibility and a form of ideological thinking that elevates technology above social relations and invests it with too much autonomous power. This way of thinking is known as technological determinism.

The problem of technological determinism

Technological determinism is a problem in the reporting of technology-related stories, but it is also an issue in journalism studies. It was an issue in the coverage of the 2011 'Arab Spring' uprisings when journalists latched onto examples of activists in Egypt and Tunisia using Facebook and other social media apps to organise protests (Post and Crone 2015). The media's fascination with social media blinded many reporters to more important factors, like student organisations, trade unions, religious groups and civil society organisations (Hirst 2012b). Technological determinism takes three main forms that are often described on a continuum from 'hard' to 'soft'. Hard determinism argues that it is technology itself that drives social change often in ways that are outside of human control; 'technology itself exercises causal influence on social practice' (Bimber 1990, 338). This is a version of 'cause and effect' positivism that searches for causality outside of mediating social relations and absent from any historical context (Rees 1998). Bruce Bimber's second category of technological determinism is the 'unintended consequences' account in which technology is 'at least partially autonomous' (340) and seen to be out of control with problematic results that compete with the positive and intended outcomes. Closely linked to this is what Bimber calls the 'logical sequence' account in which the evolution of technology follows a predetermined path 'regardless of human intervention' (341). Determinism animates technology as a historical actor independent of social relations or human actions and its logical sequence variation is the one most often associated with accounts of disruptive technologies in the sphere of journalistic activity (Hirst 2018, 29–33). This usually occurs because of the limitations of journalism itself and what Post and Crone (2015, 880–1) suggest is a 'technological imperative' that uncritically links developments in social media to a positivist account of an emerging ideal of democratic 'engagement, community and mobilisation' when, in fact, no such relationship can be demonstrated empirically. This is not a new development; the arrival of new technologies has always been met with a mix of glowing predictions about its positive impact and dire warnings about the negative consequences. To some extent this a symptom of the opposing cultural memes of utopian and dystopian visions of the future. These views are dialectical, that is related to each other and contained within one another: utopian and dystopian views can only exist in unison. Utopian futurism is based on 'despair over a current situation' and a hope that technology can fix whatever is ailing society. Dystopian gloom is based on similar rationalising but ends up predicting that things can only get worse. Both are forms of determinism based on the false premise that technology is somehow autonomous, a view that tends to ignore or downplay the roles of human agency and economics which constitute the 'social construction' of technologies (Lim 2018, 375–6).

In journalism studies, technology seems to be sometimes imbued with almost magical powers as Australian communications scholar Axel Bruns (2010, 1) explains:

> Technological determinism is rife in journalists' understanding of current changes, in fact; technology is seen as the only way out of the current crisis in journalism. First, there is the perception of an imminent threat; second, audiences are going online, and journalists perceive a need to chase them; embracing new technologies is seen as the only way to do so. So, technology has been coupled directly with progress, and this is seen as the only salvation for the industry.
>
> (Bruns 2010, 1)

Several reasons have been given for this determinist view among journalists too; digital technologies are an integral part of journalistic practice today but determinism also has deep roots in the profession and academia. At each stage when a new communication technology has emerged there have been forecasts of doom and gloom; for instance, broadcasting was going to kill newspapers, then the Internet was going to wipe out both newspapers and broadcasting. In fact, these technologies can exist quite harmoniously; what wipes out one technology and favours another is not determined by its technical characteristics but by its economic performance. It was commercial competition that killed the Beta tape format and audio cartridges, and it is commercial competition that is driving newspapers out of business in the digital age. Technological determinism is a form of what the Italian philosopher Antonio Gramsci called 'common sense' thinking, which is only a partial explanation that seems reasonable and straightforward that is then popularised as ideology. Common sense exists on the surface level, it tends to dissolve when subjected to proper scrutiny (Patterson 2016). In journalism the causal effect of technology is seen as a plausible common sense explanation for the economic crisis and a 'self-sufficient' factor that appears as an 'inevitable' and 'impersonal' force that is the direct cause of change (Ornebring 2010, 58). Contemporary researchers in the area of digital and platform journalism are now looking to move beyond a determinist approach, particularly in response to the rise of 'digital native media' that have no links to legacy media institutions or technologies such as broadcast or print and who work on subscriptions, memberships and philanthropy rather than an advertising-based business model (see, for example, Garcia-Orosa, Lopez-Garcia, and Vazquez-Herrero 2020).

The alternatives to technological determinism revolve around several conflicting ideas: the first is that technology is just a tool and has no affective power of its own; the second is technological dependency that subjugates humans to machines; the third position is more nuanced and recognises that there is a process of mutual determination between social relations and technology (Hassan and Sutherland 2017, 147–8). It might be the case that technological determinism has morphed a little in the digital age into what Hassan and Sutherland describe as 'network determinism' (151), a state in which 'it appears that we express our free will in our networked lives' but do not acknowledge our 'dependency' on automation. 'Automated digital networks now had the capacity to conceive, signpost and direct where we "go" in our networked lives. But is this really "determinism" and, if so, what kind is it?' (Hassan and Sutherland 2017, 152). This is an interesting argument and one predicated on a political economy understanding of capitalism in which the determining feature of network technologies is not technical but a *'generalized orientation'* towards commercial subsumption of our digital lives and 'the widening sphere of digital capitalism' (Hassan and Sutherland 2017, 154). This is an argument that basically suggests our choices are removed because effectively we have no choice except to be hooked in to the ubiquitous network at the expense of our privacy and our non-work leisure time as work-oriented computing colonises the privacy of our living spaces: 'As in so many other realms the needs of business trumped any (?) social and cultural considerations' (ibid.) and we become bound by 'the oppression of automation' (157).

In our view, this is consistent with the dialectical concept of mutual constitution which is appealing to us because it provides a more holistic and satisfying explanation. Technology is the result of human actions, and the direction it takes is shaped by human decision-making (for better or worse). Technology does not exist in a social vacuum and it does not determine historical change *by itself*. Therefore, the decisions that lead to the creation and eventual deployment of technologies have a social component that is ultimately determined by economic imperatives. Technologies are invented to meet a specific identified human need but only within definite social relations, and they build on previous successes or failures. This places the political economy of technology at the centre of our analysis—'profitability through "efficiency"' and 'faster means cheaper' as Hassan and Sutherland (2017, 150) note. Thus, when adopting new technologies—in this instance news-producing AI—we are inevitably adopting new social relations of production that involve market forces, potential state intervention and new cultural forms (MacKenzie and Wajcman 1999). This, it seems to us, is an appropriate analytical framework for discussing the intrusion of new technologies into the news production process—a process we begin in the next chapter and put into a more theoretical perspective in Chapters 12–16.

Drone journalism

Camera-equipped drones (technically Unmanned Aerial Vehicles, or UAVs) are now a taken-for-granted digital tool for visual journalism but their use also raises ethical issues for photo-journalists, particularly in relation to invasions of privacy and access to imagery that would not normally be available, such as seeing over high fences or through windows high above the ground (Harvard 2020). Like the Internet and other technologies, drones have moved from the military space into civilian use, including law enforcement and journalism. We could consider civilian use as perhaps an unintended but inevitable consequence as drones have become smaller, more powerful and easier to operate. Drones are often addressed as a 'disruptive journalistic technology' by those who privilege technology over other causal factors (Belair-Gagnon, Owen, and Holton 2017). While drones might solve simple technical issues for journalists but only as one new tool among many, they are not going to fundamentally alter the social dynamics of the news industry.

The mode of operation for drones—when the remote operator sees a drone-eye view—is similar to the targeting view in military operations. Some ethicists feel this itself is a worrying feature as it might provide an ethical buffer and encourage the operator to see everything in their field of vision as a 'target' (Culver 2014, 56–7). Drones have also been subsumed into what critics call the 'surveillance gaze' that draws entire populations into contact with State authorities that are not always benign in intent. This is a relatively new area of research but it confirms that UAVs present both an opportunity and a problem (Harvard, Hyvönen, and Wadbring 2020).

Despite these concerns, drones have been readily adapted as a journalistic tool and UAVs certainly broaden the scope of visual material available to journalists and news editors. Some journalism schools are now offering courses in drone journalism. Kathleen Bartzen Culver from the University of Wisconsin has outlined four key areas for ethical consideration in relation to drone use in news gathering. The safety of operators and members of the public is a number one concern particularly if the drone is being flown over a crowd and there is potential for a mishap. Accuracy and context are also concerns raised by Culver but surely it is the responsibility of the reporter to vouch for the images and to provide context. After all, a drone is really just a very agile flying camera; the operator and the journalist are responsible for editorial decisions. Culver (2014, 59) rightly points to privacy bringing 'the greatest entanglement of law and ethics' to the question of drones and journalism. This is certainly an aspect of the techno-legal time-gap in action because drones are a relatively new technology and regulation is really several years behind their actual capability and availability.

The final area of concern raised by Culver is the potential for a conflict of interest to arise if material gathered by a journalist becomes relevant for law enforcement; 'the question of whether government agencies barred from conducting their own surveillance will turn to news media as a surrogate' (ibid.). This is a valid question, and it doesn't just apply to the use of drones. Cooperation between journalists and law enforcement or government intelligence agencies is a vexed issue that has been discussed for at least 100 years. Writing in 1985, journalist-turned-academic Tom Goldstein took a very dim view of reporters 'taking the law into their own hands', or wanting 'at least to help law enforcement' (Goldstein 1985, 148). His advice, which we would echo (though perhaps for different reasons) is that this is not something journalists should do: 'A journalist is paid to write stories, not to assist the government' (145). We take up this issue again in Chapter 9. It is also a question of trust—a precious commodity in short supply these days (see Chapter 6)—as Professor Culver makes clear in relation to drones:

> Citizens already suspicious of airborne surveillance in other contexts, including military and law enforcement, cannot be expected to readily discern public-interest uses of media drones from those directed at the lowest tastes. Legitimate news gatherers run the risk of tainting their reputation by association.
>
> (Culver 2014, 63)

A 2020 study of news audience reactions to drone journalism was too small to generalise but the findings are worth noting in the context of a discussion of trust and media ethics. Audience members were willing to accept the use of drones if it is done ethically, particularly if privacy concerns were treated fairly, but 'when audiences do not think news media act ethically, they are less supportive of journalists using drones' (Duncan and Culver 2020, 108). This seems like a reasonable position; drones are not going away and their use in newsgathering is likely to increase, and viewers are now well accustomed to seeing footage from drones in a range of genres from wildlife documentaries to action movies. It is inevitable that they will become a fairly standard tool for journalists. Ensuring that they are not misused is a new responsibility and a potential source of new conflict between journalists and news consumers if they are used unethically.

Technological disruption is clearly a factor in the crisis confronting journalism today and the digital dialectic certainly creates a unique set of ethical fault lines. However, technology is not the principal cause of journalism's problems. Decisions to downsize newsrooms are not the result of decisions to embrace new technologies; they are decisions based on economic factors. Capital retains control over technological innovation and implementation to carry out its central economic purpose, to keep production costs as low as possible, and to keep its return on investment as high as possible (Umney 2018). The real driver of economic crisis—globally and within the news industry—is not innovation; it is the social, economic and political conditions that mark the period of late capitalism today. It is not technology but the crisis of profitability that drives change. Technology is central to the contradictions within the capitalist information economy, but not decisive. The machine can be a tool of oppression or of liberation, but the decisive role is played by the social relations of production (Fuchs 2019). This is a political economy perspective on the news industry and the subject of the next chapter.

Questions for discussion

1   Do you think AI will solve the 'fake news' problem? Explain your position.
2   Who in the class has access to a drone? What do you use it for? What has been your experience of the reaction of others to you flying a drone around?
3   Can you see the ethical issues around privacy and the use of drones?
4   Would you hand over your drone footage to police, if asked?
5   Would you challenge a police demand for your footage (see the case in Chapter 9)?
6   Discuss the techno-legal and techno-ethical time-gap. How worried should we be about emerging smart technologies?

Note

1   Asimov's laws have long been a benchmark for robotics and artificial intelligence. They first appeared in his sci-fi stories *I, Robot*, published in 1950. Whether or not they are enforceable is an open question. First Law: A robot may not injure a human being or, through inaction, allow a human being to come to harm. Second Law: A robot must obey the orders given it by human beings except where such orders would conflict with the First Law. Third Law: A robot must protect its own existence as long as such protection does not conflict with the First or Second Law.

5 News in crisis

The economic collapse of the news industry

Can journalism survive the Internet?

This is not a hypothetical question. In 2011, Martin published a book with this query in its title, *News 2.0: Can Journalism Survive the Internet?* (Hirst 2011). A decade later and the news industry is still trying to figure it out. As we noted in the previous chapter, it seems that AI might be the technological innovation that finally sinks journalism as a career option. Journalism still doesn't really know if it has a strong financial future. At a public meeting in Chicago on 23 February 2020 to discuss the failing health of the city's news media, the 300 or so people in the audience were still pondering this question.

> 'Eleven years ago, when we convened here, the consensus was that the financial model, the former financial model of the journalism business, was broken. And it's still broken.'
>
> (Feder, cited in Jacob 2020a)

At the meeting, veteran media columnist Robert Feder acknowledged the fundamental mistake that the pioneers of online news made in the late 1990s: '[W]e created the expectation…that news was free…and we've been trying to fight our way back ever since.' Well, that's half right, at least. Perhaps it was a mistake by the news companies—mainly newspaper publishers—who are now regretting the lost revenue and lost opportunities, but for consumers access to free news from a wide variety of sources has, arguably, been a very good development.

The undeniably true aspect of this lament from senior news industry figures is that providing free access to their content on the Internet certainly undercut their print revenues. What started as a clever marketing trick to encourage new print subscriptions turned into a sinkhole down which they poured good money after bad and which eventually drained their bank accounts, forcing hundreds of newsroom closures and the drastic downsizing of those that remained. Today's news executives are filled with regret that their peers in a previous generation made such a costly error of judgement. The contemporary lament, and attendant blame-shifting, was also on display at the Chicago

DOI: 10.4324/9780429242892-6

meeting. Editor-in-chief of the *Chicago Tribune*, Bruce Dold, acknowledged there is an ongoing financial problem for news publishers, but the threat horizon has now been shifted to the duopoly of the so-called 'platform giants'—Facebook and Google—and the collapse in the profitability of online news is now being blamed on them too.

> 'The single greatest threat facing the *Tribune* and facing every legacy news organization is the duopoly of Facebook and Google...They control 70–75 percent of digital advertising, so every organization that has been trying to make the shift from print advertising to digital has run up against this blockade.'
>
> (Dold, cited in Jacob 2020a)

There's no doubt this is a huge problem, but it is like blaming the sun for coming up in the morning and fading the curtains. The logic of capital accumulation tells us that as old industries are eclipsed and go into decline, money always finds a new and more profitable home. As investment moves from the legacy media to the new platform giants, of course there's going to be a parallel power shift. The new and emerging technology companies are growing through mergers and acquisitions and they are slowly but surely digesting their less nimble competition. Capitalism does appear to operate on the 'laws of the jungle' and, right now, the platform giants are the apex predators. It should not, therefore, be all that surprising that Jeff Bezos, whose fortune was built on the Amazon online shopping mall model, was in a position to buy the assets of *The Washington Post* for US$250 million in 2013. According to interviews he gave around the time of the purchase, Bezos wanted to save an iconic news institution, but he also believed that the online news delivery system had a profitable future—in volume sales at a reasonable price (Denning 2018).

Trust and profit: Uneasy bedfellows in the newsroom

This chapter sets out our arguments about how the crisis of profitability is central to the crisis of trust and the technological disruption afflicting the news industry. It is their dialectically combined, but uneven, impact on ethical principles and the practice of journalism that brings them together at this crossroads moment. In this chapter we outline our approach based on several key ideas within the theoretical and methodological framework of the political economy of communication and their application to a study of journalism ethics. This points to more detailed discussions in the final chapters. At the heart of the issue is a central dynamic of contradictory and competing interests that runs through the news industry. We describe this as the most significant and dangerous ethical fault line in journalism today. On the one hand, news is a public good and journalism a public service; on the other, news is produced, distributed and consumed in an economic system that values private profit over public interest. This unstable dialectic is the result of what some researchers call the news industry's 'curious position' as an economic, cultural, political, and social institution:

> On the one hand, a free press is thought to be essential for a democratic and well-functioning society, as it is through the press that the actions of the government and political elites can be revealed and held accountable. On the other hand, the media are profit-maximizing businesses that aspire to maintain and grow their audiences and that often report to owners concerned with profitability.
>
> (Archer and Clinton 2017, 2)

Everybody is aware of the difficulties involved in serving two masters well, and the issue of democratic politics facing pushback from authoritarian regimes is familiar to us today. Now, more than ever, we need a well-functioning news media; one that can help us navigate the 'fake news' tsunami and that holds rogue leaders to account. However, in many nations it is clear that public sentiment has turned against many of the once-trusted news brands. It has proven to be immensely difficult to stop the spread of fake news and to defend the public interest. The problems faced by the news industry in maintaining the public's trust in its ability to serve the public interest, while also satisfying the very different needs of shareholders and the stock market, are only exacerbated by the current conditions of technological disruption and instability in the news marketplace. But it wasn't supposed to be like this.

Even as recently as a decade ago there was a pervasive sense of optimism that the digital revolution would herald a new era of media accountability and a closer relationship between journalists and citizens. At the time, many people argued that the explosion of 'networked journalism' and news on social media would enhance the critical abilities of the Fourth Estate and strengthen the watchdog role of the news media (Beckett and Mansell 2008; Hermida 2010; Rosen 2008). There was an air of digital optimism in much of the academic literature of that period and a belief that new forms of collaboration between traditional journalists and a no longer passive audience would bring forth a new age of openness and democratic reform. Few voices were raised to offer a sense of caution, but many of them were associated with the political economy tradition. For example, the Canadian media theorist, Vincent Mosco, first offered a counter-narrative in his 2004 book *The Digital Sublime* in which he suggested that many of the optimists had been hoodwinked by the shiny new gadgets and trinkets offered up by the digital revolution. In their blindness, the optimists overlooked the tell-tale signs that the digital revolution also had a very destructive downside. In a sense, argued Mosco as the second phase of the digital revolution got under way, people have been too willing to accept the 'false promises' made by the technology boosters: 'a world in which people will communicate across borders without the filters and censors set up by watchful governments and profit-conscious businesses' (Mosco 2004, 25). With the 20/20 vision of hindsight we can see that this promise was never fulfilled.

The giant technology platforms like Facebook and Google are the new gatekeepers and for a price they will promote one message over another using algorithms whose precise formulas are closely guarded commercial secrets. Yes, there's been an explosion in the amount of content and information available via the Internet, but nation-states continue to police their cyber borders by blocking access to anything they consider dangerous or subversive of their national interest. Even in Western liberal democracies our ability to filter useful, credible information from the fake news, propaganda, and deliberate mistruths is diminished by the surfeit of source nodes available in the cascading and never-ending 24/7 spin cycle. Trying to find 'truth' in this torrent of white noise is like trying to carefully take a sip from a fire hose. We would also suggest—as a thesis to be explored in this and subsequent chapters—that the information revolution (or digital revolution, if you like) has created a new set of ethical issues for both journalists and news consumers. In this chapter we will focus our attention on the economic factors that form the bedrock of the new media reality and we'll start with an examination of why the early promise of the digital sublime has collapsed into ongoing chaos and uncertainty.

A decade of financial crisis

The financial chaos is real; paid online subscriptions do not seem to be providing a revenue cushion for any but the biggest players in each market and then, only just. It is also not a coincidence that technological disruption is a feature of the crisis; it is a method of seeking to restore profitability and thus a level of stability to the industry. Despite a decade of paywalls and subscription drives, only a small fraction of consumers is willing to pay for online news (Fletcher 2020; Mason 2020); this is more disruptive than digital technology. Even when the Nieman Lab tried to put a positive spin on the results from the Reuters Institute Digital News Report for 2020, the best it could do was to suggest that 'an increasing sliver' of consumers were willing to pay an online subscription, most of us still to consume the news for free (Hazard Owen 2020). The point is to understand why this is important for our consideration of journalism ethics. The simple answer is that as revenues decline so too does the size of the average newsroom, and so too does the diversity of news outlets. In two years between 2018 and 2020 the number of digital news start-ups that came online was matched by the number of closures. Some were small local-only sites that might struggle to attract advertising revenue (Jacob 2020b), but some have also been global brands like Buzzfeed News (BBC News 2020a) and the Huffington Post (Samios 2017). There is a global trend of news providers either closing some bureaus completely, or drastically reducing staffing levels (Waterson 2019a). Legacy media newsrooms have also been hit hard by the economic downturn in the news business and by the COVID-19 pandemic. Globally, the picture is bleak with both advertising and circulation revenues predicted to continue their downward path until at least 2024 (Mayhew 2020d). The impact of all of this bad news is that, as newsrooms shrink, the pressure increases on those who remain to do more work with fewer resources causing mistakes to creep in and corners to be cut. The ability of individual journalists or newsrooms to consider ethical issues falls in direct proportion to the job and revenue cuts.

The crisis of profitability did not spring up overnight and it certainly predates the Internet. Perhaps we can confidently say that it has been made worse by neoliberal economic policy, the global financial crisis of 2008–2009, and the news industry struggling to redefine itself in the face of competition from online sources and social media (Knowles 2018). There is no doubt that the news industry's initial poor response to the potentials and pitfalls of digital publishing have contributed to the fall in profits, and the social media giants like Facebook have contributed to an increase in the rate of decline, but the roots of the crisis go back to at least the early 1980s. This is well documented in the academic literature and it has been linked to the 'greed is good' mentality that permeated Wall Street at that time (Meyer 2004) and also to the penchant for hiring MBAs to run news operations rather than seasoned editors with 'ink in their veins' (Underwood 1993). By the mid-1980s, a number of American news publishers were facing serious debt issues and similar problems beset Rupert Murdoch in the UK and Australian markets. It is at this point that investment in news began to decline, slowly at first but as the crisis deepened more money was pulled from operations (Littau 2019).

Capitalism is a system built on competition for profits and it's a zero-sum game. If one capitalist is winning, another in the same industry must be missing out, and in January 2019 there were signs that a massive and inevitable shake-out was occurring in digital newsrooms signalled by what media commentators described as a 'brutal round of layoffs'. BuzzFeed cut 15 per cent of staff; 7 per cent were let go at Verizon the publisher of AOL, the Huffington Post, and Yahoo. Several newspapers owned by the Gannett group also suffered staff cuts in the same week, which left the 'newly unemployed' reporters 'with fewer places to go' (McArdle 2019). *The Washington Post* columnist Megan McArdle offered a very pessimistic assessment of the situation which had been humorously labelled a 'pivot to dust' by one insider. According to McArdle, there is no plan to save journalism; instead, 'we're watching the destruction of most of the nation's journalistic capacity'. McArdle was writing about the United States, but her argument applies almost universally, and certainly across the Anglophone world and Europe.

Even the new model is already broken

The digital start-ups that were going to save journalism by harnessing the enthusiasm for online distribution and social media are already in trouble. What went wrong and why did it all go south so quickly? Well, one media executive answered this question with one of his own. In a televised discussion of the job-shedding and cost-cutting at HuffPost and BuzzFeed, MSNBC presenter Chris Hayes gave voice to a deep-seated fear shared by news executives around the world: 'What if there is literally no profitable model for digital news? Or none that actually scales and endures without, say, the established readership base and brand of *The New York Times*?' (Hayes, cited in Waterson 2019a). Unfortunately, many News Establishment analysts and commentators are looking for answers in the wrong places. For some the problem is a 'digital content bubble', but this implies there is too much content and that cuts in both digital and traditional media are a necessary antidote to this oversupply. However, there is another way of looking at this issue: it is not a problem of too much content, but rather that the content is not profitable anymore.

This latter point is highlighted in an article by Emily Bell, published online by *The Guardian* in early February 2019. The headline on Bell's commentary sums up the dilemma created by the crisis in profitability: 'What 2,000 job cuts tell us: The free market kills digital journalism'. But in essence, Bell's argument is just blame-shifting; staff cuts in digital newsrooms are the fault of social media companies hoovering up the bulk of online advertising revenues. Bell articulates the issue in a sharp and succinct manner:

> The primary mistake most digital publishers made was to imagine that platform companies, and particularly Google and Facebook, had any serious interest in helping them sustain their businesses.
>
> (Bell 2019)

In fact, the news for news companies is probably worse than this. Google has a near monopoly over global Internet searches approaching 90 per cent of market share in some countries. Facebook has more than two billion active users and many of them now use the platform as their main source of news. This has created the huge hole in the business model for news organisations. Both Facebook and Google have made a profit from repurposing third-party news content without bearing any of the production costs (Hubbard 2017). The irony is though, for years the large platform companies have insisted that they are technology focused and not media companies at all (Napoli and Caplan 2017). However, the so-called platform giants cultivated news media's dependence on them for traffic (Statt 2017), and teased profit-sharing arrangements. This looked promising for both parties until the scandals surrounding Facebook's role in promoting 'fake news' about the US presidential election in 2016 caused a rethink. Smarting from the embarrassment of the fake news revelations, in January 2018 Facebook made an abrupt U-turn and changed its algorithms to promote more personal content and less third-party news to feeds. This cut traffic directed from Facebook to news websites further impacting revenues in the news industry (Meese and Hurcombe 2020). The backlash against Facebook has prompted many jurisdictions to consider new legislation to make the platform giants pay media companies for access to news. Google has also come under fire for alleged anti-competitive practices, prompting a lawsuit from the US government alleging it is using unfair monopoly tactics to dominate the search engine browser market (Rushe and Paul 2020). Both of these actions by governments represent their attempt to overcome the techno-legal time-gap by retrospectively engineering a regulatory framework to control the platform giants. It is probably too little, too late, and unlikely to alter their behaviour.

The competition between news media—both legacy print and broadcast outlets, and digital start-ups—and the 'platform giants' is real, and companies like Google and Facebook have become adept at influencing the narrative in their favour. Their methods for doing this have been described as 'corporational determinism'—a play on technological determinism—which presents the foundational aspirations of the company as coterminous with public aspiration and masking its own profit motives (Natale, Bory, and Balbi 2019). Whether the platform giants are media companies or not, they are fighting with legacy media companies over the same eyeballs and a shrinking pool of global advertising dollars. There's also a new frontier to fight over—data—and here the platform giants have an edge; so much so that we can perhaps talk about a new phase of 21st-century economic development which has been given the label 'platform capitalism' (Srnicek 2017). What makes the platform companies so important is that they are totally disruptive of old business models. The supergiants—Google, Facebook, Amazon in the Anglophone world, and Alibaba in the Chinese market—begin with a virtual monopoly and consolidate by crushing their rivals. Myspace, for example, was wiped out by Facebook perhaps because it was essentially a platform for musicians and fell behind in the tech innovation race (Lee 2011). The more commercially focused second-tier platforms, such as rideshare and food delivery apps, function in legal grey areas that allow them to push down wages for employees and skirt around analogue regulatory systems that were never designed to cope with digital disruption. In these disregulated ethico-legal gaps, companies like Uber continue to insist they are technology companies, and not in the transportation business. This is where the phenomenon we know as the 'gig economy' began. Now, casual job sites like Airtasker and Freelancer are ubiquitous and for some people provide their only sources of precarious employment. All of this disruption and the shift towards platform capitalism has had critical impacts on how the work of journalism is done—for example, the rise in precarious (part-time, casual and low-paid) employment (Waisbord 2019) and 'fragile professionalism' (Matthews and Onyemaobi 2020). For now, suffice to say that it is disingenuous for the platform giants to insist on the rapidly dissolving distinction between content production and content sharing, and to claim that they are just neutral platforms with cool and efficient algorithms that put viewers in front of content produced elsewhere (Napoli and Caplan 2017).

The role of finance capital in hollowing out the news media

> *Sports Illustrated* is being taken from all of us in an ugly and ruthless manner. The organs of the magazine are being harvested by a private equity firm that is out for blood and taking no prisoners.
>
> (Zirin 2019)

As we were drafting this chapter in October 2019, we came upon the news that one of the world's most iconic sports journalism brands was facing a limited and uncertain future after its sale to a private equity firm with no history in, or commitment to, what the magazine has represented for more than 60 years. Dave Zirin's sad and angry obituary for a title he had grown up with and loved references the intervention of a finance capital firm that can realise a short-term profit from its purchase of *Sports Illustrated* without any regard for the consequences. As Zirin (2019) argues, in the process these private equity companies 'are destroying the institutions that we rely on'. Zirin appears to be right. News accounts of the deal show that *Sports Illustrated* staff were treated badly by the new management company. Over half the magazine's employees were summarily dismissed by the new owners without notice and without any discussion (Atkinson 2019). The fate that befell *Sports Illustrated* in October 2019 is a good case study of the impacts that the influx of speculative finance capital can have on media companies.

In recent years, scholars in the political economy tradition have devoted attention to the growth of finance capital as global systemic crisis has hollowed out once-profitable industries such as manufacturing and, increasingly, news production. The global information economy is the perfect host for finance capital because the commodification of attention results in a borderless and 'space less' product that can be produced, reproduced, and shipped around the world at very little cost, but with high, even if short-term, returns on investment (Pitluck, Mattioli, and Souleles 2018). Financialisation is the process of finance capital establishing a dominant role in the global capitalist economy and exerting control over once autonomous sectors such as news publishing (Davis 2011). The more mundane issue of the intrusion of rootless finance capital into the news industry is the widening of the commerce-public interest fault line. Historically, when news companies were family-owned, or had limited shareholding, the editorial wishes of the proprietor and the mission of the newsroom were not too far apart and many of the 20th century's key news barons took pride in formally stepping back from editorial matters while maintaining effective control (Rupert Murdoch being the obvious counter example). However, finance capital is organised on very different lines and is more concerned with asset-stripping and cost-cutting than with the efficacy of the news product itself (Costa e Sliva 2014; Almiron 2010). Private equity companies have no loyalty to journalism and their business is making a profit out of restructuring industries that are in trouble, as Ken Doctor notes in his 'Newsonomics' column for Nieman Lab, the game is not journalism, it's making the numbers:

> The economics here are fairly simple: Pay no more than 3× or 4× annual company earnings, consolidate every cost you can, and keep your profit takeout steady by continuing to cut newsroom and other jobs as necessary to make The Number.
>
> (Doctor 2016)

It is almost certain that the continuing financialisation of the news industry will result in further job losses, more closures, and less diversity in journalism, which can really only be bad from an ethical perspective. This is why many people—journalists, activists, and academics alike—are placing more faith in a different sort of financial injection into the news business, philanthropy.

Can philanthropy save journalism?

In recent years several schemes have been floated to rescue journalism from the destructive cycle of boom and bust that has seen the news industry hollowed out around the world over the past 15 to 20 years. All sorts of proposals have been put forward from fully autonomous collectives like IndyMedia (which are now largely defunct; the current iteration of Indy News is a pro-gun rights and anti-Biden conservative American outfit that has colonised the name); hyper-local networks of amateur citizen-reporters to cover grassroots news under the tutelage of professionals (largely a failure); subscriptions to not-for-profit outlets like *The Guardian* (which is not strictly a not-for-profit) and various forms of philanthropic charity to support high-end public interest investigative journalism. Each of these methods, designed with goodwill in an attempt to save journalism from going down with the sinking commercial vessels that contain it, has had only limited success. In 2011, Martin posed the question 'Can journalism survive the Internet?' in his book *News 2.0*; at the time he gave a qualified 'Yes, but…' to that question. Then in 2018 he revisited the issue in *Navigating Social Journalism* in which he reviewed all that had been done in the previous decade to 'save' journalism. At that time Martin was less optimistic, concluding that efforts to rescue journalism from the economic whirlpool dragging it down were largely failing. Unfortunately, we have to reach a similar conclusion today.

Philanthropy as the saviour of journalism is not a new idea. It was proposed 100 years ago by Victor S. Yarros (1922) as the solution to what he saw as declining standards and public dissatisfaction with the news being published in American newspapers in the 1920s:

> The only feasible alternative to private and capitalistic ownership and control of newspapers is co-operative ownership and management with subsidies, for a period at least, from persons of wealth, vision and sympathy.
>
> (Yarros 1922, 417)

So, you see, this idea has been around for a long time. The question is: Can it work?

There are certainly some hopeful models currently in operation, such as ProPublica and various multinational consortia of investigative journalists who supplement their philanthropic donations by partnering with newspapers in various parts of the world to co-finance and co-publish their big investigations. The Conversation—a not-for-profit news journal started in Australia—is another digital outlet that is often cited to support a pro-philanthropy argument. The Conversation is underwritten by universities and given the crisis in global higher education that emerged in the slipstream of the COVID-19 pandemic; this source of funding may start to dry up; it also relies on the unpaid work of academic contributors. While these models are often held up as paradigm examples of how philanthropy can work to support journalism (for example, Young and Hermida 2020), they are actually quite precarious and have no guarantee of funding beyond their ability to hold the interest of their major funders; in many ways they are still subject to the whims of the market. There is also the issue of scale and sustainability, which some news sites attempt to bridge by marketing subscriptions and memberships rather than seeking donations as such, while maintaining a free online presence as well. A significant study of philanthropist-funded news media by Magda Konieczna highlights these issues but does not offer any hopeful conclusions. Charitable funding from foundations is not secure in the long term and philanthropists may prove to have only a 'limited appetite for funding journalism' (Konieczna 2020, 144).

While donor-funded news sounds good and has received a lot of support in academic circles, it does raise another ethical issue. Will reporters and news outlets funded by philanthropic sources bend their editorial line to suit the interest of the donors? This might not seem like a big issue, but in at least one reported case, the philanthropic funding caused a reporter to spend time acting as an agent of the funding agency rather than doing journalism (Malan 2018). It might be argued that this was an isolated case at one provincial newspaper in South Africa, but the potential for undue influence from donors to shape news coverage also occurs at the global level, if not deliberately at least as a result of a shared free-market ideology and finding a convenient 'fit' between the sponsor's objectives and editorial objectives (Scott, Bunce, and Wright 2017). An American study takes this concern one step further and suggests that philanthropic funding might be premised on the donor having some influence over editorial policy in relation to the operations their philanthropy supports (Ferrucci and Nelson 2019).

We are not against philanthropic funding in principle, but it is not by any means money given without some strings. There is no automatic correlation between the philanthropic values of charitable organisations and the public interest values of journalism (Browne 2010). The key point is that philanthropy comes with its own problems and does not provide a long-term or sustainable solution to the economic crisis in the news industry. The crisis of profitability is systemic: it doesn't just impact journalism; in dialectical fashion, it is both the bedrock and the curse of global financial capitalism. In the final section of this book, we will return to this issue from a more theoretical perspective to discuss the broader problem of how journalists should think about their social role as protectors and promoters of the public interest within the context of a capitalist political economy. How do journalists manage the ethical fault lines that emerge when the news commodity is valued more for its commercial aspects— as a source of profit—than it is for its public service attributes? We have already flagged this as the central ideological fault line in journalism today and one that has tremendous impact on our next topic, the trust deficit that further complicates the news crisis.

Questions for discussion

1   What have been the effects of the collapsing business model of the main-stream media in your local area?
2   Has anything been done to help it?
3   During the pandemic some governments offered assistance to ailing news titles by increasing their advertising buy. But what happens when this source of funding disappears?
4   Do you think philanthropy is the answer?
5   Discuss the ethical issues associated with news organisations accepting philanthropic donations to keep afloat (building on the issues already raised in this chapter).

6   The crisis of legitimacy

The existential crisis of trust

> When people in a society lose faith or trust in their institutions and in each other, the nation collapses.
>
> (Brooks 2020)

There can be little doubt that Western societies are experiencing a crisis of trust in institutions of government, commerce, and leadership as David Brooks outlined in an October 2020 essay in *The Atlantic*. That same month, a group of academics who teach and research in the field of 'authoritarian studies' co-signed an open letter warning that democratic norms are under threat: 'The Covid-19 pandemic has exposed profound inequalities of class and race across the globe. As the last four years have demonstrated, the temptation to take refuge in a figure of arrogant strength is now greater than ever' (The New Fascism Syllabus 2020). That the world has come to this, four generations after World War Two overturned fascism on a global scale, is troubling. It can be explained in different ways, but the most important thing to recognise is that the rise of authoritarian politicians and openly fascist movements in some countries is the result of failure. It is the failure of so-called liberal free market capitalism to resolve pressing social issues like war, climate change, inequality, systemic racism, homophobia, and misogyny. That capitalism is a failure should no longer be in doubt; even the Pope thinks the market has failed: 'The marketplace by itself cannot resolve every problem, however much we are asked to believe this dogma of neoliberal faith,' Pope Francis wrote in an October 2020 religious message. It's not just the left that thinks capitalism has failed (Bellamy Foster 2019), even the pro-market *Forbes* magazine agrees (Kobayashi-Solomon 2020). The economic and political system predicated on so-called 'free enterprise', market economics, and representative democracy is no longer fit for purpose. Even people who believe capitalism is both inevitable and workable agree that it is failing and that 'dislocation, insecurity and inequality' are all on the rise (Reeves 2019). The status quo is being questioned and social divisions are growing—between rich and poor people, and between rich nations and poor nations. It is precisely when the system cannot provide either solutions to

DOI: 10.4324/9780429242892-7

problems, or answers to genuine questions, that citizens begin to lose faith and to explore other forms of politics, including lurid conspiracy theories like QAnon, and strong leaders who promise to fix things (even though they are incapable of fixing problems and may only make them worse). People want answers, but they are not to be found in the places we might have looked for them in the past, including the news media. This is the broad background to our ethical crossroads metaphor: in folklore and in Greek mythology, a cross-roads is associated with making a difficult choice between two paths 'between worlds', one leading to salvation, the other to ruin (Mibba 2012). This ethical dilemma is the essence of dialectics in journalism.

Alongside the general crisis of legitimacy, the news industry and journalism are facing their own crossroads: an existential crisis of legitimacy. But what exactly do we mean by this? A crisis of legitimacy occurs primarily when people begin to feel that the rhetoric that is supposed to encapsulate principles and meaning to describe a phenomenon or situation no longer matches the reality—their lived experience—of the situation or phenomenon. The rhetoric of the news industry incorporates the promise that journalism embodies the public interest: that journalists can be trusted, and that the product—the news commodity—is 'fit for purpose'. However, what we witness today is a gap that 'looms sufficiently wide' (Eagleton 2007, 42) between rhetoric and reality to create a crisis in legitimacy that is too wide to be bridged by the remedial actions of the news industry or journalists. Trust is a relationship—in this case between consumers and producers—which most researchers argue is not the same thing as credibility (refer to Engelke, Hase, and Wintterlin 2019 for a dis-cussion of this issue), but trust is contingent on credibility. The more credibility a journalist or a news outlet has (in terms of its reporting record over time) the more they are likely to be regarded as trustworthy (Fisher et al. 2020)

This crisis is very much dialectically connected to the problem of trust and the fragile nexus between journalism, the news industry, and liberal democratic norms. Journalists are aware of the problem (W. Davies 2019), but perhaps not well equipped to deal with it. The system of representative democracy—which dates back to the late 18th and early 19th century revolutions in Europe and the New World—is itself in crisis, and the global economy lurches from boom to bust in a cycle that has a logic of its own seemingly beyond the control of governments. David Brooks uses the language of fault lines similar to our own to metaphorically describe the trust crisis:

> The events of 2020—the coronavirus pandemic; the killing of George Floyd; militias, social-media mobs, and urban unrest—were like hurricanes that hit in the middle of that earthquake. They did not cause the moral convulsion, but they accelerated every trend. They flooded the ravines that had opened up in American society and exposed every flaw.
>
> (Brooks 2020)

The crisis also extends beyond Western free market democracies. Two decades of war in the Middle East have not brought peace or security to the West or freedom to Palestine, and the former Soviet Union is in turmoil. Russia is embroiled in wars of its own in Ukraine, in the Balkan region, in Syria and the Caucuses. A crisis of humanity—signified by the hundreds of thousands of refugees fleeing war zones from western China, the Indian sub-continent, southeast Asia, Afghanistan, Iraq, and parts of northern Africa—has led to a growth of ultra-conservative nationalist and racist movements, some of which hold power (in Brazil, Hungary, Israel, Turkey, and Poland, for example). A tide of populist politicians making unkeepable promises—including about the 'Brexit' vote which saw the United Kingdom exit the European Union on 1 February 2020—threatens to overwhelm centrist ideals which have held nations together in the post-World War Two period.

Populism is an extremist ideological movement that seeks to prosper from division by pretending to be anti-elite and on the side of the common people. Donald Trump is a classic example of this phenomenon. His promise to 'drain the swamp' in Washington DC, saw the swamp creatures increase in numbers, and attach themselves to the Trump presidency like leeches. The dialectical gap between the promise of democracy and the reality of a system in crisis creates the space in which populist leaders can build a movement. As we saw with Trump, authoritarians deploy a rhetoric of 'us' and 'them' in which *they* create all the problems currently affecting *us*. Authoritarian populism seems to offer a simple solution—get rid of *them* and *we* can begin to feel better (Araújo and Prior 2020). Populism uses a political language that promises much, but delivers only greater division, mistrust, and economic hardship to the ordinary people who fall under its spell. Right wing populism—the type espoused by Trump and other authoritarian leaders—is also commonly based on a racist 'othering' of outsider groups (Speed and Mannion 2017).

Unfortunately, the news media can become an unwitting booster for populist politicians, creating further downward pressure on the spiral of public trust and contributing the social division, rather than bringing people together on common ground (Hameleers, Bos, and de Vreese 2019). In fact, it has been reasonably argued that there is an unhealthy symbiosis at play between populist politicians and the news media by which journalism is 'directly implicated' in the rise of populist politics (Araújo and Prior 2020, 5). Populists appear to be popular in the news media because of their performative value—they provide conflict, drama, colourful personalities, and spicy sound bites. As Perry Parks (2019) has written in relation to Donald Trump, he was given plenty of air time and front page coverage during the 2016 US election campaign *precisely because of* his unconventional and 'carnivalesque' approach to disrupting politics as usual. One key aspect of conservative populist politics—made explicit in Donald Trump's rhetoric—is that it also attempts to build up the cult of the leader at the expense of other institutions. This is clearly the case with Trump invoking 'the swamp' early in his campaign to characterise the political establishment he claimed to be the polar opposite of and in his adoption of the QAnon conspiracist meme of the 'deep state' as a rhetorical tool to disparage his perceived enemies. Trump also took this logic further by casting doubt on the honesty of various other institutions: the news media, the FBI, state governors who opposed him; Democrats; and even members of his own party.

Perhaps his most virulent populist imagery was reserved for the Black Lives Matter protestors and the 'antifa' activists whom he decried as thugs and monsters and deeply evil, even as 'a symbol of hate' (BBC News 2020b). Trump's divisive language marked out the 2020 election season too. He repeatedly and deliberately refused to criticise those who he saw as supporters, up to and including members of armed militia who carried out attacks on BLM demonstrations in his name (Bump 2020a) and later the insurrectionists who stormed the Capitol building in January 2021.

All of this means that the news media's trust relationship with its audience is under pressure. In America, the populist right has abandoned any respect for the mainstream media that it perceives as not representing its interests, preferring to live in the echo chamber of Fox News, the *New York Post* (both owned by Rupert Murdoch), and the smaller niche hyper-partisan conservative spaces of the Internet, podcasts, and cable television. Similar fractures are also apparent in European nations where the populist right is growing (Henke, Leissner, and Möhring 2020). On the other hand, there is a broader problem, one that we have been tracking for nearly 20 years. While conservatives have abandoned the mass media in favour of their own ideologically committed outlets, the broader news consuming population has been gradually reassessing how much trust it is willing to place in the news media too. When examined historically we can see this is a trend that has been developing for several decades, going back to at least the 1980s, or perhaps to the 1840s!

The long slow decline of trust

When looking at the available data and research on trust, journalism and the news media it seems we are confronted with a paradox: 'Globally, trust in journalism is on the ascent [going up]; however, this is obscured by declining trust in the news media as an institution' (McKewon 2018). This does not gel with the cumulative results from surveys we have been following for nearly 15 years which tend to show that journalists—as a cohort of professionals—do not rate well in surveys measuring trust. In the early 2000s multiple surveys ranking journalists and other professional groups (nurses, doctors, etc.) put them in the bottom quartile; at around the same trust level as real estate agents and usually below politicians. When surveys gave the results in percentages journalists were generally at 20 per cent or lower (Hirst and Patching 2005, 27–9). These numbers did not change much between 2008 and 2012 when we began to collect data from around the world. When we broadened out our search the trend was clear: trust in journalists and trust in the institution of news continued to fall on most measures (Patching and Hirst 2014, xvi–xvii). Today, the global picture is very variable; trust levels are also linked to political polarisation; the rise of populist authoritarianism is linked to broader mistrust of institutions, including the news media (Ritter and Gallup Polls 2019). A 2017 study sponsored by *The Economist* indicated that many Republican voters were prepared to believe Donald Trump ahead of reputable newspapers like *The Washington Post* or *The New York Times* (The Economist 2017)—something that is worrying perhaps, but not surprising. However, declining trust levels are not a recent phenomenon, and they are linked to public perceptions about whether or not journalists are doing a good job. Generally, satisfaction with the news media hardly ever rises above 60 per cent anywhere in the world. A February 2020 global ranking had Finland and Portugal at the top with 56 per cent with only six nations reaching above 50 per cent; notable at the bottom of the list were the United States (29 per cent), the United Kingdom (28 per cent), France on 23 per cent, and South Korea on the bottom with only 21 per cent (statista 2020). Perhaps constant invocation of 'fake news' insults from Donald Trump has affected the American figures, because Gallup reported that between 1997 and 2019, the American public's satisfaction with journalism ranged from the mid-50s to the low 40s (Brenan and Gallup Polls 2019). A 2020 survey of American views of the news media by Gallup and the Knight Foundation found 'deepening pessimism and further partisan entrenchment' with journalism 'compromised by increasing bias' (Gallup Polls and Knight Foundation 2020). Hardly a resounding endorsement, and mistrust on this scale must have something to do with perceptions that journalists and media institutions are not behaving in an ethical way.

A history of mistrust?

Former journalist Tom Goldstein (1985, 73) observed that in the mid-1980s political reporters in Washington DC were becoming too close to the politicians and officials they were meant to be scrutinising: 'It's hard for Washington journalists to maintain their distance,' he wrote. 'A lot of the problem revolves around eating'. Reporters and editors shared dining rooms in the capital and frequented the same restaurants and bars; then there were more formal occasions where political figures, editors, and senior journalists got together on a semi-regular basis such as the 'Gridiron Club' dinner in New York, or the correspondents' dinners in Washington. Goldstein finished with the comment that 'None of this does much to inspire confidence in the adversary relationship' that journalists claimed to have with political players. In the 1980s a lot of this socialising was done quietly, behind closed doors, but today the formal gatherings are lavish affairs. The Washington correspondents' dinners were— until Trump—very high profile and televised on the C-Span network. Such events take place in political cities all over the world and the journalists who attend seem to relish their close personal ties to government ministers, prime ministers, and presidents. Journalists will point to the fact that these events are for one night only and that they raise funds for charity or that it's just a bit of harmless fun. All of that might be true, but the problem is that for outsiders looking at the cocktail dresses, the jewellery, the tuxedos, the lavish food, drink, and entertainment, it seems like there is little or no distinction between the scrutinised and the scrutineers. In that environment everyone looks like a player. Such perceptions are not without merit—where there's smoke, there's fire—and the world of political reporting has a rarefied atmosphere that seems to many observers more like a cosy club than an arena where politicians are challenged by the reporters.

Today we are able to gauge trust levels through public opinion surveys and many of them we can follow over time—something we've been doing since 2005. In fact, there has been an erosion of trust across public institutions measurable in opinion polling since the 1970s that has occurred alongside what journalism scholar Michael Schudson (2019) has documented as a 'cultural shift' in journalism, from 'straitjacketed objectivity' to 'the necessity of interpretation'; the public has also changed—as reflected in our observations about populism—to embrace a more partisan view of the news media and perpetuating the information divide. Schudson also notes that the decline in trust for the news media is perhaps also a product of a general social anger, 'many people could see that an elite few were getting very, very rich while they themselves were falling behind' and with this growing inequality comes political polarization. This, Michael Schudson argues, is perhaps the cause of a backlash against journalism; it is a victim of its own success:

> [I]t also means that a lot of people are going to distrust the media, particularly when their favorite politicians…[are] openly confronted by journalistic investigation, information, or opinion…What people don't like about the media is its implicit or explicit criticism of their heroes.
>
> (Schudson 2019)

This is undoubtedly true, but it also shifts responsibility from the news media and journalists to audiences themselves and seems to imply that if only consumers better understood what reporters do, then the trust problem would go away. This idea—that somehow audiences misunderstand journalism—should not be used to absolve reporters and editors of responsibility; it may not even be true.

A different approach is taken in an Australian study by academics from the University of Technology, Sydney who write, 'Most journalists don't expect to be loved…[but] given journalists are supposedly working on the public's behalf, shouldn't they at least expect to be trusted?' Fray and McKewon (2018) continue that 'journalism's trust crisis is pressing, urgent, perhaps existential'. When a number of recent surveys and studies are examined together a very complex and contradictory picture emerges; one that shows trust differentials based on age, gender, political identification, and socio-economic factors. There are also different levels of trust allocated to social media versus mainstream news (McKewon 2018). The variations within methodologies, sample sizes, the questions asked, and the reliability of the survey overall make it difficult to focus on an accurate picture of trust levels. However, when you look at reputable polls that have been asking the same or similar questions over a period of time, it is possible to determine some useful trend data. What is clear from these longitudinal surveys is that there is a slow, steady and long-term decline in trust levels and that only around 30 per cent of respondents consistently express trust in news media (Swift and Gallup Polls 2017). Even though there are fluctuations year on year, the trend is down; the Gallup Poll from 2017 shows a decline of around eight points between 1990 and 2017 for the print media. The television numbers are worse, from a high of 46 per cent in 1993 the decline has been steady, dropping to 18 per cent in 2014 and rising to 24 per cent in 2017. This should be concerning for the news business as much as for journalists because along with a decline in trust there has been a parallel decline in revenues and profits, and this makes perfect sense: if you don't have trust in a product, why would you continue to buy it? Trust and brand loyalty also exhibit a strong correlation (Fisher et al. 2020).

It also seems likely that the economic collapse and the decline in trust levels are likely to continue because credibility and consumer loyalty are linked (Nelson and Kim 2020), and as the news industry embraces more 'robo-journalism' and relies on algorithms to both write news and service consumers—by feeding them more of what it is perceived they like—we might see this downward spiral continue. A 2017 study—albeit when robots were not ubiquitous in newsrooms—showed a correlation between a negative perception of robo-journalism and low levels of trust leading the authors to conclude that 'robo-journalism faces strong resistance' and that overcoming the trust deficit 'would seem difficult' (Schultz and Sheffer 2017, 347–9). In situations where scholars have tried to measure the impact of attempts to improve credibility and trust, the results have not been particularly promising. One German study looked at the use of 'scientific sources, statistical information and the visualization of data' and concluded that this might help grow credibility and trust, but 'the effects are small' (Henke, Leissner, and Möhring 2020, 313).

Where to from here?

A common response to the question of how the news media can repair a tarnished reputation and re-grow trust is to talk about transparency, bias, conflict of interest, and journalists 'being open about their own beliefs and values' (Fisher et al. 2020, 14). This is a necessary start, but it is questionable as to whether or not it is a sufficient condition for the restoration of credibility and trust. Fisher and her colleagues (2020, 14) also advise caution in relation to seeking answers in what audience members might think they want because there is a paradox in the self-reported evidence their study collected: 'It appears the audience wants less bias in journalism, but not necessarily more journalism' (or more journalists). As we see it, one aspect of the problem—and the difficulty in finding a workable solution—is that journalism is intellectually weak and openly celebrates its anti-theory stance. One consequence of this is that many journalists lack historical knowledge of their craft and a willingness to embrace deeper philosophical thinking. For too long, journalists have been operating on individualised notions of common sense.

> Common sense, as defined by Antonio Gramsci, is ahistorical, received cultural wisdom that appears so natural so as to be neutral. He believed there was an urgent need to develop critical outlooks that challenged common sense. As 19th-century-derived objectivity is at the core of

journalistic common sense, it is high time to subject this notion to a critical intervention in the 21st century.

(Bertuzzi 2017)

We came across Robert Bertuzzi's letter to the editor of *The Toronto Star* while searching a library database for 'Gramsci' and 'journalism'. The letter was in response to an article by *Star* columnist Rosie DiManno (2017) in which she criticised former colleague Desmond Cole for crossing the 'fundamental journalistic divide' between activism and reportage. Cole had attended a Toronto Police Board meeting and made a public statement about a police procedure he didn't like, in the process 'taking the police board meeting hostage' according to DiManno's critique. Cole (2017) resigned his position as columnist saying that he chose activism ahead of being a columnist. DiManno closed her column by writing that she 'will not even vote in any election' to avoid 'aligning myself with a political party'. This is a clear contrast perhaps expressed by two extremes here, but it is a live ethical fault line. One side is the argument that trust requires complete abstention from politics, on the other an argument that being an engaged citizen is more important than the appearance of neutrality.

In the final chapter we will return to the trust issue and look at ways in which the journalism profession and the news industry are trying to rebuild and reconnect with audiences. In that context we'll explore how crossing the line between activist and observer—in the tradition of Desmond Cole—might now be the right thing for journalists to do. This also means a return to the writing of the Italian Marxist Antonio Gramsci, himself a journalist and editor of some note. Gramsci was a leader of the Italian Communist Party and a member of parliament who was jailed by the fascist Mussolini government in 1926 (Buttigieg 2002). He died in custody in 1937 but left a remarkable legacy of notebooks compiled from his cell over a decade of incarceration. Among them is a volume on journalism that we think is worth exploring in some detail. In particular, we are interested in Gramsci's arguments about 'common sense' and what he called 'integral journalism', which can be simply defined 'as a work of cultural dissemination whose ultimate goal [is] to incite political action' (Garcia-Liendo 2016, 51). We think this is a potential way forward for serious journalists if they are willing to forego their historical reliance on 'common sense' objectivity and embrace the Gramscian notion of an 'intellectual reformation' (Robinson 2005) of journalism part of a broader effort to rebuild trust with disaffected audiences.

Questions for discussion

Research a recent example of an ethically debatable decision by the mainstream media. Then discuss these questions.

1　Is trust a precious commodity for the news industry?
2　How important is the fault line between profitability and trust?

3   Do you think the news media has some or any responsibility for the rise in authoritarian populism?
4   Can journalists help the news industry to rebuild trust with audiences?
5   What are some of the main obstacles to rebuilding trust?
6   Do you see any way to stop the level of public trust in journalism continuing to fall?

7 Journalism and social media

An ethical minefield?

Jack and Zuckerberg finally had enough

After months of flagging Donald Trump's tweets about election fraud as 'misleading' and 'disputed', Twitter finally suspended the President's account for 12 hours after concluding that his tweets on 6 January 2021 were inciting violence. The social media giant also threatened to permanently suspend Trump if the offending tweets were not taken down.

Shortly after Twitter reacted, YouTube took down a Trump video, Twitch disabled Trump's ability to livestream, and his Facebook accounts were shut down until he left office on 20 January (Paul 2021). Facebook CEO Mark Zuckerberg—who had an 'on again, off again' relationship with Trump during

Figure 7.1 Trump tweets removed—Twitter Safety

DOI: 10.4324/9780429242892-8

his presidency—cited the ex-President's 'intent' to continue undermining the 'peaceful and lawful transition' to the Biden presidency as the reason for the decision (Nover 2021). This is another example of how extraordinary the four years of Trump's presidency were for both the mainstream and social media, but many observers—us included—felt that this action was too little too late. As we wrote in Chapter 3, Trump had strategically used his social media platforms to spread disinformation, fear, and to stoke racial violence throughout his term of office. Trump also used social channels to express his constant 'fits of extreme emotion' (Coe and Griffin 2020, 11) to mobilise and energise his base. In our view, Donald Trump voluntarily gave up his right to unfettered speech when he started using his social media accounts to encourage violence and to spread dangerous false information for his own political purposes—for example, tweeting 'when the looting begins, the shooting begins', which was widely interpreted as tacit approval of White vigilantes attacking Black Lives Matter protestors in 2020 (Chen 2020). Trump explicitly used social media to overcome the bias he saw in the mainstream news media (Bissonette 2020), and also broadened his attacks on the media in 2020 to take in what he began to label 'big tech'—the social media giants—who he felt were being unfair towards him by challenging some of his more outrageous lies on Twitter and Facebook (Greve 2020). This played well with his base (Varis 2020), but ultimately did not help his re-election. It was interesting to us to see how quickly some sections of the mainstream media jumped on the anti-social media bandwagon after the 6 January riots in Washington, DC. It's not difficult to see how this was a defensive action on their part—successfully blaming social media might deflect public anger from their own role in sustaining the Trump brand for the four years of his presidency. At this important juncture—when the news media is at an ethical crossroads—blame-shifting is not a tactic that's likely to increase trust. As we argue in the concluding chapter, all the news media, on all platforms and channels, must use the current crisis as an opportunity for deep reflection, learning, and change.

Livestreaming a terrorist attack: 17 minutes of horror

The world was shocked on 15 March 2019, when a lone Australian gunman entered two mosques in Christchurch, New Zealand, and opened fire, killing 51 worshippers at Friday prayers and injuring almost as many others. As shocking as this terrorist attack was, the Facebook livestreaming of 17 minutes of graphic and violent footage from the shooter's helmet-mounted camera demonstrates some of the major issues social media raises for mainstream news media. There have been other cases of social media being used to publicise hideous crimes. Few will forget the gruesome videos of the 2014 beheading by ISIS of the two American journalists, James Foley and Steven Sotloff. In 2017 in the United States, a video of the murder of an elderly man was uploaded to Facebook and the torture of a disabled man was livestreamed. Two years earlier, again in the US, the murder of two TV journalists had been simultaneously broadcast live to air and livestreamed (Bender

2019), and it didn't end with the massacres in New Zealand. In late 2019, a neo-Nazi attacked a synagogue in Germany, killing two people and livestreaming the attack on Amazon's platform, Twitch. Nearly a year after the Christchurch attacks, and despite widespread calls by governments for action to stop social media being used as a platform by mass murderers, a Thai soldier killed at least 26 people, mainly at a mall northeast of Bangkok, and was able to post photos and videos from the scene on Facebook for almost five hours (Garvey 2020). But the Christchurch attack was different from all these other hideous incidents. The attacker had logged on to Twitter and 8chan—another mostly right-wing online message board little-known before this attack—to post photos of his ammunition and a lengthy far-right manifesto. He linked to a Facebook page, promising to livestream the pending mass shooting (Allsop 2019). In the hours after the attack the video and manifesto spread widely across multiple social media platforms. Such events are usually seen initially from the 3rd-person point of view of the news crew, and from the viewpoint of the victims. In this case the graphic video of multiple slayings was seen from the perspective of the perpetrator.

Our key concern is the challenges faced by mainstream media the world over in dealing with the gruesome helmet-cam material. It is an example of the dilemma confronting broadcast and online media when a major story breaks that triggers rolling coverage. The feedback loop that we saw develop between YouTube and broadcast news media back in 2007 (Hirst 2011) is now an entrenched and vital part of news-gathering techniques in all newsrooms. The quandary for journalists has become: How much do you show—if anything—of violent, unfolding incidents from the perpetrator's perspective? Without going into detail about which TV station showed what, and which online media embedded sections or all of the convicted killer's manifesto into their coverage, we hope there would have been some serious soul-searching during this awful event as media executives decided on their coverage, and after it, as they reviewed it. Decisions had to be made literally 'on the run' given the public's insatiable appetite for the latest on such major events. Facebook scrambled to purge its platform of the all-too-graphic material; of the 1.5 million versions of the shooter's video removed within 24 hours of the attack, 1.2 million had been blocked automatically at the upload point (Benson and Lewis 2019). Individual newsrooms were grappling with how much to show and whether to publish any of the gunman's manifesto, or link to it. As you'd expect, different newsrooms made different decisions and some faced public backlash for their treatment of the story (Mayhew 2019c; Walker and Mayhew 2019; Meade 2019; Di Stefano 2019). One local New Zealand TV network was later fined NZ$4,000 for airing segments of the massacre video described as having the 'potential to cause significant distress' (Roy 2019b). Two major media organisations—the Australian Broadcasting Corporation and *The New York Times*—published separate stories detailing the reasons for their editorial decisions. For the ABC, the test of what should be used centred on 'whether it can be done without giving the alleged shooter the platform they crave' (McMurtrie 2019). They decided not to share the gunman's footage or his 'manifesto'. For the *NY Times*: 'The manipulation of technology and use of online social platforms to document the killings, publicize them and try to inspire others to imitate him posed significant ethical challenges for our journalists running the coverage' (Ingber 2019). *The NY Times* editors decided not to run any of the gunman's video of the attack or link to it and treated the manifesto in the same way.

Many in the media believe it is part of their Fourth Estate role of informing the public about such tragedies to mention or link to perpetrators' manifestos, photos, social media posts, etc. (Greensmith and Wake 2019). But as Australian journalism academics Glynn Greensmith and Alexandra Wake warned a few days after the Christchurch massacre, reporters, in their efforts to inform their audiences, risk becoming part of the 'avalanche of unfiltered information about the perpetrator [that] cascades into the wider consciousness, spreading their twisted worldview and presenting a manual on how to attract coverage'.

Almost a year after the massacres, the convicted killer admitted to the rampage in a High Court hearing in Christchurch, ending the need for a trial. He was to be sentenced later in the year (Crystal 2020). New Zealand's major media organisations had agreed before an earlier court appearance by the killer to limit their reporting of the expected trial in an attempt to reduce the exposure of the accused killer's ideals and beliefs fearing he would use the trial as 'a platform to amplify white supremacist and/or terrorist views or ideology' (Roy 2019a). In late August 2020, he was sentenced to life without parole (Bayer and Leask 2020). The man described at 'Britain's top anti-terror cop', Metropolitan Police assistant commissioner Neil Basu, suggested in the wake of the mosque attacks that 'it was time to have a sensible conversation about how to report terrorism in a way that doesn't help terrorists' (Mayhew 2019a). The Commission for Countering Extremism, established by the British Government the year before the Christchurch attacks, issued a report on tackling 'hateful extremism' in late 2019, and in a thinly veiled swipe at the Christchurch coverage by British tabloids, called on the media to stop 'gratuitously' publishing 'titillating' details about terrorist incidents (Tobitt 2019b). Coverage by *The Mirror, Sun*, and *Mail Online* had drawn criticism at the time. Eighteen months after the attack, the horrific footage of the attack was still available online, despite efforts by governments to eliminate the sharing of it (Ravlic 2020).

You'll notice that we haven't named the gunman—that's another major ethical issue for mainstream media, and it's one on which we have a minor disagreement. Martin is not convinced that refusing to name perpetrators is effective and he wonders why it is now being applied to White supremacist terrorists when it was never applied in the case of Islamic terrorists. He thinks there's a vague whiff of racism about it. In his view, knowing who the terrorists are and what their motives are is an important aspect of combatting their twisted beliefs but in this case, Martin respects the wishes of communities who believe not naming the criminals is the right thing to do. Roger believes that naming the perpetrator only gives him (and his cause) the publicity/notoriety/ infamy he obviously craves. The New Zealand Prime Minister, Jacinta Ardern, widely praised for her compassionate handling of the tragedy, was quick to say that she would never mention the shooter's name. But should the media? In the wake of the all-too-often mass shootings in the United States, the majority of US media has adopted the practice of not using the shooter's name unless it was absolutely necessary (McBride 2019). There is an argument that using their name can glorify their actions and encourage copy-cat killers. After the 2017 mass shooting in Las Vegas that killed 58 and wounded more than 400 others, a group of 147 academics, law enforcement officers, public health experts and others wrote an open letter begging US media outlets 'to deny infamy to mass shooters' by withholding their names and likenesses when reporting on their crimes (Lewis 2019). As the first anniversary of the 2018 Pittsburgh Synagogue Shootings approached, locals offered some advice to the media proposing to cover the anniversary of the killing of 11 worshippers—avoid referring to the 'anniversary' or the 'tragedy', 'and don't name the shooter' (Conte and Ford-Williams 2019). A study of 6,337 stories on the Christchurch attacks found only 14 per cent of US publications named the shooter and almost none linked to his manifesto (Marcus 2019). However, in the land of his birth, the Murdoch national broadsheet, *The Australian*, had no problem with naming him when it ran a three-part series titled 'The killer within' in its feature section a few months after the tragic events in Christchurch. It began its top-of-the-front-page splash promoting the series with his name (Maley 2020).

The website www.nonotoriety.com was established by Tom and Caren Teves after the 2012 shooting of their son, Alex, and 11 others in a movie theatre in Aurora, Colorado. They created the 'no notoriety media protocol' with the aim of reducing the number of acts of mass violence which they believe are inspired by the prospect of media fame. It suggests, among other advice, limiting the mention of the accused's name to once per story, never in the headline and 'no photo above the fold'; a reference to the placing of any photo in the bottom half of a folded broadsheet newspaper—so that it cannot be seen in the pile of papers at a newsstand. It also urges the media to concentrate more on coverage of the victims that the perpetrator. Before we leave this topic, a distinction needs to be drawn between broadcasting 'live', which TV has been doing for decades, and 'livestreaming'. The difference is that TV stations can control their output whereas there was no regulatory oversight over livestreaming at the time of the Christchurch massacres.

Social media—'for better, or worse'?

Every journalist has a story about the 'good' and the 'bad' of social media. As far as the media is concerned, at its best, social media platforms foster public discussion of issues that are making news and provide valuable information and potential sources for the mainstream media. At its worst, journalists say, social media channels are used to abuse and harass journalists. It creates a difficult and toxic environment to work in. The online harassment is more commonly directed at female journalists, and according to the Committee to Protect Journalists (CPJ 2019c), includes 'threats of violence against the journalist and their family and friends'. The abuse can also range from very personal attacks about the journalist's intelligence, ability, gender or sexuality, and race, to threats of violence or sexual assault (Masullo and Supple 2020). It became an issue in Australia in mid-2020 when a leading television current affairs presenter shared online 'a fraction of the sexualised abuse' she received after interviewing the Prime Minister (Barry 2020; Molloy 2020). As disgusting as such online abuse is, there is also a troubling ethical dimension to the harassment. It can lead reporters to change how they write a story, as Masullo and Supple suggest, by reporters intentionally leaving out facts they fear will spark further abuse (2020). It can also lead to them seriously considering leaving the industry. A survey by the International Women's Media Foundation found that a third of nearly 600 female respondents had considered leaving the profession because of harassment, especially younger journalists (IWMF 2018). The editor of Britain's *Press Gazette*, Dominic Ponsford, summed it up at the height of the coronavirus pandemic in 2020:

> Twitter has become the sea that journalists swim in. And this week it feels like it has become so polluted that it is difficult to make more than the briefest dip without risking one's health.
>
> (Ponsford 2020)

There are many who would see a far more murky environment than a 'sea'. Ponsford went on to plead with the profession to 'distinguish professional journalism from the knee-jerk provocateurs of the "Twittersphere"'. We agree with Ponsford's general thesis, and have discussed the impact of social media on coverage of COVID-19 in Chapter 1, but kept his wider theme of 'the Twittersphere is on fire' for discussion here and to add his final comment—'Journalists should be pouring water on the flames—not fanning them' (Ponsford 2020). That's one side of the argument, not falling for the trap of giving 'oxygen' to the more outrageous assertions that inhabit the various social media platforms. The odd, the novel, the weird, the aberration, and the like, have always been criteria for what makes information 'news', but there is a point where ethics need to play a part in asking: Is this a real news story, or am I just giving publicity to something that might do more harm than good? That was certainly a conversation had in many newsrooms during the coronavirus pandemic. As we'll see soon, many journalists feel that social media is as much a curse as it is a blessing.

Millions of people use social media platforms every day to keep in touch with friends, relatives and contacts. Governments are still grappling with some of the 'down sides' of the phenomenon, like how to handle cyberbullying of children and the 'hate mail' celebrities and other newsmakers attract all too often. And, as we have pointed out in earlier chapters, what to do about the spread of 'false news' via social media. The Christchurch shooting, and others, demonstrate how authorities are also working on keeping social media platforms free of terror-related material. Another 'downside' is how to prevent social media from jeopardising an accused's right to a fair trial. Then there's the sad stories—like the twins who found out that their younger brother had died in a car crash when they opened their Facebook page on their 20th birthday expecting to read well wishes from friends (Cuneo 2010), or the final Facebook post by one of the victims of Australia's 'black summer' of bushfires in 2019–20 hours before he died as flames swept through the area (Livingstone 2019).

Today, nobody can deny that social media plays a major part in the everyday routine of mainstream journalists—even becoming 'digital gumshoes' for investigative reporters (Abdenour 2017). While initially it may have been scoffed at by seasoned journalists, social media is now an essential tool—one of many used by reporters for newsgathering and connecting with their audiences. Social media provides new ways for them to gather information and to expand the reach of their content. However, trawling through social media for a 'gotcha' moment or for writing clickbait doesn't count as journalism in our view.

When used as source material, social media creates many ethical fault lines for the news media. While some of the issues for journalists have been, or will be, canvassed in other chapters, there are several others that reporters need to keep in the back of their minds. It has long been the case that anyone with a computer, smart phone or tablet is, in the eyes of the law at least, a publisher—and many chronicle their thoughts for the rest of the world to ponder by way of blogs and social media posts, including prolific tweeter Martin. But the explosion of social media in recent years has been a 'game-changer'. Anyone with a smartphone is now a reporter, if only for their Twitter, Facebook, or Instagram 'friends'. Sometimes their efforts receive much wider exposure. It is now accepted that Twitter users regularly beat traditional media at being first with the news, especially with pictures of accidents, demonstrations or other stories where they happen to be 'on the spot' before the arrival of the mainstream reporters. Both authors have been told by former students of their being issued with 'wads of cash' by their employers to 'buy' coverage if they arrive at the scene of a story, and someone with a smartphone has captured the 'newsworthy moments'. We saw in Chapter 2 how the Black Lives Matter movement was re-born after the young woman, Darnella Frazier, recorded the final minutes of George Floyd's life with a smart phone.

Presidents, Prime Ministers, celebrities, and media commentators regularly use Twitter nowadays—some might say too often—to share their thoughts and opinions on anything and everything, unfiltered and unchallenged by mainstream media. Many journalists now tweet on a regular basis, often multiple times a day, alerting their followers to the latest news or to material coming up in order to draw an audience to their writing or broadcasting. Political journalists, as well as tweeting the latest political headline, will probably follow hundreds of other political tweeters, local and international politicians, party leaders, political advisers and lobbyists, and, of course, they'll watch what their colleagues are saying on their Twitter feeds. Journalists on other reporting rounds will follow those appropriate to their areas of expertise and interest. For the general reporter these will be many and varied. The authors, for instance, follow literally hundreds of their favourite journalists, commentators, online news sites, academics, and media executives. The time when social media was only considered a legitimate source if journalists had no other access to events has long passed. The various platforms are now an integral part of modern journalism. Research of a major newspaper in each of the UK, US, and Germany between 2004 and 2016 (analysing about three million articles) showed that the number of social media sources has increased noticeably (Von Nordheim 2018). In all three papers, journalists are using more platform content. Twitter, according to the research, although having a significantly smaller user base, was more popular among the newspapers' journalists than Facebook (Von Nordheim 2018). Among the reasons given for the increasing use of material from the major social media platforms were the facts that younger journalists have a greater affinity with the medium; there's less time nowadays for reporters to research; the oft-mentioned shrinking of the news media generally, and the ever-growing number of sources, such as politicians, celebrities, and sportspeople who use social media to bypass the traditional media 'in some cases, excessively' (Von Nordheim 2018)—like, for example, Donald J. Trump.

A tweet does not a story make...unless you're the US president

In the previous edition of this text (Patching and Hirst 2014, 201), we suggested that making a story from a random couple of tweets on a newsworthy topic—even if they were 'words of wisdom' from Rupert Murdoch—was lazy journalism. That relatively brief story quoting the media mogul was an example of what has become an all-too-familiar trend in reporting; journalists trawling through literally thousands of tweets for a comment around which to build a story. One comment from a newsmaker plus a few paragraphs of background, and there was an update for the 24/7 news cycle. In general terms, we still maintain that such stories are little more than stenography, or 'copy-and-paste' journalism. We're not trying to detract from the many citizen journalists, bloggers, and tweeters who regularly provide the continuous stream of 'news-like' material (Hirst 2011) that provides the MSM with valuable story ideas, but one 140- or 280-character comment or opinion still does not a story make. Information from social media which cannot be verified, but is published anyway on a fast-moving story, has led to some bad decisions by journalists in the past.

For about a decade all of that seemed a reasonable position to take, but then along came Donald Trump. Initially the American media was divided over whether the overnight ramblings of the candidate, and later US president, should be considered as 'news' and reported as such (Grynbaum and Ember

2016). In those early days his Twitter account was described quite accurately by Grynbaum and Ember as a 'bully pulpit, propaganda weapon and attention magnet rolled into one' (2016). The general consensus emerged that the thoughts of the President-elect (as he was then) were inherently newsworthy, and so the daily avalanche of presidential tweets began to appear in the news media (Grynbaum and Ember 2016). As it became apparent that many of the presidential tweets were either misleading or simply lies, it posed another ethical dilemma for the media: how to cover the suspect utterances of the President. Many of his tweets were attacks on them. By the end of his second year in office the President had sent out 1,339 tweets about the media that were either 'critical, insinuating, condemning or threatening' (Sugars 2019). We've discussed his frequent attacks on the media in other chapters, but the President's tweets and speeches have spawned a 'new industry'—presidential fact-checking. *The Washington Post* has kept a running tally of what it calls the President's 'false or misleading claims', not limiting it to his tweets, but covering his speeches, news conferences, and media appearances. When the major American newspaper, *USA Today*, published an opinion piece penned by the President in late 2018 attacking the opposition Democratic Party's plans for healthcare and immigration, *Washington Post* fact-checker Glenn Kessler (2018) said 'almost every sentence contained a misleading statement or a falsehood'. As the death toll from COVID-19 climbed at an alarming rate in the US in July 2020, *The Post* reported the President had made more than 20,000 false or misleading claims in his first 1,267 days in office (Kessler, Rizzo, and Kelly 2020a). At that stage a total of nearly 1,000 false or misleading claims had been made about the pandemic (ibid.). We have been watching *The Washington Post* count mount over the years of the Trump presidency but decided to call a halt to the tally in the context of this chapter in mid-2020. You would have seen the more up-to-date total in Chapter 3. The President's penchant for being 'loose with the truth' caused widespread discussion in newsrooms across the nation in early 2020 as the US mainstream media faced the daunting decision on whether to amplify or muffle Trump's endless stream of suspect tweets (Pilkington and Gabbatt 2020). Later in the election year, the President's 'love affair' with his favourite social media platform soured when Twitter 'flagged' two of his tweets with fact-check warnings was followed by the not unexpected reaction from the White House (ABC 2020b). Trump even threatened to shut down the social media platform, which, it was pointed out, he could not do unilaterally (ABC 2020c). As we noted at the beginning of this chapter, Twitter and Facebook eventually decided Trump had gone too far.

Mainstream media vs. social media

Aside from the ethical dilemmas associated with social media already discussed, there are other issues for mainstream media and individual journalists raised by the all-pervasive nature of the Internet and social media. The first is the relationship between mainstream media and the 'new chums on the block' relatively speaking—the bloggers and social media users. As social media has become so much a part of the lives of journalists in recent times, and so much makes its way into mainstream outlets, it is important to note there is a major difference between mainstream journalists and the so-called 'citizen journalists' or the 'fifth estate' that needs to be discussed. There are many online sites that uphold the ethical traditions of the profession. Many journalists who lost their jobs in the economic decline of the mass media worldwide, have turned to respected websites to publish their material, or created their own sites. But some social media platforms that are not mainstream do not always adhere to the same codes of ethics. At their worst, they can say whatever they like without needing to verify it. Most times it is simply their opinions. While both groups (mainstream and citizen journalists) hold the powerful to account, many citizen journalists, bloggers, tweeters, Facebook posters, and the like, are not held accountable—hence social media is awash with mis-information, disinformation, fake news, propaganda, and political brainwash-ing (Hamada 2018, 39). Then there's the hoaxes. A study released in 2019 that more than 80 per cent of American journalists admitted to falling for false information online (Funke 2019). The study of more than 1,000 journalists showed that only 14.9 per cent had been trained in how to best report on misinformation (2019), while all the time the hoaxes are only getting more sophisticated. The following are issues that reflect the digital fault lines and techno-ethical quandaries that journalists have to deal with in coming to terms with social media.

When a tweet is too good to be true

One of the symbiotic links between journalism and social media is the practice of embedding tweets in online news stories as a form of illustration. It is pop-ular because it gives the impression that the publication is in sync with the fast-moving Twitter world. It is also popular with publishers because it is free. In general, it is hard to argue with the efficiency of embedding and it certainly can add a little colour to a screen full of copy. However, it can also have negative consequences, particularly when harvesting tweets becomes a substitute for real reporting, or when the tweets that are being embedded turn out to be gener-ated by bots or trolls. The rule of thumb should be, to re-work a journalistic adage, if a tweet looks too good to be true it's probably bogus. Tweets should be fact-checked, and the ID of their author verified prior to embedding for publication. Journalists are not always doing due diligence on tweets regarding them as 'content' in their own right, not as sources that need scrutiny first (McGregor 2018).

Does Twitter affect news-making decisions?

While it provides so much material for mainstream media nowadays, is there an ethical argument that it is having too much of an effect on decisions about what is newsworthy? Can a Twitter storm of protest dictate what news is covered? Former *New York Times* conservative opinion writer Bari Weiss was in no doubt in her resignation letter in mid-2020 in which she accused her news colleagues of harassing her on social media: 'Twitter is not on the masthead of *The New York Times*. But Twitter has become its ultimate editor' (Weiss 2020).

The effect, according to Weiss, was an editorial process designed to 'satisfy the narrowest of audiences, rather than to allow a curious public to read about the world and then draw their own conclusions' (Weiss 2020). On the other hand, Weiss' critics suggested she was 'literally asking the *Times* to prevent people at the paper from criticizing her' (Berlatsky 2020). This high-profile case brings the double-edged sword of social media into sharp focus.

Are you being hoaxed?

Few people, except the most ardent of supporters of President Trump, would not have smiled about the 'missing thousands' at the President's election rally in Tulsa, Oklahoma, in mid-June 2020. The venue had seating for 19,000, but less than a third of the capacity turned up. It later emerged that part of the reason for the high level of 'no shows' was a campaign by teenage users of TikTok and fans of Korean pop music groups who claimed to have registered for thousands of tickets to the event and then not attended (Lorenz, Browning, and Frankel 2020). But there is a dark side to the hoaxes, too, as we saw in the earlier chapter on the pandemic. There have been many instances in recent years of deliberate campaigns of disinformation, particularly during political campaigns, like the 2016 US presidential campaign, and the Brexit referendum in the UK in the same year. One of the recent examples to come to light involved a supposed expert on the Middle East named Raphael Badani, who simply didn't exist, but nonetheless provided columns for a number of US conservative websites (Rawnsley 2020). His profile photo was taken from the blog site of a Chicago businessman to create a fake profile page (Jay 2020). According to *The Daily Beast*, Badani was part of a network of at least 19 fake personas that had spent the previous year placing more than 90 opinion pieces in 46 different US publications (Rawnsley 2020). While Arab countries have had fake online news sites pushing propaganda for years, the creation of Badani raised the bar; his stories argued strongly against the policies of Qatar, Turkey, and Iran, but were quite upbeat about the United Arab Emirates and its policies in the region (Jay 2020). Social media hoaxes are all-too-common nowadays, which raises the ethical dilemma of mistakes being made due to inadequate research or fact-checking.

Should reporters tweet breaking news first?

One of the early debates on the use of social media involved whether reporters should tweet breaking news before it was published on their employer's other platforms. One long-standing British commercial newsreader saw tweeting about a major news story as having the effect of leading 'the information thirsty to water' (Snow 2012)—in other words, a way of drawing an audience to your media outlet. And that's how most media personnel started out using the medium. Reporters wanting to disclose breaking news on social media are advised to check with their editor in case the story is an exclusive they might want to hold till later, rather than alert the opposition. Most media organisations now allow their reporters to tweet breaking news even if it is not yet on their primary service, providing they have provided 'the office' with the story. But policies may differ between organisations and new staff would be wise to consult their organisation's policy on such issues.

The need for speed?

Another aspect of social media that we think creates an ethical trap for reporters is the need for speed. The race to publish first has always been problematic as the rush to scoop rivals can lead to short cuts in reporting. It is where mistakes creep in. With the mainstream news media downsizing and cost-cutting, the temptation to cut corners can lead to errors. Add to that the speed at which 'news' circulates on the Internet and the probability of 'screwing up' increases. The damage—to reporters and lives—is greater because tweets and Facebook posts, etc. go global as soon as you hit the 'Send' key. There are any number of examples of the Internet getting it wrong. We covered several in the previous edition (Patching and Hirst 2014, 210–12), but the salutary lesson of taking that extra few minutes to be sceptical and find reputable sources rather than breathlessly reporting the latest social media post was demonstrated in the early reporting of the death of the convicted sex offender, Jeffrey Epstein, in 2019. Early Twitter reports suggested he was on suicide watch, had a cellmate, and that guards had checked on him at least an hour before he died. All wrong. Then there were the erroneous conspiracy theories, one re-tweeted by President Trump suggesting Epstein's death might be linked to former President Bill Clinton (Sullivan 2019c).

Verify it!

As with all information journalists 'receive' in the course of their newsgathering, there's a need to verify it before publication. But this is particularly true of anything gleaned from the Internet. Consider all the information that floods into media offices (or probably more correctly, into reporters' social media feeds) in times of a major emergency or during bushfires or floods? Or when journalists solicit information from the public about what is going on in a particular emergency?

We repeat, verify it before publication.

Media organisations' social media policies

Media organisations the world over have had to devise, and regularly update, policies on how their staff interact with social media—how they will use material from the likes of YouTube, Facebook, Instagram, Snapchat, and Twitter, and how they will interact with it—that is, the rules for individual journalists wanting to post or tweet. Before the end of the first decade of the 21st century, media executives seemed wary about allowing their journalists to engage with social media or to use material from blogs or other social media, but they soon realised they needed policies to cover the use of such material for news-related purposes, and to protect their 'brand' from over-zealous staff posters or tweeters. Most of the mainstream media policies cover the same areas. They invariably acknowledge that the use of social media plays an important role in the professional and personal lives of their staff, and while they are seen as efficient platforms for them to deliver content to audiences, they need policies governing their two-way use. They don't want staff to use social media in a way that would embarrass the employer, disclose any confidential information obtained while at work, break any law, or imply that the organisation approves of the personal views they express. No matter how complex a news organisation's social media rules are, there will always be blind spots, loopholes, and contradictions to be overcome in practice. The policies are constantly evolving. *The New York Times'* social media guidelines are among the most comprehensive (The New York Times 2017, updated 2020), but there are others worth perusing, like those of the BBC (BBC 2019b), the Associated Press (Associated Press 2013), and Australia's ABC (ABC 2013; ABC 2016b).

Be careful what you tweet, tell your friends on Facebook, Instagram, etc.

The first of 20 'Tips for tweeting journos' circulated more than a decade ago by Julie Posetti (2009), an Australian journalism academic who was researching the journalist–Twitter relationship at the time, reads: 'Think before you tweet—you can't delete an indiscrete tweet!' Technically, you probably can, but it may have been stored somewhere online before you do, or someone may have re-tweeted it or taken a screen shot for future embarrassment. The same goes for Facebook and Instagram posts, and what you say on your YouTube channel or blog. While news-makers' indiscrete tweets are all-too-often fodder for mass media, like politicians' ill-considered remarks, or sporting personalities 'sounding off', here we are talking about journalists falling foul of the tools of the digital era. The ethical dilemma here is when a reporter tweets something controversial, are they expressing their own opinion or are they representing the organisation they work for? It happens often, and while there have been any number examples of senior journalists and commentators 'putting their foot in it' in recent years, there are two Australians and one American who warrant special mention because of the reactions to their controversial comments.

The two Australians, who at the time worked for national broadcasters the multicultural Special Broadcasting Service (SBS) and the ABC, decided two years apart to use ANZAC Day, the day when Australia stops to remember the price paid by its military in conflicts the world over. The first chose the occasion to challenge what he considered the 'myth of Anzac Day heroism' and the other to draw attention to another group she believed should be remembered too. On that special day, 25 April 2015, Scott McIntyre, a sports reporter for the SBS, published a series of tweets from his personal account criticising what he considered the 'cultification' of Australia's involvement in World War I and the inhumane acts he claimed were committed by Allied forces in World War II, including the bombing of Hiroshima and Nagasaki (Chalmers 2015). McIntyre was promptly sacked. It emerged later that the then-Communications Minister, later Prime Minister, Malcolm Turnbull, had personally complained to the broadcaster about the 'highly inappropriate and disrespectful comments' (Meade 2015). While many were outraged at the content and timing of the tweets, others saw it as an attack on free speech:

> [A]nyone who gives a damn about the values that our soldiers allegedly died, and continue to die, for should be outraged that he was sacked for daring to express them.
>
> (Quinn 2015)

SBS maintained McIntyre had not been sacked for the tweets, but rather because the tweets contravened the broadcaster's code of conduct and social media policy by bringing the broadcaster into disrepute. McIntyre sued SBS for unfair dismissal in the Fair Work Commission claiming he had suffered loss of income, damage to his reputation, humiliation, distress, and anxiety as a result of his high-profile sacking (Bourke 2015). Almost a year later, the parties announced they had settled the case for an undisclosed amount on the morning the hearing was due to begin (Robin 2016). McIntyre resumed anti-ANZAC tweeting on 25 April 2016 (Davidson 2016).

Fast forward a year and another public broadcaster, this time it was ABC part-time presenter Yassmin Abdel-Magied who sparked a similar, but more intense, storm of protest with her 2017 ANZAC Day post on Facebook: 'Lest. We. Forget. (Manus, Nauru, Syria, Palestine…)'. The phrase 'Lest We Forget' is a pivotal line used in Anzac Day liturgy. While the ABC said the Muslim presenter's post expressed her own views on her own time about Australia's treatment of refugees on Manus and Nauru islands, and conditions in those Middle East countries, so it was none of their business, the post unleashed a torrent of criticism (Franklin 2017). For and against forces lined up, as they did in the McIntyre case, with supporters painting the comments in terms of free speech and opponents attacking her lack of tact on Australia's 'sacred' day. To her credit, when her 'mistake' was pointed out to her, Abdel-Magied quickly deleted the post and apologised (King 2017). But that was not enough for the critics, who mostly appear to have been paid employees or commentators for the Murdoch organisations. Some said the reaction from conservative politicians and commentators showed their hypocrisy over their support for freedom of speech—they demanded her resignation, and in one case deportation—because she wrote something with which they disagreed (Faruqi 2017). A month earlier, the then-Attorney General, Senator George Brandis, had said that proposed changes to the Racial Discrimination Act would stifle freedom of speech and that was 'one of the key things the Anzacs fought for' (Fine 2017). But his conservative colleagues must have missed that observation. They attacked Yassmin, leading one supporter to suggest: 'They only believe in freedom of speech if you agree with them and their narrow view of the world' (Fine 2017). Within a month the national broadcaster had axed her program (Koziol 2017). Following all the mainstream and online criticism, Abdel-Magied announced she was moving to London (Koob 2017). The experience of neither of these two is unique; it has become common for journalists, academics, and activists challenging the status quo to be not only attacked by (mainly) conservative politicians and media commentators, but also to be the target of a barrage of abusive and sometimes violent posts online (Nyst 2017).

On the other side of the world a similar ethical dilemma of 'should I raise this?' arose with a tweet by *Washington Post* reporter Felicia Sonmez in early 2020 after the tragic death of the famed American basketballer Kobe Bryant, his daughter, and seven others in a helicopter crash. Within hours of his death—and amid an outpouring of grief among Bryant fans—Sonmez tweeted an article about Bryant's 2003 rape accusation (Holpuch 2020). Initially she was suspended by the *Post* while it considered whether she had violated the paper's social media policy. The *Post*'s managing editor, Tracy Grant, said Sonmez's action 'displayed poor judgment and undermined the work of her colleagues' (quoted in Waterson 2020b). A couple of days later, after Sonmez had received more than 10,000 abusive tweets and a number of death threats, but massive support from the *Post* staff, plus other journalists and media commentators, she was reinstated with the paper admitting she had not violated their policy (Wemple 2020).

In all three cases the timing of the social media posts was criticised as inappropriate, and rather 'tacky' under the circumstances. But equally the reaction, and in the two Australian cases the ultimate results, was a definite over-reach. A few years earlier, the head of the BBC newsroom at the time, Mary Hockaday, summarised the dilemma on whether to publish something personal on social media well. In an email to staff after an editor had called a right wing political party in the UK racist and sexist, Hockaday wrote that the guidelines 'can all be summarised as: "Don't do anything stupid"' (quoted in Conlan 2014). The new BBC Director-General, Tim Davie, in his first speech to staff in late 2020, made an appeal for impartiality from the staff and was more pointed about their social media interactions: 'If you want to be an opinionated columnist or partisan campaigner on social media then that is a valid choice, but you should not be working at the BBC' (Davie 2020).

One final case worth mentioning here is that of Lewis Raven Wallace, a reporter for the NPR's *Marketplace* programme, who was dismissed from his job in 2017 for writing a blog post titled 'Objectivity is dead, and I'm okay with it' criticising the journalistic practice of objectivity (Wallace 2017). We take up this issue in later chapters, but in the context of people being harassed or sacked for social media posts this one is perhaps the worst example we've come across in some time. There is a vicious and punitive attitude in many organisations—particularly in the media and academia—towards any outspoken critic who dares to challenge orthodoxy. For organisations that claim a special form of freedom of expression for themselves, to destroy careers for acts of political speech is particularly worrying. It pays to be cautious, but what is not acceptable is the chilling effect that censorious management can have on freedom of speech.

Case study: Journalists push back against the online abusers

Anyone can be blocked from access to your social media accounts, but when you receive an avalanche of abuse, as happens often to mainstream journalists these days, what can you do? You can block offensive posts, but what if there's hundreds? What if it is an orchestrated campaign of abuse? The Australian pop culture website Junkee took matters into its own hands in mid-2020 when it decided it would not publish a by-line with stories where it considered the writer faced the risk of a tirade of abuse from the so-called 'stans'—a cross between a stalker and a fan. The decision arose after one of their writers, Joe Earp, wrote about the group One Direction and a trickle of tweets became a flood of abuse and threats—including some aimed at the writer's adopted greyhound (Stott 2020). Editorial director at the site, Rob Stott, characterised 'stan culture' as 'a toxic, vindictive swamp where fans are encouraged to outdo each other with performative displays of devotion to their hero' (2020).

A growing number of senior journalists, particularly in the US, are either cutting back on their tweeting, or abandoning it altogether in the face of unwanted abuse (Lieberman 2020). During 2020 in particular, the micro social-networking site has been a valuable platform to help mainstream journalists keep up to date with the evolving pandemic while drawing attention to the challenges they face in covering it (see Chapter 1). But as Lieberman points out, for the value journalists can gain from Twitter, they can also, as we have seen so often through this and earlier chapters, fall victim to its less savoury aspects—petty squabbles over esoteric issues, bigotry, and bad-faith attacks from anonymous users and bots (2020). An Amnesty International study of 2017 found that 7.1 per cent (1.1 million) of tweets sent to 778 women journalists and politicians were either problematic or abusive—or about one every 30 seconds (Troll Patrol Findings 2018). Put another way, one in every 14 tweets that mentioned women journalists—225,766 messages to 454 journalists—were found to be abusive or problematic (ibid.). Anecdotal evidence would suggest the figures have probably risen in recent times.

However, we also have to make the argument that sometimes journalists hide behind the threat of abuse as an excuse and mistakenly describe legitimate criticism from informed audience members as 'trolling' too. While there is certainly no room for sexist, racist, or homophobic abuse and threats of violence deserve to be treated as criminal offences, in some instances journalists need to accept criticism as the price of greater 'engagement' with their audiences. Social media has given ordinary citizens a platform to 'talk back' to journalists and to respond—favourably, or not—to the stories they produce. Many journalists have healthy egos and they love attention; they promote their stories on social media feeds and bask in the accolades of their fans. It is only right that they also accept the occasional critical comment or challenge. After all, one of the supposed benefits of social media for journalists and the news industry is greater engagement and the ability to monetise their interactions with fans through generating more 'clicks'. They can't in all fairness have it all their own way and insult their audience's intelligence while demanding 'look at me, look at me, look at me'. Our view is that criticism is legitimate but abuse is not. Strong, but polite critique can only strengthen the public sphere and help with the restoration of trust.

Questions for discussion

1   Everyone has had a bad experience with social media. Discuss some around the tutorial table.
2   It seems obvious that the social media giants are doing little to stifle abuse on their platforms. What else can do done, aside from the steps already mentioned?
3   Social media platforms like Twitter are essential tools for journalists nowadays, is it a case of 'suck it up, sunshine' when you are abused?
4   You're in the newsroom and some spectacular footage of a terrorist attack is live-streamed on a social media platform. What criteria would you use to decide what to use?
5   What's your view on naming terrorist suspects?
6   What is your favourite Internet hoax story? Share with others.
7   How should journalists respond to legitimate criticism on social media?
8   Do you block trolls and aggressive 'stans'? Why or why not?

8 Is it time to abandon privacy?

A long wait for justice

In 2014, British pop icon for more than half a century, Sir Cliff Richard, was in Portugal when South Yorkshire police raided his home in Berkshire, England. They were investigating allegations that Sir Cliff, nicknamed the 'Peter Pan of pop' for his enduring youthful appearance, had sexually assaulted a 16-year-old boy in 1986 (Barry 2018a). The BBC knew the raid was planned and arranged with police to film it. The footage put to air included helicopter images of police searching inside the singer's home. It wasn't until 2016 that police announced that Sir Cliff, who always denied the allegations, would face no charges—a long time to be under suspicion. The singer sued both the police and the BBC. The police settled relatively quickly, but the BBC decided to fight the case as an issue of press freedom. It would be another two years— almost four years after the police raid and after a two-month trial—before the 77-year-old singer would win his privacy battle and be awarded damages of £210,000 plus legal fees (Mayhew 2018b). The decision was greeted with dismay by the British media. BBC news director Fran Unsworth said it marked a 'dramatic shift against press freedom' (quoted in Mayhew 2018b). One paper saw the decision as 'profoundly dangerous and a devastating affront to press freedom', while another said the judgement was 'ominous' in its implications for what 'reporters are allowed to say, and the public is allowed to know'. Media leaders decried the decision as 'effectively handing all suspects a new right to anonymity until charged' (Tobitt 2018d). The British media saw it as setting a terrible precedent and wanted the BBC to challenge the decision. The broadcaster decided not to appeal (Mayhew 2018c). An opinion poll taken after the court's decision found the British public overwhelmingly in favour of pre-charge anonymity for suspects (YouGov Poll 2018). Few people could afford to take a media organisation like the BBC to court and risk the potentially huge legal fees if they lost. Before the trial decision, there were calls in the British Parliament—renewed after the court's decision—for a new law, dubbed 'Cliff's Law', to stop police suspects being named by the media until they are charged, but the government was unmoved (Press Gazette 2018). The arguments for and against such an obvious invasion of an individual's privacy in Sir

DOI: 10.4324/9780429242892-9

Cliff's case—a person's home is their castle, so to speak—may depend on your personal views, but they form a central theme of this chapter. Who is entitled to privacy, and who gives up that right in the pursuit of fame and fortune? The public right to know is important in terms of serious legal matters, but so to is a presumption of innocence; a tricky fault line indeed.

A few months after Sir Cliff's victory, on the other side of the Atlantic, the world's then richest man, Amazon chief executive, Jeff Bezos, was involved in a major invasion of privacy in what appeared to be an attempted blackmail of the billionaire. In this context more importantly, Bezos is the owner of *The Washington Post*. He took to the Internet to accuse the 'supermarket tabloid', the *National Inquirer*, of threatening to publish details of an extramarital affair and intimate photos of him, unless he stopped investigating the magazine (Elder and Bruce 2019). The *National Inquirer* had published an expose of the billionaire's private life a few weeks earlier, devoting the entire front page to a typical tabloid kiss-and-tell headline (National Inquirer 2019). Bezos wanted to know where they had got his 'intimate text messages' and the revealing photos. *The Washington Post* was often critical of President Trump and was one of his favourite 'fake news' targets while the chief executive of the *National Inquirer* is another billionaire, David Pecker, the co-founder of PayPal and a friend of the former President. The story got messy, as these big invasion of privacy stories often do, but our interest here is in Bezos's 'outing' of the *Inquirer's* tactics in trying to stop him finding out how they got their sleazy scoop. Under the headline 'No thank you, Mr. Pecker', Bezos detailed the *Inquirer's* approach. He claimed the tabloid's representatives said they had more texts and more photos and would publish them if he didn't stop (Bezos 2019). Bezos's eight A4-page article included an email from a *National Inquirer* executive describing various photos they were threatening to publish—mostly involving the billionaire in various stages of undress (ibid.). It was a stunning 'turning of the tables' on an opposition and one only the very wealthy could attempt.

There's another recent British case worth mentioning in this context—the events that led to the suicide of the host of British television's *Love Island*, Caroline Flack. She suffered a massive social media 'pile on' after her arrest for the alleged assault of her boyfriend, Lewis Burton, but the tabloid media also has much to answer for in their coverage of her private life (J. Smith 2020). As Joan Smith (2020) commented in *The Guardian* at the time of Flack's death, as far as Britain's tabloid media was concerned: 'It was open season on Flack—an attractive 40-year-old woman with a boyfriend 13 years her junior—from the moment news of her arrest became public.' Analysis by *The Guardian* showed that a total of 387 stories about Flack were published by the UK's national newspapers in the six months prior to her death and 99, almost a quarter, by the Murdoch tabloid—and celebrity chaser—*The Sun* (McIntyre et al. 2020). Of the almost 400 stories, a quarter were classified as having a 'negative tone' (ibid.). Imagine the impact on her wellbeing of that and the social media abuse that followed her arrest (Seymour 2020). In the context of this chapter, it is worth noting that, like the calls for 'Cliff's Law', a petition which gained more than 850,000 signatures from an angry public within a month of the *Love Island* host's death, called for the creation of 'Caroline's Law', which would make it a crime for the media 'to knowingly and relentlessly bully a person…up to a point where they take their own life' (quoted in Mayhew 2020e). Again, there's been no legislative action.

One of the more controversial invasions of privacy of a politician in Australia in recent times was the 2018 case of then-Deputy Prime Minister, Barnaby Joyce. There are several facets to this dilemma, which surfaced when a Murdoch-owned tabloid revealed that the Deputy PM was expecting a child with a much younger, former staffer. The Sydney *Daily Telegraph*, broke the story in the mainstream media with a front-page photo of the heavily pregnant woman under the headline: 'Bundle of Joyce' and a sub-heading of '"Madly in love" Deputy PM—a staunch and married Catholic—expecting a baby with former staffer' (Markson 2018). In our view there was a public interest angle that made this story newsworthy; not only did Joyce profess his Catholicism proudly, he intervened in Australia's bitter marriage equality debate to oppose same-sex marriage (Martin, McCulloch, and AAP 2018) and he had earlier argued against giving young women a vaccination against cervical cancer on the grounds it would encourage promiscuity and raised the virtue of his own teenage daughters in several public speeches on the issue (news.com.au 2018). In the eyes of many, this made him fair game for the news media.

If the Joyce baby story was in the public interest, and many Australian journalists suggested it had been an 'open secret' for months, why did it take so long to be published (Overington 2018)? At the time, the governing Liberal-Country Party coalition had a thin majority in the House of Representatives and Joyce was one of many politicians who had been found by the nation's High Court to be ineligible to sit in the Parliament because he held dual citizenship in contravention of the nation's Constitution. Prior to the publication of the 'baby-daddy' story, he had faced a by-election for his seat of New England. He renounced his New Zealand citizenship to contest the by-election and was easily returned. Might there been a different result if the voters in his conservative rural electorate knew he was cheating on his wife? Debate raged for days among the media as to whether it was ethical to publish the story of the Deputy PM's extra-marital affair. The main question at the time was: When is a politician's personal life in the public interest? Reaction to the story ranged from 'shameful non-journalism' that 'debases public life' and 'it's nobody's business except the people involved' to an affair should remain private 'until their public words don't live up to their private action'. 'Given Joyce's very vocal opposition to marriage equality and defence of the sanctity of marriage', one editor said, 'I'd say his affair with a staffer fits that bill' (Watkins 2018a). Our view is that it *was* in the public interest mainly because of the status of the person involved and the public had a right to know. Joyce was the leader of a political party, and as Fairfax journalist Jacqueline Maley commented at the time, 'his character is part of his political brand' (2018). The Barnaby Joyce affair will be discussed in other contexts elsewhere.

A recent case involving US celebrity Kanye West and his links to the Kardashian family is also worth commenting on. West has been diagnosed with bipolar disorder and in 2020 had a series of very public meltdowns leading to an alleged split in his marriage. There is huge interest in the Kardashian–West relationship, and it is at the heart of a multi-million-dollar media and merchandising empire. When West announced a short-lived campaign for the US presidency in 2018, there was even more media attention on the erratic rapper (Burton 2020). There is public interest in matters of alleged criminality or in a rapper's bid for the presidency, and then there's public curiosity in the personal lives of celebrities. Journalists are in the position of having to work out which type of interest they will put at the heart of their reporting particularly when a story lies on the fault line between privacy and fame.

What do we mean by 'privacy'?

> Privacy, however, is a concept in disarray. Nobody can articulate what it means.
> (Solove 2008, 1)

Since Daniel Solove made this observation, things have collapsed into even more disarray when it comes to understanding privacy today. Privacy falls along the digital fault line we call the techno-legal and the techno-ethical time-gap. This is simply the lag between what we are technologically capable of—such as mass surveillance—and control mechanisms (legal or ethical) that protect us from unwanted intrusion. We all leave digital footprints; sometimes these signs of our presence are benign, others can cause problems. The rise of social media and the 'share everything' approach to our personal lives leads some commentators and scholars to argue that as a society, we are moving beyond the concept of privacy. However, we argue in this chapter that several types of privacy exist, and that this distinction is important for individuals and for journalism ethics. Privacy is, as Daniel Solove writes, a 'sweeping concept', but his definition encompasses most aspects of the idea:

> freedom of thought, control over one's body, solitude in one's home, control over personal information, freedom from surveillance, protection of one's reputation, and protection from searches and interrogations.
> (Solove 2008, 1)

That's a good start, but it is obvious that both governments and corporations intrude on our privacy on a regular basis; we are under total online surveillance and anti-terrorism legislation (among other laws) removes our right to remain silent in the face of law enforcement demands for information (Greenwald 2014; Andrejevic 2007). We are also encouraged to self-disclose on social media, and many of us do it without any thought at all for the potential unwanted consequences (Tsay-Vogel, Shanahan, and Signorilli 2020). Privacy is disappearing and that's problem that journalists should think about, not just blithely add to through their own actions. The truth is journalists can't do their job of informing the public on matters of importance without invading some people's privacy. But, like so much associated with journalism ethics, it is a balancing act—the individual's right to privacy versus the public's right to know, not simply what the public might like to know. After all, we all like a good bit of juicy gossip, don't we? But the reporting of gossip, in our opinion, has no place in mainstream media.

What do journalists think is 'privacy'?

We believe it is wrong to abandon all notions of personal privacy, but for journalists there needs to be a clear distinction between privacy and secrecy. Personal secrets between friends are mostly harmless, and so too are some forms of commercial secrecy—trade secrets (Posner 1979)—but when governments and corporations, or public figures, demand privacy to shield wrong-doing, reporters have an obligation to expose them to public accountability. So, what does the public have a right to know about? This is where you need to apply a 'public interest' test. What is the public benefit in what you're about to report? Is it critical for the public to make an informed decision in an election, for instance? Or does it demonstrate a person's hypocrisy—do they flaunt their family in front of the TV cameras when it suits them for publicity purposes while privately cheating on their spouse (as we have already discussed)? The test is not 'Would the public be interested in this?', but rather 'Does the public need to know the information for an important reason?' If it fails that test, then the ethical journalist should consider ignoring the story. We know news has to have some entertainment or pleasure value for readers in order to sell and be palatable. After all, variety is the spice of life (to borrow a cliché). But that does not mean replacing worthy stories with entertaining 'clickbait'.

A number of clear distinctions need to be made between 'public' privacy and 'private' privacy and between 'privacy' and 'secrecy'. For example, there's a big difference between 'innocent' secrets, like personal details, and 'guilty' secrets, such as when governments or corporations lie to the public. In such circum-stances, it is not considered legitimate for government agencies, politicians, or business figures to claim 'invasion of privacy' in order to conceal matters that should be available to the public. In the media context, 'public' and 'private' privacy concerns the differences and difficulties the news media faces in respect of the privacy of public information—that is the levels of privacy accorded to public figures (like politicians) versus the-taken-for-granted everyday privacy 'enjoyed' by 'ordinary' citizens. In these circumstances, the issue of 'consent' is also important. A person can give informed consent to be involved in a news story, and there is implied consent if people agree to talk to you once you have identified yourself as a reporter. In effect, by identifying yourself as a reporter you are giving them the chance to say 'Go away' or 'I don't want to talk to the media', and if they do say something like that, then you are obliged to go. This situation may well rise when you seek a 'death knock' interview and the grieving relative, for instance, is too upset to talk and asks for privacy. If they don't ask you to leave them alone then you can fairly assume 'consent' unless you are dealing with children, in which case you need to seek permission from a person in a position to give it, like a parent or legal guardian. The issue of consent is important when making the distinction between the 'right' of the average citizen to say 'no', and to have their privacy respected, and public figures, who, to a greater or lesser extent, rely on publicity and exposure for their own gain, for example, through election to high office, or through sales of DVDs and books, or film or concert ticket sales. However, if your reporting is to uncover 'dirty' secrets that conceal criminality, duplicity or corrupt behaviour then you don't need anybody's permission to invade the privacy of people involved. Secrecy for the purposes of concealment of wrong-doing or to deceive the public—as either consumers or citizens—should not be protected by any right to privacy. What you do need is evidence and a solid ground to believe that exposing the nefarious dealing is in the public interest. The balance in such situations is between the privilege of privacy, the purpose of secrecy, and public accountability. There is an implied 'right to know' regarding information that should be disclosed in the public interest (Sheaff 2019).

The Taxonomy of Fame

The Australian ABC's former Director of Editorial Policies, and current Public Editor of *The Guardian*, Paul Chadwick, an award-winning journalist and former Privacy Commissioner in Victoria, teamed with a colleague at the Communications Law Centre in Australia in the late 1990s to develop what they called the Taxonomy of Fame (Chadwick and Mullaly 1997, 5–6). Chadwick and Mullaly identified five kinds of fame which Chadwick revisited for *The Guardian* two decades later in response to a 'royal intrusion' (Chadwick 2017b). The revised and expanded taxonomy is:

- fame by election or appointment (politicians, judges and others in high public office who trade some privacy for power)
- fame by achievement (film and music stars, TV presenters, sporting champions, leaders of major organisations and those who make transformative contributions in their fields)
- fame by chance (previously anonymous people randomly caught up in tragedy, disaster or, less often, good fortune)
- fame by association (people associated with those who are famous or infamous)—the spouses, children, parents, siblings who have reflected fame, but not always glory
- and royal fame (a category reserved for those born into, or who marry into, a royal family) (Chadwick 2017a).

The updated version is a starting point for a discussion of fame, and the all-too-often price of fame: invasion of privacy. As Chadwick notes, 'what makes them famous tends to be only one aspect of their lives' (Chadwick 2017a).

Public interest or public curiosity?

Few people will ever endure the pain that the thoughtless pursuit of a scoop by the BBC visited on the privacy of the much-loved Sir Cliff, the embarrassment caused to the then world's richest man at the hands of the *National Inquirer*, or the relentless attention of the tabloids and social media that proved too much for Caroline Flack, but many suffer to varying degrees at the hands of the mass media. Journalists usually justify intrusion into a person's private life by saying the story is 'in the public interest'. While an argument can be made for privacy invasion in the case of a politician if the incident is suggestive of the morals they would bring into their public life, what public interest is there in what happens between two consenting adults in the privacy of a hotel room, even if one of the participants is an international film star, music icon or sporting celebrity? This is one of those ethical 'shades of grey' that we refer to in other contexts. What one might see as not in the public interest—it's between them and their spouse, you might say—another might suggest shows the person concerned is cheating on their spouse and deserves public scrutiny of their avowed morals. But do any of these reporters chasing the latest celebrity scoop take a moment to think through the possible ramifications of their actions? To walk in their shoes? We have seen some of our former students rise to 'important' positions on tabloid television only to have themselves become the victims of their print colleagues and the paparazzi chasing a 'money shot'.

We believe that in many cases, particularly in the tabloid media, 'the public interest' falsely means 'what the public is interested in' or, more accurately, what editors *think* the public wants to know about. In many cases it amounts to little more than curiosity or voyeuristic pleasure at seeing a 'tall poppy' (like Sir Cliff) cut down and in other instances, mere titillation (What's your favourite actor been up to?). This is also linked to so-called 'influencer' culture in which the adage 'there's no such thing as bad publicity' has become a mantra and a marketing tool. The hyper-sexualisation of this type of 'news' is also of concern, particularly for women. It is an aspect of the 'pornification' of popular culture and valorisation of the male gaze (Coy and Tyler 2020). Privacy, celebrity, and the selling of fame mark an important ethical crossroads for journalists, particularly because of the growth in online 'click-bait' sites that exploit our curiosity by reporting endless amounts of gossip—usually accompanied by titillating images—dressed up as news-like information.

What remains private?

One of the bigger ethical constraints on the media involves individuals' and groups' moral rights to privacy and confidentiality. Privacy is another of those ethico-legal paradoxes we have referred to in other contexts. It simply means that there are legal, or quasi-legal, limits to what the media can, and cannot, do in relation to matters of privacy, and that these constraints can (and often do) conflict with what the media is willing to do in chasing a story. In Australia it means the media cannot access or publish some information covered by privacy laws, like medical and taxation records, for instance. There's no general privacy law in Australia—hence the renewed push for a tort on privacy in Australia in the wake of the revolting revelations of privacy invasion by the now-defunct *News of the World*. The Labor federal government in its last months in office (before losing the 2013 election) referred the issue of media invasion of privacy to the Australian Law Reform Commission, who recommended a statutory cause of action for serious invasion of privacy be enacted—(ALRC 2014)—but the new conservative coalition government rejected the proposal (Merritt 2014). Australia also has no national Bill of Rights. In the United States, the right to privacy (or perhaps more correctly, the legal remedy for the invasion of privacy) as a legal concept has developed into four distinct torts allowing the aggrieved to seek damages (Prosser 1960), but American courts have tended to side with the media, citing the overriding claims of the First Amendment rights of the US Constitution, which guarantees freedom of the press. Across the Atlantic, the United Kingdom passed the Human Rights Act in the late 1990s, taking in the European Convention of Human Rights, including Article 8 (a right to privacy) and Article 10 (freedom of expression). While the British courts have not developed a specific tort on privacy, they have used the already-established law of breach of confidence as a remedy for those who believe their privacy has been invaded. More recently celebrities have used laws around the mishandling of personal data to sue.

Privacy intrusion

While everything on Twitter is public, Facebook is a grey area when it comes to privacy. Theoretically you can control who gets to see the content you post on Facebook, but in practice most of us rarely restrict access very much, if at all. Journalists are very adept at finding ways around privacy settings and won't hesitate to do so in pursuit of a story or photo. The ethical dilemma here is where do you draw the line between telling all, and minding your own business? The discussion in later chapters on the relationship between freedom of the press, its commercial imperative, and the public's right to know, creates privacy—or the invasion thereof—as one of the most serious fault lines in media ethics, certainly as far as the public is concerned. The Australian journalists' code of ethics (MEAA 2018), the code of the American Society and Professional Journalists (SPJ 2014) and the British equivalent, the National Union of Journalists Code of Conduct (NUJ 2011) all address the issue of individuals' privacy to varying degrees.

One of the most unpopular aspects of invasion of privacy—both with the public and with many journalists—is the aforementioned 'death knock' interview. This is where the journalist seeks an interview with someone who has suffered a tragedy in their lives—a loved one may have been killed, for instance. The public is interested in the feelings of family or friends to the tragedy, but the reporter needs to approach people in such a traumatic state with the utmost tact. Often nowadays a family friend, or a member of the clergy, will agree to speak on behalf of the grieving. In Australia, the journalists' union MEAA Code of Ethics addresses the issue in Clause 11: Respect private grief and personal privacy. Journalists have the right to refuse to intrude (MEAA 2018). The British National Union of Journalists has a similar clause (NUJ 2011) and the US Society of Professional Journalists covers the area in more detail in a segment in its Code of Ethics headed 'Minimize harm' (SPJ 2014). However, these codes do not cover the now all-too-common practice of simply taking material from poorly protected Facebook pages and using it in a news story about a tragic death. This is a techno-ethical problem that still needs to be addressed. In our view, reporters should not use private social media material without permission, but it is a regular occurrence in newsrooms around the world.

Royal privacy

Paul Chadwick revisited his 'Taxonomy of fame' in 2017 after writing of the uproar over a story about a Scottish cleric urging people to pray that Prince George (William and Kate's first born) is gay because a royal same-sex marriage could help the Church of England be more inclusive of LGBT people (Chadwick 2017b). Prince William would later tell a gay group that he would be 'absolutely' fine if his children were gay (Davies 2019b). The British royal family seem to suffer most from what many see as the unwanted attention of the tabloid media, Internet bloggers, gossip magazines, online sites and social media. Every public move—and some very private ones—of the royal family is snapped by the much-maligned paparazzi, who rely on saleable photos of 'the royals' for their livelihood. People the world over seem to be fascinated by Britain's royals, and the media love them. The royals are paid from the public purse, so the argument goes that they are fair game. They will often agree to the obligatory 'photo op' when they are on holidays, on the understanding that after 15 minutes of posing for the gaggle of photographers/camera operators and responding to reporters' often shouted questions, they will be left in peace to enjoy their holiday. On official tours or other 'royal engagements' there are usually myriad of opportunities for the paparazzi to capture a 'money shot'. But let there be the slightest hint of a royal controversy or scandal and the media pack will hound them to ground—not unlike a royal foxhunt of old. That's why the photographers were outside that Paris hotel on the night Princess Diana died in 1997. She had a new lover—and a very rich one at that—and pictures of them were selling for 'top dollar'. There was much media soul-searching after Diana's death, and the media in Britain agreed to let her two boys, William and Harry, grow up without the hounding of the press. But once the boys were in their late teens, it was 'open season'.

Our previous edition (Patching and Hirst 2014, 169–73) chronicled their 'adventures' in the first half of the last decade, but a couple of more recent 'events' bear revisiting. William and Kate were furious when a French magazine published topless photos of the Duchess taken while she was sunbathing on holidays (Ravens 2012). But in this case the royals had a rare legal victory. Six years after the revealing photos had been published, a French Appeals court upheld the two €45,000 fines—the maximum allowed—for breach of privacy against the magazine, *Closer*. The magazine also had to pay €100,000 in damages to the royal couple (Davies and Agency 2018). The other major embarrassment for the royal family in the past decade also involved nudity—this time involving Prince Harry and a wild night in a Las Vegas hotel. Nude photographs of Prince Harry taken during a party in his luxury suite appeared on the American gossip website TMZ (The Sydney Morning Herald 2012). To put the story into context, the pictures surfaced as the British media awaited the judgement of the Leveson inquiry into media regulation and ethics, which they expected would establish a stronger regulatory regime on the recalcitrant British tabloids following the 'phone hacking' scandal at the *News of the World*. The ethical issue here was would the infamous British tabloids publish the photos after the attacks on their professionalism that followed the *News of the World* scandal, and pending the release of the report of the Leveson Inquiry? Initially, the papers refrained from using the photos of the cavorting prince after royal officials had contacted the Press Complaints Commission, the media watchdog then, and sent letters to British newspapers suggesting that it would be an invasion of the prince's privacy and could lead to court action. The country's top-selling daily paper, the Rupert Murdoch-owned *The Sun*, came nearest to upsetting the Palace when it front-paged a staff member conveniently named Harry, aided by one of the paper's female interns, re-creating one of the Prince's naked poses under an appropriate heading (The Sun 2012a). But that wasn't enough for *The Sun*. It announced on its website later that day that it would be publishing the actual photos the next day because its readers had a 'right to see them' (The Australian 2012).

There on the front page the next day was the 'famous' full length shot of Harry with his hands strategically placed, in what *The Sun* touted as a 'souvenir print edition' (The Sun 2012b). The move was seen as sending a message that the Murdoch tabloid would fight expected tougher media regulation. Marriage for both royal princes in recent years has led to an intense effort on their part to guard their personal privacy, especially when it involves their young children. The post-Leveson media watchdog, the Independent Press Standards Organisation (IPSO), upheld a complaint by the Duchess of Cambridge in 2016 after she objected to an online series of stories about herself and Prince George— notably a photo of the young prince on a police motorbike at Kensington Palace (The Guardian 2016). Prince Harry won a privacy battle against the paparazzi, too, when he took a photo agency to court for taking shots from a helicopter of the living and dining area of a secluded rural retreat 'and directly into the bedroom' (Press Gazette 2019). The Duke of Sussex based his case on the photographers having mishandled his personal data using what commentators said was a new weapon for the royals against the prying media—Europe's data protection regulations (Corcoran 2019). But it was the arrival of the latest royal wife, Meghan Markle, that has given the royal-watching-media the most ammunition in recent years.

No sooner had she married Harry and become pregnant than the British media decided there was a feud on between her and Kate, with royal-watchers quick to draw parallels with another pair of royal sisters-in-law, Diana and Fergie (Jeffery 2019). About the same time one British royal-watcher was suggesting that attacking Meghan was becoming a 'national sport' with the actor George Clooney suggesting the newest royal wife was being hunted in the same way that Diana was and 'it's history repeating itself' (quoted in Bennett 2019). The perennial argument that the royal family are paid from the public purse and should 'do their public duty' was brought into sharp focus again in mid-2019 when Harry and Meghan opted for a private christening for their first-born, Archie. The couple did, however, release their own 'happy snaps' of the royal occasion, including one on their Instagram account (ABC 2019a). The Duke and Duchess of Sussex renewed their 'fightback' against an 'intrusive mainstream media' in late 2019 when the Duchess announced she was suing the *Mail on Sunday* over its publication of a private letter she sent to her estranged father (Davies 2019a). At the same time, Prince Harry unleashed on the British tabloids, accusing them of a 'ruthless campaign' against his wife, and days later announced he had issued proceedings against the owners of *The Sun* and the *Daily Mirror* for alleged phone hacking. He said he could no longer watch his wife 'falling victim to the same powerful forces' which plagued his mother (Henry 2019).

Harry and Meghan's desire for something resembling a 'private life' came to an unexpected head in early 2020 when they announced—apparently without forewarning the Queen and other members of the royal family—that they had decided to step back from royal duties, giving as one of their primary reasons, hounding by the tabloid media with what they said was biased and unfair coverage (Hall 2020). It was no surprise that the Sussexes, in their initial announcement, said they would change conditions of access to their official engagements (Davies 2020). They would no longer take part in the 'royal rota' system under which accredited correspondents on UK newspapers are allowed access to royal events on a shared 'pool basis' (aimed at maximising coverage with minimum disruption to the event). The couple took their 'war' with the British tabloids a step further a few months later when they wrote to *The Sun*, *Daily Mail*, *Mirror*, and *Express* saying they will 'never again deal' with the outlets accusing them of running stories that are 'distorted, false, or invasive beyond reason' (Waterson 2020a). In early 2021, the couple took another step back from the public announcing announcing they were quitting social media in the wake of what they called 'almost unsurvivable' online trolling (Bedo 2021).

Another royal—Prince Andrew, the second son of Queen Elizabeth—was in the news for much of second half of 2019 because of his association with disgraced billionaire Jeffrey Epstein and allegations he raped one of Epstein's alleged trafficking victims, Virginia Roberts, who was 17 at the time (Harper and Bilton 2019). The Prince has always strongly denied the allegations. The scandal first arose in 2010 when he was photographed with Epstein two years after the financier had been jailed for 13 months for soliciting girls as young as 14 for prostitution. The allegations against the Prince re-emerged in July 2019 after Epstein was charged in New York with trafficking a 'vast network of underage victims' (Harper and Bilton 2019). Epstein took his own life in prison while awaiting trial. In late 2019, after Andrew disgraced himself in a long television interview, Buckingham Palace announced the Prince was 'stepping down' from his royal duties—effectively sacking him (Magnay 2019b). Again the British tabloids pulled no punches, variously describing the Prince as a 'disgrace' and an 'outcast' (Rourke 2019).

Fame by achievement

Following a close second to the royals in the 'unwanted attention of the tabloids' stakes are the A-list celebrities—those at the top of their respective sports, pop idols, and film and television stars. In most cases, the relationship between celebrities and the media is such that neither can exist without the other. Celebrities have to learn to live with the often-unwanted attention of the paparazzi. The media say celebrities are all-too-willing to call them in when they want publicity for their latest game, tour or film, so they should accept that if they openly court the media's attention for promotional purposes, then the public—through the media—is going to be interested in their private life, what they do when they are not on the field, stage or screen. The extent to which celebrities in the UK have had their privacy invaded continues to be demonstrated with the ongoing phone hacking cases following the 2011 *News of the World* scandal, involving not only the Murdoch group, but also the Tri-nity Mirror papers. One group often caught in the middle of unwanted tabloid attention is popular sportspeople. In 2019, two of the United Kingdom's leading sporting identities, cricketer Ben Stokes and Welsh rugby star Gareth Thomas, had their privacy invaded in a big way, both in the same week. There's more on the Ben Stokes story in this chapter, but basically, *The Sun* gave front-page treatment to a story about a Stokes family tragedy before Ben was born (Otte 2019). Thomas on the other hand was forced to 'go public' with his HIV status after 'tabloid interest' in the story and after a journalist had told his parents their son was HIV positive before he did (Mayhew 2019g). But equally-often it is the private lives of politicians that interests the tabloids. During his mid-2019 campaign to become Conservative party leader and thereby British prime minister, Boris Johnson became embroiled in a domestic row with his girlfriend, Carrie Symonds, that made the front page of *The Guardian* (Waterson 2019c). While the media lawyers who represented Sir Cliff said they considered the story had 'strong public interest', the newspaper (and the neighbours who provided a recording of the argument) were criticised by some sections of the media. Rival title, Rupert Murdoch's *The Sun* (a paper with a long history of kiss-and-tell stories), hypocritically described the story as 'an invasion of Boris's privacy' with no public interest justification (quoted in

Waterson 2019c). In light of the Sir Cliff decision, barrister Zoe McCallum questioned whether Boris could sue *The Guardian* for 'misuse of his private information' (McCallum 2019). She suggested that while Boris and his girl-friend had a reasonable expectation of privacy over a 'domestic altercation', she queried whether that expectation was overridden by public interest in media reporting on a probable Prime Minister's fitness for office. She felt that a judge would be unlikely to find against *The Guardian* and the practical reality would be that Boris would be 'more interested in moving the narrative onward as swiftly as possible than in pumping the story with the oxygen of a legal claim' (McCallum 2019). These issues are never black and white.

Fame by election or appointment

This category includes the likes of politicians, appointed officials like judges and the so-called 'captains of industry'—powerful people who often trade their privacy for power. As we have seen earlier in this chapter, leading politicians are continually in the news and have to accept they will have little of what the average citizen would call a 'private life'. They are also able to stand up for themselves, particularly if they are a government or party leader. In 2021 a number of Australian politicians sued a range of different media outlets over allegations of defamation. This is a disturbing trend that is no doubt meant to intimidate inquisitive journalists. In our view, elected officials are fair game.

Fame by association

This area is reserved for those whose news value rests almost entirely on their relationship with someone of worthy note. We just mentioned Barnaby Joyce. But what about his wife and four daughters—innocent victims caught up in a scandal that brought down the second-most important politician in the land? He's still a husband and father. Think for a moment what it would be like to know everyone is discussing your family's most private business? Imagine the unsavoury comments his teenage daughters would have heard at school? An Australian example emerged in 2020. It involves a connection with a sporting personality. During the trial of Arsalan Khawaja on charges relating to terrorist threats he wrote in another person's notebook (for which the other person was originally arrested and spent time in jail), the accused was regularly referred to in headlines and opening paragraphs as 'The older brother of Australian cricketer Usman Khawaja…' (Mitchell 2020). He was jailed for four and a half years in November 2020. In our opinion, the ser-iousness of the case and its 'back story' should have been highlighted more than his famous younger brother.

In the United States, a former New York congressman and mayoral candi-date, Anthony Weiner, pleaded guilty to sexting a 15-year-old girl and was jailed for 21 months (ABC 2017). He deserved it, but the media focus was also on his wife, Huma Abedin, even though she had nothing to do with his crimes. Abedin was famous because she was a close aide to Hillary Clinton and right-wing news outlets tried to smear her with her husband's crimes.

Another 'fame by association' invasion of privacy emerged late in 2019 and involved the aforementioned English cricket star, Ben Stokes, who faced a highly intrusive headline in the Murdoch London tabloid, The Sun (2019). Stokes described the story—about the double-murder of his half-sister Tracey, eight, and half-brother, Andrew, four, which happened 31 years before and three years before he was born—as 'utterly disgusting, immoral and heartless' (Magnay 2019a). Stokes pointed to the pain the story caused his mother—a 'fame by association' invasion of privacy that is hard to justify.

Fame by chance

We have left this category to last because it stirs the most emotion from the public. This is where a person is suddenly thrust into the media limelight because they have been randomly caught up in a tragedy, disaster or, rarely, good fortune. Let's discuss the last part first. Someone wins a big lottery. The public—most of whom dream of being in that person's shoes—are interested to know what they will do with all that money. It's one of those all-too-rare good news stories that we see from time to time. That's the pleasant side of 'fame by chance'—the one in many millions chance that a person's numbers 'come up'. Unfortunately, there are far more examples of the controversial side of this category, where someone finds the media pack on their doorstep because they have become involved in a tragedy or disaster. This is where our 'person in the street' can readily relate to the one in the news. They know how they would feel if they were suddenly in the same position—grieving a lost loved one and the seemingly callous media wanting them to talk about their feelings. The aftermath of a terrorist attack is a classic example of this category of fame. The Kerslake report into the aftermath of the 2017 Manchester Arena bombing, in which 22 men, women, and children died, found that most of the families of those killed or injured in that attack had 'negative media experiences' (Tobitt 2018b). These experiences included: being 'hounded' by the press; 'taking a photo of my sister when we were getting the news'; 'The press were not respectful of grief'; and the suggestion that 'the Press got hold of family members' mobile phone numbers and "bombarded" them' (cited in Tobitt 2018b). In the wake of that report, the Independent Press Standards Organisation (IPSO), the independent regulator of most British newspapers and magazines, published guidelines for reporting major incidents when they occur, in the immediate aftermath and on subsequent anniversaries (IPSO 2019). The media's performance in the aftermath of the Manchester terrorist attack is not new; similar criticisms have been levelled after other major news events. We believe that ordinary people caught up in a big story should not have to face the onslaught of a media pack without there being a very high level of *real* public interest in the story. While there was legitimate interest worldwide in the Manchester attack, it didn't justify the behaviour of some journalists.

What can the reporter do about it?

In this chapter we've detailed a few of the appalling cases of how some sections of the media cover people who, for one reason or another, either permanently or fleetingly, fall into one of the five categories of fame. One of the reasons the media give for covering 'the rich and famous' is that they made their fortunes from the public watching their television show, going to their movies, watching them play whatever sport they excel at, or buying the merchandise they endorse or the artworks they produce. So, the public, in a way, 'owns them' and therefore has a right to know every little detail about their lives. But do we really? If it were you, how would you feel about people reading or seeing the sort of material we've been talking about? What would your parents or children think? It might not be an issue for the average university journalism student, but stories have a very long 'shelf life' on the Internet. It could be you some day. One of the authors was told that as soon as students learned he was about to join that university, 'we jumped online to check you out'. This is a good time to raise John Rawls's veil of ignorance, behind which 'it is possible to walk in the shoes' of the person whose privacy is about to be breached. According to Patterson and Wilkins (1994, 118–19), behind the veil of ignorance 'freedom of the press…becomes equal to freedom from unwarranted intrusion into private life'. Is this a proposition that, as journalists, we can live with? Perhaps, but we have a problem with the veil of ignorance. It suggests that all people should be treated equally, which clearly doesn't happen, simply because of the news value of prominence. The mayor of a city, for instance, is a far more newsworthy person than our long-suffering friend, the person in the street. The former will appear in the local paper far more often that the latter. Overall, in a society where—as the late artist, Andy Warhol, said— everybody gets their '15 minutes' of fame, journalists need to be very mindful of the public interest test when thinking about reporting on private matters. Just because something is available via a social media account with weak privacy settings does not mean it is open slather for reporters to just take and use. On the other hand, if someone is keeping a secret because knowledge of what they're hiding constitutes a crime or unethical behaviour then—subject to the public interest test—you should feel free to pursue the story.

Case study: Pre-Christmas chaos at Gatwick airport

As many as 350,000 airline passengers had their Christmas travel plans thrown into chaos in 2018 when a drone was allegedly spotted near the busy London airport at Gatwick, forcing its closure. Distressing as that might be for the thousands left stranded at the airport, imagine what it would be like to pick up a Sunday paper the next day to see your partner and yourself identified as 'the morons that ruined Christmas' (Gallagher 2018). That line was in the page one headline in *The Mail on Sunday*, complete with a photo of the suspects, husband and wife Paul Gail and Elaine Kirk. *The Sunday Express* identified the couple, too, with a different photo under the headline: 'Revealed: Gatwick drone suspects' (Torro 2018). Gail and Kirk also featured on the front pages of three other British national papers. The couple had been arrested on suspicion of being responsible for disrupting take-offs and landings at Gatwick with a drone. It soon emerged that they were innocent. They were released without charge by lunchtime that Sunday. Within days there was even the suspicion that there was no drone (Magnay 2018). Kirk and Gail were not celebrities, just a young couple with no claim to fame except a 'suspicion' their drone 'might be the one'. The Conservative Party MP who'd been pushing for 'Cliff's Law' in the wake of his privacy invasion by the BBC, Anna Soubry, renewed her call, saying that the couple should never have been named at that early stage in the investigation (Tobitt 2018c). Both Sir Cliff and the couple were exonerated of any wrongdoing, yet all three had their reputations tarnished and their privacy violated by media coverage (Hacked Off 2019).

Questions for discussion

1   The British tabloids are notorious for their 'kiss-and-tell' exposes of the rich and famous, anyone from members of the royal family to stars of sport, stage, screen, and the music industry. They claim 'public interest' when really it is 'what the public is interested in'. What's the difference?

2   Is there an ethical difference between public interest and public curiosity?

3   What could be done to restrict the media to really reporting 'in the public interest'?

4   Background yourself on the findings of the Leveson Inquiry in the UK, and the regulations of IPSO. What's your considered opinion of media regulation in the UK?

5   How much privacy do 'people in the news'—like a Prince accused of rape—deserve? What about the impact on other relatives who've done nothing wrong?

6   The royal family are paid from the public purse. Do they deserve privacy for their 'affairs', be they financial or personal?

7   What about pop stars like Sir Cliff Richard or Kanye West?

8   Research the case of the Australian entertainer, Rolf Harris. Why do you think the mainstream media didn't identify him as soon as he was arrested?

9   Now consider the case of Paul Gait and his wife Elaine Kirk. Should there be 'special circumstances' for 'ordinary' (we mean no offence, just a form of comparison) people?

10 Mainstream media has long been criticised for disproportionate coverage of major stories, like the Manchester terror attack (Murrell 2017). For instance, at the same time as the terrorist attacks in Paris in 2015, there were also terror attacks in the Middle East and Africa that received scant coverage. Why might that be?

11 What are the important differences between secrecy and privacy? Are some forms of secrecy 'innocent' and some problematic?

9   Dubious methods

The Al Jazeera 'sting' on Australia's right-wing One Nation party

Australian television audiences were stunned in March 2019, when the national broadcaster, the ABC, aired a programme titled 'How to sell a massacre'. The programme was produced by the Qatar-based Al Jazeera network who sent an Australian reporter under cover for three years—yes, *three years*—primarily to expose the strategies used by the powerful American gun lobby, the National Rifle Association (NRA), to promote firearms ownership. In the process the journalist uncovered executives of a far-right Australian political party, One Nation, soliciting a donation from the NRA to help soften Australia's tough gun laws (Walker and McKenna 2019). Using hidden cameras, the reporter, Rodger Muller, secretly recorded officials, James Ashby and Steve Dickson, meeting the NRA and other conservative US lobby groups. The pair appeared to be seeking up to AU$20 million in donations for One Nation (Berkovic 2019). As part of the elaborate sting, Rodger Muller created a fake pro-gun group in Australia as a plausible cover story (2019). While the effects of the deception had political ramifications for One Nation, we are interested here in the debate that arose over the ethics of the 'sting'. The programme divided journalists over the covert methods used to gather the material. Former Al Jazeera journalist, and head of journalism at Queensland University, Peter Greste, acknowledged that the story was in the public interest, but labelled the undercover investigation as 'crossing the line' because the journalist took part in 'actually creating the story' and not simply reporting it (Truu 2019). Greste spent 400 days between late 2013 and early 2015 in an Egyptian jail with two other Al Jazeera staff on 'trumped-up' charges of political interference. It was clear that the 'One Nation' story was gathered on hidden cameras and by using deception. So, was it ethical and justified? Two senior Australian investigative journalists—Chris Masters, formerly of the ABC's *Four Corners* programme, and *The Australian*'s award-winner Hedley Thomas—both maintained the deception could not be justified. In an email to the ABC (Australia) programme, *Media Watch*, Masters said: 'We don't lie to tell the truth. We don't pretend to be anyone other than journalists, and we are not law enforcement detectives or

DOI: 10.4324/9780429242892-10

international spies' (quoted in Barry 2019a). Thomas said that while the story was powerful, it arose from 'a deceitful and manufactured method from start to finish' (quoted in Barry 2019a). The presenter of *Media Watch*, Paul Barry, had a different view, telling his audience that the ethics of the 'sting' boiled down to public interest and a fundamental question: 'Do we deserve to know that a national political party wants to weaken our gun laws? For me, the answer has to be yes' (Barry 2019a).

Another journalism academic, Andrew Dodd, said the question was whether the public's right to know was so important that it justified the deceptive conduct and breaches of privacy (Dodd 2019). He concluded that the public had a right to know what a publicly funded political party was doing. The story received international attention when a *New York Times* reporter, Isabella Kwai, questioned whether deception was right or wrong for investigative journalism (Kwai 2019). While she talked to the same two journalism academics already mentioned, she also approached her paper's Standards editor, Phil Corbett, who cited their Ethics Guide which said staff reporters 'should disclose their identity to people they cover' and 'may not record conversations without the prior consent of all parties to the conversations' (quoted in Kwai 2019). All the reporters, editors, and academics seemed to leave the door slightly ajar, saying there were rare exceptions to the widely accepted rules. Different news organisations interpret those rules differently at times, depending on the implications of the story. Undercover reporting, 'sting' operations and secret recordings have a place in journalism, but only when there is a strong public interest justification. For the record, our view is that the deception was totally justified because of the high public interest in the story. Ethical reporting is about maximising exposure in the public interest, not slavish adherence to rigid principles. In this chapter we also discuss undercover reporting, phone hacking, plagiarism, fabrication and, in the case study at the end of the chapter, look at the vexed question of whether the media should co-operate with police.

Journalism under cover

> I always want to take the position of the victim, to expose myself to what I am going to write about. I distrust those who think they can imagine how some people live without trying it for themselves.
> (undercover journalist Günter Wallraff, cited in McDonald and Avieson 2020)

The German journalist and writer Günter Wallraff is not well known in the English-speaking world, but for more than 50 years he has practised undercover journalism as a form of political activism. He often disguised himself as a worker and took menial jobs in order to expose poor working conditions or corruption. Willa McDonald and Bunty Avieson argue that Wallraff's deceptions are ethical using the framework of 'standpoint theory' which posits that valuable insights can be gained from reportage that adopts the point of view of the oppressed and marginalised. While Wallraff is a classic exponent of the craft of undercover reporting, he stands in a long and proud tradition that includes George Orwell (*The Road to Wigan Pier*), the American writer Barbara Ehrenreich (*Nickel and Dimed*) and several muckraking journalists of the past, such as Nelly Bly who famously went undercover in a New York 'mental asylum' in 1887 to expose its mistreatment of patients:

> 'Nearly all night long I listened to a woman cry about the cold and beg for God to let her die. Another one yelled, "Murder!" at frequent intervals and "Police!" at others until my flesh felt creepy,' Bly wrote about her first night at the institution in her exposé for Joseph Pulitzer's *New York World*.
>
> (Bernard 2019)

These examples are exceptions, in the sense that their work often results in book-length reportage, but each of them highlights the important work that undercover journalism does. We believe that there are very few cases where day-to-day journalists need to use deceptive methods—like not identifying themselves—to get stories, but we don't rule it out completely. The key question that exposes this ethical fault line is: Is it appropriate for journalists to deceive someone to get to the truth?

Those who take the moral higher ground argue that a journalist should never lie or purposely deceive anyone in the process of gathering newsworthy material. But that's too simple an answer for something as complex as the ethics of investigative journalism. Ethical decision-making in general involves deciding on a course of action after weighing up the options, several of which can have both positive and negative consequences. The Australian MEAA Code of Ethics poses problems for the investigative journalist faced with having to use deception to get that important exposé: 'Clause 8: Use fair, responsible and honest means to obtain material. Identify yourself and your employer before obtaining any interview for publication or broadcast' (MEAA 2018). The American Society of Professional Journalists (SPJ) and the British National Union of Journalists (NUJ) are less dogmatic:

> Avoid undercover or other surreptitious methods of gathering information unless traditional, open methods will not yield information vital to the public.
>
> (SPJ 2014)

> Clause 5: Obtain(s) material by honest, straightforward and open means, with the exception of investigations that are both overwhelmingly in the public interest and which involve evidence that cannot be obtained by straightforward means
>
> (NUJ 2011)

There's a fine line between legitimate investigative reporting and using less-legitimate methods to get a story. Definitions and practices vary from organisation to organisation, but in general, 'dubious' methods include disguising your journalistic identity and the use of undercover techniques. Some of these methods are, in fact, illegal. One of the more common methods is for the journalist to pose as someone they are not for a period of time, living undercover, and then writing the story once they are back in the office. Examples include reporters living with street kids, or in a Housing Commission flat ('the Projects' in American parlance), to get the story about hardship in those circumstances. Tabloid current affairs television programmes regularly use hidden cameras to get material for their stories, like the doctor who prescribes medications too readily, etc., but it is a long way from that rather tacky practice to some of the high points of investigative journalism which have led to major legal inquiries and criminal charges against 'big fish'. That's part of the problem—the daily current affairs TV programs are all-too-ready to 'bend the rules' for a story that amounts to little more than embarrassing someone and claiming the moral higher ground for their actions—while the serious current affairs programmes, like the BBC's *Panorama, Frontline* on PBS, or the ABC's *Four Corners* rarely use deceptive methods to gain major stories that often have serious legal and political ramifications. In the following we consider some of the most obvious methods of deception and offer our opinions of their validity and value to reporters.

Identifying yourself

News reporters interview people every day. They have no problem ringing a politician, athlete, a celebrity, a union or business leader, or simply walking up to someone in the street, identifying themselves as a reporter and seeking information for a story. Investigative journalists, on the other hand, maintain they couldn't do their job if they had to immediately identify themselves each time they approached someone for information. Reporters often use the line that there is no other way for them to gain the trust of the people who are the subjects of their story as the reason for not identifying themselves from the start, or they argue that the source would refuse access to a journalist if they identified themself before trying to get the story. Some journalists see it as a legitimate tactic in investigative journalism not to identify themselves from the start. The justification in such circumstances is usually the argument of the 'greater good', using the overriding principle of the public's 'right to know' to justify their deception. But there is an equally valid argument that by denying the 'subjects' the right to refuse (or agree), they are at the very least misleading them.

This is an issue on which the authors have a slight disagreement. Roger believes there are very, very few circumstances—nothing is absolute in a discussion of ethics—that justify journalists misleading sources by either not identifying themselves or pretending to be someone they are not. He has heard all the arguments, but still feels that stories gained by deception are 'tainted'. He acknowledges that some of the biggest investigative stories have involved some form of deception, but still questions whether the result justifies the deceptive means that were used to get it. He knows many will disagree with him—especially those of the 'investigative journalists' club'—but that is his ethical stance. On the other hand, Martin believes that deception is acceptable if it leads to the exposure of a larger 'lie', such as government blunders or deception, significant criminal activity, or corporate malpractice on a major scale. He says that using subterfuge to trap a lying politician or to expose a commercial scandal is obviously in the public interest, and crusading journalists are not being unethical if they use deception to gather evidence. Martin is a firm advocate of 'standpoint' activist journalism but adds the caveat that the 'public interest' test threshold must be very high to avoid the gratuitous use of deception. On one point the authors agree: deception used against 'ordinary people' who have no chance to give informed consent to being questioned, or might be unnecessarily embarrassed by exposure, is not justified. How would you feel if everything you said in a casual conversation with someone ended up in a newspaper (or on TV or radio)? If you knew that what you were saying was being recorded for possible later use, you might answer some questions quite differently, certainly not in the sometimes flippant way people—including journalists and academics—often discuss issues.

Before the 'One Nation' sting, the most commonly cited exponent of dubious methods in gathering his scoops was the British journalist Mazher Mahmood, better known by his nickname, 'The Fake Sheikh', so-called for his propensity for wearing Arab robes in some of his more memorable stings. We discussed his methods in an earlier edition (Patching and Hirst 2014, 60–2). Among the notable subjects of his stings were: the Duchess of York, Sarah Ferguson; the Countess of Wessex, Sophie; the then-manager of the British soccer team, Sven-Goran Eriksson; and three members of the Pakistan cricket team. He boasted he had 'nailed scores of paedophiles, arms dealers, drug peddlers (and) people traffickers' in his 20 years at the notorious *News of the World* (O'Carroll 2016). But the world of the (in)famous undercover reporter came crashing down in late 2016 when he was sentenced to 15 months' jail after being found guilty of tampering with evidence (changing a police statement) in the collapsed drug trial of reality TV star, Tulisa Contostavios (Davies 2016). It was reported after the two-week trial of Mahmood and his driver that News Corp UK was facing more than 45 civil claims related to his stories (Davies 2016).

Phone hacking

It probably goes without saying—given the coverage of the *News of the World* phone hacking scandal in the United Kingdom in 2011–2012 and the widespread repercussions in the form of the ongoing huge pay-outs to those who had their phones hacked; the closure of the offending newspaper; the arrests of journalists and others; and the Leveson inquiry into media ethics in the UK—but we will say it anyway: phone hacking is illegal and unethical. It is gaining information by deception and involves a massive invasion of a person's privacy. There is no instance where hacking into someone's phone to listen to their voice messages can be justified.

However, there are important legal and ethical distinctions between hacking a phone and using recordings of phone calls in your story without the consent of the person being recorded. Legally the situation is complicated by different rules in different jurisdictions and you must always check the legal situation where you are before deciding to use a surreptitious recording in a news report. Generally, one of two situations will apply: either use of the recording without the permission of everybody on the call will be illegal under all circumstances, or its use will be okay legally as long as one of the parties to the call knew it was being recorded. This is legally important because it means that the reporter cannot tap a phone line and listen in, but they can use material legally recorded by one of the parties to the call. The best example to illustrate this came in January 2021 when then-President Trump was recorded demanding Georgia state officials 'find' him enough votes to overturn the state's certified election result. The recording was leaked to the news media by Georgia secretary of state Brad Raffensperger and was embarrassing for Trump (Gardner 2021). *The Washington Post* was able to legally—and ethically—use the recording because Raffensperger was on the line. We also think there's no doubt that the story passed the public interest test; the President was trying to steal an election he lost—and breaking the law—while falsely claiming that someone else had stolen the election from him!

Copyright

Copyright is mainly a legal issue, but there are ethical aspects too. An important distinction that journalists need to understand is that copyright does not exist in an idea, but in the expression of that idea (Pearson and Polden 2019, 403–4). In other words, there is nothing to stop journalists from getting information or ideas for stories from other sources—like your story—and then creating their own version of that information. They do it all the time. Mainstream media monitor each other's online sites and broadcasts for story ideas. We will discuss plagiarism next, but commercial TV current affairs programmes are forever 'ripping off' each other's ideas for stories, often only to discredit them. But to repeat: copyright does not reside in the facts of a story, but rather in their form of expression in a particular newspaper, magazine, online, or broadcast form. That's the case with the basic facts or idea of a story (or the circumstances), but how much of a person's original created work can you 'take', even with attribution, before it would be considered an infringement of copyright? Neither of the authors are lawyers so we suggest you seek expert legal advice. In most copyright jurisdictions there is the 'fair dealing' clause, which allows the use of some part of an original work for journalistic purposes. It also protects university lecturers using original material as examples in class. It's the same clause that allows the TV stations to run excerpts from another station's programme or highlights of various sporting events from other station's coverages in their TV news programmes, even though the 'opposition' might have paid a billion dollars or more (or a lot less in the post-coronavirus environment) for exclusive rights to the live broadcasts of the games. Discussion of copyright and its possible infringement leads us to one of the more serious ethical dilemmas, which has become more prevalent in recent years—at least more people are being caught out—that of plagiarism.

Plagiarism

All three professional organisations we've been quoting—the Australian MEAA, the British NUJ, and the American SPJ—are unanimous in their condemnation of plagiarism. Plagiarism is the use of another person's work without attribution—copying their original material, perhaps changing a word here or there, but basically reproducing their work and calling it your own. We are amazed that it happens so frequently nowadays. With the modern technology available, what makes journalists think they will get away with it? University students know that if they submit their essays through a programme like Turnitin, plagiarism will be easily detected. There are plenty of members of the public who might vaguely recognise a familiar sentence or phrase in a story, then run an online search of it and find the original. ABC-TV's *Media Watch* regularly exposes plagiarists. The Internet, which had made plagiarism far easier to do (a simple 'copy and paste') has also made it easier to detect, and social media platforms like Facebook and Twitter give frustrated journalists to opportunity to 'out' thieving colleagues.

One of the biggest plagiarism/deception cases so far this century involved *The New York Times* and self-confessed serial plagiarist and fabricator, Jayson Blair. The *Times* is one of the most respected papers in the US—despite ex-President Trump's criticism—yet on 11 May 2003, on page one, below their slogan 'All the news that's fit to print', was an embarrassing headline and admission; 'Correcting the record: *Times* reporter who resigned leaves a long trail of deception' (Barry 2003). The resulting four-broadsheet-page, 7,000-word investigation showed errors in half of the 73 articles Blair had written over the previous seven months (Dalton 2003). What continues to amaze us, is the seniority and public profile of some of the journalists who get caught plagiarising other people's work or passing off barely disguised media releases as their own work. The former *New York Times* executive editor, Jill Abramson—one of the most famous names in American journalism—was forced to apologise in early 2019 in the wake of a plagiarism scandal surrounding her then-new book, *Merchants of Truth: The Business of News and the Fight for Facts* (Pullman 2019). She denied the plagiarism by claiming some parts of her book weren't 'appropriately and fully attributed' (Jones 2019). Also in America three years earlier, the then soon-to-be (Republican) first lady, Melania Trump, was embarrassed when her speechwriter was caught out plagiarising part of a speech of her predecessor, the then-current first lady Michelle Obama's 2008 speech to the Democratic National convention (Marans 2016). As if to prove our earlier point about the ease with which you will be caught out, Melania's plagiarism was first noticed by a recently laid-off journalist watching her speech from a Los Angeles Starbucks (Borchers 2016).

In Australia, few weeks go by without a journalist tweeting about their story being 'ripped off', usually by an online site. There was a major blow-up in mid-2014 when the Murdoch-owned News Corp labelled local online competitor, *Daily Mail Australia* as a serial plagiarist and its reporters as 'copy snatchers and parasites' (Meade 2014). News Corp sent a legal letter to the *Daily Mail* asking them to stop using its content or face a lawsuit. The letter cited ten examples of stories it said the online site had 'lifted' from News Corp tabloids (Markson 2014). What particularly annoyed News Corp was that their content is behind a paywall, while the *Daily Mail* offerings are free. In a tit-for-tat response, the *Daily Mail* responded offering several examples where News Corp had 'lifted' their 'exclusives' (Robin 2014). Media lawyers at the time suggested News Corp would have an 'uphill battle' winning a copyright action against the *Mail* (Greenslade 2014). News Corp journalist Jane Hansen's 2018 tweet tells a familiar story:

> Rose at 3am, drove 5 hours to Port Macquarie to respectfully write about Sinead McNamara's funeral, filed, drove back. 829k round trip, back home at 7.30pm and whole thing RIPPED OFF by @DailyMailAU who, I can tell you WERE NOT there. Thieves.
>
> (@janehansen2000 2018)

Accusations against *Daily Mail* continued off and on until late 2018 when ABC TV's *Media Watch* host Paul Barry tweeted out a call for journalists to provide examples of their having had stories 'ripped off' by the *Mail*. A week later he devoted the entire programme to the *Mail's* plagiarism (Barry 2018b). Barry said the programme had received 'well over 100 replies' to the request for examples. He told his audience that 'while all the media steal stories from time to time, the *Daily Mail* does it on an industrial scale' (ibid.). Another form of 'stealing another's work' surfaced at the height of the coronavirus pandemic in April 2020—dropping in on another media organisation's Zoom meetings (called 'zoombombing'). This incident involved Australian journalist Mark Di Stefano, who had built up a reputation for breaking stories in his homeland for the ABC and Buzzfeed before joining the *Financial Times* in London. He was accused of listening to the audio feed of confidential video conference calls by *The Independent* and its sister title, *The Evening Standard*, on the financial impact on the two London papers of the COVID-19 virus and breaking the news on Twitter as the staff were hearing it (Sweney 2020). Initially he was suspended from the *Financial Times*, but later tweeted he'd resigned (Fenton 2020) and was soon back at work for another website as its technology reporter (The Information 2021).

Fabulism

We mentioned the 'Jayson Blair Affair' briefly in reference to plagiarism, one of his major sins, but *The New York Times* reporter didn't stop at taking others' material and calling it his own. He was also a 'fabulist'—he made up stories. By his own admission, Blair (2004) filed stories from places he never visited, quoted people he never spoke to, and described details he never saw (Rosen 2003). Blair selected details from photographs to create the impression he had been somewhere or seen someone, when he had not. By an amazing twist of fate, it was another former *New York Times* colleague, Macerena Hernandez, who helped bring him down. She'd written a story for the *San Antonia Express-News* about the death of a soldier in the Iraq war, and after reading Blair's version of the story believed he had 'stolen' her story and dobbed him in. Before the Jayson Blair affair, the best-known case of fabrication involved *The Washington Post*, another major American newspaper. It was the *Post*'s investigation into the Watergate Affair that played a major role in forcing President Nixon to resign—a high point in modern American journalism. But it was another *Post* reporter, Janet Cooke, who wrote a story in 1980 titled 'Jimmy's World' in which she looked at drug-taking among young children. Cooke claimed to have interviewed an eight-year-old heroin addict called Jimmy. The story caused a furore and won Cooke a Pulitzer Prize. No sooner had she taken delivery of the award than she and her embarrassed newspaper had to announce they were returning it; the story was a fabrication. There was no 'Jimmy'; Cooke unconvincingly claimed he represented a 'composite' of child addicts. The whole story was fiction (Hirst and Patching 2007, 223).

As we touched on briefly in Chapter 6, a more recent example of a senior reporter simply making up stories came to light in late 2018 when *Der Spiegel*, Europe's biggest-selling news magazine, admitted one of its star reporters had fabricated facts in his stories for years. The award-winning journalist, Claas Relotius, resigned from the German magazine after admitting making up parts of his reporting for a decade (The Australian 2018). According to the magazine, Relotius fabricated interviews and facts in at least 14 articles. The next issue after the revelation of fabrication contained a 23-page feature on what happened under a plain front cover which said (translated from the German): 'Tell it like it is. On our own account: how one of our reporters falsified his stories and why he was able to do it' (Tobitt 2018a). Then, of course, there are the 'exclusives' so often found in the 'gossip magazines' that bear little resemblance to the truth. The laughable nature of such magazines was demonstrated in a finding by the Australian Press Council—the nation's print watchdog—in February 2020. The Press Council had been asked to adjudicate on a *Women's Day* front-page splash on 27 May 2019, which screamed 'PALACE CONFIRMS THE MARRIAGE IS OVER! WHY HARRY WAS LEFT WITH NO CHOICE BUT TO END IT' and the 'story' on an inside page headed 'THIS IS THE FINAL STRAW! Bombshell revelations about Meghan push a distraught Harry to breaking point' (APC 2020). We all know to take gossip magazine contents with the proverbial grain of salt, but the Press Council seemed to accept that they simply published lies: 'The Council acknowledges that celebrity and gossip magazines are purchased for light entertainment, with readers not necessarily assuming that everything presented is factual. Accordingly, some latitude is given for factual exaggeration and inaccuracies' (APC 2020). The Press Council did, however, find that the headline 'made a statement that was blatantly incorrect and not supported by the article's contents' and said that it was more than just an exaggeration, it was misleading (ibid.). The APC adjudicators added that since 'the Palace' did not make a complaint to the Council, there was no need for a correction. That from the organisation that is supposed to uphold journalistic standards in Australia! There are no excuses for plagiarising or fabricating a news item—news is fundamentally about truth and accuracy. Decades ago, reporters and editors might have thought they could get away with it, but not nowadays. Someone will find the original quote or challenge the veracity of the story. There's enough 'fake news' in the world without reporters adding to the mix with their own fabulism.

Conflicts of interest

Conflicts of interest can arise in a variety of situations but most often they involve a reporter having a personal or financial interest in the story they're reporting. Some are obvious such as 'insider trading' when a journalist uses information about the stock market that's not generally available to the public to enrich themselves. Others, such as accepting gifts are not so easy: When does accepting hospitality or a small present tip over into bribery or inducement that comes with strings?

The issue of gifts and inducements offered to journalists to influence their writing is also a major ethical issue and covered in most Codes of Ethics:

> Clause 4: Do not allow personal interest, or any belief, commitment, payment, gift or benefit to undermine your accuracy, fairness or independence.
>
> (MEAA 2018)

> Refuse gifts, favors, fees, free travel and special treatment, and avoid political and other outside activities that may compromise integrity or impartiality, or may damage credibility.
>
> (SPJ 2020)

> 8. Resists threats or any other inducements to influence, distort or suppress information and takes no unfair personal advantage of information gained in the course of her/his duties before the information is public knowledge.
>
> (NUJ 2011)

In practice, though, the rules are regularly broken *in house* by journalists and their editors. Many journalists see nothing wrong with accepting some 'freebies' from sources. After all, they take their sources to lunch from time to time to 'pump them' for information (if they have the luxury of time, that is) and may send them a 'bottle of something' along with the corporate Christmas card as an annual 'thank you' for services rendered. So why not let the source offer the same hospitality? And why not accept the fancy folder, pen, notepad, etc. and hospitality at a conference? These 'freebies' seem petty, but there is not such a big jump between that and the free tickets to 'the big game' or live theatre, the autographed copy of the star's new book, and further down the spiral to cheap holidays or free trips. Nowadays mainstream media pay their own way and have policies about accepting gifts. Basically, you can keep the pen and notepad, but anything worth more than, say, AU$50 (some put the bar higher, at AU$100) has to be handed in. What happens to the more valuable 'freebies' varies, but usually the reporter can either 'buy' it for a reasonable price, or it is auctioned in the newsroom with the proceeds in either case usually going to charity, or the item is donated to a charity to use in their fundraising. But what if you are offered a free trip to inspect a new mine site on the other side of the country (or overseas) and the mining company says they'll put you up in a nearby city in a fancy hotel for a couple of days 'while you get a feel for the project and what it will mean for the area'? Such offers of free flights and accommodation are usually acknowledged nowadays in the coverage. That's not the problem, and there are plenty who will point out the 'freebie' if the organisation doesn't mention it. It is how you feel a few months later when someone who entertained you on the visit to the mine, or whatever, calls. We're not singling out mining enterprises; tourist destinations often offer free flights and accommodation in return for mention in the paper's travel section. What do you do when a source/host contacts you asking a favour? Perhaps asking you to overlook an unfavourable story. Do you feel at all obligated to the source? That's one type of compromising position. Another is a conflict of interest at its very basic level. For example, you are asked to write a story about a problem at a sporting or service club of which you are a member. Your membership may well compromise your objectivity—particularly if the story is going to show your club in a less-than-favourable light. In such cases you need to make your chief of staff or editor aware of the potential conflict of interest and let them decide a course of action. They should hand the story on to someone else who is not a member of that club. There is another form of freebie in political reporting that is also ethically suspect, but widespread; it is called 'the drop'. A 'drop' is a story briefed to favoured reporters by a political staffer usually working for a senior politician. A 'drop' offers the reporter an exclusive but it is done behind closed doors to disguise the source. When journalists become dependent on 'the drop', they are effectively bought off by the politician. If the journalist writes a critical story, the drops will stop.

Do you work for the police?

There's another ethical dilemma that involves general reporters and investigative journalists alike. Would you hand over to police the video or still photographs you had taken in the course of covering a story? Let's say you were at a demonstration and it turned ugly, and some of the demonstrators destroyed property. The police want your coverage to help identify the offenders. Do you hand it over? It might earn you 'brownie points' with the police that you might be able to 'cash in' at a later date—that is, call in the favour for some information you badly need—but is it ethical to become an extension of the law? In most cases it usually comes as an informal request. While we have no problem with the police reviewing any images that were used by the various TV channels in their regular news and current affairs programmes, they could just as easily have had them recorded, but what about the off-cuts—the material not used? Surely the police don't consider the electronic media an extension of their evidence-gathering resources?

Sometimes the police will seek a court order demanding journalists hand over material. In 2013, *The Guardian* destroyed hard drives of information given to the paper by NSA whistleblower, Edward Snowden, rather than risk legal action by the British government (Borger 2013). This is where it gets very tricky and a good legal firm should be involved in any decision or negotiation with authorities. In the United States in 2020, at the height of the 'Black Lives Matter' demonstrations that followed the murder of George Floyd by police officer Derek Chauvin, journalists in Cleveland faced just this dilemma. The local County prosecutor's office subpoenaed from two local media outlets, *Cleveland.com* and the *Plain Dealer*, any reporters' photographs, video, and audio recordings that showed 'potential criminal activity' during the city's 30 May riots (Shaffer 2020). *Cleveland.com* Editor Chris Quinn said he planned to turn over material already published, as had been done in the past. The Committee to Protect Journalists (CPJ) called on the prosecutor's office to withdraw the subpoena. Editor Quinn told CPJ they intended to fight the demand for unpublished material (CPJ 2020c). A newsroom's relationship with local police, and the extent of any cooperation between journalists and law enforcement, are active fault lines in journalism ethics. Our discussion of BLM in Chapter 2 and material covered in Chapters 13–16 sheds light on this issue at this ethical juncture. Given the troubled reputation of police in relation to racism and other issues, to what extent do they deserve or merit cooperation from journalists who want to pursue truth and act in the public interest?

As we have seen, there are plenty of unscrupulous methods and potentially harmful ways in which reporters can use disguises, technology, and just plain lies to get stories and impress their editors and their audience. One heartening thing, though, as these examples demonstrate, plenty of the 'perps' are getting caught, often in the glaring spotlight of unwanted publicity. But not all of them are found out. While ever a degree of fame and fortune might await the dishonest, the temptation is always there to cut corners and invent facts or sources, just to get a story. Our advice is: *don't do it!* If you are considering using a hidden recording device, ask yourself: 'Is it worth it?' and certainly make sure you are aware of the legal as well as the ethical implications. If your editor or producer attempts to pressure you into doing something that you're not comfortable with, consider saying 'No', but first get advice from colleagues you trust and/or from your professional association or union.

Chequebook journalism

Put simply, chequebook journalism involves buying exclusive rights to a story to improve newspaper or magazine sales or broadcast ratings. It is becoming less common in mainstream media nowadays because of the parlous economic state of the industry, but it can still be seen on commercial current affairs television programmes, and among gossip magazines and some tabloid newspapers. While it has a long history among the British 'red top' tabloid newspapers and American supermarket magazines, and to a lesser extent in television current affairs (especially stories of the 'kiss-and-tell' sex scandal variety), serious mainstream media have almost always resisted the temptation to 'buy the news'. We chronicled the history of chequebook journalism in Australia in a previous edition (Patching and Hirst 2014, 78–89), but there are a few points worth mentioning in the context of this 'dubious practice'. We talk elsewhere about the economic fault line in modern journalism—the quest for profit overriding the public information functions of the media—chequebook journalism demonstrates this fault line and taints the information it buys.

The biggest cheques so far

The benchmark for chequebook journalism in Australia was set in 2006—and it is unlikely to be surpassed in the current economic climate—when the Nine Network and its stablemates at the time, *Women's Day*, the *Australian Women's Weekly* and the now defunct news magazine *The Bulletin*, reportedly paid coalminers Todd Russell and Brant Webb AU$2.6 million for the rights to the story of their 14-day ordeal of being trapped underground during the Beaconsfield mine cave-in in Tasmania (The Australian 2010). It was—and still is—a huge sum, when most 'exclusives' in Australia tend to go for much, much less. The British Royals, as we saw in the previous chapter, are always big news, as are photos of them in unguarded moments. In 2013 photos emerged of the Duchess of Cambridge on holiday in the Caribbean in a bikini showing her 'baby bump'. The oft-mentioned *Women's Day* was reported to have paid about AU$150,000 for the Australian rights to the photos (Hornery 2013). Several other magazines around the world were believed to have also paid large amounts for the photos and others in Australia were believed to have made offers. British media were restrained, honouring their 'gentlemen's agreement' not to invade the Royals' privacy. The editor of *Woman's Day* at the time, Fiona Connolly, offered an interesting rationale for publishing the photos. She said the royal family should be pleased with the photos because the Duchess looked happy and healthy after what the editor called a rocky start to her pregnancy (The Australian 2013). The former Australian Deputy Prime Minister, Barnaby Joyce, was the centre of another controversy in mid-2018 when he and his new partner agreed to appear with their new-born son Sebastian in a supposed 'tell all' interview on the Seven Network's flagship weekly current affairs programme, *Sunday*, for AU$150,000 which he said would go into a trust fund for the child (Farr 2018). The episode raised some of the ethical issues associated with chequebook journalism. For instance, should politicians, already taking a public salary, charge the media for exclusive interviews? One political commentator described the deal as a 'new low for Australian politics' with 'the nasty and confronting ingredients of a tacky spectacular soap opera' (Farr 2018). An editorial in Brisbane's morning tabloid, *The Courier Mail*, left no doubt about its opinion when it said the deal was 'not just a bad look—it's a line you don't cross' (The Courier Mail 2018). Few of his parliamentary colleagues supported his decision to 'go public' for money. Australia's *60 Minutes* is also famous—notorious?—for chequebook journalism, but how can networks continue to pay for stories when they're haemorrhaging advertising dollars?

Just another business expense?

Some media companies see chequebook journalism as just another business expense. They justify the payments because they believe exclusivity brings higher sales or ratings and improves their financial bottom line. The counter-argument is that the economic benefit is short-lived. TV ratings or magazine sales might spike, but it rarely lasts. In the current economic climate, it is likely those who hold the purse-strings are sure to be asking more questions before approving payments for exclusives. Aside from the general odiousness of 'paying for exclusive rights', there are several other issues associated with chequebook journalism that warrant consideration. How much is paid for the 'exclusives' is rarely disclosed publicly, but most figures quoted in the media by their opposition are educated guesses, in some cases because they were involved in the bidding war, too, or spoke to a source that was. This is another of the murky aspects of chequebook journalism—the precise details are usually kept from the consumer.

Another issue is that bought stories are often not as well researched or fact checked as those that result from investigative journalism or the everyday work of seasoned journalists. These stories may simply be written to the audience's perceived tastes—salacious and emotional. While it might not be a problem when the source is simply recounting what happened while they were trapped down a mine, or escaping the jaws of a Great White shark (in which case the 'feeding frenzy' is on the part of the competing tabloid media), it's another thing if the story has wider, perhaps political, implications. Is there an element of 'getting square' and making a packet at the same time? What about when chequebook journalism leads to the arrest of the reporter on kidnapping and assault charges? This happened to an Australian *60 Minutes* crew when they paid private detectives to 'rescue' children from their father in Lebanon and it all went horribly wrong. The children's mother—an Australian—had enlisted

60 Minutes with a sob-story of family breakdown but entering a foreign country with intent to kidnap children is way beyond the pale (Chain 2018). It's not just dubious methods, it is criminal conspiracy.

Whatever way you spin it, chequebook journalism compromises honest and ethical journalism. How do we know that what we are being told 'exclusively' is the whole truth and nothing but the truth, as the witnesses swear in those television courtroom dramas? Once a person is being paid for their story, they may feel an obligation to 'perform' to earn their fee. Who's to say they won't 'gild the lily' or exaggerate their story to give the paymaster value for money? Who's to say the reporter concerned won't 'coach' them on what might be the most quotable answers? Paying for exclusive rights is another nail in the coffin of journalistic credibility. We have mentioned elsewhere the low level of credibility journalists 'enjoy' and paying people for their stories does nothing to enhance it. The final category of chequebook journalism is the 'kill fee'. This is the practice of paying for a story in order to bury it. The source is paid and signs a non-disclosure agreement, but the story is never published. Once again—of course—the most relevant example features Donald J. Trump and the tabloid *National Inquirer*. In 2018, as part of investigations into alleged corrupt payments from Donald Trump's election funds, the *National Inquirer* admitted it had paid a 'catch and kill' fee to a former 'Playmate' Karen McDougal to suppress a story about an affair between her and Trump. Prosecutors alleged the money amounted to a 'secret in-kind contribution' to Trump's 2020 re-election campaign (Swaine 2018).

What do the ethics codes say?

In Australia, the MEAA Code of Ethics covers chequebook journalism in clause 7:

> Do your upmost to ensure disclosure of any direct or indirect payment made for interviews, pictures, information or stories.
>
> (MEAA 2018)

The British NUJ does not mention chequebook journalism in its Code of Conduct (NUJ 2011), but the IPSO Editors' Code of Practice in the UK leaves to door open for payments for news:

> Editors invoking the public interest to justify payment or offers would need to demonstrate that there was good reason to believe the public interest would be served. If, despite payment, no public interest emerged, then the material should not be published.
>
> (IPSO 2018)

Writing for the prestigious *Columbia Journalism Review*, John Cook (2011) suggested that for American journalists chequebook journalism falls into the same moral category as paying for sex. The SPJ Code of Ethics leaves no doubt:

[D]o not pay for access to news.

(SPJ 2014)

Is it ever OK to pay for stories?

The committee that framed the current 12-point MEAA Code of Ethics (2018) thought there was an argument, in certain circumstances, for people to profit from their misfortune. Our view should be fairly obvious from the tone of the discussion thus far. We see no merit in the practice but accept that it is a fact of life in tabloid television and gossip magazines. However, some believe it is only fair that media organisations pay if big stories translate to higher ratings or circulation, which in turn means increased revenue. Why shouldn't the people at the centre of the news benefit? After all, they created the increased revenue. Others argue that chequebook journalism allows people in the spotlight to tell their story on their terms rather than being subjected to the chaos of 'all in' media conferences. Charities sometimes benefit from chequebook journalism when celebrities are paid for exclusive interviews and donate the money. Maybe there is a case for some payment for 'important stories', to cover reasonable expenses for the person(s) involved, but they are all-too-often overshadowed by other stories obtained by the size of the cheque that amount to little more than audience titillation. Reporters and editors should ask themselves a number of important questions about the use of payments to sources before they head down that road:

- How important is the story and do we need it to beat the opposition? Basically a commercial decision.
- Is the source's information accurate, or is this an invitation to be ripped off? There have been instances where newspapers have paid for allegedly good stories only to find out later that they have been sold a dud, or a pack of lies. As mentioned earlier in this book, one famous case involved Rupert Murdoch buying and hastily publishing the fake Hitler diaries in 1983.
- Do the rights of so-called 'ordinary people' differ from those of public figures and celebrities as we explored in Chapter 8?

In general, we do not like the practice of chequebook journalism, believing it is too open to abuses like the botched 'rescue' of children in Beirut, or 'catch and kill' operations that protect dubious characters from rightful public exposure. It is clearly an active fault line and one that opens up at the ethical crossroads where journalism and the news industry find themselves today.

Case study: How far do you go in helping police?

Ukrainian security forces staged the elaborate 'murder' of Russian dissident journalist, Arkady Babchenko, in Kiev in May 2018 in what was said to be a sting operation aimed at foiling a Russian assassination plot. They used make-up and pig's blood. They shot bullet holes into one of the journalist's sweat-shirts, and even took him to the morgue (Barker 2018). One of Russia's best-known war reporters, and a strong Kremlin critic, Babchenko, 41, fled Russia in early 2017 because of death threats. Ukrainian security told him their Russian counterparts had ordered his murder. As part of the elaborate hoax, a photo was released of Babchenko lying face down in a pool of blood with apparent multiple bullet wounds in his back. We are not interested here in debating whether the staged murder was a political 'coup' for the Ukraine or a propaganda win for Russia, but rather what damage such behaviour does to journalism. As Australian ABC foreign correspondent Anne Barker commented at the time, 'in today's era of fake news, his complicity in staging his own murder risks further eroding trust in journalists around the world' (2018). Friends and colleagues of Babchenko questioned the value of such a hoax, and its impact on the media. Reporters Without Borders denounced the hoax as a 'pathetic stunt' (cited in Barker 2018). Former senior journalist and academic, commentator Roy Greenslade (2018), said it was 'impossible to see any value in the…elaborate faking of his death' and the episode had 'done a disservice to truth, and to journalism' (2018). A *Guardian* editorial titled 'The Guardian view on a journalist's return: The death was fake, the damage was not' criticised Babchenko's involvement in the sting 'not as a reporter', they acknowledged, 'but as a potential victim' (2018). But the paper kept the best comment for the final paragraph:

> At a time of cynicism and deliberate manipulation, when 'fake news' is the rallying call of those seeking to bury facts, and when lies are proven to spread faster than the truth, such injuries [to truth and to journalism generally] are more serious than ever.
>
> (Guardian Editorial 2018)

Questions for discussion

1 Put yourself in Babchenko's shoes. Security forces suggest they fake your death to draw out a Russian hit squad. Would you play along?
2 What if it was a Western security agency making the approach?
3 How would you feel, as a friend or a member of Babchenko's family? You're mourning his death, and suddenly he's not dead?
4 What, if any, journalistic benefit can you see from the hoax?
5 Broadening out the discussion, what would be your attitude (as a member of the mainstream media) towards helping the police with their enquiries?
6 Would there be a cut-off point? Where you would draw the line?
7 Why should the media help the police or security forces?
8 Is chequebook journalism ever justified? Explain the circumstances in which you might consider paying for a story.

9   Undercover journalists like Nellie Bly and Günter Wallraff have made a huge impact with their reportage but the technique is also open to misuse. When is it okay to use undercover reporting tactics?

10   Discuss the legal and ethical implications of using surreptitiously recorded phone calls in your reporting.

11   What do you think of our idea for a high standard in the 'public interest test'? Is it always easy to meet this standard?

10 The importance of whistleblowers and source protection

International condemnation follows Australian police raids

Within the space of two days in June 2019, Australian federal police raided the home of a senior News Corp political journalist in Canberra and the Sydney headquarters of the national broadcaster, the Australian Broadcasting Corporation, trying to establish who leaked stories that supposedly damaged national security. The day before the first raid, Sydney radio presenter Ben Fordham received a call from the federal Home Affairs Department asking him to 'out' the source of his story about several boatloads of asylum seekers trying to reach Australia (2GB 2019). It would later emerge that police had also planned to raid the Sydney headquarters of News Corp, but decided to put the raid on hold in light of the furious reaction to the other raids (Lyons 2019). The Australian media was united in their condemnation of the raids as an attempt to intimidate journalists and, more importantly, their sources (Harvey 2008).

Overseas reaction was equally vociferous. The London-based ex-pat human rights barrister, Geoffrey Robertson (2019), asked of his fellow Australians: 'How did we become so out of sync on press freedom, invasions of which are the sign of a second-rate country?' *The New York Times* headed their news coverage 'Australia may well be the world's most secretive democracy' (Cave 2019), and in an editorial suggested: 'Like the Trump administration, the Australian government seems determined to frighten whistle-blowers into silence and to undermine the core journalistic tool of source confidentiality', describing the raids as 'straight from the playbook of authoritarian thugs' (New York Times 2019). *The Washington Post* used the headline 'A bad, sad and dangerous day', and noted the raid 'comes at a time of growing concerns of eroded press freedoms around the world' (Elfrink 2019). The BBC was quick to support its Australian counterpart, calling the raid 'deeply troubling' in an official statement and echoing *The New York Times*' concern: 'At a time when the media is becoming less free across the world, it is highly worrying if a national broadcaster is being targeted for doing its job of reporting in the public interest' (BBC statement cited in BBC 2019a). The United Nations rapporteur on the state of freedom of opinion and expression around the globe, David Kaye, went as far as to suggest 'Australia leads the Western world on media restrictions' (Miller 2019).

DOI: 10.4324/9780429242892-11

What sparked the raids?

News Corp journalist Annika Smethurst's home in Canberra was raided over a story she wrote more than a year before under the front page headline 'Let us spy on Aussies', which said the federal government was considering expanding surveillance powers to allow for 'monitoring Australian citizens'—in other words, domestic spying—at that stage banned by law (Merritt 2019). Seven federal police spent many hours searching her home, famously including rifling through her 'undies drawer' (Harvey 2019). The next day it was the national broadcaster's turn as the federal police sought further information on a series published in 2017 titled 'The Afghan files' about Australian special forces being investigated over possible war crimes[1] (Knowles, Worthington, and Blumer 2019). The second raid was odd as the confessed whistleblower on the Afghan files story, David McBride, had already been committed to stand trial for leaking the information to the media. The warrant served on the ABC related to 'allegations of publishing classified material contrary to the Crimes Act 1914' (Bradley 2019). The police worked their way through more than 9,000 files and left after eight hours with two USBs (Kaye 2019). The Smethurst and Afghan files stories clearly embarrassed the Morrison federal government. Initially it was thought the raids were intended to track down those who had leaked the stories, but as the investigation dragged on, it became obvious the Federal police were also investigating whether the journalists involved in producing the stories had committed criminal offences (Knowles 2019). David McBride had been questioned about whether the two ABC journalists involved knew they might be breaking the law (Knaus 2019b). Both News Corp and the ABC said they would challenge aspects of the raids in the courts (Shanahan 2019a). The ABC lost their challenge to the validity of the search warrant in the Federal Court, described by one former senior ABC staffer as 'a crushing defeat' (Holmes 2020). Smethurst and News Corp were partially successful in their challenge to the High Court. While the High Court ruled that the AFP warrant for the raid was invalid on a technicality, it was a hollow victory because the Court did not order police to destroy the material seized, exposing the reporter and her source to possible prosecution (Karp 2020). Almost a year after the raid, the AFP announced no one would be prosecuted over the News Corp story (Hayne 2020a). The Federal Attorney General at the time, Christian Porter, had offered a ray of hope to the three journalists facing possible federal charges by announcing a few months after the raids that prosecutors would need his formal approval to charge a journalist (Worthington 2019). In mid-2020, it was revealed the AFP had asked prosecutors to consider charging one of the ABC journalists, Dan Oakes (Hayne 2020b). Three months later the Commonwealth Department of Public Prosecutions announced there was no public interest in pursuing a prosecution (ABC 2020a). The following day Oakes expressed his relief at the decision and noted that McBride still faced charges, suggesting: 'Embarrassment should never be reason enough for journalists or whistleblowers to be prosecuted' (Oakes 2020).

Within a couple of weeks of the raids, three of the nation's most powerful media executives, in a rare show of unity, made a joint appearance at the National Press Club to push for an overhaul of media protection laws (Shanahan 2019b). The media executives thought they had initially been given a reasonable hearing by the federal government—it had announced a parliamentary inquiry into press freedom. But then the Home Affairs Minister at the time, Peter Dutton, declared 'nobody is above the law' and rejected requests from the ABC and News Corp to rule out charging the journalists at the centre of the raids, leading to further media criticism in their news pages and bulletins (Samios and Ferguson 2019) and a scathing editorial from the News Corp flagship, *The Australian* (The Weekend Australian 2019). The announcement of the inquiry, to be conducted by the parliamentary joint committee on intelligence and security (PJCIS), was greeted with scepticism by media commentators, one suggesting it was like 'letting the fox guard the henhouse' (Muller 2019). It was the same government-run committee that signed off on national security laws. Both authors are firmly in the camp of the sceptics. Martin pointed to three previous government reports on potential media reform which saw minimal changes and wrote the result of the inquiry was: 'more likely to reflect the restrictive culture of FOI law and entrenching the right of government secrecy than to give us any form of genuine reform and a guaranteed free press' (Hirst 2019b). On the eve of the parliamentary inquiry, Home Affairs Minister Peter Dutton issued a direction to the AFP that effectively told them to avoid raiding or investigating journalists who had been leaked confidential information (Shields 2019). The senior media executives that had appeared at the National Press Club again presented a united front to the inquiry calling for changes to the laws they saw as inhibiting press freedom and 'criminalising journalism'. ABC News Director Gaven Morris told the inquiry that the raids meant the broadcaster could not 'absolutely' guarantee protection of sources (Samios and Vitorovich 2019). When senior public servants appeared before the inquiry a day later, government MPs on the committee suggested that journalists who were leaked confidential documents should submit their work for approval by government media officers (Keane 2019). The inquiry received plenty of submissions from the media and other interested parties, including the nation's journalism educators.

While the inquiry was taking evidence, the media launched a coordinated campaign pushing their demands for change. On 21 October 2019, the major News Corp and Nine mastheads censored their front pages, blacking out the majority of the text alongside red 'secret' stamps (Doran 2019). A TV campaign had been unleashed the night before. Day after day, for weeks, the print and broadcast media continued to run stories on how the public's right to know what the federal government was doing in their name was being stifled by national security laws. The report of the Parliamentary Committee was finally released in May 2021, but it offered little comfort to the media. Among a minimum of concessions, the report recommended restricting who could issue warrants against journalists, a review of the classification of restricted documents

(Doran 2020; Meade 2021). The four Labor (opposition) members of the committee said the recommendations 'do not go far enough' (quoted in Ananian-Welsh 2020). Media observers have long believed the powerful national security laws were being abused to crack down on anyone who embarrasses the government, particularly whistleblowers. The information contained in the stories at the centre of the raids was in the public interest—surveillance powers on their own citizens on home soil, more asylum seekers heading towards Australia, and possible war crimes—later confirmed—by Australia's armed forces. All were issues embarrassing to the federal government (Johnson 2019) and stories that needed to be told. Other critics of the earlier raids, including opposition politicians and media executives, said that—like all governments—the coalition government 'leaks like a sieve' when it suits them using the infamous 'drop' system (see Chapter 9), pointing to other leaks favouring the government that had not been investigated (Karp 2019b; Mitchell 2019). The cumulative effects of the raids and the Right to Know campaign saw Australia's World Press Freedom Index rating in 2020 drop five places from the previous year to 26th. The MEAA Media federal president, Marcus Strom, said the slump was an indication that 'overseas observers are recognising what Australians already know: that press freedom in our country is under sustained assault' (MEAA 2020).

And it wasn't just happening in Australia

A few weeks before the Australian police raids, a freelance reporter in San Francisco, Bryan Carmody, declined to reveal a source who provided him with a copy of a police report. Soon after, ten armed police officers searched his home taking notebooks, computers, cameras, phones, and a copy of the police report (Rosenberg 2019). California's shield law protects journalists from contempt of court charges for refusing to disclose their sources and the State Penal Code supposedly provides that 'no warrant shall issue' for any item protected by the shield law NORCAL, (SPJ 2019). The raid centred around a leaked report detailing the circumstances of former San Francisco Public Defender Jeff Adachi's death. After a fortnight of public outrage over the raid, Police Chief Bill Scott apologised, admitting the search was probably illegal and called for an independent investigation into the episode (Sernoffsky 2019). A CNN commentator and newspaper columnist described the raid as a 'stunning intrusion on press freedom, similar to what we see in autocratic regimes' (Ali 2019).

A few weeks after the Australian raids, police in the United Kingdom launched an investigation into who leaked the confidential memos from Britain's ambassador to the United States, Sir Kim Darroch, which famously described the Trump administration as 'clumsy and inept' (Siddique 2019). The reaction from the former President eventually led to the Ambassador's resignation. Almost comically, British police asked the anonymous person who leaked the sensitive memos to 'turn themselves in and stop wasting detectives' time' (Taylor 2019). Assistant Commissioner Neil Basu drew criticism from editors, cabinet ministers, and lawyers for advising 'social and mainstream' media against publishing leaked government documents and suggesting they return any they have in their possession (Baynes 2019). As if they would. After the usual conspiracy theories about how *The Mail on Sunday* had received the memos, a 19-year-old journalist, Steven Edginton, claimed he was behind the scoop, saying 'a trusted source read out to me an astonishing letter written by Sir Kim in June 2017' which contained the disparaging comments (2019).

Why source protection matters

This chapter argues that source protection is a critical issue for journalists, one that continues to create headaches for them, particularly those who cover issues like defence, government surveillance and national security. We also look at shield laws for journalists and the protection of whistleblowers. With the advances offered law enforcement agencies by the digital surveillance technologies, whistleblowers exposing those important stories about what Western governments are doing (or planning) appear to be a threatened species. However, as much as we hate to throw a bucket of cold water over anyone's passion for journalism and willingness to be fined or possibly go to jail to protect their source, you should know that the court system has long felt it has equally valid reasons for demanding reporters 'give up' their sources in certain cases. The differences over confidentiality go to the heart of journalistic ethics because the keeping of promises and trust are crucial for the reporter seeking the honest pursuit of 'truth', 'fairness', and 'balance'. Here we truly have fault lines with consequences. Protecting sources, like the conflicts around privacy canvassed in Chapter 8, involves that grey area of intersecting legal, ethical, and philosophical issues that we call the 'ethico-legal paradox' and which is often the source of ethical fault lines. The paradox emerges because it is usually a legal inquiry that demands journalists name their sources, while in ethical terms, there is a compelling argument that source protection also protects the public interest. This paradox is clearly evident in the fact that governments rely on often-outdated espionage laws (De Carteret 2019) as well as the latest surveillance technologies in their attempts to control whistleblowers and shutdown unwelcome leaks. By adopting such heavy-handed tactics, police have made most of the legal protections for journalists' sources all but redundant. It is almost impossible to disguise your digital fingerprints when dealing with sources. The flippant suggestion a few years back that journalists might have to revert to the 'Watergate days' of surreptitious meetings in underground car parks—where Woodward and Bernstein met their main source in the scandal, the famous 'Deep Throat', former FBI Associate Director Mark Felt—may well come to pass.

Sources: The lifeblood of serious journalism

Serious journalism is about getting information into the public sphere that those in power would prefer was kept secret. Exposure can lead to inquiries, resignations, and even bring down governments. At another level it can lead to police investigations, court cases, and the jailing of offenders. At the very least, disclosures can spark serious public concern and debate that forces governments, private corporations or individuals into action. But it is not above governments or private industry to take extreme measures to protect their 'secrets' and find out who is leaking them. They regularly invoke 'national interest' or 'commercial-in-confidence' arguments to counter whistleblowers' revelations. Journalists invoke their respective industry Code of Ethics to justify protecting the identity of their sources.

> Aim to attribute information to its source. Where a source seeks anonymity, do not agree without first considering the source's motives and any alternative attributable source. Where confidences are accepted, respect them in all circumstances.
>
> (MEAA 2018)

> Consider sources' motives before promising anonymity. Reserve anonymity for sources who may face danger, retribution or other harm, and have information that cannot be obtained elsewhere. Explain why anonymity was granted.
>
> (SPJ 2014)

> 7. Protects the identity of sources who supply information in confidence and material gathered in the course of her/his work.
>
> (NUJ 2011)

The source relationship—a two-way street

The relationship between journalists and their sources is a two-way street. The journalist needs sources to get those elusive 'scoops', and the source needs the journalist to get their message to the wider community. Such relationships are built on trust and reliability, often developed over many years. Much of that trust on the source's part comes from their belief that if they pass on important information and ask for anonymity, that any guarantee will be honoured by the journalist. The quality of journalism across the Western world would be the poorer if stories based on information gained from sources that need to remain anonymous were eliminated. Not every source demands anonymity. Few do. Most of the work of the everyday newsroom journalist involves ringing their sources—those with whom they have probably had countless dealings—and talking about potential stories and what they can add to what the reporter already knows. It is not all 'guarantee me confidentiality or I won't talk to you' negotiations. The 'two-way street' we have referred to means that the sources are usually just as keen to get their information into the media as the journalist is to write it. It is here that you and the source need to realise the conditions under which you are talking: whether what they say is 'on the record', 'background'; or 'off the record'.

There might be degrees of 'background', but these are the three main cate-gories of the source–reporter relationship. It is important that both reporter and source have a common understanding of the meaning of these terms to avoid confusion and possible embarrassment. 'On the record' means that anything the person says can be quoted directly or paraphrased in a story, and directly attributed to the source. This happens every day at hundreds of media con-ferences around the world; a VIP calls the media in to make an announcement and expects to be quoted. It happens in thousands of conversations between journalists and their regular sources. It is the most common source–reporter relationship. 'Background' means that the information is being offered to help the reporter put the story into context, and it is intended for publication, but not to be directly attributed to the source. It might be used without attribution in a story; it might be used carrying a descriptor of the source, without directly identifying them; or it might provide another thread of inquiry for the reporter to follow up. The most controversial is 'off the record'. This means that the source is giving you information confidentially, perhaps as a favour, and it is not intended for publication, certainly not in any way identifying the source. It amounts to the source giving you a 'heads-up' or 'tip-off' on a potential story, but they don't want to be associated with the final publication. The best advice is always to seek information 'on the record' and, where possible, confirm it with another source. Verification of 'off the record' information is vitally important but difficult given you can't tell anybody where your tip-off came from.

Source security: An international issue in the Digital Age

Journalists and media researchers the world over have for years been pointing out the serious issues surrounding source confidentiality in the Digital Age. One of the leading academic researchers in the area, Australian Julie Posetti, has written, or co-authored, two major reports: 'Protecting journalism sources in the Digital Age' for UNESCO (Posetti 2017); and, more recently, 'The Per-ugia Principles for journalists working with whistleblowers in the Digital Age' (Posetti, Dreyfus, and Colvin 2019). The UNESCO report takes a global look at the issues for sources we have been highlighting in the Australian context—the problems of surveillance, data retention and the broad anti-terrorism laws, and the affects national security laws are having on whistleblowing in general—and examines how these can undermine the confidentiality protection jour-nalists can offer sources. The Perugia Principles were developed after a round-table of 20 international journalists and experts in Perugia, Italy, in April 2018, as a guide for journalists working with whistleblowers. The report details 12 principles, including the need to protect sources, to provide safe ways for them to make first contact, and to recognise the costs of 'whistleblowing' to the whistleblower. The principles also cover the need to verify any material offered and advises using encryption for communication. Among the other steps the principles suggest are: explaining the risks of exposure to the source;

determining the biggest threats to the reporter and the source; and under-standing what steps are needed to protect both. The other principles involve more technical and legal aspects of source protection, but all are explored in detail in the publication (ibid.).

No source, no story, but at what cost?

The prominence of WikiLeaks, Julian Assange, Edward Snowden, Chelsea Manning, and Reality Winner has led to a renewed debate about the use of 'whistleblowers' by reporters. On one side are those who demand that Assange and Snowden be brought to the United States to stand trial for espionage. The more hot-headed among this group have even called for the two to be given the death penalty as 'traitors' (Winkler 2017). We discuss the Julian Assange situation in the case study at the end of this chapter. But the treatment of Assange, Snowden, Manning, and Winner by various government agencies is indicative of the treatment whistleblowers face if caught. The Reality Winner case also had further repercussions that led to two of the founding editors of *The Intercept* parting ways with the publication. Glenn Greenwald announced his resignation at the end of October 2020 citing claims that his reporting had been censored due to 'mandated ideological and partisan loyalties' towards the Democratic Party. Greenwald also cited his anger at the way *The Intercept* handled the Reality Winner case, accusing the publication of responsibility for the whistleblower's arrest and subsequent imprisonment, which he called 'an embarrassing newsroom failure' (Greenwald 2020). In mid-January 2021, Laura Poitras publicly announced that she had been fired from *The Intercept* at the end of November 2020 after she too raised concerns about the handling of the Reality Winner leaks. Poitras (2021) referenced a 'cover-up', a 'multitude of mistakes,' and 'egregious disregard for source protection' in her 'Open Letter' revealing her dismissal. The company that publishes *The Intercept* has always denied mishandling the Reality Winner leaks and issued statements denying the claims made by both Greenwald and Poitras (Ellison 2021).

In Australia, at the time of writing, there were three serious cases involving government whistleblowers before the courts. We've already mentioned the case of David McBride, who did not dispute at his committal hearing that he leaked the 'Afghan Files' to the ABC (Karp 2019a). Another whistleblower who took his story to the ABC (and the former Fairfax media), Richard Boyle, initially faced 66 charges and a possible 161 years in prison for exposing abuses in the Australian Tax Office over their dealings with small business and indi-viduals (Ferguson 2019). That potential prison term would have been just 20 years short of the sentence metered out to Australia's most notorious serial killer, the late Ivan Milat. The Commonwealth later dropped 42 of the charges (Khadem 2020). The final case before the courts is the 'Witness K/Collaery case'. A former Australian Security Intelligence Organisation (ASIO) officer, who can't be named (and his lawyer, Bernard Collaery) are charged over their roles in revealing a covert Australian spy mission to bug the Timor-Leste government during sensitive oil and gas negotiations in 2004 (Knaus 2019a). It was revealed in August 2020 that the federal government had spent almost AU $3 million pursing those whistleblowers through the courts (Knaus 2020a).

Source protection: Those who went to jail

Protecting the sources of important information is a fundamental tenet of journalism, a principle on which serious journalists should be prepared to end up in court or maybe jail. Though it doesn't happen often in Western countries, a few brave souls have spent time behind bars for protecting their sources and many more have rallied to support colleagues who have been jailed. In 2005 a *New York Times* reporter, Judith Miller, was jailed for refusing to identify the source of a story she wrote that divulged the name of a CIA operative (Liptak 2005). In the US, about 20 journalists have been jailed or fined for not divulging sources or cooperating with police inquiries since 1970 (Reporters' Committee 2019). In Australia, when *Courier-Mail* journalist Joe Budd was convicted of contempt and sentenced to 14 days' jail in March 1992, his editor, Des Houghton, spoke at a rally in his support: 'The day journalists get into the witness box and spill the beans is the day that people will stop giving us vital information about wrong-doing in public office' (quoted in Hurst and White 1994, 150). Budd was one of several Australian journalists jailed for refusing to reveal sources' names in the 1990s. Sources need to be certain that the journalist will not reveal their name under any circumstance, otherwise there will be far fewer whistleblowers willing to 'blow the whistle'. Guaranteeing a source confidentiality is not an action to be taken lightly. It can have very serious consequences. A journalist should not guarantee confidentiality too readily.

Source protection needs careful consideration

There are many issues that need to be considered before a journalist agrees to grant confidentiality to a source—a course of action that could conceivably lead to the journalist spending time in jail, although that is far less likely in jurisdictions that have introduced varying forms of shield laws. The question of maintaining confidences, it can be argued, relies on the 'public good' defence. In this context using information provided by a source on the basis that they won't be revealed is a 'greater good' than not using the material because the source refuses to be named. On the other hand, some might argue that if a source does not have to reveal his or her identity, they might be inclined to make things up, or 'embellish' the story to make it more appealing to the reporter. Because journalists are reliant on sources and some sources are reluctant to go on the record and be named, this relationship of dependence has consequences for the reporter. The same is true for the source: if the reporter 'burns' them they, too, may, as we have already seen, face serious consequences. It is a difficult fault line to straddle safely.

Are you authorised to leak that leak?

In this discussion, we need to distinguish the different ways confidential information is relayed to a reporter by a source. The practice is called 'leaking' a story. There are 'authorised' and 'unauthorised' leaks. 'Authorised' leaks usually involve someone in authority in an organisation—for example, a company CEO, a political leader (or one of their media advisers)—taking a journalist aside and telling them something by way of 'background', which in journalism jargon means 'information that can be used, but not attributed to the source by name'. This is the 'drop' and it is used every day in Washington, London, and Canberra, and political capitals around the world, to get the political messages of the day out when the source doesn't want to be publicly named in the story. Australia's top political writers were divided in late 2017 over whether journalists who were alerted to an imminent police raid on union offices should have revealed the source of the tip-off. The controversy arose after Alice Workman (2017), working at the time for Buzzfeed, revealed that journalists had told her they were tipped off about the pending raid so they could be there with cameras, by a member of the staff of conservative federal Employment Minister, Michaelia Cash. Minister Cash had spent most of that day vehemently denying to a Senate committee that she, or her office, had been the source of the tip-off. Then she had to correct the record when it was revealed the tip-off came from one of her staffers, David De Garis (Meade 2017). Some journalists felt their colleagues were on a 'slippery' slope if they revealed the names of confidential sources of stories (McCauley 2017). They cautioned against making an exception to the rule that sources were sacrosanct, saying the disclosure of the source's name could threaten the flow of information on 'background'. The raid was on the offices of the union of which the then opposition (Labor) leader, Bill Shorten, had been a senior executive, so the raid was, in part, to embarrass him and a political point-scoring exercise by the conservatives. For journalists, it boiled down to an ethical dilemma over whether to report the truth—that is, the Minister was misleading a Senate committee—or protect a source. Up against the 'don't burn a source on any account' group were those who looked no further than the first clause of their union's Code of Ethics: 'Report and interpret honestly, striving for accuracy, fairness and disclosure of all essential facts' (MEAA 2018). It wasn't a cabinet leak, they said, or a whistleblower telling them something in the public interest. It was a Ministerial staffer trying to score points against the opposition leader. It was the equivalent, some said, of putting out a media alert to set up a photo opportunity (Meade 2017). We believe that 'outing' the source in those circumstances was the ethical thing to do. It's an example of using the 'drop' as a form of media manipulation, and often involves the idea of payback: 'Use this material and next time we have something good, you'll be (among) the first to know.' Other types of this form of media manipulation include what is called a 'selective leak' by which the source hopes to ingratiate him/herself with a journalist by leaking an important story. It appears to be a 'win–win' situation.

The journalist gets exclusive access to a story in a highly competitive environment and the source can virtually guarantee favourable treatment for their story. But the 'authorised', almost 'official', leak is very different from the 'unauthorised' leak that usually involves someone further down the 'food chain', who wants to see something their organisation is doing that they believe is corrupt, illegal, unethical, or even dangerous, exposed through the media.

Quality, motivation, or a means to an end?

One of the important issues to consider before agreeing to confidentiality with your source is the quality of the information. Is it an important story? Is it something that the public *really* needs to know? Does it justify anonymity for the source, or could you get it from other sources without having to betray the originating source? Can you get the same information on the record from someone else? Does the story pass the 'public interest' test to a standard that warrants confidentiality? If you can't answer 'Yes' to at least most of those questions, then there are other issues to consider before agreeing to guarantee your source's confidentiality. For instance: What is the motivation of the source? Ask yourself: 'What's in it for them?' Are they motivated by the highest ideals of a whistleblower—seeing that important information gets into the public arena—or are they simply after revenge against an institution or individual? Is the source trying to hide behind the journalist's ethical stance that they won't reveal his/her name to ensure they can evade any responsibility for what they have said? If you are at all concerned, you need to weigh up the decision on confidentiality, probably in consultation with your superiors. A second issue is the validity of the information: Is it true? Could the source be lying? In 2019, Buzzfeed had to apologise and reach a settlement with former Australian politician, Emma Husar, after publishing unfounded allegations of sexual misconduct that implied the then-MP was a 'slut'. Buzzfeed reporter Alice Workman published the story based on documents leaked to her that turned out to contain false and unsubstantiated allegations against Husar (McGowan 2019). While the source has never been confirmed it is widely believed that it was a person with a strong motive to discredit Husar. Could they be putting the best 'spin' on the story they can by ignoring relevant facts? You must always do your best to verify the information by cross-checking and trying to corroborate it with other sources. Another problem arises here—you might 'tip off' someone strongly associated with the story if you delve too far for verification, and that person might attempt to deflect the impact of the story by releasing a similar story to your opposition, thereby possibly negating your 'scoop'. It is common practice for those affected by leaks to try to establish the identity of the confidential source by saying: 'Reveal your source or we'll know it's not true.' We have mentioned that journalists don't enjoy high credibility among the public at large, and the repeated use of 'confidential sources' doesn't do much to enhance that reputation. Why should the public believe you if your credibility isn't much higher than that of a used-car salesperson?

The ethical issues that came to light at the time of the 2010 WikiLeaks document 'dump' are also worth mentioning in this context. Melbourne media ethicist, Denis Muller (2010), identified five major issues raised by the Wiki-Leaks cables release:

- What should be done with material that is reasonably suspected of having been unlawfully obtained?
- What can be done to verify the genuineness of the material?
- What harms might be done by publication?
- What can be done to minimise those harms?
- What public interest is served by publication?

If you can answer these questions positively in the broader context of any material that comes your way from a source that demands confidentiality then go ahead and publish, but be prepared for a backlash, especially from anyone embarrassed by the release of the information.

Before we move on from the discussion of a reporter's relationship with a source, there's another point to be made. That's the issue of getting too close to a source. The reporter who covers any round on a regular basis, from politics to courts and sport, gets to know the important sources on more than just a professional level. They might exchange small gifts at Christmas (in the case of the reporter often paid for by the office) and share the odd drink or three. It becomes an ethical issue when the source becomes the story (or a major part of it) for the wrong reasons, and you feel sorry for your friend on a personal level. Is that likely to influence how you write the story? It shouldn't—the source should realise that you have a job to do—but if you think it might, discuss it with superiors or colleagues in the newsroom. They might decide to pass the story on to another reporter.

Shield laws offer some protection

Shield laws which are supposed to protect confidential sources from having their names revealed by journalists have been enacted in many jurisdictions with varying effect. As we have seen continually through this chapter, the protection of sources is one of our 'grey areas' and fraught with contradictions. A shield law is a specific piece of legislation that applies protective conditions to the journalist–source relationship. Unlike whistleblower legislation, which specifically protects a source, the shield law can also apply to a reporter, but they lack uniformity. In the United States, journalists have the Constitutional protection of the First Amendment and most of the 50 states have specific shield law legislation, but a federal shield law at the time of writing had yet to be enacted. In the United Kingdom, reporters enjoy protection from divulging their sources under the Contempt of Court Act. As legal scholar Anthony Fargo wrote in a paper on the American shield law situation in 2018, legislators face a series of hurdles, the most pressing of which is to differentiate legitimate news and journalism from the purveyors of 'fake news'. It would be a mistake, Fargo (2018) argues, to extend shield protections to rogue propagandists.

Serious debate about the need for shield laws began in Australia in the mid-1990s because of the jailing of journalists mentioned earlier. Journalists were divided along interesting fault lines by the debate. Some argued for a form of legislative 'shield' to protect journalists, but others were equally convinced that to do so could have the opposite effect, creating an offence of non-disclosure in all but the most restricted circumstances. The journalists' union, the MEAA, and a coalition of the proprietors, through their pressure group, the 'Right to Know Coalition', continued to pressure federal politicians until they introduced legislation after the federal election in 2010. Both Houses passed a shield law in early 2011 that saw source protection extended beyond the traditional news media. The federal law defined 'journalist' to include anyone 'engaged and active' in the publication of news in any medium. This would include bloggers, citizen journalists, independent news organisations, and presumably, university journalism students. But that very broad definition of what constitutes a journalist, and their publication, is not included in the state shield laws. At the time of writing all Australian states and territories, except Queensland, had introduced shield laws. Also, a journalist needs to have guaranteed anonymity to a source for the shield law to apply and the laws do not automatically guarantee protection. Courts can still rule against shield law protection if they decide that the public interest in revealing the source's identity outweighs any adverse impact on the informant and the media's ability to report and comment (Pearson and Polden 2019, 326). Protection of sources and whistleblowers, freedom of information and the public's right to know, and the right of a reporter not to reveal their sources are all important principles. However, like most issues in journalism ethics, the contradictions between these principles lead to fault lines and conflicts. Each of them must be weighed in the context of the utilitarian argument of the 'greater good' and the public benefit of disclosure or secrecy.

Case study: Julian Assange: Journalist, whistleblower, or traitor?

The ABC's flagship current affairs television programme, *Four Corners*, in promoting a two-part special in mid-2019, referred to Julian Assange as 'one of the most influential figures to emerge this century' (Brissenden 2019a). While some of his many critics might dispute that description, few would challenge the opening line of part one of the programme: 'Few people have had an impact on the history of this century quite like Julian Assange, and few have been as polarising' (Brissenden 2019a). WikiLeaks and its founder, Julian Assange, were virtually unknown before they became household names the world over in 2010 with the release of the 'Collateral Murder' video. It showed American forces in Iraq in 2007 firing from an Apache helicopter on unarmed civilians killing two Reuters journalists and nine others (WikiLeaks 2010). The video was part of a huge cache of confidential American military documents about the Afghanistan and Iraq wars and diplomatic cables—which contained some undiplomatic analysis of world leaders and their countries—leaked to the whistleblowing website by former US army intelligence analyst Bradley (later Chelsea) Manning. Manning served seven years of a 35-year sentence for leaking the classified material before being pardoned by President Obama during his last days in office. At the time of Assange's arrest in London in 2019, Manning was back in jail for contempt of court for refusing to testify to a grand jury about the WikiLeaks founder (Fossum, Shortell, and Kelly 2019). Manning was released from prison amid reports she had attempted suicide in early 2020, after a judge ruled her appearance before the grand jury was no longer needed, but her release came at a price: the judge refused her request to cancel US$256,000 in fines imposed for her refusal to testify (Pengelly 2020).

Within weeks of the 2010 release of 'Collateral Murder', some of the biggest media organisations in the world were teaming with Assange to publish thousands of incident and intelligence reports from the Afghan War. The contents were hugely embarrassing to the United States government, and the military claimed the leaks put lives at risk. The release of more confidential reports about the Iraq war and thousands of diplomatic cables would follow. But it would be his private life that would see Assange seek political asylum in the Ecuadorian Embassy in London in 2012. Assange had visited Sweden in late 2010 and, as a result, one woman accused him of rape and another of sexual assault (Addley and Woolf 2012). Sweden sought Assange's extradition from London for questioning, but he and his supporters maintained that his removal to Sweden would be followed by onward extradition to the United States and possible espionage charges which they feared could lead to the death penalty (Addley and Woolf 2012). While in the Ecuadorian Embassy, Assange continued to embarrass various governments with the release of more than two million emails, including details of international trade deals and evidence of how America was tapping the phones of foreign leaders (Brissenden 2019b). On the eve of the 2016 Democratic Party convention to 'anoint' Hillary Clinton as their presidential candidate, WikiLeaks released thousands of damaging emails that had been hacked from senior figures in the party—a move that helped the Trump campaign. Hillary Clinton was US Secretary of State when WikiLeaks released the diplomatic cables in 2010, so there was a history between the presidential candidate and the WikiLeaks founder. To cut a long story short, Assange's days in the Embassy were numbered with a change in government in Ecuador in 2017 and the new administration's desire to form a positive relationship with Washington. After spending nearly seven years in the Embassy, Assange was dragged out by British police in April 2019. He was jailed for 50 weeks for jumping bail in Britain and seeking asylum. The United States government charged him initially with helping Manning to hack a classified government password, and with efforts to protect her identity (Sullivan 2019b). Six weeks after Assange's removal from the Embassy, the US Justice Department announced it was seeking his extradition on the one hacking charge and 17 espionage charges (Brissenden 2019b).

The initial treatment of Assange and the pending US hacking charge caused a major outcry in Western media. Journalists and media commentators were concerned that if the government could charge Assange for his interactions with Manning, then the same charge could be levelled at almost any media organisation, especially those who had published the Afghan and Iraqi war logs and the diplomatic cables (Sullivan 2019b; Reidy 2019; Rusbridger 2019; Cullen 2019; Rundle 2019; Williams 2019). Concern reached a new level with the announcement of the espionage charges, each carrying a ten-year sentence. If convicted, Assange could spend the rest of his life in an American jail. The media was flooded with opinion pieces about the dangers to journalists posed by the new charges, which some saw as criminalising investigative journalism in the US (Goodman and Moynihan 2019; Raban 2019; Sullivan 2019a; Turley 2019; Barns 2019; Bacon 2019; L. Johnson 2019; Barry 2019b; Shapiro 2019).

Assange became very ill while locked up in a British prison awaiting a decision on his extradition case (ABC 2019a). His trial at the Old Bailey lasted four weeks with a decision due on 4 January 2021 (Press Association 2020). In early 2021, a British judge ruled against Assange's extradition to the US over concerns for his mental health and his risk of suicide (BBC 2021). The judge ruled that while the US prosecutors had met the tests for Assange to be extradited for trial, they were incapable of preventing him from attempting to take his own life. The US was expected to appeal the decision in what was seen as a victory for Assange, but not for journalism or freedom of the press.

Throughout all of this saga has been the question: Is Julian Assange a journalist? The Walkley Foundation, which hands out Australia's national journalism awards, certainly thought so when they awarded WikiLeaks and its founder a Walkley Award 'for its outstanding contribution to journalism' in 2011. On the other side of the debate is former journalist-turned-academic Peter Greste maintained that while he has 'a certain sympathy for Assange', he 'is not a journalist, and Wikileaks is not a news organisation' (2019). The main reason for him saying Assange is not a journalist is the way he handled the dump of leaked diplomatic files:

> Instead of sorting through the hundreds of thousands of files to seek out the most important or relevant and protect the innocent, he dumped them all onto his website, free for anybody to go through, regardless of their contents or the impact they might have had.
>
> (Greste 2019)

Peter Greste, and those on that side of the debate, maintain that when journalists receive confidential information it comes with the responsibility to 'seek out what is genuinely in the public interest and a responsibility to remove anything that may compromise the privacy of individuals not directly involved in a story that might put them at risk' (Greste 2019). At the time of his lengthy trial there was more support for Assange, the journalist (Cockburn 2020; Nagy and Barns 2020; Osborne 2020). The Ex-*Guardian* editor, Alan Rusbridger, who worked with Assange on the original cache of confidential military documents before falling out with the WikiLeaks founder, described the extradition case as 'disturbing' with 'worrying implications for all journalists' (quoted in Mayhew 2020b). As we wrap up writing this book, we still do not know the ultimate fate that awaits Julian Assange. All we can add is that we think he is a journalist and that he is entitled to due process. It is shameful that he has been a hunted criminal for the past few years for doing public interest reporting. You don't have to agree with all of Assange's methods to understand that locking him up under conditions that amount to torture and threatening him with a long jail sentence in a US military prison is wrong on every level. Julian Assange has now spent nearly a decade locked up for the crime of journalism.

Free Julian Assange!

Questions for discussion

1 Is Julian Assange, in your opinion, a journalist? What evidence do you base your decision on and why?
2 Or is he a whistleblower? What evidence do you base your decision on and why?
3 Or a traitor? What evidence do you base your decision on and why?
4 How would you characterise the activities of WikiLeaks?
5 What is your personal opinion of Assange and does it differ from your professional opinion?
6 Take the position of Alan Rusbridger, the editor of *The Guardian* at the time of the 2010 WikiLeaks collaboration. He's written about how difficult Assange was to deal with. How would you handle him and the masses of confidential information he was offering?
7 What about Chelsea Manning? When she was sent back to jail in May 2019, the judge also ruled that she be fined US$500 per day after 30 days and US$1,000 per day after 60 days (Fossum, Shortell, and Kelly 2019). Is she a victim here, or a traitor?
8 Research some of the opinion pieces cited earlier in this chapter. Was the escalation of the charges against Assange to espionage a one-off, or just part of President Trump's war on the mainstream media?
9 What dangers do you see for journalists in general if Assange is extradited to the United States?
10 If you had collaborated with Assange on the original cache of military secrets, and they were published in your newspaper, do you think the US government might come after you, too?
11 Research the Reality Winner case and read what Glenn Greenwald and Laura Poitras say about how *The Intercept* handled her case. Also read the

company's responses. Do you think mistakes were made? Who made the mistakes? Could things have been handled in a better/different way?

12 Research shield laws in your state, territory, or federal jurisdiction. Do they exist? Are they adequate? How could they be improved?

Note

1 In November 2020 a highly secretive internal investigation was completed and the Australian military's top brass revealed that Special Forces soldiers had been involved in at least 39 murders of Afghan citizens (Knaus 2020b). This was a complete vindication of the reporting by the ABC and other media outlets.

11 Journalism under threat

Time magazine recognises the danger

Time magazine took the unusual step in late 2018 of issuing four versions of the cover of its annual Person of the Year issue—each with a different photo. Under the banner of 'The guardians and the war on truth', the magazine told the stories of a number of journalists not for the stories they had covered, but rather for the risks—in some cases fatal—of doing their job (Vick 2018). One cover photo featured *The Washington Post* correspondent Jamal Khashoggi who was murdered in the Syrian embassy in Istanbul. Another showed Philippine journalist Maria Ressa, editor of the crusading online news site Rappler, who had attracted the attention of President Duterte by covering (among other stories) the violent drug war and the extrajudicial killings that have left, according to *Time*, some 12,000 people dead (Vick 2018). In mid-2020, Ressa was found guilty of cyber libel charges, a verdict that could lead to six years in jail and, at the time of writing, was free on bail pending an appeal (Ratcliffe 2020). Another cover pictured the staff of the *Capital*, the Annapolis (USA) newspaper suddenly thrust into the headlines when five of their colleagues were killed by a gunman who walked into their newsroom and opened fire. The final cover showed the wives of two Reuters journalists, holding photos of their husbands, Kyaw Soe Oo and Wa Lone, who at the time were serving a seven-year jail term in Myanmar for documenting the massacre of a group of Rohingya Muslims. The Reuters pair were finally freed by presidential pardon in May 2019 after serving 500 days (Mayhew 2019d). The lengthy *Time* cover story chronicled a number of other journalists either in jail or under threat around the world. A few days before *Time* was drawing attention to the dangers facing journalists, human rights lawyer Amal Clooney declared that the media was 'under attack like never before' (Mayhew 2018a). In one of her first reports on media freedom, Amal Clooney called on all governments to 'sanction those complicit in the killing or arbitrary imprisonment of journalists to 'shift the default from impunity to accountability' (Tobitt 2020a). Charlotte Tobitt (2019a) had reported a couple of months earlier research finding that 'freedom of expression had "reached a ten-year low around the world"'. Ms Clooney, later to be named the United Kingdom's special envoy on media

DOI: 10.4324/9780429242892-12

Danielle Muscato (she/her) ✅   ...
@DanielleMuscato

First they came for the journalists

We don't know what happened after that

#protests2020 #GeorgeFloydProtests #GeorgeFloyd

12:32 AM · Jun 1, 2020 · Twitter for Android

Figure 11.1 First they came for the journalists—Danielle Muscato

freedom, went a step further at the Defend Media Freedom conference in London in July 2019, openly blaming President Trump's rhetoric for hastening the decline in press freedom worldwide (Mayhew 2019b). Clooney resigned her special envoy's position in late 2020 over what she described as the UK government's 'lamentable' plan to override Britain's international treaty obligations in the EU withdrawal (Brexit) agreement (Bowcott and Boffey 2020).

Collectively, the four cases highlighted by *Time*—and others in the accompanying cover story—demonstrated two frightening trends that emerged in the latter part of the last decade. As we have highlighted in the Introduction and other chapters, one trend was the continuous berating of the media by Donald Trump. It emboldened dictators the world over to dismiss any media criticism as 'fake news' and in some cases take brutal action against their critics, including journalists. In the past few years we have seen an alarming increase in attacks on news media, and often physical assaults on journalists, in what most would be considered 'safe' countries, like the United States. Aside from the deaths at the *Capital* in 2018, the cable TV network CNN, received an explosive device in the mail—one of more than a dozen sent to prominent Democratic Party politicians and donors by fanatical Trump supporter Cesar Sayoc—and also had its New York offices evacuated because of a bomb threat (Chavez 2018). The same October 2018 week that Jamal Khashoggi was butchered, Bulgarian journalist Viktoria Marinova was killed a few days after interviewing two journalists who were arrested while investigating the misuse of European Union funds (Watkins 2018b). In 2017 Maltese investigative blogger/journalist Daphne Caruana—who had been writing local stories from the revelations in the Panama Papers—was murdered with a car bomb (ibid.). Maltese millionaire Yorgen Fenech was charged with masterminding Caruana's murder (Garside 2020). As we have already mentioned in Chapter 2, the Press Freedom Tracker has been chronicling attacks on journalists in the US associated with the renewal of the Black Lives Matter demonstrations that followed George Floyd's death in late May 2020. In 2020 there were nearly 900 attacks on journalists covering the protests, comprising at least 120 arrests, 222 assaults (160 by law enforcement agencies) and 544 other press freedom violations. The police attacks included the use of tear gas, pepper spray, and rubber bullets (Press Freedom Tracker 2020b).

In the line of duty?

It is shocking that we have to include a chapter such as this in a book about journalism ethics, but the dangerous situation for reporters today is a direct effect of the crises we have already discussed, and an issue that marks out the ethical crossroads at which we find ourselves. War zones have always been dangerous, but more reporters are killed and injured today outside of conflict zones directly as a result of their reporting challenging vested political and economic interests. These threats to the security and safety of journalists, are what we describe as 'anti-journalism' scare tactics. Some of the threats arise within the authoritarian legal regimes emerging in several countries and they are an explicit attempt to criminalise the methods of investigative journalism. We've also included suggestions about how journalists might keep themselves safe and the importance of supporting non-governmental organisations (NGOs) like the International Federation of Journalists (IFJ), the Committee to Protect Journalists (CPJ), and Reporters Without Borders (RSF), in the light of recent tragic events. That major international organisations committed to keeping journalists safe now have to turn their attention to the protection of journalists in so-called democratic countries illustrates the scale of the legal, ethical, judicial, legislative, and physical dangers that are now part of the news media's everyday experience. The price of seeking the truth and holding the powerful to account has been far too high in recent decades.

In mid-December 2020, the Committee to Protect Journalists reported that a record high of 274 journalists were in jail around the globe for doing their job (Beiser 2020). They further reported later in the month that the number of journalists murdered in retaliation for their work more than doubled—from 10 in 2019 to 21—in 2020 'as criminal gangs targeted reporters working in violent but democratic nations' (Dunham 2020). Reporters Without Borders reported the statistics in a similar way, saying that while the number of journalists killed in countries at war had continued to fall in 2020, more were being killed in countries not at war (RSF 2020). According to the CPJ, 1,340 journalists were killed because of their work between 1992 and mid-2019 (CPJ 2019b). The IFJ reported that more journalists were killed in 2018 than any of the previous three years (IFJ/IFEX 2018). While Afghanistan (16 media killings), Mexico (11), Yemen (9), and Syria (8) headed the list of countries most deadly for journalists, the United States came in as the equal sixth most deadly country for journalists, because of the five deaths at the Annapolis newspaper (ibid.). The alarming trend of 2018 was reversed somewhat in 2019, when, according to Reporters Without Borders, the international death toll among journalists dropped to 49—the lowest for 16 years (Mayhew 2019e). The CPJ put it even lower (The Torch 2019). At the end of 2019, CPJ reported that for the fourth consecutive year, at least 250 journalists were behind bars around the globe (Beiser 2019). The world's worst jailers of journalists, according to the CPJ were, what we call 'the usual suspects': China, Turkey, Saudi Arabia, and Egypt (Beiser 2019).

Nine out of every ten journalist killings go unpunished, with the United Nations in recent years nominating a day in early November as 'International Day to End Impunity for Crimes against Journalists' (Beniac-Brooks 2018). Two of the countries constantly in the news for their actions against journalists are Turkey and the Philippines. Turkey is regularly among the leading jailers of journalists. The Philippines rates highly in the annual indexes of the most dangerous countries in the world for journalists, but in recent years has been using the judicial system to intimidate investigative media, like the aforementioned online site Rappler and its crusading editor, Maria Ressa. In 2016, Philippines' President Duterte said he would have no problem killing journalists whom he felt were corrupt. 'Just because you're a journalist you are not exempted from assassination, if you're a son of a bitch,' Duterte said. 'Freedom of expression cannot help you if you have done something wrong,' he added for good measure. When so-called democratic leaders can make such vile threats, is it any wonder that gullible followers take it upon themselves to harass, threaten, beat up, or worse, reporters on the street? It is not far in time, nor intent, from Duerte's explicit threat and Trump's thinly veiled threats, to so-called 'patriots'—actually 'domestic terrorists'—smashing camera gear stolen from an AP news crew or scrawling 'murder the media' on a door in the Capitol building during the Washington DC 'MAGA insurrection' of 6 January 2021 (News Laundry 2021).

The murder of Marie Colvin

'The price of truth' was the page one headline in the London *Times* when it reported the death of the revered foreign correspondent, Marie Colvin, and her photographer in a rocket attack in Syria in 2012 (The Times 2012, 1). Hers was one of the first in the modern era of State-sanctioned killings of journalists in conflict zones. The famed reporter had been due to leave Syria the day she died, but 'she wanted one more story' from the besieged city of Homs. London's *Daily Mail* reported at the time that Syrian government forces had been ordered to deliberately target foreign journalists (Walford and Ramdani 2012). Also on that *Times* front page, the paper reproduced part of Colvin's address at a 2010 church service to commemorate war reporters who had died since the turn of the century (2010). She spoke graphically of the dangers for the foreign correspondent in a conflict zone:

> Covering a war means going to places torn by chaos, destruction, and death, and trying to bear witness. It means trying to find the truth in a sandstorm of propaganda when armies, tribes or terrorists clash. And yes, it means taking risks, not just for yourself but often for the people who work closely with you. In an age of 24/7 rolling news, blogs and twitters, we are on constant call wherever we are. But war reporting is still essentially the same—someone has to go there and see what is happening. You can't get that information without going to places where people are being shot at, and others are shooting at you.
>
> (Colvin 2010)

On the last day of January 2019, an American court handed down a civil verdict that the Syrian government had deliberately targeted and killed Colvin (Bowcott 2019). The judge wrote in her statement of findings that the journalist and her photographer were murdered as part of a systematic campaign by the Syrian regime 'for the purpose of silencing those reporting on the growing opposition movement in the country' (Hilsum 2019). Colvin's family had filed a civil suit against the Syrian regime two years earlier (Priest 2016). The regime was ordered to pay the family US$300 million in punitive damages (Bowcott 2019), a payment they are unlikely to see.

The deliberate targeting of journalists in war zones continues. Journalists from the British-based Sky News network were attacked by forces of the Assad regime in mid-2019. Their correspondent reported being 'tracked, targeted and fired upon by regime forces' in Idlib province (Mayhew 2019f). The CPJ reported at the time that three journalists had been injured in the attacks (CPJ 2019a). Working as a foreign correspondent—reporting back to your home country on major news events around the world—is seen by many as a glamorous job, at the top of the journalistic food-chain, and much sought after. While the story of the final assignment of Maria Colvin is a sad and sobering tale, there is a job to be done covering major conflicts around the globe. It is a very difficult and dangerous job. Those few sentences from Colvin's 2010 speech represent a mantra for the foreign correspondent. They do it because someone has to. It is a vitally important role for a journalist. Someone needs to tell the rest of the world what is going on, and in Syria in recent years it has been a very dangerous occupation, as it has in the other countries we have mentioned.

On the same day as Colvin's 2010 speech, the then head of the international news-agency Reuters, David Schlesinger, challenged the need for journalists to put themselves in danger in a speech to the International News Safety Institute in London. He asked whether in an age when a gunship can fire up to four kilometres, and a drone can be piloted from half a world away, journalists could justify the risks of being 'in the midst of things' (Schlesinger 2010). He said that sometimes the benefits of transparency and understanding dictate that journalists 'must be right there', but added: 'Sometimes those benefits are not there and the reasons for being in harm's way are less noble: competitive pressure, personal ambition, adrenaline's urging' (Schlesinger 2010). Schlesinger kept his most sobering thoughts for the end of his speech: 'We have to be ready to lose the shot to avoid being shot. We must be ready to lose some stories to avoid losing yet more lives' (2010).

In the decade since Schlesinger's speech, the number of journalists killed 'for doing their job' has ranged from the 20s to 74 annually. Anyone who receives the Committee to Protect Journalists' (CPJ) emails, follows their Twitter feed or receives their weekly email newsletter, *The Torch*, will know how dangerous being a journalist in general, and a foreign correspondent in particular, can be in some countries. The Committee sends out daily reports of journalists being assaulted, arrested, jailed, harassed, kidnapped or killed. It has become standard practice for the CPJ to issue a 'Journalist Safety Kit' for covering a major story, like a conflict or a national election. The guide offers advice on how to prepare their digital devices as well as how to handle online harassment and trolling and how to store and secure their materials. On personal safety, the kit offers advice on how to report safely in a hostile environment like rallies and protests. There is also advice on dealing with trauma-related stress and managing stress in the newsroom. Following a series of incidents where journalists in America were physically assaulted and verbally abused at Trump political events and rallies, the CPJ felt the need to put together a 'safety kit' for journalists covering such events in 2020.

The war reporter through history

Most of the time during major conflicts the news media plays a number of roles—sometimes simultaneously—being patriotic, critical, informative, and full of propaganda from 'their side'. This is a good example of the 'dialectic in journalism' that we discuss in Chapters 13 and 14. It is a fault line that resembles an ethical minefield for journalists. For most of the 20th century, news organisations were expected to 'do the right thing' and report only favourable material to the public 'back home'. Phillip Knightley's seminal book, *The First Casualty* (2003), provides one of the best historical accounts of war correspondence; the 'first casualty' in the title is the truth! We explored the history of media reporting of conflict in a previous volume (Patching and Hirst 2014, 94–100). Much of the recent change in military–media relations had its genesis in the post-Vietnam period of the late 1970s and the Falklands 'war' between Britain and Argentina over possession of a few small islands in the south Atlantic in 1982. The military considered that the foreign correspondents covering Vietnam were given too much freedom in where they could go and what they could see and report. The British military restricted the media covering the Falklands conflict. Primarily it was the sheer isolation of the Falklands that helped the military limit media access to the battlefield. But while that may have worked for that conflict, it would be the massive advances in technology that helped journalists get closer to the action in later conflicts. What becomes clear from an historical and contemporary perspective is that media coverage of war is, for the most part, far from objective. Journalists 'choose' sides constantly sometimes in a conscious way—a political choice—and sometimes unconsciously—the pull of patriotism or belief in the 'national interest' (Ravi 2005). This means there is always a fine line between reporting and propaganda because all of us have a 'vested interest' in the outcome of the conflict, one way or another (Nohrstedt et al. 2000).

War correspondents have always taken risks—typified by the approach of journalists like Marie Colvin and her photographer. Many of the best operate on the edge, without necessarily getting the sanction of the 'allied' commanders. This freelance style has become more common as news demands increase with the 24-hour news cycle, and as the equipment has become even more portable. The laptop computer has replaced the cumbersome satellite dish of old (although they are more portable, now, too) and audio and stills are easily obtained by mobile phones.

The start of the second Gulf War in 2003 saw a new twist in the traditional media—military stand-off. The American military offered places with the front-line units to scoop-hungry war junkies. The 'embedding' of reporters with American and British military units took full advantage of the latest generation of lightweight equipment to put journalists in tanks and trucks. It might have seemed like the military was giving the reporters full access, but most correspondents soon realised that 'embedding' was cleverly designed to reduce the threat of any independent reporting. It is believed that between 500 and

700 journalists were 'embedded' with combat units of the American and British forces in that conflict. The Australian military did not adopt the practice until late in the second Gulf War, but it has become common practice for Australian journalists to spend a week or two with their combat troops in Afghanistan in recent years.

But the 2003 conflict was the first time since World War Two (1939–1945) that journalists—and in this case, perhaps more importantly, camera crews with portable satellite technology—were on the front lines with the advancing troops. It seemed like a 'win–win' situation for the media and the military. Journalists and camera crews were at the centre of the action, reporting on battles as the coalition advanced through Iraq. But reporting from the front lines has its disadvantages. Apart from being possibly shot at and killed—which has become an even bigger issue in recent years, especially in Syria—there's the discomfort, the constant danger of injury, and the restricted view of what's happening elsewhere in the conflict. An added ethical dilemma for the embedded journalist emerged in late 2004 when an American television crew filmed one of their marines shooting dead an apparently unarmed Iraqi as he was lying on the floor of a wrecked Fallujah mosque (The New York Times 2004). The correspondent with the NBC crew that filmed the shooting, Kevin Sites, said the mosque had been used by insurgents to attack US forces the previous week. But a wounded and unarmed Iraqi? Do you really want to show your soldiers in such a light? *The Australian*'s media section the following day carried a cartoon showing the Iraqi pleading with the Marine 'Don't shoot' while the Marine was turning back to the TV cameraman with the same plea (The Australian 2004).

Reportage or propaganda

Throughout history, popular support 'back home' for war is something that had to be 'prepared' according to military timetables, like battle plans and supply lines. In times of war, the media's critics often accuse it of being a government propaganda tool. Others regard support for the government as simply being patriotic. People want information, and relief from the anxiety they feel about the uncertainty of a major conflict, particularly for those whose relatives or friends are 'over there' defending 'our' freedom. The media can also play a vital role in any conflict by supporting one side or the other. Journalists must avoid being turned into an arm of military propaganda, willingly or unwillingly.

The question for all media, once the troops are 'over there', is whether challenging the government policy that sent them there equates to *not* supporting the troops? How would *they* see it, reading criticism of their deployment online? Should we automatically support our troops once they are in a foreign war zone? The difficulty is separating the political debate from support for the military. Does the media no longer challenge the government's decision to send troops into dangerous situations once the decision has been taken? It is a major role of the media to keep the public informed of such important debates and decisions. There were major media debates in 2003 in the US, UK, and Australia over the second Iraq war. The debates were long and wide-ranging, and with the benefit of hindsight perhaps they should have been even longer and more wide-ranging.

The question of when simple reporting tips over into propaganda is controversial and deeply problematic. In our view, it is an aspect of journalistic ideology that needs to be questioned. Too many journalists are too quick to rally behind their country's flag in times of military conflict and 'trade wars' without questioning the moral, economic or political implications of doing so. It is too often a patriotic knee-jerk reaction; war is hardly ever in the public interest. This is a lesson that should not need repeating following the disclosure of the lies behind the 'Weapons of Mass Destruction' (WMD) subterfuge that dragged the US and its allies into a costly, long, immoral, and probably illegal conflict in Iraq in 2003. Many of the trust issues that the news industry is dealing with today first surfaced during the period in which the lies of George W. Bush, Tony Blair, John Howard, and others were made public for the first time. This was 'fake news' manufactured by governments and amplified by a compliant news media (Hirst 2011, 30–2). That this issue was not decisively resolved for journalists following the collapse of the WMD lies points to the profession's problems of epistemology—methods of knowing—and ontology—our body of knowledge—that we discuss in later chapters.

In Chapter 10 on whistleblowers, we discussed the federal police raids on the headquarters of the ABC in Sydney aimed at gathering material on their series of reports, 'The Afghan Papers' about Australian special forces being involved in war crimes in Afghanistan. At the time of writing, a major government report on the special forces' actions detailed at least 39 murders of Afghan civilians by Australian soldiers that would be investigated as suspected war crimes. A highly decorated military hero, Ben Roberts-Smith, was at the centre of many allegations, which he vigorously denied. There was outrage in Australia when this news broke, just as there was in America when news of the 1968 My Lai massacre in Vietnam and the 2004 abuse of inmates at the Abu Ghraib prison in Baghdad. Each is an example of the ethical dilemma for the foreign correspondent/war reporter that we have already outlined. But these stories need to be told, even if we would prefer it was the 'other side' committing the atrocities or abuse. We want to think of 'our side' as being the 'good guys' in the conflict, trying to free people from oppression and tyranny, and fighting for justice. It is disappointing in the extreme on a personal level when members of 'our side' are shown to be party to such atrocities.

The oxygen of publicity

In 1988, former British Prime Minister, the late Margaret Thatcher, remarked that governments needed to find some way of 'starving terrorists and kidnappers of the oxygen of publicity' (Crawley 2008). The metaphor was used in an address to the American Bar Association in London in the wake of a TWA airliner hijacking in Beirut (Hirst and Patching 2007, 96). It is believed that the 'Iron Lady' was speaking in the context of depriving republican and loyalist organisations in Northern Ireland access to the British airwaves because they were seen as terrorists, not freedom fighters. Many at the time thought that Sinn Fein and the IRA were the main targets (Crawley 2008). But Thatcher's remarks have come to symbolise the symbiotic relationship between terrorism and the mass media: stories about terrorism sell, while simultaneously providing the terrorists with the publicity they crave. There seems no answer to this issue; media organisations know that coverage of conflict and terrorism 'rates', so they are unlikely to stop covering these major stories.

This creates new ethical fault lines for journalists reporting from the front line of a conflict that has become known as the 'War on Terror'[1]. There was a gruesome episode in late 2014 when video emerged on YouTube of the beheading of American freelance journalist James Foley by the Islamist militant group, ISIS (The New York Post 2014). Newspapers the world over carried stills from the video of the macabre execution in the Iraqi desert, usually on their front page, showing a hooded ISIS fighter in black and Foley, in a yellow prisoner-style jumpsuit, at different stages of his grisly murder. Sydney tabloid, *The Daily Telegraph*, for instance, showed the execution scene, but with the knife well away from Foley's throat (The Daily Telegraph 2014). The most gruesome front page of the Foley killing, published by the Rupert Murdoch-owned *New York Post* and which showed the knife at the journalist's throat moments before his death, drew the most criticism. Other beheadings of media personnel and aid workers would follow at the hands of ISIS. It would take years to bring the killers to justice. Only in late 2020 were two ISIS fighters extradited to the United States to face trial for their roles in the murders of two journalists and several aid workers (CPJ 2020b). The killing of the journalists again highlighted a perennial dilemma for media: How much do you show of such barbarism? In the wake of the Foley execution there was considerable discussion about those various front page photos in a debate about media restraint and media excess (Weir 2014). Put another way: 'Damned if you do, damned if you don't.' Some were angered by the brutality, while others thought it necessary to highlight the barbarism of ISIS. Part of the issue is that such material, published on the front page of a tabloid newspaper, without warning, leads to a strong possibility that children or vulnerable people might see a violent propaganda photo of a man moments from death (Smith 2014). Some likened it to 'death porn', an issue raised a few years earlier over the grisly images of the body of Libyan dictator Moammar Gaddafi at the height of the Arab Spring of 2011 (Jefferson 2011). As would become the 'norm' in such events in later years, within minutes screen shots from the video were appearing on social media—exactly what the ISIS terrorists had wanted (Abbruzzese 2014). Terrorists have continued to use the Internet and social media to publicise their terror, not only inflicted on journalists, but on the world at large, as demonstrated in the Christchurch mosque massacre of mid-March 2019, discussed at the beginning of Chapter 7. Journalism scholar Kasun Ubayasiri makes a strong case that there needs to be a 'paradigm shift' in how such events are reported. This involves less focus on the actual event and more attention being paid to the motivations behind the acts. Ubayasiri also suggests a very practical measure; reducing the propaganda impact of the event by not showing the types of images we've discussed and explaining to audiences 'the publication's refusal to be a vehicle for ISIS propaganda' which would be 'exposing ISIS rhetoric' and be a form of 'harm minimisation' (Ubayasiri 2017, 10).

James Foley and the others publicly beheaded by ISIS had been taken prisoner or kidnapped by the terrorist group. The possibility of being kidnapped, being held for ransom (or worse), and guaranteeing publicity for the group that kidnapped them is a very personal dilemma. The CPJ's Frank Smyth (2013) listed among the motivations for the diverse array of groups that kidnap journalists—militants, rebels, criminals, and paramilitaries—a number of reasons why journalists are taken. They include ransom, to deliver a political message, to influence coverage, to extract information from the captive journalist or concerns over espionage, and the suggestion that they might be spies (Smyth 2013). The dilemma for the journalist's superiors is do you not publicise the fact that the staff member has been kidnapped in the hope he/she will be returned promptly, or do they publicise the kidnap like they would any other person? The case study at the end of the chapter takes up this perennial dilemma.

A major issue for female correspondents

Aside from the very real physical dangers associated with attempting to cover the conflicts associated with the Arab Spring, a major danger emerged for women covering those stories—sexual assault. Top CBS *60 Minutes'* foreign correspondent Lara Logan suffered what was termed a 'brutal' sexual assault lasting about 40 minutes at the hands of a mob of Egyptian men while covering the downfall of President Hosni Mubarak in early 2011 (ABC 2011). Within months, the CPJ had released a report titled 'The silencing crime: Sexual violence and journalists' (Wolfe 2011). The issue had been rarely reported until the assault on Ms Logan and her courageous decision to talk about it. It prompted an outpouring of commentary about the dangers that female correspondents face around the world (Mirkinson 2011). In the four months between the Logan assault and the release of the *CPJ* report, the report's author, Lauren Wolfe, interviewed more than four dozen journalists who had undergone varying degrees of sexual violence. Many said they had been worried about reporting the assaults for fear they would be reassigned or prevented from taking risky assignments in the future (Mirkinson 2011). As was noted in Chapter 7, physical attacks on female journalists have been joined by widespread attacks online.

The bias of familiarity

Another major ethical issue for the journalist in a foreign country—and for his/her audience 'back home'—is trying to understand the local culture. There is certainly a bias of familiarity involved, similar perhaps to what we discussed in Chapter 2 when White reporters make mistakes in covering the Black Lives Matter movement because they do not understand the lives of Black people and haven't thought it necessary to educate themselves. In an international context, the clash of media and cultural understanding was graphically illustrated in 2012 by what can only be described as three shocking incidents.

The first, a three-minute video showing a man said to be a member of the Taliban, fatally shooting—in front of a cheering crowd—a woman accused of adultery, was given the Western tabloid treatment by *The New York Post* (2012). While this is a vile and disgusting act that no moral person could condone, the headline—'Watch: Taliban thugs execute woman for "adultery" near Kabul'—is inflammatory, to say the least. Headlines like this feed into anti-Muslim sentiments and are weaponised by racists (von Sikorski, Matthes, and Schmuck 2018). Two months later, there were protests in a number of countries over an anti-Islam video produced in the United States (The Daily Mail 2012). The low-budget trailer for a movie titled 'Innocence of Muslims' sparked furious anti-American protests across the Islamic world. The reaction was similar to that in 2005 when a Danish newspaper, *Fyllands-Posten (Jutland's Post)* published 12 cartoons depicting the Muslim prophet Muhammad. The drawings had been commissioned by the paper to accompany an article on self-censorship and freedom of speech after Danish writer Kare Bluitgen had been unable to find artists willing to illustrate his children's book about Muhammad for fear of violent attacks by extremist Muslims. While the original publication of the cartoons raised a storm of protest, it was nothing to the reaction to their re-publication in later months in Europe and around the world. Muslims regarded the cartoons as deeply offensive. There's no doubt the cartoons were offensive, but the debate soon became 'hijacked' by extremist Muslims on the one side rioting in protest that saw lives lost in several countries, and those supporting 'freedom of the press' argument on the other. The third 2012 incident also involved the Taliban. They shot a 14-year-old girl in the face after she championed the rights of girls to be educated in Pakistan. The girl, Malala Yousufzai, was targeted, the Taliban said, because she was 'pro-West' (Elliott 2012). She was very seriously wounded and was airlifted to the United Kingdom for specialist treatment. She recovered fully and was the co-recipient of the Nobel Peace Prize in 2014.

Most Western journalists, foreign correspondents included, would struggle to understand how these incidents could happen and would have no trouble writing condemning accounts. But we can't always assume that we know or understand everything about different cultures or religious beliefs. While it might be hard to understand, it is part of the media's educative function to try to explain the religious or political motivation behind such actions. While in no way condoning the actions, it is important to try to understand them and put them into context. Usually, such actions are those of an extremist minority, like ISIS, and bear little resemblance to the beliefs of the majority. All-too-often journalists will carry their own cultural bias into their reporting of such upsetting stories and settle for the 'usual suspects' by way of sources for comment on such offensive stories. It is no coincidence that each of the incidents briefly mentioned earlier involves Western coverage of Islamic communities. Many Muslim communities have good reason to be mistrustful of Western journalists and many journalists are ignorant of Islam. News coverage of Islam is often 'stereotyped and unbalanced' (Heeren and Zick 2014). Throughout the last 20 years there has been far too much blanket condemnation of Muslims in the media for the acts of a few ideologically motivated terrorists. Media scholars are now active in addressing the fault lines and arguing for greater respect on both sides (Rahman 2016).

Reporters are often 'first responders'

Away from conflict zones, reporters are often called upon to deal with suffering, death, and widespread human misery. In many situations where there is dramatic tragedy unfolding, journalists are early on the scene along with the 'first responders', police, ambulance officers, and fire brigade staff. Emergency services professions were quicker than the mainstream media to realise the traumatic effects of being among the first on the scene of a tragedy. They have had courses for many years to teach their staff how to cope with what they encounter at such events. Journalists, too, can be considered 'first responders' subject to the same traumatic emotional consequences. The major news organisations realised some time ago they had a duty of care to journalists sent to horrific events and have instituted training programs to help them cope with such events. Research shows that journalists are affected by what they witness and need appropriate training on how to handle the awful situations they sometimes encounter. In 1991, the Dart Center was established in the United States and has since spread to other countries to research the effects of trauma on journalists; it has amassed many useful resources for helping to combat those effects, including a number of resources for would-be foreign correspondents. While the major media employers are now helping their staff cope with covering traumatic events, freelancers have to fend for themselves. They often find themselves covering major conflicts—like Afghanistan—without a major news organisation behind them. They need to prepare for such events. But as has been noted, it is not only foreign correspondents that can suffer the effects of reporting on tragedies. One of the groups sometimes overlooked are regional journalists. Working for a non-metropolitan media organisation—the local newspaper, radio or TV station—the journalist gets to know the local newsmakers. Often there are 50 or less major news sources in the area, and the reporter will literally 'bump into them' professionally and privately from time to time. What happens when a familiar source is involved in a serious accident? As an example, imagine the acute loss the local Sunshine Coast (Queensland) journalists felt at the sudden death of 'Crocodile Hunter' Steve Irwin in 2006? The larger-than-life character had provided many stories for the local media and been a popular and valuable source. Many would have seen him as a friend and felt his loss deeply. The research talks about the cumulative effect of witnessing tragedy—typified by the 2019 case involving the crime/court reporter at *The Age* discussed in the next section—but regional journalists, often those early in their careers, need to realise the potential to suffer the effects of witnessing repeated trauma.

Post-Traumatic Stress Disorder

Respected ABC (Australia) foreign correspondent Peter Lloyd is (to use a cliché) a textbook example of what can happen to a reporter who is overwhelmed by the emotional stress of covering disasters, assassinations, and human misery. Lloyd was arrested in Singapore in mid-2009 and charged with drug offences that carried up to 20 years in jail and the possibility of being caned (O'Brien 2008). The charges were later downgraded, but Lloyd spent 100 days in a Singapore prison. He recounted the awful experience in a memoir titled *Inside Story: From ABC Foreign Correspondent to Singapore Prisoner #12988* (2010). Lloyd talked openly about how he turned to drugs to help him sleep and to 'settle his demons'. As his lawyer explained to the Singapore court, like many addicts, Lloyd was not a drug abuser. He used the drugs as a form of self-medication to cope with his mental illness, PTSD (Lloyd 2010, 177). Lloyd recounted the cumulative traumatic effects of reporting some of the biggest stories in southern Asia in the early years of the 21st century. In those years, before *he* became the news story, according to the blurb on his book, Lloyd had:

> stood among the gruesome human wreckage laid out in an improvised mortuary after the 2002 Bali Bombing and joined Thailand's disaster recovery workers collecting the bloated flotsam of the 2004 Boxing Day Tsunami. And he was there for the worst atrocity in Pakistan's history, a 2007 suicide bombing attempt on Benazir Bhutto's life, two months before she was finally assassinated
>
> (Lloyd 2010, back page)

As he recounted early in his memoir, one of what he called the 'guilty secrets of journalism' (ibid., 55) is that 'for us to have a really good day, someone else must have a very bad one', and he had seen more than his fair share of the bad ones. Lloyd returned to the ABC in radio current affairs—a remarkable recovery.

It is not only journalists working overseas in 'trouble spots' that can be exposed to traumatic events. In what was described at the time as a landmark ruling that would have international consequences for media companies, an Australian court ruled in February 2019 that a journalist for the Melbourne newspaper, *The Age*, be awarded AU$180,000 for psychological injury suffered during the decade she covered the Victorian capital's notorious and bloody 'gangland wars' and later days and days of court listening to graphic accounts of horrific crimes (Ricketson and Wake 2019). The Victorian County Court was told the journalist, identified in court only as 'YZ', attended 32 murder scenes, but found it increasingly difficult to report on events involving the death of children, like when a father threw his four-year-old daughter off a Melbourne bridge. The court found that the paper had failed in its duty of care to the journalist as she was repeatedly exposed to trauma and increasingly showed signs of psychological injury. Her lawyer, Bree Knoester, said it was the first successful court action of its kind in the world (Watkins 2019). Three months after that finding, *The Age* filed papers in the Victorian Supreme Court in an attempt to overturn the ruling (Varga 2019), and had a partial victory. The Court ruled that while the judge was right to award damages to the journalist, the question of the size of the payout should be re-assessed (Akerman 2019). After a six-year battle, YZ reached a private settlement with *The Age* in March 2020 (Yates 2020). In 2012, a Walkley Award-winning photographer had sued the same newspaper after she covered the first anniversary of the 2002 Bali bombings (Farnsworth 2012). The newspaper was accused of failing to provide a safe workplace and breaching its duty of care, but the case was dismissed.

Being a foreign correspondent can be rewarding and exciting, and covering important global stories is often a career goal for journalists who love being at the centre of things. We have no problem with this and recognise the important job that reporters do under often difficult or dangerous conditions. Our advice is simple:

- Go for it! BUT: Don't get yourself into situations that you do not understand and are not prepared for.
- Take all the survival training that's on offer; make sure you are well-equipped, physically, intellectually and psychologically, for whatever the story throws your way.
- Before you decide to become a war correspondent read up on the approach known as 'peace journalism' that eschews the 'us and them' dichotomy of traditional war reporting and instead has a focus on 'shared problems', 'human rights abuses on both sides', and the 'visible and invisible effects of war-related policies' (Ewart and O'Donnell 2018).

Case study: Who'd be a journalist in a conflict zone?

Kidnapping has long been a tool of the terrorist, the warlord, the common criminal and, in recent times, of insurgents in the military conflicts in Syria and Afghanistan. People are taken captive to fund the group's activities, or to force government action, like the withdrawal of troops or the release of prisoners. But there is another dimension to this life-threatening issue: What if the person kidnapped is a professional colleague or friend? Just as journalists are increasingly becoming the targets of pirates and assorted villains, they are also routinely being kidnapped in the world's trouble spots. The reaction by the media to a kidnapped correspondent varies. Let's look briefly at five different examples.

In October 2008, Canadian Broadcasting Corporation (CBC) reporter Melissa Fung was kidnapped in Kabul, Afghanistan, but it would be a month before the public knew of her desperate plight and her safe release. That's because the CBC, the Canadian military, and the office of then Canadian Prime Minister, Stephen Harper, pleaded with the Western media not to report it (Kidder 2008). Fragile negotiations for Fung's release could be instantly derailed by any publicity, the broadcaster, military, and Prime Minister's office argued. They felt that panicked kidnappers could simply kill her to dispense with the danger of a raid by special forces if the incident became 'big news' (Loong 2008). 'No news story is worth someone's life' is the succinct policy of the Canadian Press wire service aimed at guiding the reporting of kidnapping and terrorism stories (Kidder 2008). Journalists and their managers alike went through much soul-searching during the weeks of Ms Fung's captivity over what's more important—the safety of the kidnap victim or the free flow of information (Loong 2008).

July 2009 saw *New York Times* journalist David Rohde, and his Afghan colleague Tahir Ludin, escape from the Taliban in Afghanistan after being held captive for seven months. Although word had spread quickly in the previous November that Rohde, Ludin, and their driver had been kidnapped, *The New York Times* convinced news organisations around the globe to keep a lid on the story with a simple appeal: The kidnappers had demanded silence. By defying them, the media could be signing the reporter's death warrant (Hoyt 2009). The *NYT*'s public editor at the time, Clark Hoyt, wrote that some readers and even some journalists 'see hypocrisy when a news organisation subordinates its fundamental obligation to inform the public to its human impulse to protect one of its own' (2009). The Poynter Institute's Kelly McBride said the paper's defence of the total news blackout 'made the job of every free journalist in the world harder' and accused the paper of putting their 'loyalties to a few in front of the larger journalistic principle of truth telling' (2009). She said the paper had indicated that when a life was in danger, journalists should avoid reporting the truth until the life is secure, setting a standard journalists couldn't possibly uphold.

More public was the case of the BBC's Alan Johnston, the respected Middle East correspondent who was kidnapped in Gaza City in the Middle East in March 2007, just two weeks before his contract was due to end. He was held for nearly four months by a Jihadi organization called the Army of Islam. The BBC mounted a major international—and very public—campaign to try to secure his release, and he was eventually freed unharmed in early July (BBC 2007). After his release, Johnson told his story to the BBC (Johnston 2007) and in a book titled *Kidnapped: And Other Dispatches* (2011). As the publicity for the book noted:

> When Alan Johnston, the last western journalist to remain in Gaza, was kidnapped by religious terrorists—millions of people, from the backstreets of Gaza, to London, New York and Johannesburg, felt the need to express their anger and their determination to see him free.
>
> (Johnston 2011)

Johnston had spent his 114-day ordeal largely alone in a tiny, windowless room with only a radio for company. He said he had been threatened but he was physically assaulted only in the half-hour before his release (Chulov 2007).

In a slightly different scenario, what happens when the journalist goes missing and it is up to the relatives to find a ransom? Australian photographer Nigel Brennan and Canadian journalist Amanda Lindhout were kidnapped outside the Somali capital Mogadishu in August 2008 and held captive for 462 days (Elliott 2011). Brennan and Lindhout were released after more than 15 months, after Brennan's family finally raised the AU$1.1 million needed to secure the release of the couple, including generous donations from family members, former Australian Greens political party leader, Bob Brown, and entrepreneur Dick Smith. Brennan's sister-in-law, Kellie Brennan, said, 'we had to keep everything out of the media, because if the Somalis knew they would up the ransom' (Elliott 2011). The couple were released in November 2009. Brennan said that during his 15-month ordeal he'd been chained up and pistol-whipped; his colleague said she had been beaten and tortured (ABC 2009). Amanda Lindhout told the media she was repeatedly raped and that she and Brennan converted to Islam in order to please their captors. At one point, Lindhout contemplated suicide in order to end her ordeal (Mann 2018). The story is told in Brennan's book titled *The Price of Life* (Brennan, Bonney, and Brennan 2011) and in Lindhout's memoir, *A House in the Sky* (Lindhout and Corbett 2014).

While most of the examples thus far have been from more than a decade ago, here's a more recent case. British photojournalist John Cantlie was first captured by ISIS forces in July 2012 but escaped a few months later. He returned to Syria the following November, only to be kidnapped along with James Foley, the American journalist mentioned earlier who was beheaded by an Islamist terrorist in 2014. But Cantlie was different. He was used by ISIS to create English-language propaganda videos and was last seen at the battle for Mosul in December 2016 (Philp 2019). As you can see from the preceding reference, he made the news again in 2019 with word that he may still be alive, much to the surprise of his family. The British government said they believed he was still being held captive at that time by the terrorist group somewhere in Syria.

Questions arising from the case study

1   Put yourself in the position of a kidnapped journalist. What would you want your bosses to do? Publicise your kidnapping widely, like the case of the BBC's Alan Johnston, or keep quiet and negotiate like a couple of the others?
2   Now put yourself in the position of the news organisation's editor. Debate how you would reach your decision? Publish or keep quiet?
3   An Australian engineer, Douglas Wood, was kidnapped by insurgents in Baghdad in 2005. His plight was covered in newspapers 'back home' for the six weeks of his captivity before his rescue by the American military.

What's the difference? Why publicise his captivity and not that of 'your friend, the kidnapped journalist'?

4 You are reporting from a Middle East trouble spot and a colleague is kidnapped. What would you do? Is there any difference when it's a friend, and not you?

5 Nigel Brennan was freed after his family raised the ransom and paid it to the kidnappers in Somalia. How do you feel about paying kidnappers? Does a political motive differ from a financial demand?

6 Most Western governments have a policy of not dealing with terrorists (notably not paying ransoms). Where does that leave the family of the kidnapped journalist?

7 The Australian Foreign Affairs Department said at the time of the Brennan kidnap that changing its policy (of not paying ransoms) would undermine Australia's policy, and indirectly result in more Australians overseas being targeted. Then Defence Minister Marise Payne confirmed the policy in late 2019 when she called for international cooperation to cut off the millions of dollars said to be flowing to terrorist organisations in ransoms (Harris 2019). Do you agree that paying a ransom only leads to others being kidnapped? What would you do?

8 Is Cantlie a captive or an active ISIS agent? Does the suggestion he might be working 'for the other side' make a difference?

Questions for discussion

1 Should a journalist put loyalty to nation above their duty to report without fear or favour?

2 The saying 'Patriotism is the last refuge of a scoundrel' is attributed to the famous English orator and writer Samuel Johnson in 1775. Was he right to think this?

3 How can reporters prepare themselves for potentially dangerous assignments? Check out the resources at the International News Safety Institute, the Dart Center, and any others you can find to help you answer this question.

4 How can journalists respond to authoritarian leaders who think it's okay to kill reporters or have them murdered?

Note

1 In this context—a war without end, or clearly defined enemies, and fought over shifting terrains in multiple locations—our comments about the problematic nature of the journalist's role are even more sharply posed.

12 Journalism, ethics, and philosophy

One foot in history

> The press within a half century has become the chief medium of enlightenment;
> it has awakened the masses to full perception of their powers, and has established
> the fact that an alert and aroused public opinion is irresistible, the mightiest force
> evolved by modern civilization.
>
> (Ochs 1906, 38)

At the beginning of the 20th century, the emerging modern incarnation of
journalism was thought to have an important role in public life. According to
publisher of *The Philadelphia Public Ledger*, George W. Ochs, journalism was
'the chief medium of enlightenment'; a very philosophical proposition that
many journalists today would scoff at. Ochs also noted that the successful
journalist in 1906 needed 'the knowledge, the comprehension, and the depth
of intellect' to fully understand the complexities of a simple news story:
'extracting its real meaning, interpreting the relation it bears to events that may
have preceded or its influence upon what may follow' and 'deduce the real
import of a current event' (ibid., 44). Ochs argued that senior editors must each
have a specialist knowledge (economics, foreign affairs, etc.), but also 'diversi-
fied attainments to be able to properly discuss any subject' (ibid., 45) with
'expert knowledge and critical judgment' (ibid., 48) and possess 'the sagacity
and judgment of a skilled tactician' (ibid., 49) that is gained through 'a thorough collegiate education' (ibid., 51). What is not required, according to
George Ochs, is 'dry philosophy' and 'overwrought scholasticism' (ibid., 52).
However, the good newspaper editor, in Ochs' view, does need to grasp 'certain fundamentals' of academic instruction in a wide range of disciplines from
civics, to sociology and political science, history, the sciences, international
affairs, and literature imbibed from a 'range of reading with breadth of learning'
(ibid., 52) and a 'keen knowledge of human nature' (ibid., 53).

Today, nearly 120 years after George Ochs outlined the necessary intellectual
attributes of a good journalist, the research literature that takes in journalism
and philosophy is very underdeveloped and has not had much scholarly attention over the past 40 years, particularly not in English. However, history could

DOI: 10.4324/9780429242892-13

have been written differently if a simple idea proposed in 1928 by Charles D. Johnson had been adopted. Mr Johnson seriously proposed that schools of journalism—which had been in existence then for about 25 years—should be renamed as schools of *journalology*, much like schools of sociology, biology, and theology. Journalology would be a 'new science' that embraced the teaching of news production and research into journalism as a category of knowledge (Johnson 1928, 385). It is possible that Mr Johnson was joking when he wrote: 'Let's have departments of journalology presided over by journalologists.' But we can see his point: the study of journalism should be considered analytically and separately from its practice. Unfortunately, the proposal did not survive beyond Mr Johnson, and the knowledge gap between working journalists and the scholarship of journalism has been widening ever since. Instead of a unified theory of journalism, what we have seen over the past 100 years is various attempts to lasso journalism studies to other disciplines (most recently post-modernist cultural studies in the late 1990s (Hartley 1996), an attempt that was resisted and eventually foundered (Hirst 1998a, 1998b) and to other theoretical frameworks such as John Dewey's social responsibility thesis or Habermasian notions of the public sphere (Coleman 1997). Long-time journalism scholar Michael Schudson (2013, 159) writes that the 'philosophy of journalistic pro-fessionalism' is 'riddled with self-deception'. We would add that it is also marked with disciplinary overcrowding, epistemological confusion, ontological overload, undiagnosed idealism and a normative rationalism that taken together obscure the field behind a thick ideological fog. Pierre Bourdieu (1998) perhaps came close to a theory of journalism as a totality, or at least as a field of praxis that is related to, brought into being by, and subservient to economic and political power (Champagne 2005).

Ethics and philosophical thinking

The contemporary debate about journalism ethics takes its general contours from thousands of years of philosophical thinking. The morality of decision-making has been a cornerstone of philosophy for two millennia. Ethics is the philosophical study of what constitutes *right* and *wrong* and an exploration of what separates 'good' from 'evil'. Even a relatively contemporary idea like 'freedom of the press' can be traced back to a philosophical argument about the right to speak (Steel 2012), or perhaps more importantly, the right to be listened to and taken seriously when speaking in public about matters of public importance. Journalists claim this right for themselves, and this implies a number of consequential rights and responsibilities. We also make it clear in the following pages that earning the right to speak on behalf of the public and defending journalism from those who would like to see it silenced are problematic ideas that are often misunderstood, mis-interpreted, and riddled with mistaken beliefs—on all sides.

Throughout the ages, ethical questions have also been questions of power and control. Who gets to decide between those who can speak and those who cannot depends almost entirely on who carries the biggest stick; who has the biggest army and, ultimately, who has the most money. Wealth has always bought the privilege of speech, beginning with ancient Greece where slavery was common despite the grandeur of its classical arts and architecture and fabled origin as the birthplace of *democracy* (Nafissi 2000). Even Aristotle thought democracy was going too far if it didn't give a more entitled place to the wealthy Athenian elite (Jordović 2011). It is not so different today; the freedom to own a press—even a digital media space—is expensive and not really equally available to everyone. We will return to this topic in a discussion of 'press freedom', and we touch on the complex relationship between ethics, wealth and power in the news media in Chapter 14, but before we get too deeply into that subject, a brief historical diversion into the world of ideas is necessary.

We begin with ideas because the world is presented to us first as a series of ideas. It appears as though ideas shape the world we live in, and history is often presented to us as a contest of ideas. Even great and destructive world wars are explained this way. According to this idealist version of history, World War Two was about two opposing ideas—'Freedom' versus 'Fascism'; the very material economic causes of war such as—colonialism, imperialism, and competition, are downplayed or ignored in this narrative. A similar narrative is often used to explain the Cold War that raged for 50 years between 1945 and the collapse of the Soviet Union in 1989; that was a war between 'Freedom' and 'Communism'. Today, world history is sometimes explained as a clash of ideas between 'Freedom' and 'Terrorism' or a 'clash of civilizations' (Huntington 1993). At best these are partial explanations, at worst they are misleading. In Chapters 13 and 14 we explore the contradictions between philosophical idealism and philosophical materialism in more detail, but for now we'll assume that ideas have an intrinsic power of their own; in this way we can explain principles without cluttering the picture with too much history, economics or theoretical baggage.

The philosophy of ethics

When it comes to defining a philosophy of ethics, we are simply talking about a form of reasoning that gives us insights into how to behave under certain conditions. In journalism this philosophy is usually written up into a 'code', a list of principles that are supposed to govern the power of journalism in a responsible way. Unfortunately, codes are pragmatic and cannot adequately represent the complexity of philosophical reasoning. In this chapter we explore the more esoteric thinking that has led to written prescriptive codes of ethics, because through understanding a more theoretical model of ethics and embracing dynamic forms of thinking we can arrive at an informed judgement of the value (or otherwise) of the more static ethical 'rules' and how to apply them.

Ethics is a branch of philosophy and it is important for journalists to consider their ethical stance from this perspective. However, journalism ethics is not esoteric, nor purely of academic interest. The philosophy behind journalism ethics translates into everyday decision-making under sometimes difficult or confusing circumstances. Ethics is a historically evolving field of enquiry and also of application. Not only are old problems and issues being constantly reinterpreted in light of new information, new problems are being considered in light of pre-existing interpretations. This is good and important because the world is changing around us and our ethical thinking must catch up, adapt, and even be ahead of the curve. This is why we want you to consider ideas like the *techno-legal* and *techno-ethical time-gap*. Sure, drones are useful, but they also bring with them new ethical dilemmas and challenges. Yes, algorithms might help solve the 'fake news' problem, but at what cost? Of course, it is entirely possible for robots to produce news copy, but does that mean they should? If we're not careful, ethics gets left behind, and less ethical decisions may come to dominate. At some point it becomes too late to do anything about it.

We start from the position that understanding the intellectual and philosophical roots of journalism ethics is a good thing. However, this does not mean a long and boring treatise on the history of philosophy; rather we will deal briefly with a series of important ideas and then ground them in the here and now. For us, ethics is the application of principles and values to real world situations. Ethics is applied philosophy, and journalism ethics is philosophy applied to the practice of journalism. The principles behind most ethical systems are deeply rooted in the Western tradition of philosophy and therefore they adopt many values associated with the Enlightenment and re-interpretations of the classical Greek and Roman philosophers of Antiquity. For example, the concept of 'objectivity', central to normative iterations of journalism ethics, has its roots in the dialogues of Socrates and Plato. In this sense, objectivity is formed in a dialectical relationship with subjectivity and 'subjective experience' (Hassan and Sutherland 2017, 62–4). There are several important traditions in the philosophy of ethics and all of them are reflected in contemporary ethical reasoning, in codes of ethics and in ongoing debates about practical ethical dilemmas (see Chapters 7–11). Of course, traditions are changed and reinterpreted throughout history, and we'll discuss that process in the next two chapters. For now, the philosophical traditions we need to consider in relation to journalism are a rights-based system, virtue-based systems founded on duty and obligation, a system of utilitarian ethics, and the theories of consequentialism (Baumane-Vitolina, Cals, and Sumilo 2016). Sometimes these theories go by other names, but if we stick to these simple terms it's easier not to get them confused. None of these traditions—alone or in concert—can really be described as a philosophy of journalism, but they are key principles on which most contemporary debates about journalism ethics are built; for that reason, it is worth providing a brief explanation before moving to a more holistic theory of journalism that might be described as a systemic philosophy.

Rights, obligations, and consequences

Ethics is a complex area of thought that, over 2,000 years, has produced several major positions which are simultaneously complimentary and antagonistic. A rights-based system of ethics begins from the proposition that humans have certain inalienable rights or what are sometimes called natural rights. These rights can be, and sometimes are, encoded in legal statutes, international law, and some constitutions; this makes them enforceable. Virtue systems begin from the principle that certain actions are intrinsically good and therefore humans should always seek to act in ways that are virtuous. Principles such as honesty in affairs of money and truth in human relations are the foundation of virtue ethics. Utilitarianism is more of a social ethic that has at its core the idea that actions should result in the greatest good and the least harm for the greatest number of people. Consequentialism is grounded in the belief that actions have consequences and therefore if the outcome of an action is just, then the action is justified. However, there is often some overlap in the values expressed in each theory and in practice they are actually mixed together. It is almost impossible to have a complete system of ethical reasoning without blending some aspects of rights, virtues, and consequences into a coherent thread. The relationship between all of these traditions is, in fact, dialectical (see Chapters 13, 14).

Despite their overlap, there is a fundamental clash between rights, obliga-tions, virtues, and consequences that cannot easily be untangled. Our first fault lines—a series of contradictions in journalism ethics—occur between antag-onistic systems of thinking about ethics: rights versus obligations; virtuous action versus consequences. A rights-based approach posits that journalists are imbued with a professional right to seek information, ask questions, and report their findings to the public, without fear or favour. It is what John Merrill described as the 'imperative of freedom' (Merrill 1990). In the same vein of freedoms and rights, the public has a right to information. This takes concrete shape in the formula 'a right to know', which is a catch-cry to defend at least one version of press freedom (Stiglitz 1999). A virtue ethic requires an indivi-dual to always act in a way that is morally good. If obligations or duties are paramount, then a journalist has an obligation to report truthfully and to behave honestly, it becomes a duty to the public and to the institution of journalism. When consequential thinking is paramount, a journalist must be conscious of both wanted and unwanted outcomes or repercussions when their story is published. It should be clear that, in reality, ethical thinking is quite complex and a reporter needs to consider all of these principles in order to arrive at an ethically sound decision (Suarez Villegas 2015).

In keeping with the theme of historical continuity, we can trace the ethical systems of duty, consequence, and virtue to the philosophers of ancient Greece. An ethical system based on duties is known as a deontological ethic from the Greek root *deon* meaning duty and it is predicated on a duty to do what is right from a moral perspective (Alexander and Moore 2016). Virtue ethics is linked to Aristotle and is a deontological approach in that it requires a person to behave in a virtuous or morally sound way at all times and in all dealings with other people. Virtue theory begins with a very individual question: 'What kind of person do I want to be?' The answer supplied in this tradition is that everybody should act in good faith and in ways that they would like to be treated. It goes further and adds that virtues are universal and largely non-negotiable. Aristotle's 'golden mean' is often cited as an example of virtue ethics where the morally right approach is the middle ground between two extremes. Virtue theory emphasises a person's good character and suggests all their actions should reflect these attributes (Christians, Ferré, and Fackler 1993). Virtue theory asks reporters to internalise their ethical code and to embed it in their thinking so that it becomes existential—an intrinsic part of their being (Merrill 1989, 1996)—usually through a process of training and socialisation into the norms of journalistic behaviour learned on the job (Quinn 2007).

Deontological ethics imposes a limit on our freedom of choice. We might *choose* to do something, but if it is not the morally responsible thing to do, we should *choose not to* do it. The 18th-century German philosopher, Immanuel Kant is considered the founding father of modern deontological ethics and today we talk of a 'Kantian' *moral imperative* to always do the right thing. Kant's imperative also relies on being universally applicable and posits that we should not treat people as a means to an end, or take advantage of them to serve our own interests (Sanders 2003). In journalistic terms, the categorical imperative and universality of Kantian ethics means that reporters should not take unfair advantage of sources or put them at risk for the sake of a story (Hirst and Patching 2005). A system based only on a deontological ethic can seem quite rigid because it imposes on us a duty to live by strict moral rules that cannot be broken even if the consequence is something good. In other words, it is not the outcome that determines the moral value of an action, but the rightness of the action itself. For example, a deontological ethic would place any dubious action—for example, using stolen documents—by a journalist in the 'forbidden' basket, even if the result was a scoop that brought down a corrupt politician. Karen Sanders (2003, 19) points to a flaw in Kantian ethics: it does not explain the moral significance of emotions and only operates at a level of cold logic. We agree that this is a fair point because there is an emotional element in most news stories. How can it be otherwise when reporting on events that involve humans, perhaps the most emotion-driven species on the planet?

Ethical systems in which the action or consequence is paramount are known broadly as teleological ethics, from the Greek root *telos* or (end point/outcome). Jeremy Bentham and John Stuart Mill are 19th-century British philosophers most closely associated with the teleological systems of consequential and utilitarian ethics. A consequentialist believes an action is good if it results in a net amount of good. Consequentialist ethics, commonly known as 'utilitarianism', posits that the 'greater good' is in an action that benefits the most people and harms the least (Sinnott-Armstrong 2019). In an outcomes or consequence-based ethics, the morality of the action is less important than the effect of the action (Baumane-Vitolina, Cals, and Sumilo 2016). So, a teleological ethicist would say that using stolen documents to prove corruption would be morally defensible because the end result is that a corrupt official gets caught. In this scenario, an ethical journalist would first have considered that the corrupt official might face heavy penalties as a result of the exposure and decided to do the story anyway because the consequence is acceptable. However, this raises the question of how broadly a journalist should consider the idea of 'consequences'. If the jailing of a corrupt official leads to suffering for that person's family, is the exposure still justified? This is where John Stuart Mill's principles of utilitarianism become relevant. Utilitarianism posits that the greater good might come from the corrupt official being exposed, so any harm to innocent family members is less than the potential harm to more people if the official continues in their corrupt behaviour. This is just one of the many moral dilemmas that arises if we attempt strict adherence to only one set of principles. Utilitarianism sounds good in theory, but in reality would you like to be the journalist who causes anguish to innocent people even if one guilty person is caught? Mill's utility principle is altruistic and asks us to examine the broader context of our decision-making; it does not rely on an individual being motivated by some inner adherence to being a good person. Utilitarianism is therefore linked to the idea of a social contract and in journalism we can clearly see that this is a contract between the journalist and the audience. This is an obligation on behalf of the journalists and editors that they will supply truthful facts and context to news consumers (Hirst and Patching 2005).

We have always argued that a system of 'sustained moral reasoning' is one fundamental requirement for ethical journalism (Hirst and Patching 2005, 17). It is necessary, but it is not sufficient (Korkonosenko 2013). As we've suggested here, trying to establish a philosophy of ethical journalism on the basis of only one model of moral reasoning is never going to work. What we've come to recognise is that it is necessary to add more elements and complexity to our theoretical understanding of how ethical systems interact, in order to create a viable model of ethical thinking that can be operationalised by working journalists and taught to journalism students. Each time we've approached this subject in our writing on ethics (Hirst and Patching 2005, 2007; Patching and Hirst 2014), our understanding has grown and our reasoning—we like to think—has become a bit more sophisticated. Each time we've added more historical context and attempted to embellish our theoretical arguments. We now think it is time to reframe our thinking again and tackle a deeper question: Is there such a thing as a philosophy of journalism? What follows in the rest of this chapter and in the two that follow, is our attempt to provide a path towards answering this question. Of course, others have previously dealt with this problem, and we acknowledge and celebrate the work that has been done (Merrill and Odell 1983; Zelizer 2004a; Muhlmann 2010; Hearns-Branaman 2016b), but it is an issue that does not seem to receive the attention it deserves from either working journalists or journalism scholars. This is a pity because journalism and philosophy are closer than you might think.

Why philosophy is useful in journalism

> How can it be that journalism and philosophy, the two humanistic intellectual activities that most boldly (and some think obnoxiously) vaunt their primary devotion to truth, are barely on speaking terms?
>
> (Romano 2009)

This question was posed by Carlin Romano in *The Chronicle of Higher Education*, and it's a good one. Romano makes several good points in answer to his rhetorical query: philosophers think journalism is intellectually inferior, 'superficial intellectual goods'; journalism developed after many philosophical debates of the Enlightenment were settled; philosophers are too insular and journalists too arrogant to ever get along and, our favourite, journalism students—according to professors of philosophy—are not smart enough to grasp high-level concepts. Meanwhile, journalists wrongly think of professors as 'pointy-heads' who are out of touch and irrelevant to modern life. No wonder then, that journalists and philosophers tend to talk past each other rather than engage in conversation. 'Both groups,' argues Romano, 'twist the screws into each other too reflexively'. Romano is both a philosopher and a journalist, and he makes a very agreeable point when he writes: '[W]e need journalists who scrutinize...their own preconceptions...and how their daily practice does or does not resemble art or science.' To do this, journalists need to sharpen their 'intellectual instincts' and discuss 'Wittgentein's instantiation of conceptual journalism as a philosophical method' (Romano 2009). That last point might be a little obscure, but generally we agree. Journalists need to engage with philosophy, to see journalism as an extension of philosophy and to see themselves as 'quotidian intellectuals'—the intellectuals of the 'everyday' (Hirst 2012a).

In our view, the gap between journalism and philosophy should be remarkably narrow and easily bridged. That the gap remains as wide as it is today is another reason why we argue that journalism ethics is at a crossroads. Journalism can either continue as if it's business as usual, or it can subject itself to a thorough re-examination of its entire way of thinking (epistemology) and what it believes itself to be (ontology). Journalism—and journalists—need to think in more philosophical terms about the world, and about their own future. Journalism and philosophy need to be closer together, and recognise their common interests if trust is to be re-established. In simple terms, philosophy and journalism are both concerned with the six basic questions of Who? What? When? Where? Why? And How? Like philosophy, journalism is a body of knowledge with its own historical traditions and its own ways of seeing the world; it sits most comfortably within the social sciences or humanities and it has—in common with these disciplines—its own theory about how it knows itself and justifies what it knows as 'truth'. In other words, journalism has an epistemology (Hearns-Branaman 2016b). An epistemology is a theory about how we come to know things about the world and how we go about finding evidence to support our hypothesis (Audi 2011). Epistemology is a philosophical exploration of how we know certain things are 'facts' or 'true' (Steup and Neta 2020), and according to Robert Audi (2011), epistemology cannot be fully appreciated except as a philosophical undertaking that links to 'the philosophy of mind', 'the phenomenology of perception', and 'the nature of belief' (xiii). Thus, we find there is a pathway between journalism and philosophy, right back to Plato and the ancient Greeks. The modern link is to thinkers of the Enlightenment and the philosophers who helped forge the intellectual tools for the revolutionary upheavals of the 17th to 19th centuries (Hobsbawm 1996; Stephens 2007; Patching and Hirst 2014; Hearns-Branaman 2016a, 2016b).

Why is this important? Because understanding philosophy is useful for journalists. Understanding philosophy can make journalism better (Attia 2017). The corollary reason is that the crises discussed in the first section of the book are expressions of a crisis in the epistemology of journalism. In other words, we think that journalists have lost their way because they have forgotten how to *think about journalism* in any critical or self-reflective way. Journalism has spent decades trying to shake itself loose from its philosophical foundations in favour of pragmatically clinging to a short-term cycle of daily renewal that situates the practice of journalists in a 'perpetual present', excluding any reflection on past practices that might guide future directions, and honouring a discourse in which the ability to think historically is no longer valued (Jameson 1990, 231; Baumbach, Young, and Yue 2016, 155).

The epistemological problem whereby journalism is unable to place itself into an historical context is a reflection of the daily practice of journalism itself. The object of journalistic knowledge is the 'new', the 'just happened', the 'yet to happen', the 'current affair'. Journalism is one of the few intellectual practices that must effectively re-invent itself each day. The story is always what's in front of you, not what has been left behind in history's wake. This constant search for the 'new' and the 'next' shapes the journalistic mind by rewarding the 'scoop' and the 'exclusive' and being first, and by devaluing 'old' news and relegating the past to the dustbin of history. The fast pace of journalism and its neglect of history does not lend itself to valuing introspection and philosophical speculation about the meaning of truth, or the foundations of ethics. In a world that values the perpetual present, history and philosophy are usually invoked to 'justify the present, and only rarely to challenge it' (Lewis 2009, 43). It is important for journalists to occasionally step back from the brink of the perpetual present and to help you to do this, let's turn our attention to the reasons why journalists should take philosophy a little more seriously.

Everything that we have talked about so far in this book—objectivity, truth, credibility, ethical behaviours, rights and responsibility, censorship, and the social purpose of news is, at its core, an issue of philosophy. We agree with John Merrill and Jack Odell (1983, ix) that philosophy should be 'the foundation of modern journalism' because '[p]ilosophizing in journalism helps us design meaningful definitions for ourselves which can help us in our work'.

Why don't journalists take philosophy seriously?

Tom Goldstein had a long career in journalism before joining the staff at the University of California. In his view, journalists are 'almost inarticulate on the subject of what they do and why they do it' (Goldstein 1985, 18). This is perhaps a little unfair; reporters today probably do have something to say about why they are journalists and about what it is they do. However, their responses to these inquiries are likely to be fairly shallow and couched in pragmatic or rhetorical phrases. In other words, journalists are not that interested in deep philosophical inquiry. This is unfortunate because journalists have—by their own account—an important role to play in defending and promoting democracy in support of the body politic and the public interest. Some journalists may be offended by what we're about to say, but we have to be clear about where our starting point is: At best, most journalists only have a cursory understanding of democracy and their role as society's watchdogs over powerful interests. As former *Guardian* editor Alan Rusbridger wrote in a rather shallow introduction to his dictionary-like book *News and How to Use It*, journalists like to think they have a good understanding of truth and power but adds 'we seldom like to reflect on our own power', noting that journalism 'always struggled to describe itself honestly, if at all' (Rusbridger 2020a, xi–xii). Journalists take little interest in theory or philosophy, and this is evident in Rusbridger's book, which he admits 'is in alphabetical form and is, inevitably, quite subjective and a bit random'. It is! The explanation of 'Bias'—you might think a huge and interesting philosophical topic for journalists—gets a short half-page entry containing the wisdom that 'Bias can be boring…Bias also sells' (ibid., 8). The problem is that reporters and editors are short-term thinkers, driven to chase 'news' from one deadline to the next, and in this environment an ideology of anti-intellectualism flourishes (McDevitt et al. 2018a).

Unfortunately, as Michael McDevitt's team discovered, it seems that this ethos also exists among journalism students. If you're a journalism student reading this book, we hope to change your mind. If you're a journalism trainer in a newsroom or academia, we also hope to convince you to take journalism a little more seriously (Zelizer 2004a), even though '[t]he premise that students act as agents of cultural hegemony in control of ideas is unlikely to sit well with JMC educators' (McDevitt et al. 2018b, 783). The findings of McDevitt et al. should be alarming for everyone reading this book, particularly since another piece of recent research suggests that journalism graduates are being hired into newsrooms to lead a process of change and to commercially engage a new younger demographic with the news product (Broersma and Singer 2020). How can these two ideas sit comfortably next to each other? Digital natives who graduate j-school with an anti-intellectual bias are hardly well-equipped to handle the complex negotiations required of them to be innovative and entrepreneurial or 'bring new ideas to the table' (Broersma and Singer 2020, 1). We hope that by outlining some thoughts about recoupling journalism with the idea that journalists and editors are public intellectuals (Hirst 2012a; McKnight and O'Donnell 2017), we can help bridge the gap. It seems that not taking themselves, or journalism, too seriously (or seriously enough?) is a global issue for journalism students. While specific research projects have uncovered a variety of motivations among journalism students, in general the literature tends to highlight that young people are motivated towards the profession more by aesthetic values and self-interest rather than ethical, altruistic, philosophical, or political concerns (Coleman et al. 2018).

A study of Danish students in 2010 found that political motivation was of limited importance in their decision to study journalism, and less important than factors of convenience (working close to home, for example) or prestige (high salaries, fame, etc.). This study also concluded that Danish journalism students would not be 'future left-wing missionaries' either (Hopmann et al, 2010, 670). A comparative study conducted among journalism students in Cuba, Ecuador, and Venezuela also pokes holes in the myth of journalism being a left-wing profession. Journalism students in these Latin American nations see the media as being mostly about entertainment and their motivations are not idealistic, but 'based on limited information about the reality of the profession, a stereotyped image of their prestige and the adventurous lifestyle'. The 'possibility to act as defenders of citizenship in the face of abuses of power' is a lower priority (Alonson et al, 2019, 480). A study of Spanish and British students reports that they shared a similar motivational preference for channelling their creative energy into the supposedly glamorous genre of feature writing over socio-political idealism (Sanders et al. 2008). Coleman and her colleagues conducted a survey and series of focus groups with American students seeking to understand their motivations for studying journalism and their conclusions support the idea that it is aesthetics not politics that draws them to the news as a career: 'Extroverted Writer describes students interested in self-fulfilment and maximising their own talents. Most college students are still focused on themselves and satisfying their own desires for self-realization' (Coleman et al. 2018, 812). This study summarises student motivations as still being centred on self-interest and, to a lesser degree, on altruism, 'but more are more motivated by fame than before' (ibid., 813).

A more global study covering eight countries revealed some significant national differences, but overall, the strongest motivating factors for students were that they 'simply liked journalism', followed by a self-belief in their own creative writing ability. The study reports that these two factors were 'by far the most prominent in each country' (Hanusch et al. 2015). Perhaps we're seeing the effects of an age gap here and the dialectical process of generational change under way. Perhaps the views of these students change after graduation when they are more exposed to an established institutional journalistic culture. Perhaps, but not necessarily. An oft-cited study from a decade ago notes that British journalism students were more likely to use what we call ethically 'dubious' actions (such as paying a source or using hidden cameras) than older journalists who'd been in the industry for a while (Sanders et al. 2008, 143). There is definitely a changing of the guard in newsrooms (Jackson, Thorsen, and Reardon 2019) and perhaps, in another ten years, news culture will be so dramatically altered that this discussion will seem very old-fashioned and a little bit pointless. It raises another question too: Will there be anyone left in the news business who sees any importance in defending journalistic values and the democratic function of the press? This is a live debate (Pingree et al. 2018) as we see a global rise in authoritarian leaders attacking the news media as 'fake' or as an enemy of the people. We cannot afford to descend any further into the dark underworld of media populism (Kraemer 2014) that validates an anti-intellectual view of the world and feeds authoritarianism.

As we described earlier, we believe the crisis situation is too serious for journalists to continue sitting on the sidelines in the belief that their claims to neutrality will protect them from the authoritarian instincts of the Donald Trumps of the world, the global collapse of the news industry, the technological tsunami, the 'spiral of cynicism' (Bants et al. 2010) or the crisis of trust. We also don't think that ignorance is a defence; it is not good enough to say: 'We didn't know at the time.' Being a journalist comes with baggage and the heaviest piece of luggage is labelled 'Responsibility'. Journalists have several suitcases of responsibilities and the best way to manage them is through first recognising that journalists are as much public intellectuals as those rarefied individuals we call philosophers. This is the real meaning of the preamble to the Australian journalists' Code of Ethics:

> Respect for truth and the public's right to information are fundamental principles of journalism. Journalists search, disclose, record, question, entertain, comment and remember. They inform citizens and animate democracy. They scrutinise power, but also exercise it, and should be responsible and accountable.
>
> (MEAA 2018)

Like philosophers, journalists rely on a set of first principles; like philosophers they search, disclose, record, question, comment, and remember; like philosophers, they have to inform citizens and animate democracy; like philosophers, journalists both scrutinise power and exercise it.

We believe that journalists, journalism educators, academics, and students should be treating the profession like a branch of philosophy. This means paying more attention to philosophy itself—in particular, paying more attention to a philosophy of journalism. We are not being flippant in saying this. The research into student motivations for joining the news profession confirms that altruism plays second fiddle to self-centred motivations. The growing literature covering this topic has consistently shown that to be the case; now it seems that younger Millennials and Gen Z students entering the profession after gaining a university qualification lack idealism when it comes to the values of journalism. Instead, they seem motivated by a pragmatic and transactional ideology of self-interest and are not motivated by a desire to change the world (Jackson, Thorsen, and Reardon 2019, 119). As Jackson and his colleagues conclude: 'A question for journalism educators is the extent to which they encourage such aspirations or challenge them.' We think that shifting attention to the intellectually demanding discipline of philosophy within the curriculum might help—it certainly can't do any more harm than teaching journalism students how to operate drones or do their own coding. The alternative is that we'll have armies of journalists who can cover celebrity weddings, and very few who can expose the crimes of the rich and powerful. Journalists should be front and centre in writing this first 'rough draft of history' (Shafer 2010), and they cannot do that without some intellectual rigour and philosophical commitment to their profession.

Besides lacking a unified philosophy of journalism, we also face the problem of the news media's hostility to academics and public intellectuals, which makes it difficult to convince journalists to even take philosophy seriously. Former journalist turned academic philosopher Kenneth Goodman made the point in 1989 that the relationship between journalists and philosophers has long been built on 'mutual distrust':

> Few journalists know or care as much about philosophy as about govern-ment, crime or other journalistic staples. And few philosophers have lucid ideas about how journalists work, or the sorts of things that interest them or strike them as suitable for publication.
>
> (Goodman 1989, 35)

Unfortunately, we think this is still true today. If anything, it's perhaps worse; our survey of the current state of journalism leads us towards pessimism and the conclu-sion that one of the defining features of today's journalists is a deep-seated hostility towards anything remotely intellectual. For Goodman, the issue is the lack of jour-nalistic engagement with philosophy as presented in the news pages; for us the bigger issue is journalists' rejection of any philosophical self-examination of what they are doing. It is problematic that journalists are not inclined to 'apply philosophical rigor to the treatment of news developments' (Goodman 1989, 36). Goodman makes another salient point about reporters' and editors' disinclination to discuss philoso-phical issues about their own profession; 'there is already epistemology and meta-physics in the paper; it is just of a very low order', offering opinion 'uninformed by analyses' that only 'rarely' moves 'beyond the superficial' (38). As David McKnight and Penny O'Donnell (2017) point out, there is a certain paradox between the role of journalists as public intellectuals and the apparent anti-intellectualism of the pro-fession. We will turn our attention to this topic in the next chapter where we discuss what kind of philosophy is best suited to a foundation for the renewal of journalism in response to the existential crises of profitability, disruption, and trust.

Questions for discussion

1 What qualities does a good 21st-century journalist need?
2 Are these vastly different from the list proposed by George W. Ochs?
3 Having read this chapter, will you take philosophy more seriously?
4 Do journalists have a role as public intellectuals?
5 What can you do to become more philosophically aware?

13 A crisis in epistemology and ideology

The crisis in journalism theory

The currently accepted orthodoxy in journalism, as both practice and theory, suffers from what some scholars call 'epistemic relativism' (see Durham 1998). This is evident in the so-called 'post truth' and postmodern present where all points of view are rendered equally valid and belief trumps facts. Truth has become subjective (Wagener 2019), rather than based on any verifiable empirical observation of reality. Barbie Zelizer points to this 'epistemological uneasiness' in her 2004 article 'When facts, truth, and reality are God-terms: On journalism's uneasy place in cultural studies'. Cultural studies is a discipline which valorises 'relativity, subjectivity, and construction', over journalism's claims to truth (Zelizer 2004b). The 'epistemological uneasiness' identified separately by Zelizer, Durham and Stephen Ward (2020), is focusing attention on the concept of objectivity as an ideology of journalism. This should not be surprising because objectivity has been a contested area of journalism's philosophical cannon for most of the last 100 years (Schudson 2001; Ward 2004; Maras 2013; Wallace 2019). The late 20th century 'cultural turn' that made postmodern relativism hegemonic in media and cultural studies has further destabilised the epistemology and ontologies of journalism by calling into question 'the very notion of demonstrable broad-based truths' (Gade 2011, 75). Journalism scholars have noted this but have not been able to counteract it in any meaningful ways. We argue that this is because they—and the news media—are invested in the ideological belief that objectivity, as messy and difficult as it is, is still something worth pursuing and clinging too. There is a lot more to say about the problems of objectivity, and we will return to it soon in Chapter 16.

In the first section (Chapters 1–6) we laid out our explanation of a series of crises impacting journalism on a global scale. Two of those crises were immediate in the sense that they arose out of current conditions that did not previously exist—the COVID-19 pandemic and the local response to the extra-judicial killing of Black Americans at the hands of an institutionally racist police force. The first described crisis is obviously global; the second—coalesced into the slogan 'Black Lives Matter'—began in a series of local protests and quickly spread beyond the United States as oppressed communities of colour around the world, and their allies,

DOI: 10.4324/9780429242892-14

responded with their own similar stories. Within a matter of weeks, 'Black Lives Matter' became a global cause much like the 'Me Too' movement that generated worldwide reactions to revelations that women in the entertainment industry had suffered sexual assault at the hands of powerful men (Hillstrom 2019). The 'fake news' crisis had been simmering for some time (see Hirst 2011), but since 2016 it was given added impetus by President Donald Trump, who made it a constant refrain of his term in the White House. The second grouping of crises—of profitability, declining trust, and technological disruption—has deeper roots in the news industry. These crises have been active individually for a number of years, if not decades, and we attempted to show in our analysis how they are linked and mutually constitutive of each other. In this chapter, we see that each of these problems is also linked to the crisis in epistemology—a crisis that sits much deeper as an unresolved contradiction within journalism itself as both an institution and a social practice. We will show how this crisis in epistemology is manifest within journalists themselves and expressed by how they think. One glaring problem that speaks to the critical importance of the crisis of epistemology is the debate about 'objectivity'. Steven Maras (2013, 199–200) describes it as 'tensions around our historical conceptions' of objectivity, and 'changing paradigms'. Stephen Ward (2004, 161) questions traditional objectivity as 'an incorrect theory of journalistic inquiry, built upon an indefensible epistemology'. Maras does not raise epistemology directly, but he cites the work of Meenakshi Durham (1998, 117) on the need to re-invent journalistic epistemology as a way of resolving the 'hotly contested' notion of objectivity.

Journalism has perhaps always faced a crisis of epistemology, inherent in its internal relations which express the 'duality of the news commodity' (Hirst 2003). In a capitalist society, journalism is both a 'symbolic product' with ideological power, and a source of surplus value (Wayne 2003, 21). This contradiction is central to journalism and the cause of volatile ethical fault lines. It is a product of how journalism has developed historically and within a totality of social relations determined, in the last instance, by economic relations of production. The first grouping of crises explained in the first section (Chapters 1–6) is an expression of the crisis of epistemology. In the language of this chapter, the first group explains appearances, while the crisis of epistemology is a crisis of the 'internal determining relations', and 'the fundamental self-contradiction' or 'inner self-negation' (Pavlidis 2010, 86) of journalism as a way of thinking and a way of being (praxis). Our intention here is to explain this deeper, philosophical crisis using the explanatory tools of the dialectic and materialism. In doing this, we have to acknowledge the work of John Calhoun Merrill, who first introduced what he called 'the dialectic in journalism' to the scholarship of journalism studies in the 1970s and '80s.

There's a lot to absorb in this chapter, and we introduce some new terminology that may be unfamiliar. In this chapter and the next we will unpack our assertion about the form and development of crises within journalism and give you context for the new terminology—*internal relations, contradiction, totality, social relations, materialism, idealism, mutual constitution, relations of production, appearance, essence*, and *dialectic as method*. This last term refers to a method for thinking about journalism ethics and the process of change that occurs over time as ethical principles are developed, modified in practice, and discarded in favour of new ones. We argue that in order to fully understand this process we have to grasp the relationship between the social conditions in which journalists operate and journalism is practised, and the ideas and ideals which motivate and form our thinking about ethics.

Historically, argues Stephen Ward (2020, 1), the journalist's ideals of truth and objectivity were based on 'long-standing common sense realism', and epistemology that 'exuded confidence in the power of journalistic observation…[and] in psychological dualism' the separation of facts from opinions or 'values'. These ideals are under strain, Ward says, but worth defending. 'To deny truth and objectivity undercuts every attempt to assert a proposition, including the proposition that there is no truth or objectivity' (Ward 2020, 2). The 'real issue', Ward writes, is not that truth and objectivity are invalid as 'general notions'; rather it is to 'properly understand and improve' these ideas and 'how to apply them in practice' (ibid.). This is right, but not for the reasons Ward puts forward.

From epistemology to ontology

> The single biggest challenge facing Western journalism today, and especially American journalism, is not economic or political, it is ontological.
>
> (Ryfe 2019, 206)

If we are right that the journalistic method—its epistemology—is flawed, then it stands to reason that the knowledge produced using this flawed method must also be, at least in part, wrong as well. Thus, we arrive at the second philosophical problem within journalism: a mistaken ontology. An ontology is a basic theory about the fundamental nature of the world and how that world functions (Mussachia 1977, 257). Ontology is 'the study of what there is'; it is also a theory about how to settle 'questions about what there is in general', which takes us into the area of both objective reality and beliefs about that reality (Hofweber 2020). So the ontology of journalism, according to David Ryfe (2019, 206), is 'the question of what journalism is, and is for, and how it is to be distinguished from an array of other news'.

Former editor of *The Guardian*, Alan Rusbridger (2020a, x), comments that the once-reliable 'official script' of mainstream journalism is no longer working, and the news industry is 'more fragile than ever'. It shouldn't come as too much of a surprise, given what we've written about the various crises currently impacting on journalism, that there is angst, debate, and some confusion about what journalism even stands for today. David Ryfe is right to point to economic problems as one cause of the ontological crisis: good 'explanatory' journalism is expensive to produce and this difficulty is compounded when the business models are failing. This, says Ryfe (2019, 207), means the purpose that journalism has held for itself for the past century—essentially its Fourth Estate role—is no longer viable. He then asks the million-dollar question: If the Fourth Estate model is dysfunctional, 'then what other options are left?' Ryfe suggests that journalism might adopt an affirmative role, 'to affirm the norms, values and beliefs of the communities it serves' (2019, 207). But what if those norms, values, and beliefs are holding that community back? Isn't the role of journalism in that case to challenge rather than affirm these things? After critiquing this option—'it may more often lead journalists to sanction a community's prejudices' (ibid.)—Ryfe falls back on what he calls 'a thinner, but perhaps more realistic, conception…the practice of *reporting* the news' (Ryfe 2019, 208, emphasis in original). This strikes us as a form of surrender and Ryfe perhaps sees it that way himself: 'If journalism is merely what journalists do, then the field cannot be defined by a broader public service mission' (ibid., 209). The pessimism of Ryfe's conclusion is stunning: 'There is one more possibility, or course. It is that journalism loses cohesion…There is nothing natural or inevitable about its existence, and perhaps its time has passed.' The ontological crisis is, Ryfe concludes 'journalism's greatest challenge' (ibid.).

Ryfe's brief article, published in *Journalism*, is itself a good example of both the ontological and the epistemological problems. Ryfe cannot see a way out of the ontological impasse because he does not have the epistemology to see past the formal logic of appearances and so he is left oscillating between contradictions he can't even fathom. He is blind to the inner relations of journalism that create the crises in the first place. A second attempt to grapple with the issue of journalism's fractured ontology brings us back to a discussion of technological determinism and the role of non-human 'actants'[artificial intelligences] in the production of news such that 'the very definition of journalism needs to be reconsidered.' According to Primo and Zago (2015, 39), 'such an ontological turn certainly has important epistemological consequences' too. The determinism in this view is explicit in the link the authors make between the history of journalism and the history of technology. They argue that technology has been the developmental force that drives change in journalism: 'The history of journalism is tied to the evolution of technology,' such that 'technologies are inherent in journalism' (ibid., 40). As we argued in Chapter 4, technology is important, but it is not the dominant or determinant factor in the history of journalism. It can only ever be deployed within social relations and according to particular determinations of economic relations expressed in the commodity form of news. Therefore, we reject the central premise in Primo and Zago's paper that technology 'also *does* journalism' (ibid., emphasis in original). This is problematic from our materialist standpoint and the duality of the news commodity. From our perspective, any suggestion that a machine can produce journalism that has exchange value—a value that accrues to the capitalist in terms of profit—is deeply flawed. Machines themselves only contain the value of the labour that went into their production and it is only human labour—exploited as a commodity—that can produce a surplus for the capitalist to appropriate. As the Marxist economist Ernest Mandel notes, machines can increase the productivity of labour, but new value can only be produced by living labour (Mandel 1990). Second, there is an objection based on the human essence of news. A robot may well be able to compile sports results or tabulate numbers on a stock exchange index, but would you really trust a machine to understand and sympathetically report on the Black Lives Matter movement or Trump's attempted insurrection in January 2021?

From this, we can see that the ontological distortion which takes hold in Primo and Zago's thinking is evident in the formulation 'journalism is not made of a social substance, nor is it fundamentally a human process…A news story is not solely the result of social forces,' the machine becomes an 'actor' in the news process (Primo and Zago 2015, 42). In their discussion of these issues, Primo and Zago call for 'significant epistemological revisions' with repercussions for 'ethics, ideology and value judgment' in journalism. The 'ontological mistake' they argue is to believe that 'journalism is a practice restricted to humans' (ibid., 46). The extension of this argument is that the assumed epistemology of journalism is directly 'challenged by the ontological premises discussed in this paper,' 'we may conclude that nothing can be said to be journalism in itself' (ibid., 48). We agree that Primo and Zago have identified the right problem, but we think the answers lie a long way from their machines and algorithms. In our view, a journalist is an embodied 'social relation,' 'not a thing, a technical entity' (MIR Chile 1971, 133). The doing of journalism takes place within a complex matrix of social relations that connect the journalist to commodity production, to the ideological structures of meaning that create and maintain class rule, to the State, and to the subaltern social groups: 'the journalist becomes a link, a communicating vessel, a distributor of bourgeois knowledge and ideology' (ibid.). This is not a role that AI can currently play.

Alex Primo and Gabriela Zago certainly present a challenging view that does send shockwaves through the normative ontologies and epistemologies of journalism theory and practice, but by redefining human-centred journalism out of the picture in favour of some sort of human–machine hybrid network they reduce the whole social object and social nature of news to algorithmic rigidity. An entire issue of the journal *Journalism* was devoted to this topic in 2015 with a focus on 'materiality', which looks to study objects used in the production of journalism (Anderson and De Maeyer 2015). The approach of several authors in this special edition is to elevate objects (particularly software and AI) to a determining role in 'journalistic practices' (Rodgers 2015, 23). Far from tackling the problems of epistemology and ontology, this approach elevates the fetishism of commodities to the level of theoretical insight. In the end, this is an attempt to solve philosophical issues by crude mechanistic methods and by redefining the essential social and human element out of the news production process. This becomes another undialectical and one-sided solution that cannot ultimately resolve the contradictions in the social relations of journalistic practice. One note of caution in the special edition of *Journalism* is raised by veteran theorist Michael Schudson (2015, 64): 'I worry only that this theory like any approach…needs to work hard not to become untweakable itself…but it should do that without fetishizing itself.'

The advocates of materiality and technological determinism are not alone in attempting to produce a new machine-readable ontology for journalism. The search for suitable tools began in 2004, via a project called NEWS funded by the European Union (EU). NEWS stands for News Engine Web Services to help news consumers (clients of NEWS) by using semantic web functionality to choose content to push to them. The linguistic framework to be embedded in the News Engine algorithms is what the researchers on this project are referring to as an ontology. It is essentially the coding that allows the machine to make some sense of what it is processing and then decide what to do with it (Fernandez-Garcia and Sanchez-Fernandez 2004). AI-produced journalism is a current fad for the technophiles, but there is a serious side to such innovation. As machines replace human labour in the newsroom, more journalistic output can be achieved with fewer workers involved (Liu and 36Kr 2020). Capitalism has always sought to intensify the rate of exploitation through the application of technology to the production process; there is no reason to think such measures are not being applied in the news industry. The fruits of this work are now well embedded in the artificial intelligences that power so-called 'robot journalism' discussed in Chapter 4, the purpose of which is as much economic as it is technological. The key conclusion from this discussion is that 'materiality' is not the same theoretical approach as 'materialism' although Rachel Moran and Nikki Usher (2020; see also Usher 2018) make a half-hearted attempt to reconcile them. Materialism—coupled with dialectical thinking—emphasises the materiality of social relations rather than fetishizing technological objects which are themselves capital goods used up in the production process. Unlike materiality's focus on objects, materialism takes as its starting point the productive forces and relations of production that form the economic base of society out of which 'all political and ideological phenomena of intellectual life' are generated (Pannekoek 1942). This is why the study of journalism ethics must also include a study of the political economy of journalism. We will return to the issue of materiality versus materialism in Chapter 15.

Reification and ideology in the epistemology of journalism

The reason why Primo and Zago make fundamental epistemological and ontological mistakes in elevating machine-made journalism and downplaying the social relations of news is the same mistake made by the scholars mentioned earlier who recognise the breakdown of orthodoxy but cannot resolve it. Their error is the product of idealistic and undialectical thinking. The physical, or surface properties, that are first observed are mistaken for the essential, but partially hidden, social forces that create the contradictions. Schudson and Ward see the problem of objectivity as a problem of journalistic thinking about the world, rather than as a fault line embedded in the very social relations of news production. For them, and for most journalism scholars, the solution is to develop a new theory, rather than address the actual relations of production. This is the essence of 'conceptual idealism'; the idea that our thinking about the world exists independently of our social place in the world, and independently of our relationships with objects: 'objects conform to the understanding and not the understanding to the objects', and 'reality is a creation of thought' (Ruben 1979, 59, 68). Ruben notes that idealism 'limits knowledge to the world as it appears and never as it is' (ibid., 97).

We can name the process of mistaking the surface appearance of a thing or phenomenon for its essence as *reification*. What we mean by this is that every aspect of an object or social relationship comes to be represented in our thinking by the purely physical properties that our senses pick up. When we use this type of reified thinking, we lose sight of the contradictory internal relations that hold a thing or phenomenon together, and the object or relationship appears to be static, natural and inevitable (Burris 1988), rather than an amalgamation of dialectical tensions that are in constant flux and motion. Reification is itself a dialectical concept that helps to explain the power of ideology (in the sense of 'false consciousness[1]') as the contradiction between 'objective social relations and the subjective apprehension of those relations—in a society dominated by commodity production' (Burris 1988, 23). That last point about a society dominated by commodity production is useful in understanding reification because in materialism the most obvious form of inverted thinking occurs around what Karl Marx called the fetishism of commodities, or more commonly 'commodity fetishism'. This is the process caused when 'the market interposes itself' in relationships between people, such that 'human and class relations appear as relations between…inanimate…commodities' (Rees 1998, 94). The 'marketplace of ideas' is a form of commodity fetishism specific to the communication industries in general and to journalism in particular:

> In the marketplace, the products of labour meet and exchange according to unconscious market forces beyond human control. The actual relations between people—the social dependencies between producers in a complex society—are obscured behind the relations of things, which are apparently autonomous…[and] the exploitative wage relation between labour and capital appears as a fair deal between equal parties.
>
> (Gartman 1986, 168)

The 'marketplace of ideas' uses this form—explicit in supermarkets, shopping malls, and car dealerships—extrapolated into the realm of cultural production, or the production of meaning and ideas. According to the Hungarian Marxist Georg Lukács, modern bourgeois literature and philosophy are attempts to solve the problem of reification at the level of ideas (cited in Gartman 1986, 168). Knowing this helps to situate the work of John Merrill and Jack Odell when they write about philosophy and journalism or the application of Hegel's dialectic to a study of journalism practice. John Merrill, in particular, tries hard to persuade readers of *The Dialectic in Journalism* that the alienation of journalists from philosophical thinking can be resolved—in terms of his triadic formulation *thesis, antithesis, synthesis*—through the application of what he calls 'responsible use of press freedom': 'only when the journalist realizes that both freedom and responsibility are equally necessary for authentic journalism will journalism reach a maturity that will be satisfying to everyone concerned' (Merrill 1989, 243). Unfortunately, and despite his best efforts, Merrill ultimately falls into the trap of reification himself by uncritically accepting the 'marketplace of ideas' formulation. This makes him incapable of fully grasping the importance of a political economy method that digs beneath the superficial appearance of a smoothly functioning marketplace, to fully understand the dialectic of contradictory internal relations that bind journalism and the news industry to capitalism and therefore to reproducing the class relations, inequalities, exploitation, and alienation that are roiling away just below a seemingly calm surface.

Thinking about contemporary journalism

John Merrill has a few things to say about the dismissive attitude that journalists and journalism scholars can sometimes display towards esoteric subjects like theory and philosophy. One aspect of Merrill's writing that we admire is his willingness to make a strong and compelling argument that there is actually a philosophy of journalism and that it is a living, changing thing, not some timeless prescription written on tablets of stone or a yellowing sheet of paper. 'Too often,' Merrill declares 'scholars and practitioners' display an 'anti-dialectical propensity' under the 'gravitational pull of either-or thinking' (Merrill 1989, 9). This is a serious charge that is perhaps still relevant today. A search of journal databases produced a handful of reviews of Merrill's book in the media and communication journals and one review of an earlier iteration of our own work on journalism ethics that was encouragingly honest (Thomas 2014). We found one article about journalism with the word 'dialectics' in the title, but it did not appear anywhere in the author's keywords, or in the body of the essay (Slot 2018). A second article with the promising title 'Professional confidence and situational ethics: Assessing the social-professional dialectic in journalistic ethics decisions' (Berkowitz and Limor 2003) used the word 'dialectic' three times in the body, but each mention was of the contradiction between 'professional ideals' and the 'profit motive', and the 'journalism–business' dialectic. This is similar to our conceptualisation of the duality of the news commodity as the source of many ethical fault lines. We agree that this is an important antinome in journalism, perhaps the most important, but Berkowitz and Limor did not explain or theorise this idea in any meaningful way. Berkowitz used the same formulation in a 1993 journal article about work roles and news selection techniques in local television which reveal 'the tension between business imperatives and journalistic ideals' (Berkowitz 1993, 67). While it is useful for Berkowitz to empirically demonstrate the existence of this antinome, there is little attempt in his article to approach the problem with dialectical thinking. Our search did uncover a book chapter published in 2019 with the title 'Power, place and the spatial dialectic of digital journalism' (Hess and Gutsche 2019). Disappointingly, though, there was no discussion of the dialectic in the body of the essay. The only mention of the term 'spatial dialectic' was in the third paragraph to define it in relation to the work of another scholar. This reference also reinterpreted the idea of the dialectic to strip it of the meaning ascribed to it by Hegel and other dialectical thinkers.

However, our search was not entirely in vain. In his 2016 book *Journalism and the Philosophy of Truth*, Jesse Hearns-Branaman takes up a useful argument about the 'relational dialectic' between 'realism' and 'pragmatism' in the formulation of a journalist's heuristic vision, or worldview. The author's dialectical thinking is evident in the way he uses the terminology and his understanding that the dialectic is an 'unresolvable' but 'productive' tension between thesis and antithesis—in this case realism and pragmatism (Hearns-Branaman 2016a). We also found an interesting article on fake news in the *Journal of American Folkore* that discussed the issue of President Trump always claiming he was 'only joking' when some of his more confounding statements were questioned by invoking 'the dialectics of humour'. This is an excellent use of the concept to critique the 'only joking' claim which 'cannot be dismissed outright, but it cannot be taken at face value either,' creating 'endless uncertainty' and allowing the President's proxies to accuse those who are not laughing of lacking a sense of humour, while using the laughter of Trump's supporters to create 'a feeling of solidarity' and cement their loyalty to him (Marsh 2018).

It is interesting to see the dialectic deployed this way in relation to journalism, but from outside the academic field of journalism studies. However, it is not uncommon for this to be the case. In more critically focused communication studies, the use of dialectical reasoning as a lens for examining various media practices is more established. Importantly, critical scholarship in the political economy of communication acknowledges the importance of the dialectic in its material circumstances. The Marxist communications scholar Dana Cloud (2006, 53) has noted that 'dialectics poses something of a problem for communication scholars', and she's right. It is problematic for communications scholars because they have neglected it for too long. Our aim in the next chapter is to reintroduce a dialectical approach to the study of journalism and ethics, starting with a review of John Merrill's work in this area from the 1980s.

Questions for discussion

1　Have you ever considered journalism and philosophy together?
2　Combining theory and practice is known as *praxis*. Do you think praxis is important for journalists today?
3　What do you think now of concepts such as epistemology, ontology, and ideology?
4　How can journalism begin repairing its problems of epistemology and ontology?

Note

1 In materialist theory 'ideology' has several meanings (See Eagleton 2007), several of which are relevant to this book. Here we are using 'ideology' to mean the mental map or worldview that all of us have that helps to (at least partially) explain the world around us. 'Common sense' as we use it in Chapter 17 is a form of ideology in this sense.

14 (Re)introducing the dialectic

Hegel and Merrill

The dialectic in journalism—a forgotten hero

> No condition in journalism is permanent. At every stage of journalistic practice and conceptual concern a contradiction arises, and this clash of opposites results in a new synthesis or moderated idea or state.
>
> (Merrill 1989, 7)

The late American journalism scholar John C. Merrill applied a form of the idealist Hegelian dialectic to his own study of journalists and ethics. We think that Merrill's work deserves more attention and recognition than it generally gets in contemporary journalism studies and we hope to rescue it from neglect. Merrill introduced the Hegelian concept of a 'dialectic' into journalism studies in the 1970s, but it has not been widely adopted. It is time for Merrill's work to be 'rediscovered' and updated for the 21st century. The concept of the dialectic—the interplay of opposing, but mutually constitutive social forces that shape society and govern how societies and economies are structured, change, and evolve—was first argued by Socrates, but really came into modern philosophy via Georg Hegel and, later, Karl Marx (Rees 1998). This chapter builds on the work of Merrill and offers a critical appraisal of how new dialectics shape journalism and the news industry today. Merrill (1989, 4–5) summarises the workings of the dialectic in four short words: 'Paradoxes abound in journalism.' He continues, '[C]onflicts and disagreements are healthy, not unhealthy.' The dialectic is a concept almost as old as philosophy itself and we usually link it to the sixth century BC Greek thinker, Heraclitus, whose work we really only know from a few preserved fragments. Heraclitus began with the idea of flux—that is, nature is in a constant state of change—and it is summarised in his apocryphal observation that we never step into the same river twice. This is a simple statement but obviously true: as the water flows past us we step into it as it's moving and so each step is in a 'new' river. When Merrill applies this concept to journalism, he is acknowledging something as equally simple as it is profound: 'Flux is king in journalism. Dynamic thinking and dialogue is essential to journalistic progress' (Merrill 1989, 8). The dynamic thinking Merrill refers to here is the other aspect of dialectic that we need to

DOI: 10.4324/9780429242892-15

consider and that is a method of thinking dialectically, or for shorthand purposes *dialectics*, which we can express as a logical way of thinking about movement towards change in both nature and in society.

What is the dialectic?

The dialectic has its origins in ancient Greek philosophy. It is a term developed from the Greek *dialektike* and *dialektos*—which translate as conversation, discourse, and the art of debate (Kovel 1998, 475). The dialectical method involves acknowledging the interrelated nature of the physical and social worlds as a 'totality in a constant process of change' (Rees 1998, 42). The essence of the dialectic as method is not simply restating it as a series of mechanical laws that govern how social formations develop, regress, and change. Rather, an understanding of dialectical thinking 'rests on a profound enough grasp' of all the laws of natural and social life to be able to 'put them to work, and the willingness to try working with them'. The value of the dialectical method is 'the heightened ability to deal with reality' (Finkelstein 1967, 64), to subjectively act to change the objective world, rather than simply reflect it back with sociological accuracy. To be effective, dialectical methods of thinking should be applied to concrete problems that objectively exist outside of consciousness (subjectivity). The foundation of the dialectical method must be 'the reality it analyses', documented 'from actual economic life and history' (Finkelstein 1967, 64).

Dialectical thinking is a method for describing and analysing the world through observing how the potential for change—paradox, flux, and flow—is already present as a set of internal contradictions within objects, events, and relationships in their history, their present, and their future development (Pavlidis 2010, 75). Dialectical thinking begins with the surface appearance of an object, event or relationship but then proceeds to study its *essence*, 'the essential relations governing it' and then reconsiders and interprets appearance 'based on the knowledge of the essence', revealing the 'internal dialectical relations' that set it in motion (and hold it in place) (Pavlidis 2010, 88). This inherent set of contradictions—the *internal relations* of a thing, or event—is often described as a 'unity of opposites' in that the tension of the contradiction not only has the potential to change something, but it is also what holds it together: 'Dialectics explains the genesis of movement and development by the struggle between internal opposites proper to all things and phenomena' (Schaff 1960, 241). At the core of a dialectical process of development and change is its dynamism and continuous movement. The dialectic is also a method for studying and analysing the world: '[D]ialectics is the study of things which are in a constant state of change' (Thatcher 1991, 129). The Marxist theoretician, Bertell Ollman (2003a) describes 'the subject of dialectics' as 'change, all change, and interaction, all kinds and degrees of interaction'. This means that we have to subject the idea of the dialectic itself to the scrutiny of observing it as a thing that is in a constant state of change throughout the history of thought. Dialectical thinking is based on the fundamental assumption that nothing is eternally fixed or outside history, and therefore there is a perpetual state of movement and flux in the world: '[D]ialectical analysis proceeds from the assumption that everything in life is in constant motion, that everything is inter-related rather than rigidly schematic and systemic' (Landy 1986, 53).

The dialectic situates the world in its natural and social totality and in a state of flux. In this state, the action of one element will likely impact on another creating a series of small, *quantitative*, changes that, over time, establish the potential for more significant *qualitative* change. When applied to the history and development of human society, a materialist dialectical 'tries to account for the structure as well as the dynamics of the entire social system, including both its origins and likely future' (Ollman 2003a, 10). Ollman continues to define dialectics by both what it is not: 'an all-purpose explanation', or 'formula' and what it is: 'a way of thinking that brings into focus the full range of changes and interactions that occur in the world' (ibid., 12) and also recognising that 'reality is more than appearances' (ibid., 13). Dialectics asks us to think about the world in terms of objects, processes, and relationships that exist in a totality with connections extending everywhere. More often than not, dialectical relationships and connections involve a contradiction, a sort of negative relationship that is itself overcome (negated) through the process of resolution. However, the dialectical process is not linear or sequential; instead, everything carries its own contradiction as part of being what it is. The 19th-century philosopher who first developed a systematic approach to the dialectic was Georg Hegel, and his term for the idea of internal contradiction was the *negation of the negation*, or the *unity of opposites* which he characterised as 'an internally contradictory totality in a constant process of change' where the parts of the whole (the totality) 'mutually condition, or *mediate*, each other' (Rees 1998, 7). Hegel is less popular than he perhaps should be in philosophical circles but his contribution to understanding how and why ethical imperatives change in response to changes in the social world should not be underestimated.

The double motion of the dialectic is derived in translation from Hegel's German in which the word *aufhebung* (sometimes *aufheben*) contains the double meaning of both preserving (being) and removing (non-being) at the same time. Deepa Kumar (2006, 76) explains that Hegel's term 'incorporates both aspects of being and nothing…and invokes motion'. The English word *sublation* is often used in this context to mean the partial transformation and preservation of the two sides of the dialectical relationship (Bhaskar 1993, 12). The new phenomenon emerges from the dialectical clash of opposites, and the new entity contains them (in a new form) at the same time as it negates (overcomes) the earlier forms (Maybee 2016). This process can be understood simply in this more straightforward explanation: 'Every object develops through the interaction of two opposing forces, whose conflict is resolved by their synthesis in a new object on a higher plane' (Fremlin 1938). Thus, the dialectic is not just a method of analysis—though it is that—it is also an organising principle for the social world:

It is important to remember that even for Hegel the dialectic was not a method that one simply applied to phenomena. Things in themselves are dialectical. Therefore, dialectical thinking simply requires seeing things as they are...not only to see them in terms of established fact, but rather, to see them in terms of their unactualized potential.

(Farr 2008)

This passage brings us to a further point of departure; 'things in themselves are dialectical' and we must see things 'as they are'. In other words, we must look at the actual, physical world to understand how the dialectic works in action and we must put human beings into the world to understand the historical process of 'subjects acting on and transforming the world' (Fracchia 1999, 171). This dialectic involves the following elements: scientific determinism (thesis)— human choice (antithesis)—recognising that choice is limited by the basic laws of nature (synthesis). Humans become free through 'uncovering an understanding the laws of nature, society and thought' (Novack 1980).

What's important for the material form of the dialectic, as Bool Chand reminds us, is 'the basic stuff of the universe is matter...an objective reality existing outside of and independent of the mind...matter is primary, since it is the source of sensations and ideas, while the mind is secondary, being itself a reflection of matter' (Chand 1944, 15). As George Novack (1980) writes, 'the rationality of nature and human history is bound up with matter in motion'; it is the dialectic in nature that sets matter in motion, creating 'cause and effect'. However, we cannot leave it there because to do so leaves us once again in a non-dialectical bind. The material world is important and exists outside of our mental construction of it, but at the same time, our consciousness is more than a reflection of matter. Human consciousness grows out of the material world, but it is not just a reflection of it. It is *consciousness*—our subjective thoughts about the material world—that allows us to act within the world and to act upon it, and in fact, to change it.

To put this another way, which relates the concept more directly with a discussion of journalism ethics: human subjectivity (our consciousness) is the product of our physical interaction with material nature (the objective world). Nature exists outside of our consciousness of it, but it is only through consciousness (subjective thought) that humans can understand the world and effect change within it. Only 'verified scientific knowledge' provides us with the tools to 'control and change the world around us' (Novack 1980). All of us can only act in accordance with the conditions of our lives, we cannot shrug off the cause-and-effect relationship that exists between subjectivity and objectivity.

The constant movement forward in nature and in society ensures that there is both continuity (things that stay close to their original form) and change (the appearance of new things or ideas). The element that draws together continuity and change is the contradiction. Dialectics takes as its starting point the state of flux that nature embodies. Following the work of Hegel, Frederick Engels articulated the dialectic of nature and showed how it operates according to three 'laws':

- the law of the transformation of quantity into quality and *vice versa*
- the law of the interpenetration of opposites, and
- the law of the negation of the negation.

The first of these laws is simply explained by considering that all objects on the earth—including the very planet itself—are made up of atoms, which join together to form molecules, which then aggregate further into animate and inanimate objects; into living beings, into plants, and into the various elements and compounds that make up rocks, soil, and all of matter. There is a qualitative difference that occurs in nature—the product of Heraclitus' process of flux—which is at the same time both random and purposeful. As Engels noted in his classic work *Dialectics of Nature*: 'All qualitative differences in nature rest on differences of chemical composition or on different quantities or forms of motion (energy) or, as is almost always the case, on both' (Engels 1883). The concept of precarious balance is important in understanding this first dynamic law of the dialectic. The totality of the object is held in place when the opposing forces or elements that constitute it are in balance but it is a state always in prospect of immanent collapse. For example, ice remains a solid if the atmospheric temperature around it remains at or below freezing point. When the surrounding air begins to warm up—say, when the sun hits frost on the grass—the ice will melt. Similarly, when water is heated, the equilibrium between it and the surrounding atmosphere is altered. The water boils and heated steam rises from the surface; if this heated steam comes into contact with a much cooler surface it will condense back into its liquid form. Hegel applied this logic to his analysis of European society around the time of the French revolution and the rise and the fall of Napoleon. He observed first-hand how the pressures released by the French revolution and Napoleon's attempt to conquer the rest of continental Europe destroyed the equilibrium of social power in the more feudal and backward provinces of Germany. This was one aspect of the dialectic in operation by which 'gradual changes in the balance between opposed elements suddenly results in a rapid and complete change in the nature of the situation' (Rees 1998, 9).

Engels second law, 'the interpenetration of opposites', sounds difficult, but it can be stated more succinctly as: *objects or ideas that appear to be total opposites of each other are actually connected in a way that makes them dependent on, and able to modify, each other.* Hegel described this law as 'the unity of opposites' where one element is reliant on another for its stability, but this reliance is also an antagonistic relationship that creates an internal contradiction. Hegel's famous example from *The Science of Logic* (1811) is the paradox of being and nothingness (non-being). Hegel establishes a thesis (being) and an antithesis (non-being) and asks us to consider them in isolation. He then argues that thinking of *being* and *non-being* in isolation from each other is impossible because each contains the idea of the other. In other words, being can only exist in relation to nothingness (non-being), and non-being can only exist in relation to existence itself (being). Hegel's synthesis is the idea of becoming—that is, everything is in the process of becoming nothingness and non-being is always in the process of becoming something. We call a thing in the process of becoming *immanent* to place it at a moment in time; a moment which is, itself, 'an endless activity of becoming and producing' (Hegel 1811, cited in Gottfried 1980, 424). As Engels and other Marxists have explained this idea, it translates into the notion that change is brought about when contradictions cause a substantial conflict that needs to be resolved. Translated into social life, this suggests that contradictions exist in any society—most emphatically between those with economic or political power, and those without—and it is the resolution of such conflicts that brings about social change (Pickard 2006).

This leads us to the third law of dialectics, the 'negation of the negation', which also relies on *thesis, antithesis*, and *synthesis*. Thesis is the first idea or thing; its antithesis is its intellectual or physical opposite that is in contradiction with the first, and the synthesis is the creation of a new idea or thing based on the resolution of the contradiction between the first two elements. The essential feature of this third law is that it is not simply the destruction of the old; it is also a positive form of motion towards something qualitatively new (Boger 1991). The negation of the negation leads to 'new and distinct situations' developing 'from contradictory circumstances', but in such a way that 'aspects of the old circumstances appear, transformed, as part of the new conditions' (Rees 1998, 9).

Internal contradiction is the fundamental cause of development and change; this is the 'movement of opposites' (Mussachia 1977, 258). The essence of a thing can only be known by understanding its contradictory internal relations. One of the internal contradictions will be determinant, but also subject to the mutual constitution of all internal relations (ibid.). Generally speaking, the two sides of a contradiction are not in equilibrium; one aspect is dominant. The sides of a contradiction can only exist as a condition of each other's continued existence, the 'unity of opposites'. Under the right conditions, the contradictory aspects of a thing can transform into their opposite. The resolution of contradiction occurs in a new unity but with its own contradictory internal relations 'at a higher level', 'thesis-antithesis-synthesis, also the 'negation of the negation' (Mussachia 1977, 259; see also Schmitt 1988, 443–5). The logic of dialectics describes the motion inherent in apparent stability and also negates the thesis of analytical philosophy based on the formal logic of non-contradiction and external relation (cause and effect). Analytical philosophy posits that each thing is essentially unique and independent of every other thing; by contrast, in a dialectical world, everything can only exist in relation to other things in a state of 'interaction, motion and change [and] are not merely self-subsistent' (Sayers 1984, 142). As Sean Sayers points out, the ontology of dialectics does not deny the reality of distinctions, but rather suggests that these distinct aspects are the result of internal and contradictory relations that bind things to each other. He uses an example from the sphere of production to illustrate this: a machine stands independently on the floor of a factory and appears to be a thing in and of itself. However, this appearance conceals the fact that the machine has been produced somewhere else and therefore embodies the labour of the people who put it together and the expenditure of capital used up in its construction. Thus, one inner relation of this machine is the store of value it represents. The machine is also a force in the production process (another of its hidden inner relations) only when it is put into motion in the factory by workers commanded to do so by their employer—who is also the capitalist owner of the machine. In order for this to happen, the machine is set within a series of social relations that include capital and labour bound together by class relations and that foreshadow the using up of stored value and the production of new value. If the machine is removed from these social relations (its history and its future potentialities), then it is 'no longer…a productive force, but merely in its abstract material aspect…a physical object'. In other words, a machine is *only* a machine 'as an instrument of social production, as a productive force [and]…only in certain relations of production' (Sayers 1984, 145). Formal logic is blind to this aspect because it assumes the machine is totally represented by its appearance in and of itself.

More importantly, this ontology comes into play when applied to the study of human society at various levels of generalisation, all the way from a consideration of the species, down to the unique daily activities of an individual (Ollman 2003a, 59–172). So far, we have not looked closely at the concept of *generality*, but it is a reference to the materialist schema for examining particular aspects of the human condition. It is worthwhile outlining its salient features at this point because it usefully references another epistemological error in the journalistic method. The levels of generality move from 1 through to 7 with 1 being the most specific and 7 being the broadest. Bertel Ollman sets out the following 'levels' of generality from the most specific to the broadest:

Level 1: '[W]hatever is unique about a person and a situation.' At this level, Ollman writes, 'the here and now, or however long what is unique lasts, is brought into focus' (Ollman 2003c, 88)

Level 2: '[W]hat is general to people, their activities and products because they exist and function within modern capitalism, understood as the last twenty to fifty years' (ibid.)

Level 3: 'Capitalism as such constitutes level three' (ibid.). This level of generality is where Marx' analysis of abstract production relations occurs 'anywhere that these relations obtain and [constituting] the entire four hundred or so years of the capitalist era' (ibid., 89).

Level 4: Class society, 'the period of human history during which societies have been divided up into classes base[d] on the division of labour' between an exploiting and an exploited class (ibid.).

Level 5: The 'human condition', 'all human beings and the entire history of the species' (ibid.).

Level 6: The animal kingdom and humans' relationship to other creatures. (ibid.).
Level 7: This is the most abstract and encompasses all that we know and don't know about nature itself, including qualities such as mass, movement, chemical composition, etc. (ibid.).

The final observation we need to make about dialectics in general is that contradictions and conflict in nature, and in journalism, are fixed at moments in time. In other words, they are historically contingent. This does not mean that they can be instantly resolved at the time they first arise. In nature it can take generations before a new genome (a synthesis of interaction in existing genomes) can express itself. The same is true in the social world; a contradiction (thesis—antithesis couplet) can take decades to reach resolution or synthesis. In terms of revolutionary change—such as the transition from Feudalism to Capitalism— resolution can take centuries of incremental dialectical clashes. Applying these dialectical processes—albeit in Hegel's idealistic fashion—to the practice of journalism is the basis John Merrill's enduring contribution to the scholarship of journalism ethics. For example, the interpenetration of opposites (sometimes referred to as the *unity of opposites*) is evident in this observation from Merrill:

> Absolutes and extremes are unproductive in journalism if they are honoured as static values. They must be looked upon as *means*—as instruments of opposition and friction—that lead to a new and better journalistic idea or essence.
>
> (Merrill 1989, 8 [emphasis in original])

At a glance we can easily relate this to the contemporary situation in journalism and the news industry where the process of digital disruption has exploded the old certainties of print and broadcast news and created something totally distinct—digital journalism. Digital journalism is a new form with its own appearance, but it contains within it all of the tensions left by the old contradictions, and it also contains new ones. For example, the interactions between journalists and audiences can be good, bad or awful and everyone is still figuring out how to make it work (Hirst 2018). The only new certainty is that we cannot undo the present to return to the past. We need to bear this in mind when discussing Merrill's contribution to our understanding of the dialectical processes at play in the development of journalism because the issues and problems he identified at the time of publication of *The Dialectic in Journalism* in 1989, are still playing out today. In other words, for many of the antinomes—the competing theses and antitheses Merrill identified as being in contradiction—the synthesis, or resolution, has not yet fully manifested. The dialectical fault lines that Merrill expressed as the contradiction between journalists' 'freedom' and journalistic 'responsibility' are still active, though in true dialectical fashion, they do not present today exactly as they did when Merrill was observing and writing about them.

Contradiction, dialectic, and change in journalism

The central concept in the philosophy of dialectics is the contradiction. We have already mentioned this as the idea of fault lines in journalism—the fissure or crack that results from unreconciled forces pushing and pulling against each other. Ethical issues often exist along these fault lines (Hirst and Patching 2005, 1). We have always considered the contradiction between the news industry's reliance on the profit motive and its purported adherence to reportage in the public interest as the central ethical fault line: 'The economic function of the news media tends to dominate, determine and undermine any democratic function of information delivery,' we wrote in the second edition of *Arguments and Cases* (Hirst and Patching 2007, 31). We expanded on this again in *Arguments and Cases for the Twenty-First Century* to examine the paradox (contradiction) inherent in journalistic thinking between the ethical values of neutrality, fairness or objectivity and journalists' self-identification with the ideological construct of the 'marketplace of ideas': 'Most journalists rarely challenge their deeply held assumptions about the nature of democracy and the market, or the social values associated with them,' we argued at the time (Patching and Hirst 2014, 44). In this chapter we want to expand our arguments about the importance of the dialectics that operate within journalism— what John C. Merrill (1989, 6) called the triadic movement of the contradictions in journalism from thesis—to antithesis—to synthesis through 'the logic of movement, of evolution, of change'.

Merrill himself seems to express a contradiction of internal opposites when he asserts that journalists have both an 'antidialectical propensity' (1989, 9) and also have dialectical instincts 'whether they realize it or not' (ibid., 10), and he's right. It is almost impossible not to think dialectically, even unconsciously, because our dialectical world demands it. The unresolved tension between these internal opposites is what holds together the current epistemological paradox that characterises journalistic thinking and practice. As Merrill notes, dialectical thinkers are likely to be 'more in tune with reality', but more often than not it is 'often overlooked or underemphasized' by journalists who are used to treating the world as a series of discrete objects, events, people, and thoughts. In this mistaken epistemology, the world is understood to be only a series of singular events and unconnected ideas, in which both cause and effect seem to be externally imposed rather than existing as internal relations of the objects, events, people, and thoughts themselves. This is why understanding the theory of internal relations is important to dialectical thinking. An example of internal relations in this sense is the idea—floated earlier—that the crisis of epistemology has always been a feature of journalism since at least the mid-seventeenth century. This problem is inherent in journalism. It is part of the internal relations that make up the essence, or true self of journalism. This contradiction will always find its expression in journalism, even if it is not always apparent to journalists or those who study it. The surface expression—the appearance—of this essential contradiction is evident in the many crises we've already discussed; but they are only expressions of the deeper essential crisis. The *essence* then can be defined as the sum of contradictory internal relations that make up the whole of something—whether an object, a relationship, or an idea (Ollman 2003a, 70); it is what gives the appearance of a thing its character; it 'brings into focus an extended set of internal relations' (ibid., 79). Thus, we can now begin to flesh out the crisis of epistemology by suggesting—in accordance with dialectical thinking—that journalism is too focused on appearances and fails to account for internal contradictions within 'the horizon marked off by our sense perceptions' so that 'what strikes us immediately gets taken as responsible for the more or less hidden processes that have given rise to it' (Ollman 2003a, 80).

The clash of antinomes in journalism

> The fundamental dialectical theme…is freedom and ethics in a critical tension that results in a higher synthesis—the ethical use of freedom.
>
> (Merrill 1989, 38)

In Merrill's application of the dialectic to a study of journalism and ethics, he identifies one key paradox as the defining contradiction generating friction and driving change: 'the thesis (freedom) is presently being attacked by the antithesis (social control)' creating a 'dialectical cauldron' from which 'a synthesis of social responsibility' is emerging. The synthesis for Merrill is always a middle way, a rebalancing of the dialectic tension. In this case, he sees the resolution (synthesis) of the clash between freedom and social control as 'a moderated and socially concerned use of journalistic freedom' (Merrill 1989, 7). However, we know that this synthesis will only become a new antinome—a thesis to be 'buffeted by new antithetical winds—either from the anarchistic direction or from the totalitarian direction' (ibid.). While Merrill was astute enough to know that the 'precise nature' of the new dialectic 'is impossible to foresee at this moment [1987]' perhaps we see it more clearly today as the rise of what we broadly term citizen journalism on one hand and concerted attacks on press freedom by authoritarian populists on the other (Hirst 2018).

For John Merrill the dialectical struggle for synthesis occurs at the level of ideas, or perhaps journalistic ideology. The antinomes are described in idealist terms as freedom (thesis) and responsibility (antithesis) and the synthesis as a hybrid responsible exercise of individual (existential) freedom. In this schematic the resolution of the contradiction comes through 'seeking the middle ground' (Merrill 1989, 34). Merrill's idealistic and metaphysical formulation only sees the dialectic operating at the level of antinomies in thought; thus, resolution is also in the realm of thought. This resolution also results in a synthesis that is a balance between the two opposing thoughts. Thus, in Merrill's idealistic triad *freedom–responsibility–responsible exercise of freedom* nothing has fundamentally changed between the thesis and the antithesis; they are merely brought into harmony in the synthesis. However, this is a misunderstanding of how the dialectic actually operates in the real world. The resolution of a contradiction will not necessarily result in equilibrium. In fact, it rarely, if ever, actually does and this is because in the real world it is rare for two antinomes to share power equally. Instead, what tends to happen is that the synthesis will fall closer to whichever of the two antinomes exerts the stronger force on the contradiction. In Merrill's terms, authoritarian impulses today push the resolution of 'responsible freedom' towards more government control, not less. The resolution of a dialectical contradiction does not create equilibrium; it generates a new fault line in which the synthesis itself becomes a new antinome, a thesis in search of its antithesis. A new thesis is immanent with the inevitability of its impending clash with its opposite.

Merrill's individualism

A close reading of *The Dialectic in Journalism* reveals a great deal about John Merrill's own worldview and it shows him clearly caught up in the ideological belief system common to American scholars of his period. He has a very positive, normative and supportive view of journalism as practised in a 'free market' economy and a very negative view of its supposed antinome, 'collective' journalism as practised behind what was then the so-called 'Iron Curtain'. In this regard Merrill is no different from the mainstream of American communication scholarship that was born in the 1960s and continues today (if somewhat challenged by liberal critical studies). However, to his credit, Merrill (1989, 14) was also critical of American journalism 'adjusting itself to its capitalist context, wallowing in conformist muck and mire'. This was clearly frustrating for him; he had long held to strong libertarian beliefs and initially wrote a very one-sided polemic arguing for complete and unfettered individual freedom for journalists in his 1974 book, *The Imperative of Freedom*. For *The Dialectic in Journalism*, completed more than a decade later, Merrill chose to present, as he saw it, 'the entire dialectical process' and, while still politically libertarian in outlook, he also partially—and perhaps unwillingly—concedes that the so-called 'marketplace of ideas' (the Holy Grail of libertarian theory) perhaps does not function in the ideal way that theory suggests it should.

Merrill is right to draw our attention to the application of Hegelian dialectics to contemporary journalism, even if he is mistaken in some of the specifics and his prescriptive conclusions. Hegel's idealist and metaphysical exposition of the dialectic is limited by a circularity of thinking that cuts it off from the material reality of the physical world and the social role of humans within it, as John Rees explains in his book, *The Algebra of Revolution*:

> Contradictions in Hegel are merely intellectual contradictions to be resolved merely by intellectual methods. The real world exists only as a foil to intellectual development, the means by which intellectual thought is clarified to itself.

> (Rees 1998, 67)

In our view, this critique of Hegel can be applied to Merrill's work in which the central contradiction holding back the development of ethical practice in journalism is theorised as an intellectual stand-off between 'freedom' and 'responsibility'. The resolution of this dialectic is the practice of 'responsible freedom'. In true Hegelian fashion, Merrill believes that by merely thinking this through the contradiction is overcome and the middle ground—here a simple blending of responsibility and freedom—provides a stable foundation for the change he is advocating. Unfortunately, it's not that simple. History shows us, time and time again, that reality is messy, that inequalities in wealth, position, and distribution of power and the existence of commercial competition within the capitalist system will confound even the most rational of intellectual arguments if material conditions are not accounted for.

Marx and Engels were critical of Hegel while, at the same time, recognising his important and original contribution to the theory of dialectics. The dialectic of Hegel is idealist because it follows the general thesis laid down by the Greek philosopher Heraclitus in the 6th century BC in which the essential element is 'essence'—the abstract ideal of an object or relationship. As Merrill writes of Hegel's formulation: 'ideas constituted the essence of all reality, and as ideas developed, the rest of reality was moved forward' (Merrill 1989, 8). This is an important point, as one of the most enduring debates in philosophy is between idealism and materialism. The idealist view of history is that shifting ground in the development of thought and knowledge is the 'ultimate cause of the historical movement of mankind (sic)' (Plekhanov 1899, 21). The materialist alternative is that human thinking 'is itself changed' by the process of history in response to the conditions of life (ibid., 31). Plekhanov continues on this point, concluding that, from a materialist perspective 'at the basis of these complex dialectics in mental phenomena lay facts of a social nature' (ibid., 33).

Despite its idealist limitations, for us Merrill's exposition of the dialectic in journalism is very useful because it shows clearly that there is a philosophy of journalism and that change occurs when opposing forces come into conflict as ethical antinomes. However, Merrill's theory is limited in that it applies the dialectic only to a clash of ideas and he is relatively silent on the impact of external forces on the 'spirit' of the dialectic. In the end, Merrill accepts as a social given that the marketplace of ideas will be the final arbiter in resolving contradictions. This is true in one sense, but not in the way that Merrill understands it. Merrill's theoretical understanding is bounded by his own libertarian ideology and his faith in market forces. We have to move beyond this in order to fully grasp how the dialectic works in the field of journalism. Merrill is critical of Marxist thinkers but what is remarkable is that Merrill takes the Hegelian dialectic as far as he does. John Merrill is unique among normative late 20th-century journalism scholars in that he takes 'capital T' Theory seriously and recognises the importance of a holistic theoretical framework to scaffold a discussion of journalism ethics. Merrill's work on the dialectic in journalism is sadly overlooked by most journalism scholarship today. We have some disagreements with Merrill, particularly the idea that the resolution of a dialectical contradiction is a compromise 'Golden Mean' where the two opposing ideas—in Merrill's Hegelian schema—find common ground. However, we also think his work on the application of dialectical thinking and the dialectic working within the practice and ethics of journalism is of profound importance. We appreciate Merrill's efforts to popularise the use of a dialectical method to develop his theoretical insights into journalism and ethics and we acknowledge the groundwork he's done in situating both journalism and journalism ethics within the broader field of philosophy.

In Merrill's Hegelian formulation of the dialectic in journalism, the key unit of analysis is the individual journalist, and the resolution of the contradictions—between freedom and responsibility, for example—happens at the individual level, through the 'moral progress of the journalist' which is motivated by 'the spirit of the dialectic' (Merrill 1989, 176). However, we are arguing that ethical dilemmas must be resolved at the collective level, which is only possible if we situate Merrill's dialectic within the theoretical paradigm of historical materialism that 'replaces philosophical sophistry and disputations around abstract concepts with the study of the real material world' (Pannekoek 1942). In the next chapter we complete our journey along the tributaries of the dialectic by moving from the metaphysical word of Hegel's 'spirit' to the material world of political economy.

Questions for discussion

1 Can you relate the idea of the dialectic to our simpler version of 'fault lines'?
2 Can you think of any contradictions in journalism that operate dialectically?
3 What is your understanding of idealism and materialism?
4 Discuss the idea of thesis—antithesis-synthesis. Can you locate this process at play in journalism today?

15 'Standing Merrill on his feet'
Journalism and materialism

The material dialectic

> The mystification which dialectic suffers in Hegel's hands, by no means prevents him from being the first to present its general form of working in a comprehensive and conscious manner. With him it is standing on its head. It must be turned right side up again, if you would discover the rational kernel within the mystical shell.
>
> (Marx 1873)

In the previous chapter we examined how John Merrill successfully used a metaphysical and idealist Hegelian dialectic to investigate the contradictions within the practice and philosophy of journalism. Our critique of Merrill mirrors Marx's critique of Hegel: we must stand Merrill back on his feet. In order to do this, we must situate the current turmoil evident in the field of journalism in a concrete social reality. That is to say we must study the crisis afflicting journalism not as an idea or simply a clash of principles (freedom versus responsibility, for example) but as a series of antinomes/contradictions mobilised within and by the system of news production itself (the internal material dynamics of the news industry). We also have to situate journalism within the contradictions and crises that animate the entire social system that is global capitalism. It is on this point that the materialist formulation of the dialectic diverges from the Hegelian or idealist view advocated by John Merrill. This means we must add to the dialectic the tools and methods of *materialism*. By materialism we do not mean the commonly held definition that invokes the idea of a person consumed by consumerism to the exclusion of all else; instead, we define materialism as a way of viewing the world in which the concrete, sensuous objectivity of the world exists *a priori*. In Marx's famous phrase, 'being determines consciousness' and it is our constant interaction with the material world that structures our thinking. A materialist analysis makes use of abstract concepts but it recognises that there is a social relationship between the abstract and the concrete, 'within the social formation itself' (Garnham 2006, 204). Central to materialism is the methodology of political economy which begins from the proposition that humans are involved in a 'constant material exchange with nature' through the mechanism of labour (ibid.).

DOI: 10.4324/9780429242892-16

With this in mind we can now briefly outline the ontology of materialist dialectics based on the foundation of an '*objective* reality', namely the principle that 'the existence of the world is independent of the mind', and a '*material reality* in which the mental [thought and mind] is a particular form of the material', such that the 'concrete particulars of the world' are not just mental constructs in and of themselves (Mussachia 1977, 258). In other words, things exist whether we think about them or not and '*Yes, the tree does fall in the forest even if there's nobody there to witness it.*' In the course of our discussion, we will also show how the logic of the materialist dialectic stands in opposition to the idealism of metaphysics and the rigid externalities of formal logic (Schaff 1960; Sayers 1984; Schmitt 1988). The materialist standpoint also has implications for what we understand as 'truth' and 'objectivity'. Truth is based in material reality and exists regardless of what we think about it. Therefore, a materialist ontology insists that the existence of class as an abstract concept is just as real as the trees that make up the forest. Classes exist as abstract ideas because of the very concrete social relations of production within the political economy of capitalism. Class is an abstract concept, but it is based on empirical evidence—for example, the observation of inequality in income, the lived experience of workers, and the existence of poverty alongside vast wealth. Thus, political economy operates at Level 3 in our hierarchy of generalities because it is concerned with the material conditions and operations of the capitalist economy.

This typology of levels—discussed in Chapter 14—is also relevant here because one of journalism's epistemological problems is that it is most often operating at the wrong levels of generality. Commonly journalism operates with a mixture of Level 1 and Level 5 analysis. Individuality and individual freedoms (for example) are assumed to be Level 1 characteristics unique to each person seen in isolation; this is coupled with a leap straight to Level 5 where the immutable principles of human nature are assumed to operate. The problem with this is that the very important levels of analysis—contemporary capitalism at Level 2; the conditionality of capitalism at Level 3; and the history of class society at Level 4—are ignored, dismissed as not relevant, or seen to be only of interest to left-wing crackpots (Friedersdorf 2017). Thus, political economy, capitalism, and class are literally written out of the story except in purely sociological terms that serve to slot isolated individuals into convenient income or educational brackets as a way of organising Level 5 problems. The reality is that we are living in Level 3 conditions and obviously under the influence of the dialectics at play within Levels 1 and 2. It is at this level that the problems and crises we discussed in Chapters 1–6 exist, and it is at this level that they will have to be solved:

> For example, if social and economic inequality, exploitation, unemployment, social alienation, and imperialist wars are due in large part to conditions associated with capitalist society, then they can only be understood and dealt with through the use of abstractions [concepts, categories and mental constructs] that bring out their capitalist qualities...Not to do so, to insist on sticking to

levels one and five, leaves one blaming particular individuals (a bad boss, an evil president) or human nature as such for these problems.

(Ollman 2003c, 91)

We can close this discussion of materialism by pointing out, for example, that the experience of young Black American workers facing harassment and fearing for their lives when challenged by the police for the offence of 'driving while Black' (Harris 1999) is a problem that exists clearly at Levels 2 and 3 of our generality. Thus, racism has a material and concrete existence, it is not just an idea. Racism is the objective reality—the lived experience—of Black people in America today with material and measurable impacts on their lives.[1] This reality can only be understood as a specific product of American capitalism with the racial fault lines inherent in class oppression; this means that journalists must recognise it as an issue at that level and comprehend it accordingly. The hopeful sign is that this might now be happening. As Lewis Wallace (2019) points out, the real victory will be keeping it going and changing America for the better.

Fixing our attention on the right level of generality—in this case the third level of capitalism itself—means that the production of goods and services—commodities, including journalism—can be properly understood only when it is not 'abstracted and isolated from the social relations in which it is exercised' (Sayers 1984, 145). Seen in the abstract, isolated from the social relations in which they exist, humans all have a capacity to labour, but it is the social relations—including class membership—that determines the conditions under which people will work. At the concrete level of the society in which we exist, our individuality and other human characteristics are determined by social relations which are, to a large extent, internal: '[A]ll the properties which things have exist by virtue of their relations…of the thing to another thing' (Sayers 1984, 152).

Having outlined the specific level of generality at which we are operating, we can return to a brief discussion of the materialist dialectic and journalism that begins from the following proposition: 'The materialist dialectic is, in outline, a set of claims about the nature of mind, of meaning and of truth. It also has implications for the theory of practice' (Schmitt 1988, 454). If journalism also has claims to being the study of meaning and a search for truth it additionally, even if only indirectly, must have a theory of mind and a 'theory of practice'—which we suggest is the same thing as epistemology. As we've already suggested, the deeper crisis—the crisis of its internal relations—in journalism is the flawed epistemology based on analytical philosophy and formal logic which attempts to explain the world only as a series of discrete things that are tangentially but not dialectically related. One step forward towards correcting this is to set the ontology and epistemology of journalism firmly on a foundation of materialism and the dialectical method. We offer this as a solution because we think that journalists can gain from a process of dialectical reasoning which sees the growth of knowledge as a process of 'mutual interaction and conflict between theory and experience/practice' (Boger 1991, 28). As we have noted—and referenced other scholars who discuss similar ideas—journalism is experiencing its own crisis of theory and, in our view, this can only be resolved through the dialectical struggle of journalists testing theory against experience and practice. This is the subject of the final chapter in which we discuss rebuilding the trust between journalists and audiences, and reimaging a journalism more suited to the period of extended economic, social, and political crisis that is now upon us. In this chapter we will take Merrill's dialectical thinking and stand it the right way up by linking it to an analysis of the material conditions—the political economy of news—in which ideas about ethics and journalism are developed, challenged, and changed.

Capitalism and political economy

This text is based on the foundations of political economy, in particular the intellectual field of the political economy of communication. This extends from a deliberate choice we made over 15 years ago when our first collaborative effort was published (Hirst and Patching 2005). We laid out our reasoning by pointing to what we still consider to be 'the fundamental and glaring fault line within journalism', which we said could be found in the 'dual nature' of news as a commodity in a capitalist economy:

> News has a sale price and is a source of profit to those who control its production and distribution. At the same time, news is the circulation of public information for the benefit of the public.
>
> (Hirst and Patching 2005, 55)

News is an example of the duality of cultural production more generally; 'it produces both commodities for exchange on the market and objects with cultural meaning' (Nixon 2012, 442). Without a political economy approach this critical fault line is difficult to see, let alone understand or navigate. A political economy approach to journalism ethics is valuable because it brings our discussion into the physical and social space of the newsroom, and it also invites us to look at the broader social meaning of news and its function within the parameters of a capitalist economy. Using this critical dialectical method we are able to penetrate the appearance, which we have characterised as the 'marketplace of ideas' (covered later in this chapter), and begin to analyse the internal relations of the news production process. Ethical decision-making occurs in the daily routine and non-routine functions of gathering and publishing newsworthy information, not in a social, economic or political vacuum and not between the pages of a philosophical text. Political economy focuses our attention on two key aspects of news production, and both are critical to our arguments about ethics. The first area is what we might call the institutional environment, or the political economy of the news industry. The second area is how the production of journalism is itself organised, the 'relations of production' if you like. We call this the political economy of journalism. Both of these areas come together when we focus on the dual nature of the news commodity.

Fifteen years ago, there was no real need to separate the institutional political economy of news from the political economy of journalism; they were the same thing. Journalism was then produced almost exclusively inside institutional newsrooms that were themselves located in large media organisations whose business was packaging and selling audiences to advertisers. Newspaper companies produced newspapers, and broadcasters in radio and TV tended to offer a variety of programming in which news and current affairs played a leading role in the early morning and early evening time slots. Television had experienced the disruption of cable news a decade earlier in the mid-1990s but the news industry was, in the mid-2000s, still relatively secure. The Internet was seen as a marketing tool for the print and broadcast product and not something that could stand alone or be monetised. Stand-alone web-based news outlets were few and far between; the only one that is still around today is perhaps Drudge Report. In recent years, that has all changed. In 2005, social media platforms like Twitter hadn't yet been invented and sites like Facebook were in their infancy. In 2005 'TheFaceBook' was one year old and membership was limited to American college students. Facebook did not go fully public until 2006. The political economy of the news industry and the institutions that make up its establishment core have all been shaken by the digital revolution (Hirst 2011, 2018). The news industry is no longer able to conduct 'business as usual' and hasn't for some time; all the old certainties have been disrupted by the operation of new dialectics—the contradictions brought into play by digital technologies and the crisis in profitability. The impact on journalism has also been profound and we feel the need to discuss this separately from the institutional issues in order to fully explain how and why the changes have been so profound. As we discussed in Chapters 4, 5, and 6, the very definition of journalism and the notion of who is and who is not a journalist have also been shaken loose from their traditional foundations. A lot of this movement has come from outside the institutions of the news industry themselves in the form of the platform giants discussed earlier but also through new modes of doing journalism such as 'citizen', or 'amateur' or 'ambient' journalism that can exist without any connection to the legacy news institutions (Hirst 2018). Here we link the past, present, and future of these institutions to the broader *totality* of capitalism itself.

The political economy of journalism

> Conflict between journalistic performance and the economic role of the press is perhaps the most knotty ethical problem.
>
> (Burd 1978, 5)

The biggest fault line in journalism today, and the cause of nearly all of the others—the determinate internal relation, if you like—is the conflict between the commercial interests of the news business and the public interest responsibilities of journalism as an institution. This is what makes the news industry so unstable today and leads to the 'fragility of contemporary journalism' (Moran and Usher 2020, 9). In the late 1970s, Gene Burd was highly critical of what he described as the 'boosterism' of news bosses who promoted their own business interests as being identical to the interests of the city, state or nation where they operated. This fault line remains today, but in most scholarship about journalism and the news industry it is either ignored, downplayed, put in the 'too hard' basket or normalised. In the 21st century the myth identified by Burd; that 'the corporation does not affect news' or direct coverage is still a convenient one, and in fact it is still 'essential to corporate credibility' (ibid.). The major difference between the 1970s and today is that audiences have greater media literacy—partially thanks to social media (Hirst 2018)—and are arguing back in ways that excite some journalists and upset others (Hirst 2019a).

Jill Gordon (1997, 244) reminds us that we 'must at least proceed cautiously' if we expect the commercial news media to encourage or defend 'unpopular opinion'. This is good advice because one of the central and most active fault lines in the news media is between the commercial interests of owners and shareholders and the supposed public service mission of journalism to speak truth to power and uphold the public interest. This is an important idea to hold on to and it is reinforced when we begin to further unpack the metaphor of the marketplace of ideas. One of the central tasks of this book is to explain the link between the various crises afflicting the news industry and the need to re-examine the ethical foundations of journalism. We think the link is very strong, but it is not always visible or clearly articulated. In our view the crisis in profitability—the focus of Chapter 5—has a direct impact on ethical practice because of the directive power that economic control bestows. The political economy of journalism also deals with the questions of power and control because it situates the news business and the practice of journalism within the totality of capitalism as an all-encompassing social system. In this context power has two particular aspects: the power to control and direct the production of news, including directing how journalists work; and the power of the news media as one of the 'consciousness industries' (Nixon 2012)—journalism, entertainment, broadcasting, publishing, theatre, and other forms of cultural production—to legitimise the inequalities and class-based power relations inherent in capitalism, and to disguise or normalise the alienation and exploitation that characterise capitalist relations of production (Mosco 1996; Murdock and Wasko 2007; McChesney 2008; Hirst, Harrison, and Mazepa 2014).

Within the political economy tradition, it is recognised that news is a commodity that shares its identity with other common commodities. News is produced under the general conditions of commodity production in a capitalist society. As such, it is sold to consumers and it generates a profit (return on capital invested) for the owners of media capital and the shareholders in the industry. Additionally, audiences are commodified and sold to the advertising industry. This is how we think the term 'marketplace of ideas' should be understood, but often this term is used to suggest that somehow there is an equal exchange between suppliers and consumers—the supposed 'law' of supply and demand—and that (according to this 'law') the best information will rise to the top and be in higher demand, while low quality information will not be able to hold its spot in the 'marketplace'. This is another example of an explanation that goes no further than appearances and does not allow the observer to see the actual essence of unequal power exchange that keeps the market active and profitable. As a dialectical methodology, political economy rejects the simplistic marketplace of ideas explanation as a form of reified thinking.

The news as a commodity

> [T]here is no solution that could not be found in the solution to the riddle of commodity-structure.
>
> (Lukács 1923, 65)

The main reason that the marketplace of ideas metaphor is so powerful is the same reason that it is essentially false: news is a commodity and in a capitalist economy, every commodity has a dual nature. On one side, journalism has a *use value*; it serves a function and consumers find it useful. In the case of news, use value is the delivery of information that can help people navigate their daily lives (the weather, important news about where they live, etc.). But the news is also a commodity with what political economy calls an *exchange value*, which simply put is the value of one product measured against all other products. In the marketplace of ideas, the use value is the surface appearance of the commodity and its exchange value is its essence but hidden away within the internal relations of the object. The Hungarian Marxist George Lukács insisted that a study of the 'structure of commodity-relations' can 'yield a model of all the objective forms of bourgeois [capitalist] society' because it should be regarded as the 'central, structural problem of capitalist society in all its aspects' (Lukács 1923, 65). Karl Marx devoted nearly 800 pages to discussing the commodity in Volume 1 of *Capital*, but here we try to distil all of this thinking into our own discussion of the duality of the news commodity.

Here we return to the key concept deployed by Lukács—*reification*—to understand the dual aspects of the journalistic commodity. Reification explains why cultural memes like the marketplace of ideas have such a powerful and central role in ideology. Reification also has a duality in relation to journalism. The first is that the various facts, analyses, interpretations, and opinions offered for consumption tend to confirm the marketplace of ideas metaphor to news audiences. Reification makes it appear that the consumer makes their selection based on their own taste and preferences and purchases accordingly. The relations of production—the class location of news workers, their role in the production of surplus value (profit), and their ideological function—are hidden from view. For the journalist, reification is expressed in the ideology of objectivity that masks the alienation of the journalist from their work:

The journalist, portrayed as a privileged member of society, a romantic figure, is in reality twice damned by the nature of his [sic] practice in capitalist society: condemned first of all to be unable to recognize himself in his own product, and then condemned to be an agent of the ideological alienation of the exploited sectors which consume his product.

(MIR Chile 1971, 132)

The process of reification is also the product of alienation and commodity fetishism (Fogarasi 1921, 153) in that the journalist is cut off from taking pride and pleasure in their work because of the division of labour in large, impersonal mainstream newsrooms. In a simplified sense, journalism has several bureaucratic elements that are adopted by reporters to make their jobs easier and to guarantee a steady supply of useable material (Windschuttle 1988, 275) and this also leads to a certain bureaucratisation of thinking. In particular, following Lukács (1923, 78), we can note that this involves adapting their worldview 'to the general socioeconomic premises of the capitalist economy'. In other words, it is epistemologically and ontologically easier to operate as a journalist—developing sources, following a round, establishing routines—if you also adapt to the prevailing and dominant social and ideological norms. This is also a form of reification; the journalist becomes engrossed in surface features—in appearance—and any story can be covered using a 'formal and standardised treatment' remote from 'the qualitative and material essence' of the situation being reported on. Reification also explains why journalists continue to cling to the ideal of objectivity even while acknowledging that it is flawed to the point of being unworkable (Ward 2004, 2020). To some degree, the frustration that journalists feel with this quixotic quest for perfect objectivity might help to explain the ingrained cynicism common to many journalists and which is the result of their alienation. The journalist—as worker—is also subject to commodification that splits their 'labour-power' from their humanity; 'so the press transforms the journalists' (Fogarasi 1921, 150). The reporter's ability to produce news is separated from them; it becomes something external, 'a thing, an object' (Lukács 1923, 78) that is sold in the marketplace too. The insight Lukács provides here is telling: the split in the psyche of the journalist brought about by their capitulation to bureaucratic methods 'invades the realm of ethics' and reinforces the 'reified structure of consciousness' (ibid., 79). 'This phenomenon can be seen at it is most grotesque in journalism,' Lukács observes, before continuing:

Here it is precisely subjectivity itself, knowledge, temperament and powers of expression that are reduced to an abstract mechanism functioning autonomously and divorced both from the personality of their 'owner' and from the material and concrete nature of the subject matter in hand. The journalist's 'lack of convictions', the prostitution of his [sic] experiences and beliefs is comprehensible only as the [result] of capitalist reification.

(Lukács 1923, 79)

Journalists themselves are therefore victims of commodity fetishism in which their own relationship to their work appears to them as an object of 'ghostly objectivity' that 'stamps its imprint upon the whole consciousness' in which their innate intellectual abilities 'are no longer an organic part of [their] personality, they are things which [they] can "own" or "dispose of" like the various objects of the external world' (ibid.). The reality is that journalists are mostly objectively working class, even if their ideological outlook rejects this idea.

Journalism, journalists, and class

> [T]here is a capitalist press written in by so-called proletarians for real proletarians…The capitalist press is an ideological weapon in oppressing the proletariat.
> (Fogarasi 1921, 149)

This line from Hungarian journalist and socialist Alabert Fogarasi perfectly expresses the dialectic of class in journalism. We see in this brief statement the outlines of a contradiction that has shaped journalism for most of its modern history. The dialectic of class cuts through journalism in several ways. First, the content of news and news institutions are biased towards and supportive of the capitalist ruling class, and the information needs of the working class marginalised (Kumar 2004, 16). Second, by and large journalists are objectively members of the working class—they do not own any means of production, they work for wages, and they are subject to the reified consciousness that is an expression of commodity fetishism. Despite this, the work they do for the capitalist press helps the ruling class to reify the existence of an entire class, to keep itself in power and to subvert any thoughts of revolution or insurrection into safer forms of expression such as meaningless consumption, sexual fantasy, alcoholism, and drug addiction. In other words, journalists tend to act against their own class interests. This is the sense in which the Chilean MIR group (MIR Chile 1971, 133) argues that journalism is a social relation 'between the dominant classes and the dominated classes' and the journalist *as social relation* is 'a transmission belt for the mechanisms of domination'. Martin wrote his PhD thesis on this topic and he called it *Grey Collar Journalism: The Social Relations of News Production*. 'Grey collar' invokes a class location somewhere between 'blue collar' workers and 'white collar' managers or bureaucrats, and expresses the contradiction within the lived experience of journalists: they occupy a location in the class structure of capitalism that makes them grey collar workers, but they also give expression to reification because ideologically they align themselves with the ruling class. This is to say that journalists do not identify with the working class even though their economic and political interests align with those of the workers' movement; instead they take their cues from the ruling class and help to 'dominate the ideology of the ensemble of classes' (Fogarasi 1921, 149). Class is an important concept in political economy, it is more specific than an amorphous 'public' and it is directly tied to economic inequality. The class nature of journalism is hidden behind the reified veil of the marketplace of ideas.

The marketplace of ideas

One of the most influential—but flawed—ideas about journalism is the framing of the news media as a 'marketplace of ideas' in which it is projected as an uncontroversial fact that the consumer is sovereign, and that competition will impartially determine which news outlets do well—and coincidentally make profits for shareholders—and which ones will fail because they are allegedly not doing a good job. Through the process of reification—that hides from view the class relations of journalism and the audience—the market is ideologically transposed into a level playing field in which all competitors begin with an equal chance of victory. The only concession to any external influence over the smooth operation of the market is a supposed 'invisible hand'.

The concept of a marketplace of ideas has its roots in both ideology and political economy. In the contemporary context its importance in the realm of journalism ethics can be traced to a famous case in the US Supreme Court in 1919 at the height of the First World War and ruling class hysteria at the successful workers' revolution in Russia. The original case involved four Russian immigrants with sympathies for the Russian Bolsheviks. The four were convicted of sedition and sentenced to 20 years in jail for publishing a political leaflet which called for a general strike if the US militarily intervened against the revolution (it did, along with Australia, the UK, and 12 other nations). The supposed crime of the four men was violation of the 1917 Espionage Act, which criminalised 'disloyal' speech about the United States (O'Neill 2009). The case went to the Supreme Court on appeal, which the four men lost 7–2. The idea that free speech is a 'free trade in ideas' and that 'the best test of truth' is the acceptance of an idea 'in the competition of the market' was expressed by a dissenting judge, Oliver Wendell Holmes, and supported by his colleague Louis D. Brandeis (Abrams et al. v. United States 1919). The fallacy of the marketplace metaphor as articulated by Holmes and Brandeis is well observed by the legal scholar Vincent Blasi (2004, 7) in his rejoinder to Holmes' 'marketplace of ideas' remarks when he comments 'the market for ideas would seem to be especially divergent from the economists' ideal'. Blasi then lists his objections, including inequality in access 'to the channels of mass communication'; distortions in the way ideas are 'bought and sold'; the ways in which some ideas are 'more easily packaged' as propaganda; differences in 'such capacities as articulateness and comprehension' among individuals; and, finally, 'the costs created by speech are seldom borne by the speakers'. In his detailed exegesis on the Holmes marketplace of ideas metaphor, Vincent Blasi spends several pages on a detailed—if undialectical—critique before rounding on himself and concluding that the concept aligns with a generous interpretation of the First Amendment protection of political speech. However, along the way, he offers some commentary that, when read in the context of commodity fetishism, tends to discredit the marketplace metaphor. For example, he acknowledges that the market only affords an appearance of equality, 'in that a pauper's dollar buys as much as a prince's,' and that markets can be distorted by unequally distributed wealth (2004, 42); further it 'does not offer the prospect of a just distribution of opportunity to persuade' (2004, 45).

In a more historical context, the notion of a marketplace of ideas as a metaphor for the exercise of free speech is often attributed to the 19th-century political economist and philosopher of liberalism, John Stuart Mill. Mill published a book of philosophical essays, *On Liberty*, in 1859 and is perhaps best known for the ethical concept of utilitarianism—of individuals doing what is best for themselves and therefore creating the best collective outcome—and for being a champion of individual liberty (Schapiro 1943). However, Jill Gordon (1997) provides a close textual reading of Mill which convincingly argues that he would not support the marketplace of ideas metaphor as being an accurate representation of his views. She writes: '[T]he marketplace has become a paradigm for all freedoms we value, but this paradigm...stems from an ideological framework that Mill did not share' (Gordon 1997, 245). Gordon provides an eloquent rebuttal to Schapiro's positioning of Mill as a champion of the market and reminds us that the neoclassical economic theory rests on too many untenable assumptions, chiefly that economic decisions are somehow made in a social vacuum of equilibrium and full rationality. Central to the metaphor of a rationally operating and balanced market is the idea that somehow 'truth' would emerge from 'the free competition of ideas in the market place' (Schapiro 1943, 154). While this is an appealing idea, it has no basis in the actuality of the market which is far from balanced or rational because it 'responds to forces of power, whether it be in terms of wealth, influence or sheer numbers, and truth is not necessarily generated from any of these sources' (Gordon 1997, 241)

Commodity fetishism in the marketplace of ideas

> The laws of reification insure that the journalist...as a simple personification of journalism, follows the laws, carries out his functions mechanically and unconsciously...every intelligible structure is remade into a commodity...[the journalist] not only does not notice this...but is not even in a position to notice it.
>
> (Fogarasi 1921, 151)

In the ontology of materialism and the dialectic, the marketplace of ideas can be understood as an expression of the fetishism of commodities. This expression is a shorthand way of talking about how the appearance of goods in the capitalist marketplace is ideologically disconnected from the inner relations of the commodity form; such that the human labour used up in their production is rendered invisible and social relations assume 'the fantastic form of relation between things' (Marx 1867, 165). Products, consumer goods, and commodities appear as ready-made and as expressions of consumer demand rather than as products of social human labour. As consumer products became more readily available in the 19th century they took on an almost mystical aura and 'served to ground and give objective form to one's own individuality' (Henderson 2002, 5). Commodity fetishism has been described as a 'condition of subjectivity' for modern individuals who see themselves mirrored in objects (Mulhern 2007, 479). When applied to ideas, commodity fetishism presents them as disembodied from the social conditions in which they are created; or, as Karl Marx writes in Volume 1 of *Capital*, 'the products of the human brain appear as autonomous figures endowed with a life of their own' (Marx 1867, 165). Perhaps this is best explained by using the commodity fetishism lens to look at the concept of the marketplace of ideas itself.

The first thing to note is that the idea has been misattributed to John Stuart Mill and that this mistaken attribution is now held to be a truth that is repeated whenever the notion is discussed. This is itself a form of fetishisation of the idea such that it becomes an object of faith that can 'attract the gaze while obstructing the vision' (Mulhern 2007, 489). Mill (1806–1873) was one of the most influential bourgeois thinkers, famous for his work *On Liberty*, a defence of freedom of speech (Macleod 2020). By asserting that he developed, or at least approved of, an idea is a way of legitimising it and shielding it from criticism. In other words, in misattributing the idea to Mill, we are gently being directed to not look any further into the content of the idea. The second important attribute is to see how the idea has been stripped of any social relationships that might undercut the assumption that markets operate smoothly based on individual choices made on a level playing field on which suppliers can only respond to consumer demands. Through the process of reification embodied in the fetishism of commodities, the market becomes a metaphysical space stripped of its internal relations and removed from political economy.

In this idealised scenario, ideas compete with each other only on their own merits removed from any attachment to centres of social power; 'processes and relationships appear as things, and quality is reduced to quantity' (Mulhern 2007, 480). One idea is presented as just as valid as any other, and rational individuals, without prejudice or bias, then choose the best of the available ideas and therefore a 'truth' is revealed. In a sense, if truth and morality can be left to the market choices of consumers, we can argue that this view tends to absolve the journalist of any ethical responsibility. Perhaps the most misleading assumption at the heart of the marketplace metaphor is the idea that there is a necessary link between competition and the idea of something being considered right and truthful. On what basis can it be asserted that unfettered competition always leads to the best outcome? This is certainly an odd way to test the reliability and trustworthiness of an idea. An idea might be very attractive and popular in the marketplace, but that does not guarantee it is either the truth, or that it is the best possible idea. For example, as Charles Lawrence III (1990, 468) noted in an article about regulating racist speech, when the marketplace of ideas was being upheld as an honoured principle by Justice Holmes in 1919, 'the racial inferiority of non-whites was one of its chief commodities'. In a prescient comment that still holds true, Lawrence then added, '[E]ver since the market opened, racism has remained its most active item in trade' (ibid.). The historic experience of Black communities in America certainly undercuts the marketplace of ideas rhetoric: 'We have seen too many demagogues elected by appealing to America's racism,' Lawrence wrote in 1990 (468); it is true today too. The marketplace of ideas is full of such distortions; it mutes and devalues the speech of minority groups on the basis of race, ethnicity, sexuality, gender-identity, and religious belief, among many other limitations (Lawrence III 1990; Cole 2017; Wallace 2019). If we just accept a commodified view of information exchanges, our choice is reduced to simply selecting from a range of prefabricated opinions. This might reduce the burden of having to think for ourselves, but it also works to make us passive recipients of knowledge, rather than the generators of our own new thoughts. It induces 'passivity' and makes us a 'subject population' rather than active creators of our own destiny (Mulhern 2007, 480). In the following chapter we will review how reification distorts some of the important foundational beliefs of journalism as an institution and the stories that journalists tell about themselves.

Questions for discussion

1   What do you understand of the 'duality' of news as a commodity?
2   Discuss the concepts of commodity fetishism and reification. Do they make sense when applied to news?
3   Is the marketplace of ideas a useful concept for understanding news?
4   Is a class analysis of journalism and journalists useful to understanding the news crisis today?

Note

1   We are not minimising racism in other contexts here and acknowledge that it is a lived experience for oppressed and marginalised groups in many societies. Racism also structures the lived experience of White people and other oppressor groups too, but in different ways that extend or constrain their margin of privilege over people of colour.

16 Dialectic in action
Revisiting key issues in ethics

Putting dialectical reasoning to the test

In this chapter we will explore several current and active fault lines in journalism ethics using some of the methods for dialectical reasoning set out in the previous chapters. Our purpose in doing this is to demonstrate where we see problems with the epistemology and ontology of journalism and how thinking dialectically helps to unpack the issues in a more productive way. The topics chosen for this chapter all link together and form the backbone of journalistic ideology today. Our review starts with the concept of objectivity because for perhaps a century or so it has been a central element in ethical schemas. We then move on to a discussion of press freedom—or, more commonly, freedom of the press—which has a long and storied history. From there we transition to a discussion of the Fourth Estate which signifies journalists' self-perception that they are the last ones protecting democracy and the public interest from the predations of the powerful and unscrupulous.

Using the dialectical and materialist method discussed earlier, we will set out the basic working model for each concept as currently operating and then offer a critique that takes us beneath the surface appearance to reveal the inner relations that activate the dialectic and set in motion the contradiction, animating it as an ethical fault line. Here we are once again using dialectic in the double sense explained in the previous chapters as both a method of investigation and as a term defining the process of movement towards change embedded in the object being investigated: 'Dialectic is both—it is a method of thought, but it is also more than this, namely a specific structure which belongs to the things themselves' (Lecture No. 1, May 1958, Theodor Adorno 2017 (1958), 1).

The dialectics of objectivity

> If journalistic objectivity is an ideal, it is surely a complex one. What does it mean to strive for an ideal that can never be attained? Does it mean the ideal is worthless, or does it represent the ultimate in journalistic virtue?
>
> (Maras 2013, 1)

DOI: 10.4324/9780429242892-17

Steven Maras is an Australian media academic and his book *Objectivity in Journalism* is among the most recent scholarly investigations of objectivity in English. The Maras text and Lewis Wallace's *The View From Somewhere* (2019) provide the context and background for the exploration of objectivity in this chapter. The purpose of this exegesis is to answer two basic questions about objectivity: What are its internal relations that determine how it develops and changes? and How are these relations evident in the key ethical fault line involving objectivity? Maras provides some clues as to where we might look for answers in the history of objectivity in specific 'cultural formations', and 'the professional aspirations of journalists themselves' requiring a 'philosophically and historically nuanced view of how the concept has been defined and what it allows us to do' (Maras 2013, 2). As a professional mantra, objectivity, became attached to journalism at the beginning of the 20th century at a time when the more partisan press of the 19th century was butting heads with the marketing and advertising needs of the growing merchant capitalist class (Stephens 2007, 251–7). Mass industry needed mass audiences for advertising and this economic need was best met by performing a kind of journalistic neutrality that eschewed a formal tie to politics but that was—at every level—imbued with the politics of capital accumulation. This historical view is necessary to unpack why objectivity is such a contested idea that's difficult to pin down in practice and why it moved from having a 'positive connection' to 'the processes of democratic deliberation' to becoming 'part of the problem not part of the solution' from the 1950s onwards (Maras 2013, 3). In our first text we wrote that objectivity is a 'key component of journalistic ideology' whose purpose was 'to mask, disguise and legitimate the authority of society's powerful ruling groups over weaker sections of the population'. For good measure we added that the conflict around determinations of objectivity established 'one of the most volatile fault lines' facing journalism (Hirst and Patching 2005, 40). We see no reason to change our view but, at the same time, it is important that we acknowledge a dialectical shift in the profession, and in the scholarship of journalism, such that objectivity is problematised 'not only as an unattainable standard but also as an undesirable norm' (Boudana 2011, 385).

One issue that arises is pinning down objectivity with a workable definition. This is absolutely necessary because over the years it has moved in and out of fashion in the ethical lexicon of journalism, but it has not moved very far conceptually. Objectivity has always been linked to notions of bias, balance, fairness, facts over opinion, the separation of the journalist from the news being reported, and emotional detachment. In a sense, the ideology of objectivity does a lot of work in shaping our understanding of journalism, and for most people it means that reporters are neutral and take no active role in shaping the news that they faithfully represent the public. However, this view is open to challenge. It is not a simple matter of bias being somehow imposed over neutral facts by bad actors attempting to mislead the public, and who must somehow be held to account by fearless and impartial Fourth Estate observers. There is no way that *facts* as such can be separated from *values*. As Greg McLaughlin

(2016) notes, 'bias' is not simply a matter of individual prejudice or beliefs getting in the way of objectivity, 'bias is not in the eye of the beholder but is structured within the entire news process' (39). In other words, bias is an inevitable feature of journalism reified by commodity fetishism and the pro-systemic and largely unconscious worldview of reporters and editors.

Why, if objectivity is such an important and foundational principle of jour-nalism, is it so widely criticised and misunderstood as one of the 'great confu-sions' (Massaquoi 2016, 19) in practice? We think that the answer—at least partially—can be found in our assertion that the epistemology and ontology of journalism are broken, as seen in previous chapters. To refresh your under-standing of our position, we can say that both the methods (epistemology) and the body of knowledge (ontology) of contemporary journalism are problematic because they are undialectical and idealist. The specificity missing in this global framing of objectivity is any sense of the political economy of news production. In other words, we have to examine objectivity not as a purely cultural con-cept, but within the Level 3 framework of capitalism and its necessary relations of production. Steven Maras (2013, 15) does make an effort to introduce some elements of the inner relations that generate movement within the concept of objectivity by noting that there is a link between it and 'commercialism' and that the introduction of objectivity into journalism was an early 20th century response to 'technical, economic, cultural and social problems'. In this chapter we aim to take this analysis several steps further.

There have also been several attempts to link journalistic objectivity with 'scientific objectivity' using a hypothesis and test model rather than an 'inter-pretive' method of 'factual objectivity' (Post 2014), and by privileging the ideas of 'transparent method', a 'pluralistic search for consensus', and 'trained judg-ment' (Fahy 2018). Using feminist 'standpoint theory' as her guide, Sandra Harding has argued for an even harder version of 'strong objectivity' in scien-tific epistemology that is also, paradoxically, based on 'strong reflexivity' that privileges 'democracy-advancing values' (Harding 1993, 71–3). This is the ultimate outcome of the problematic mistakes evident in journalistic episte-mology. The objectivity problem really needs to be turned upside down—or 'right side up' if we follow Marx's analogy of how Hegel's dialectic should be treated from the previous chapter. From within its current epistemological fra-mework, objectivity is seen as an internal and personal ideal or belief that a journalist—and journalism—should adhere to, or at least strive to adhere to. To do this requires that journalists have an internalised 'objective' viewpoint and attempt to report without any of their own beliefs interfering or getting in the way of their supposedly clear-eyed view of the world based on 'hard facts' and 'stripped of all interpretation or bias', a 'sort of passive stenography' (Ward 2020). However, such a viewpoint is already warped by ideology, and as Ward and others nave noted, conforming to it is a difficult, if not impossible, task. Therefore, the supporters of an objective viewpoint argue, journalism needs to 'reconstruct' a new epistemology that clears away these problems with objec-tivity as currently constructed. We agree, but differ perhaps on why and how such a reconstruction can be achieved. We start with a materialist perspective that says objectivity is not to be found in consciousness. Objectivity cannot be a state of mind or a point of view. Instead, truth and objectivity exist in the material world and are independent of our beliefs.

The problem is that journalistic objectivity begins in subjectivity and idealism, in an attempt to make the world fit a preconceived pattern that is deemed 'objective' but in fact relies on a superficial intuition. This is the commonsense approach currently taught to journalism students and embedded in journalist's self-conception of their Fourth Estate role. As Hartle (2017) notes, this is a 'form of objectivity that conceals' rather than reveals the actual social conditions of the totality (28). What we are presented with here is 'the illusion of objectivity' that effectively conceals the 'fluid and dynamic social relations' that constitute the economic and political system of capitalism. Hartle has a neat expression that sums up this process as it is constituted in journalism: 'the ontological fallacy of abstracting objects from their constitutive processes', which creates 'a static visual reproduction and confirmation' of reified ideologies, '*a reification of the objective world*' (ibid., 29). In other words, the objectivity of journalism is actually a construct of reified consciousness that is not capable of 'rooting social facts in social practice' or of 'relating to fellow human beings as co-producers of social reality' (ibid., 30). Journalism's self-conception as being somehow ideologically objective is itself an idealistic construct existing only in a journalist's head, that has become fetishized even though it represents no more than a myth, 'removed from the concrete conditions of history and social existence' (Kieve 1983, 64). In the realm of journalistic practice, objectivity cannot be willed into existence, it can only be assessed through 'a detailed and concrete analysis of human history and social existence' (ibid.).

Towards a materialist objectivity

From a materialist perspective, objectivity is a quality of material reality, not subjective consciousness. As George Novack (1980) has written: 'The external world exists regardless of our relations with it and apart from the uses we make of its elements.' For a journalist using the materialist method, objectivity must start 'from the ground up,' and 'not the other way around' (Kieve 1983, 60) from subjective thought. Objectivity is determined by the 'materiality of social life' (ibid., 62), not from the mental perspective of the journalist. As materialist philosopher Peter Binns (1973) puts it: '[O]bjective truths are not *uncovered*, so much as *created*…in the act of us making them they become revealed' (5). Truth is not possible without 'a clash of different views, a struggle of beliefs…without error' (ibid.). The scientific process is the making of truth through overcoming error and the gradual discovery of truth over time. Therefore, truth is a function of materiality reflected in thinking, but it is a reality that exists independently of our ability to conceive of it in thought: 'truth is objective…not dependent on the subject…intentions or will' (ibid.).

The other internal relation that drives this view of journalistic objectivity is the realisation that a human being cannot *be* objective, it is a rational impossibility. We all look at the world from within an epistemology and ontology—whether we acknowledge it, or not—so we can only *see* the world subjectively. We look at the world with a point of view. The questions about what we see, how we see it, and how we choose to interpret the world can only be answered from our subjective position. Within the current epistemological and ontological frameworks of journalism, the 'objective' journalist views the world as a static given and fixed quantity rather than 'a complex determination of many underlying elements' (Binns 1973, 5). On the other hand, when we see the world through the materialist lens—and incorporate the totality into our conceptual worldview—we can see the world as it is: an infinite and dynamic reality 'developing according to objective laws' (Spirkin 1983). It is the world that has an objective existence as a concrete accumulation of social relations and subjective truth is 'the accurate reflection of the object in the consciousness of the subject' (ibid.). Reality is more than a simple accumulation or summary of 'all the existent things' including immutable ideas about the world (Binns 1973, 5) but objective journalism cannot see beyond this piling up of things. If we choose to see the world only as a series of piled up objects and ideas—as in Merrill's idealist construction of the dialectic in journalism—and these ideas 'have no correspondence in reality', then they 'have nothing to do with the truth' (Spirkin 1983). Similarly, the current methodologies of journalism privilege the narrow intellectual frames of the individual and the positivist—the obviously observable facts—rather than looking at the bigger and more complex picture of the social totality. For the materialist thinker any contradictions in thought are reflections of contradictions in the material and social life of the thinker which is an expression of the 'ontological and epistemological primacy of matter' (Binns 1973, 6). In other words, the right way to view the world is not *mind over matter* but *matter over mind*.

When see the world from the standpoint of dialectical materialism and we acknowledge that truth is a process of discovery, rather than a fixed quantity rooted in the obvious, we can also see how truth can be both *relative* and *absolute* at the same time. Truth is relative because it reflects the objective world only within 'certain limits, certain relations' (ibid.). Science itself is relative truth because it is always incomplete: 'The mountain of knowledge has no summit', Spirkin reminds us. Relative truth has nothing to do with your subjective point of view; you cannot bend truth just by believing something different. Belief does not equal truth; 'relative truth is objective truth' (Spirkin 1983). In George Orwell's *Nineteen Eighty-Four*, the character Winston is tortured until he finally comes to believe that $2+2=5$ because that's what Big Brother wants him to believe, but it did not make it true. $2+2=4$ was true for Big Brother just as much as it is for us today. The objective truth of *Nineteen Eighty-Four* is that Winston's belief system was the product of the way he was treated within the totality of the dystopian post-war society in which subjective truth is inverted:

> To know and not to know, to be conscious of complete truthfulness while telling carefully constructed lies...to use logic against logic...to forget

whatever it was necessary to forget…to apply the same process to the process itself…and then…to become unconscious of the act of hypnosis you had just performed.

(Orwell 1988, 31)

Here Orwell is indirectly exploring the concept of reification: 'All that was needed was an unending series of victories over your own memory. "Reality control", they called it: in Newspeak "doublethink"' (ibid.). To rescue journalism from its contemporary crisis involves journalists—and audiences—recognising their own version of doublethink and overcoming it through careful consideration of the materialist and dialectical epistemology that brings us to a fuller understanding of truth. Instead of accepting Big Brother's mantra 'Who controls the past controls the future: who controls the present controls the past' (Orwell 1988, 31). we have to remember that truth 'about the objective world' can only be discovered and confirmed through coming to terms with the totality, 'the interplay and opposition of forces which govern our life and action' (Binns 1973, 4). Facts may themselves be value-free on one level—in the sense that $2+2=4$ or that gravity exists, and the earth is a rotating sphere—but the presentation of facts cannot exist in such a vacuum either value-free or outside of ideology. Steven Maras (2013) seems to acknowledge this when he writes, 'objectivity also operates as a form of judgment' (14). Anthony Nadler (2016, 36) is right to point out that throughout the 20th century, objectivity played the role of legitimising 'ideological frameworks articulated by powerful officials'. One consequence of this has been to compromise press freedom—perversely celebrated by some journalists who relish their insider status—and therefore contributing to declining trust.

What is press freedom?

[A] few successful press giants are not the best guarantee of press freedom.

(Chopra 1980, 1656)

Securing a workable and meaningful definition of press freedom has been the Holy Grail of philosophers, legislators, media owners, journalists, writers, and consumers of news for over 250 years, but it is much easier to understand in the abstract than as it actually exists in material circumstances. In principle, press freedom is linked to democratic forms of government, the public's right to know, and holding governments to account for their actions. In this abstract definition, there is an almost perfect link between a free press and a functional democracy. It is 'an instrument of democratic control' (Sorabjee 1986) ostensibly in the hands of the people. As such, many authors contend, a free press underpins 'popular decision-making and the balance of power between government and society' (Voltmer 2014, 157). These ideas are now deeply embedded in general ideology and are used extensively to justify the professional identity of journalists (Himelboim and Limor 2008), particularly when they are being criticised for allegedly not doing their jobs well. So deeply entrenched is a public belief in the concept of press freedom—no matter how well it might be understood—that for the past 60 years it has been considered an axiomatic element of Western representative democracy (Graber 1986). So much so that is barely subject to question. However, freedom of the press is not a licence for unethical behaviour, and it is not an excuse to trample over the rights of other people. There has to be some balance, and our preference has always been the public interest test. As we indicated in our discussion on privacy (Chapter 8) there is no blanket rule against invasions of privacy, and journalists have every right to press public figures on their private actions when they impact on public life (Wilson 1990). We also made an argument that privacy and secrecy are not the same thing and that, sometimes, exposing secrets is the right thing to do in the public interest. So, how do we assess whether or not something is in the public interest and should be exposed through reporting? In other words: How free is the press actually? This question is really about the ethical principles of utilitarianism, and public interest has to be measured using the concept of 'the greater good'. When the benefit to the broadly defined public outweighs the right of an individual or group of people to keep information private or secret, then the public interest test has been met. The public interest is not the same as 'what the public is interested in', and we have to insist on this point because we've seen too many cases where lazy journalists justify clickbait stories on the basis that this is what audiences want. Journalism must serve the public interest. This is a fundamental and founding principle of the 'Fourth Estate' model. However, there is evidence that this model is flawed, perhaps even broken.

In our view we need to understand the idea of press freedom from the perspective of dialectics and materialism. Of course, there is an ideal and an important principle to be defended in the idea of press freedom, but it does not, and cannot, occur in a social vacuum. Freedom of the press is very much a product of political economy and in a class society which is based on inequality, freedom of the press is not equally distributed. As Pan Chopra noted, competition between a limited number of giant media companies does not constitute press freedom. Therefore, we have to subject the practice of press freedom—as well as the ideal—to a dialectical 'cost-benefit analysis' (Graber 1986) to uncover the hidden antinomes that make up the internal relations of press freedom.

Press freedom is not just an idea, it has both an economic and a political materiality. In the marketplace of ideas, the economic aspect tends to get lost under the weight of commodity fetishism. It is simply assumed that the owners of the press hold the right to use their power for whatever purpose they choose. The media owners exercise their freedom, and the imperfect functioning of the market is supposed to guarantee the public interest. We have sufficiently demonstrated the fallacy of this argument already in Chapter 15. The freedom of media capitalists is the simple freedom to make a profit through selling the news commodity and to pursue their own class interests at the expense of the vast majority of the public. In Randall Benzanson's memorable phrase: 'Today, the business of news is business, not news' (Bezanson 2001, 20). In the ideology of the marketplace, the only recognised impediment to press freedom is the potential for political or policy interventions that might curtail the economic and political freedoms of the media owners. As we've already established, the news media's relationship with the State power of governments is never straightforward, it is always dialectical, under pressure and subject to modification. Some form of market-based and imperfect press freedom is generally accepted by most democratically inclined governments, but exceptions, caveats, and restrictions are always kept handily in the bottom drawer, or embedded in legislative and regulatory fine print, to be pulled out and acted upon as and when it becomes 'necessary in a democratic society' and when responding to 'a pressing social need' (Munro 1991, 104). What's missing in the normative account of press freedom being freedom from government intervention in the running of the news media is an understanding of how the State acts to defend and extend the property rights of capital at the expense of the working class. In this context, freedom of the press is a property right exercised by the owners of media capital, not news workers and the actions of the State reinforce this property right. The history of First Amendment legal cases before the US Supreme Court—which we've noted gave us the 'flawed metaphor' of the marketplace of ideas—bears this out over many decades. Commercial speech, such as advertising, has been placed squarely under the protection of the First Amendment and so too has the money power of well-funded lobbyists and political action committees at the expense of the rights of citizens, minorities, and social movements (Parsons 2019; Dwyre 2020; Baker et al. 2020). The First Amendment to the American constitution has become a cornerstone of media freedom in the United States even as the meaning and value of the actual clause itself are constantly fought over, and 'free speech' is a legal and ideological battleground.

The First Amendment was adopted in 1791 as the first clause in a ten-point Bill of Rights:

> Congress shall make no law respecting an establishment of religion, or prohibiting the free exercise thereof; or abridging the freedom of speech, or of the press; or the right of the people peaceably to assemble, and to petition the Government for a redress of grievances.

These famous words have come to represent an unbridled approach to freedom—implying a right to do and say anything—but in practice and in reality the American legal system has, over a period of more than 200 years, imposed some limitations on the broadest interpretation of freedom. The same is true in the Anglophone world of common law and unwritten constitutions.

The ideological principle of press freedom is regarded as unassailable; at least until some unavoidable crisis renders it malleable. If it functions properly, a free press can hold to account the powerful and act as a watchdog on the excesses of both government and business or other powerful institutions. However, as we've discussed in earlier chapters, this ideal and theoretical model does not function to capacity and has not done so for at least half a century. Writing in 1986—well before the triple crises of technology, trust, and profitability that we identify—American political scientist Doris A. Graber noted that on an examination of its record over 200 years, the US news media had failed to live up to the principles and protections afforded it by the First Amendment and had not adequately performed its watchdog functions which, over time, had 'diminished its contributions to the vigor of American democracy' (Graber 1986, 258). Any discussion of journalism ethics has to come to terms with the ideas surrounding the troubled concept of 'press freedom', or 'freedom of the press'. Of course, we mean news media when we say 'press', but this idea has been around for a long time. In fact, revolutions have been fought to enshrine the 'right' to media freedom in political and constitutional structures. The most important revolutions in which a version of press freedom was a key demand were the Industrial Revolution in Britain and political revolutions against the old order in France, and the United States during what British historian Eric Hobsbawm (1996) described as the 'age of revolution' from 1789 to 1848. The leaders of these upheavals were, in each case, the most enlightened and for-ward-thinking members of the bourgeoisie, a class based on mercantile and industrial capital that was chafing under the restraints on trade, labour, and investment imposed by the collapsing feudal order. Freedom for *their* press was an important weapon in the fight against the remnants of aristocracy. The bourgeois philosophers and intellectuals constantly argued against censorship and set up small magazines or periodicals that would eventually be shut down by government decree.

To a large degree it was this process of being involved with short-lived radical newspapers that drew the young Karl Marx into political activity while he was still a student of poetry and philosophy (Rees 1998; Alizadeh 2019). Marx wrote for and edited a number of German publications which honed his journalism, writing, and politics. However, Marx also recognised that once the bourgeoisie had gained sufficient power to enable them to supplant the old aristocracy as a new ruling class, their concern for press freedom lessened in proportion to their growing grip on the machinery of State. This was particu-larly obvious in France during the period of the Second Republic when the ruling Party of Order reimposed a censorship tax on newspapers to prevent them from publishing anything that the National Assembly might consider offensive or defamatory, as Marx noted in his commentary on the French revolution; 'the provisions concerning caution money killed the so-called revolutionary press' and turned once argumentative and political magazines into safe and perfunctory literary magazines, in which 'every article sank to the level of an advertisement' (Marx 1850, 73).

Karl Marx was a champion of free speech and press freedom, and his views were most cogently set out in a series of articles he wrote in May 1842 that were published over several weeks in the *Rheinische Zeitung* newspaper pro-testing the censorship of the press by the Prussian state (Sanders 2009). As we've already discussed, Marx's method was to approach the question of press freedom dialectically—as a product of historically situated social relations—and bound up with the political economy of publishing as generally constituted in a class society (abstraction at Level 4). Using this approach, Marx discussed the paradox at the core of debates about freedom of the press in 19th-century Europe and also provided universal insights that we can fruitfully employ today in our own discussion. Marx's exposition (1842) of the dialectical fault line that animates the internal relations of press freedom is easily explained in his own words: '*The primary freedom of the press lies in it not being a trade…*Of course, the press exists also as a trade.'

This is a key idea in any deliberation of what we mean when we talk about a free press. The commonsense meaning that most people would agree with is that the press should be free from government interference and that the highest expression of this sentiment is the First Amendment to the United States constitution guaranteeing such freedom. However, Marx is not, in this quote, directly addressing State censorship, though he deals with it extensively in his series for the *Rheinische Zeitung*. Marx's concern here is what he sees as the commercial limits imposed on press freedom by ownership structures that are bound up with the class interests of the capitalists (the bourgeoisie). In the context of Marx's writing there was a pressing and current debate in May 1842 about legislation to determine who can be an 'authorised' writer on certain subjects. The conservative Prussian state found itself confronted by a restless bourgeoisie that was economically dominant, but that lacked commensurate political rights. There was, therefore, an unsteady alliance between the aristocratic class which controlled the State apparatus (but that was a waning economic power) and an economically powerful bourgeois class that was pushing for political autonomy. The bourgeois traders, merchants, and industrialists were unhappy and felt excluded from political power (Sanders 2009) but, to a large degree, the burghers were reliant on the stability provided by the Prussian state apparatus. Marx's position was that the friction between the aristocracy and the bourgeoisie resulted only in 'soulless bargaining and haggling as to *how much freedom freedom of the press ought to have*' (Marx 1842). At both a theoretical and a practical level, this question articulates one of the most enduring contradictions in journalism. Where does media freedom exist and with whom does it reside? This is an important—and ultimately political (Okulicz-Kozaryn 2014)—question, and there are several answers each of which creates its own set of antinomes with their own thesis, antithesis, and synthesis.

Who does media freedom apply to?

Any definition of freedom has to account for the idea of both positive and negative freedom. Freedom from is a negative freedom in that it implies only that there is no constraint imposed on the speech or actions. On the other hand, freedom to is seen as a positive freedom because it gives express permission for certain forms of speech or action (Merrill 1989, 19). This is a paradox for journalism ethics because we must use both types of freedom to ascertain who exactly benefits from, and has access to, the freedom available to 'the press'. The idea of *freedom from* and *freedom to* has been described as the difference between objective freedom and subjective freedom. *Freedom from* implies living without restraint, while *freedom to* implies choices (Okulicz-Kozaryn 2014). Some of these forms of media freedom are overlapping, but some of them are also juxtaposed and totally incompatible. On a simple level there are four possible sites where media freedom might be said to reside and each one sees freedom operate in slightly different ways but predominantly as either a negative or positive expression of freedom. Which location and which version of media freedom one chooses is dependent, to a significant degree, on the ideological worldview adopted as a lens to look through. In order to come to a full understanding of the complexities and contradictions involved in the determination of who gets to exercise media freedom, whether it is a positive or negative expression of freedom, what it means and why, we should start with some simple Level 5 abstractions: the individual journalist, the social collective of journalists, the institution, the citizen, the society, the corporation, and the State.

The simple, most libertarian, view of media freedom is that it applies uniformly to all journalists individually and it is a freedom to act according to one's own moral conscience (Domingo 2015). This is a Kantian version of freedom as a universal value that gives human beings their autonomy in the world (Demenchonok 2019). In this formulation, the single journalist is free to decide for him or herself what stories to report, how to report them, what angle to take, who to talk to and not talk to, which 'side' of the story to promote, and which to demote or ignore. At this level of abstraction, the journalist is the social actor who embodies both the negative freedom of having no constraint put on their actions or their speech and the positive freedom of having a 'right' to carry out the functions of a journalist (news gathering, reporting, having special access rights, etc.) in whatever form they choose. Merrill (1989, 30) adheres to this view of what he calls 'journalistic autonomy', or the 'separation of press and state, an independence…from government—a form of institutional freedom'. This is a problematic formulation because it is predicated on the false assumption that the State is a neutral arbiter rather than the locus for political power. The problem arises when conditions of formal freedom (Level 5) are privileged over actual social conditions (Levels 3 and 4) in which the formality of freedom is restricted by, for example, dictatorship, racism, sexism, or real economic inequality (Hamilton 2013).

The Level 5 corollary of Merrill's insistence on journalistic autonomy is obviously that these individual rights also hold for the collective journalist—for all journalists and at all times. The freedoms bestowed on the individual journalist are enjoyed by all journalists, without exception. This can then be further extended to the institution of the media and it is at this level where the idea that the institution of the news media embodies the ideals and the duties of the Fourth Estate. The Fourth Estate formulation also introduces the idea of responsibility alongside media freedom. However, it is a particular manifestation of responsibility and not necessarily how the term will be used in relation to general ethical codes or principles. In relation to the Fourth Estate, the responsibility is to carry out its duties on behalf of the general population of citizens—that is, the population constituted politically—and to use its freedoms to hold to account powerful social actors. In a market economy such powerful social actors are usually considered to be the political and commercial leaders and decision-makers.

Level 5 abstraction leads us to consider the media freedom embodied in individual citizens and in the social collective of citizens that are said to make up 'society'. Individual citizens and the collective citizenry have a right—a positive press freedom—to be given as much truthful information as they require in order to make informed decisions about things like what they consume and who they elect to powerful positions of political leadership. The negative freedom is freedom from being lied to and misled in ways that make them act against their own best interest. So, we see that there is a compact—a form of social contract—between the institution of the news media (constituting the Fourth Estate) and the collective citizenry. The news media has an institutional role to deliver to the social citizens an honest, factual, and truthful account of the workings of society—usually considered to be the economy and the government—that allows them to operate in their own best interests. This is what constitutes the idea of the public interest around which the news media and the population can gather on agreed terms.

All of this appears to work well in theory. However, as we've previously discussed, at levels 3 and 4 of abstraction, the political economy of the news industry in a capitalist economy, and the powerful interests of the capital-controlling class, distort our perfect model and distort any value-free assumptions on which it is built. Thus, we have to introduce the corporate news entity into the mix. The institution of the news media is a Level 5 abstraction that obscures the really important underlying structure of individual and competing nodes of media capital. Therefore, we must account for the general principles of media freedom as they are abstractly applied to these capitalist news enterprises at levels 3 and 4. At this point we must revisit another abstract concept that is loaded with ideological value, but which actually has very little value to use in terms of explanatory or theoretical insights. As previously discussed, the 'marketplace of ideas' is a construct that attempts to describe capitalist political economy according to the so-called laws of supply and demand. In the context of this chapter, the market is seen as a guarantor of press freedom.

In this construct, the freedom of the media is said to be embodied in the figure of the business owner who is free to do whatever he or she pleases with the capital and human resources at his or her disposal. Thus, if a media owner wishes to place their newspaper, radio or television station at the disposal of a particular political ideology or party they are free to do so and—in theory—the 'market' will determine the value of this action by either buying the product on offer or rejecting it. The business owner has the negative freedom to deploy or dispose of their asset without restraint and the positive freedom to endorse any ideology, individual or idea they want to, no matter how whacky. Unfortunately, Merrill's own positivist ideology means that he ends up defending market-based journalism in the most undialectical way:

> The press libertarian wants to retain *the traditional or pure nature* of press freedom…in wanting individual journalists, *or at least the media managers*, to be able to act in accordance with their own rational self-determination.
>
> (Merrill 1989, 32 emphasis added)

Merrill laments that the power of 'press managers' to exercise untrammelled editorial freedom is being circumscribed by talk of responsibility and reimagining press freedom 'as belonging to the people' (ibid.). However, consistent with his libertarian and individualist thinking, he is also capable of recognising that press freedom in a Level 3 market economy 'is not a democratic concept at all' but is 'tied in with economic control and power, and it lies in the hands of a press power elite' (ibid. 35). It is Merrill's inability to close this dialectical loop that leads to his theoretical mistakes.

Existential freedom

John Merrill is an individualist in keeping with his essentially libertarian world-view. For him, personal freedom—both positive and negative—is the most valuable asset to be treasured by journalists. Merrill (1989, 23) describes this as 'existential freedom', the freedom 'to act, to choose, to make one's self through choices and actions'. However, the ability of the journalist to be truly free in an existential sense also has limitations imposed on it at levels 3 and 4–the capitalist economy. Merrill recognises this as 'the difficulty of personal freedom in the workaday world'. As materialists we would add that the working world of the journalist is constrained by political economy; by the social relations of news production, and the inescapable antinomes that these relationships generate.

It is at this point, we argue, that Merrill's idealism loses touch with the material reality of the 'workaday world'. According to Merrill (1989, 24), the existential journalist must try to exercise the greatest personal freedom 'in spite of such difficulties' because of the 'inescapable responsibility' they bear to act only in accordance with their own individual and personal morality. Failure to achieve the noble ends of existential freedom is explained as journalists being in fear of freedom because they do not want to 'assume responsibility for [their] decisions' in a 'personal fight' (Merrill 1989, 25) for what they believe is right. Merrill also sees failure in a journalist's decision to seek collective support from colleagues and peers rather than 'choosing to make a stand alone'. We reject this formulation outright. For us, banding together in a union or other voluntary collective association is actually a source of strength for journalists and we take up this argument in the concluding chapter.

As we've argued from the beginning, Merrill embodies an idealist conception of history and dialectical change. He sees the synthesis of the antinomic paradox as some sort of balanced or middle way between two extremes. In our view this is a misreading of the dialectic, particularly in its Marxist application as a material manifestation of social forces. Writing about what he saw as key trends in attempts to regulate journalistic freedom in the 1980s, Merrill (1989, 36) laments the rise of 'press councils, journalism reviews and journals, ombudsmen and codes of ethics for journalists'. Today we tend to take most of these things for granted and perhaps even regard them as improvements that help guide journalistic behaviour and even enforce standards. Certainly, there is an infrastructure in place that formalises complaints processes and allows members of the public to speak directly to media organisations and have their concerns addressed. However, Merrill (1989, 36) didn't see it this way. Instead, he expresses his displeasure that journalists were becoming 'little more than cogs in the corporate wheel', whose main freedom 'is the freedom to quit and seek another job'. This leaves us wondering how he might view social media today as an arena where news consumers engage directly with individual journalists in often acrimonious exchanges and where non-professional citizen-journalists are able to report or offer opinion unmediated by editors and not filtered through traditional newsroom procedures. As we've noted already, tradition often becomes institutionalised and embedded in collective consciousness as an ideology. In the case of journalism and journalists, this tradition is formalised in the gatekeeper role of the Fourth Estate.

Gatekeeping and the Fourth Estate

> The first ethical entanglement is presented by the idea that the newspaper is a civic actor and business and political institution.
>
> (Burd 1978, 3)

Journalism has long claimed for itself the mantle of gatekeeper and protector of the public interest. These twin roles—claimed as essential to a democratic politics—are often referred to by the symbolic idea of the Fourth Estate. However, the conceptualisation of journalism as a Fourth Estate is highly problematic, even though it is an aspect of professional ideology that most journalists cling to and fiercely defend. The Fourth Estate mindset is also closely related to the idea that journalists are 'gatekeepers' who fact-check information to promote the public good and who carry the burden of responsibility for maintaining social adherence to 'the broader civic good or civic goal of democracy...that survives only through broad public access to reliable accounts of what is going on in the world' (Singer 2008, 63). However, as we've argued previously, the concept of the Fourth Estate is an aspect of the reification of journalism, part of a 'narrow caste consciousness' that ascribes to journalists 'a modest independent power' that stands 'next to others' but that is independent and powerful only in appearance (Fogarasi 1921, 151). The *essence* of the Fourth Estate is that the power and influence of the news media is really a result of journalists embracing the powerful, doing their bidding while maintaining a veneer of objectivity and independence.

The ideology of the Fourth Estate reflects the closeness of politicians and correspondents in the press gallery, despite its largely mythical reputation as a noble challenge to the powerful in defence of the public interest. The term 'Fourth Estate' was actually used to mock the political reporters rather than praise them. According the 19th-century British historian Thomas Carlyle, it was Edmund Burke who coined the term:

> Burke said there were Three Estates in Parliament, but, in the Reporters' Gallery yonder, there sat a *Fourth Estate* more important far than they all... Literature is our parliament too...Whoever can speak, speaking now to the whole nation becomes a power, **a branch of government** with inalienable rights in law making...the requisite thing is that he have a tongue which others will listen to; this and nothing more is requisite.
>
> (Carlyle 1841, 194; italics in the original, bold by us)

Carlyle was pointing out to his readers the relatively new idea that the news media had power too: '[T]he Press is to such a degree superseding the Pulpit... and much else...with palpably articulated, universally visible power' (ibid., 196). Carlyle ends this passage with the opinion that the press perhaps had too much power:

> What the best arrangement were, none of us could say. But if you ask, which is the worst? I answer: This which we now have, that Chaos should sit umpire in it; this is the worst.
>
> (Carlyle 1841, 196)

A generation later, the Irish socialist critic Oscar Wilde laid down his own observations of the Fourth Estate in an essay written in 1891:

> Somebody—was it Burke?—called journalism the fourth estate. That was true at the time, no doubt. But at the present moment it really is the only estate. It has eaten up the other three. The Lords Temporal say nothing, the Lords Spiritual have nothing to say, and the House of Commons has nothing to say and says it. We are dominated by Journalism. In America the President reigns for four years, and Journalism governs for ever and ever. Fortunately, in America journalism has carried its authority to the grossest and most brutal extreme. As a natural consequence it has begun to create a spirit of revolt. People are amused by it, or disgusted by it, according to their temperaments. But it is no longer the real force it was. It is not seriously treated.
>
> (Wilde 1891)

In the 130 years since Wilde's spiteful observation, the idea of the Fourth Estate has been stood on its head, mostly by journalists and scholars of journalism so that, today, this less flattering view is hidden from history. However, we are also perhaps seeing the emergence of a new 'spirit of revolt' against a less-than-satisfactory Fourth Estate. This revolution plays out on social media where prominent journalists are challenged and questioned. Some respond well to criticism and others use their own powerful corporate platforms to denounce their critics as ignorant trolls. We are not downplaying the fact that some journalists—particularly women—receive violent abuse on social media that is unwarranted and abhorrent (Posetti 2020), but there is a place in the news 'conversation' for reasoned and well-argued critique. There is a difference between demanding that journalists be accountable to readers—which ideally enhances consciousness on all sides—and abuse and intimidation. The inability to tell the difference between accountability and intimidation leads to journalists seeing themselves as above criticism and dialectically, to the violent 'Murder the Media' ideology of modern fascists. Intimidation is meant to silence journalists and also encourage hostility towards them. Such silencing was the whole purpose of Trump's deliberate attacks on the media throughout his presidency. For Trump discrediting the news media was a means of destroying the independent political consciousness of his supporters. He was telling them that only he could be trusted to tell the 'truth'. However, when journalists dismiss their critics as too ignorant to have an opinion they are acting on the worst aspects of their professional ideology that situates them as an elite. Neither hating journalists and calling for them to be silenced by violence, nor journalists' open scorn for readers and viewers who challenge them, does anything to help restore public trust in the news media.

The trust problem goes back a long way and so too does the problem of 'ethical entanglement' in which the role of the supposed 'detached observer' and Fourth Estate crusader for truth and justice is 'augmented by its ties and support to established authority' (Burd 1978, 3). This is particularly interesting in the hypocrisy it reveals among the ranks of some journalists. Senior editors and news managers often participate in political functions on committees and commissions associated with ruling class interests—business roundtables and the like, or on boards or inquiries—but they frown on journalists having any political affiliation of their own. Participation in the business of capitalism is seen as a legitimate exercise of press freedom and civic responsibility. (Good examples can be found in Burd 1978 and Goldstein 1985.) At the same time, journalists who choose to take their activism to the streets, in anti-war protests, or to support Black Lives Matter are marginalised, criticised and fired from their jobs. (Examples in Burd 1978; Wallace 2020 covers his own sacking in detail.) As Gene Burd noted (1978, 9), perhaps 'the paradox is explained by differences in perception about what is political involvement'. Anything that falls into what Daniel Hallin (1989) so accurately described as the 'sphere of deviance', such as participation in social justice movements, is frowned upon while membership of conservative think tanks is encouraged and even applauded: '[I]f a citizen-reporter supports the government, it is "safe partisanship" and not called activism' (Burd 1978, 10).

In summary, within the paradigm of the Fourth Estate the ideology of objectivity—itself an unsound concept constructed as a self-justifying catch-all excuse by journalists—normalises the relationship between the institutions of the so-called 'free' press and the authority of the State apparatus and leadership of the ruling class. In other words, the news media should be seen 'as an actual fourth branch of government', because it is 'not uncommon' for the news media to give itself a role in the prevailing power structures through having senior political reporters actively embedded in the halls of power leading to a whole host of 'ethical enigmas' (Burd 1978, 4). The final question remains: What can we do about this sad state of affairs? That trust between the news media and the public needs to be re-established is not in doubt, but how do we begin this process given everything that has gone before? The crises in the world that need to be reported and explained, the crises of appearance (finance, technology, trust) that are crippling public interest journalism, and the essential crises of epistemology and ontology outlined in the previous chapters are issues that must be addressed. The penultimate question then is: How do we make change that will stick? We turn our minds to answering this query in the next and final chapter.

Questions for discussion

1   Is objectivity still a useful concept for journalists?
2   Where does objectivity reside? Is it a property of the material, real world, or is it a mental construct in a journalist's head?
3   How are subjectivity and objectivity related?
4   How relevant is the Fourth Estate model for journalism today?
5   What is press freedom and who has it today?

17 Rebuilding trust in journalism

An ethical imperative

Can we fix the trust problem?

> [T]he current state of scholarship around trust in journalism is also broken.
>
> (Usher 2018, 564)

Journalism ethics is at a crossroads, serious scholars are beginning to recognise the epistemological and ontological crisis in journalism studies, and there is almost universal agreement among both producers and consumers of news that trust in journalism and journalists is declining. The question that it seems nobody has yet been able to answer is: How are we going to fix it? The answer lies in a close examination of the social relations of news production using the methods outlined in the previous chapters. In this chapter we want to be a bit more positive and discuss how trust between journalists and audiences can be restored.

The Knight Foundation and the Aspen Institute produced an expensive, glossy report on the troubling issue of trust, journalism, and democracy in February 2019 but in our view its recommendations were no more than motherhood statements (Knight Commission on Trust, Media and Democracy 2019). The Knight Foundation is one of the most influential think tanks producing endless reports on the future of journalism, but it cannot move its institutional thinking beyond lukewarm suggestions that the news industry needs to expand its revenue base and 'recommit' to ethical values. Another round of calls for newsrooms to 'diversify' in terms of hiring beyond the typical young, middle class, white male limits of convenience is going to have little to zero impact on news organisations already strapped for cash. The plea that 'leaders and new media entities must act responsibly and serve democratic principles' can only fall on deaf ears when the so-called innovators like Buzz-feed News are already downsizing their global operation just seven years after launching with high hopes and a huge amount of fanfare and goodwill. The report's recommendations about citizenship and rebuilding democracy are written within an entirely American context, but they are weak and almost meaningless even within that narrow remit. Civics education has existed in the American school curriculum for nearly 100 years, but today it is in sad decline

DOI: 10.4324/9780429242892-18

(Shapiro and Brown 2018). A systemic failure to engage students and inculcate even basic knowledge of government and politics won't be fixed by the Knight Foundation report. The call to 'reach across political divides' is unrealistic in a nation fractured by the very existence of Donald Trump in the White House, and encouraging a 'year of national service' and volunteering is a joke in a nation where many people have to work two jobs just to meet their monthly bills.

The crisis of trust is system wide and system deep. The news industry cannot fix the problem because it is part of the problem. The Knight Foundation's commission of eminent practitioners and scholars cannot fix the problem because they are embedded in the broken system and represent the News Establishment (Hirst 2018, 7–27). Current directions in journalism scholarship can't fix it because they are stuck in the epistemologies and ontologies of the marketplace, the Fourth Estate, and defending a hopeless ideal of objectivity. Restoring trust in journalism, so that it can effectively reclaim the mantle as a force for democratic change, requires a root and branch rethink. It cannot be wished into being by the Knight Foundation or any other well-meaning and philanthropic group of news insiders.

The journalist's quandary

Our colleague and friend, Professor Ian Richards, wrote a book about journalism ethics with the title *Quandaries and Quagmires*, which is a nice metaphor for how to imagine the tangled web of rights, obligations, consequences, and possibilities that any discussion of journalism ethics brings up. Ian notes that a focus on ethics often creates a 'consistent thread of anxiety among many journalists' wary of public criticism and reluctant to delve too deeply into ethical quicksand. Quandaries and quagmires is a nice metaphor for thinking about expressions of the dialectic in journalism. Like us, Richards also criticises 'a strong thread of anti-intellectualism' in the news profession (Richards 2005, 4). However, we think there's another reason why journalists are reluctant to investigate their ethical thinking too closely. It is uncomfortable because such a reflection would force them to confront some common, but unhelpful, myths about their own behaviour and their role in society. Tom Goldstein addresses this particular quandary directly in *The News At Any Cost*, and his theory is that the most difficult contradiction for journalists is to decide whether their job is 'to watch the world or to help change it'; 'journalists must decide to what degree they should be involved in the events they cover' (Goldstein 1985, 30, 32). This is good advice, but it is redundant to the extent that journalists cannot help but become involved and most, if not all, are involved in the stories they cover, even though they'd rather not admit it to themselves. The journalists' quandary today centres on how to rebuild public trust in the institutions that provide the news. There are two basic positions—though variations exist on a wide spectrum—involving differing conceptions of the role that journalists and news institutions play in meeting what is assumed to be journalism's 'democratic responsibility' (Coddington and Lewis 2020). On one side are the so-called 'traditionalists' who wish to return to a form of objective, neutral, and simply informative reporting; on the other are those who want journalism to be more 'engaged' with audiences. This is an interesting new fault line or, as Merrill would say, a new 'antinome' and a new contradiction that expresses the dialectic in journalism. However, it is important to explore both sides of this fault line in some detail before expressing any judgment on which approach—if either—can offer journalists a way forward out of the crisis of trust.

The editorial choices made in the newsroom shape the ways in which a story will be covered. Many editors and journalists like to maintain the polite fiction that their decision-making is done without emotion and without any regard to slanting the coverage in terms of politics or ideology. But no journalist or editor can function outside of their own mental maps of the world. Journalists are imbued with ideology. The very structures of the system—the social totality we discussed in earlier chapters—impose their own structures on our thinking (see our chapters on journalistic epistemology). These mental routines become so embedded that they come to define us—unless we make a conscious effort to think past them. It is the comfort of these ideological routines—what we often call *common sense* [1]—that underlies the problem of anti-intellectualism. This highlights again what we mean by a problem of epistemology in journalism: the uncritical reproduction of society *as it appears to be*, but not in its *essence*. This failure is a product of an uncritical consciousness that has not grasped the importance of the dialectical method (Nixon 2012, 447).

In philosophical terms, we can illustrate this problem by distinguishing between two types of thinking, or what Immanuel Kant called *Understanding* and *Reason*. Understanding is a shallow form of thinking that mistakes 'individual and random features' that are fixed on the surface of an object (*appearance*) for the dialectical unity of opposites that constitutes its real essence and relationships with other sensuously perceived phenomena. On the other hand, Reason reveals the 'essential relations…that determine [the object's] birth and evolution, but are not available to purely 'sensuous knowledge' (Pavlidis 2010, 89). It is thinking at the level of Reason that, ironically, brings thought back to the level of the concrete. We say *ironically* because the very concept of journalistic objectivity holds that it is the sensuous—that which can be perceived with the five senses—that constitutes the concrete. However, the irony is removed when we consider the triadic movement of dialectical thinking which begins with the sensuous reality—*appearance*—then abstracts and generalises to discover the internal contradictions that show us *essence* and then moves up again to the concrete, but this time reality seen as 'a system of internally interwoven concepts' (Pavlidis 2010, 92). Translating this back into our discussion of objectivity we can say that Reason contains elements of a healthy subjectivity in which the thinker is aware of their own position vis-à-vis both the objectively real world and their own position in it. As Periklis Pavlidis notes, Reason can be defined as refined Understanding, as 'thought which studies itself': 'At the level of Reason, the effort to comprehend the object is associated with critical examination of the way the concepts are constructed…

[and] every concept acquires a meaning...only through it link with other concepts' (Pavlidis 2010, 93).

This distinction—between Understanding and Reason—is important because without the conscious engagement of our mental faculties it is impossible to perform any really critical or dialectical thinking. Without breaking with the commonsense mode of thought it becomes impossible for journalists to see past the horizon of today's news agenda. Common sense is not a strong intellectual foundation on which to position journalism. It is too often, as the Italian Marxist, Antonio Gramsci, noted in his *Prison Notebooks*, 'fragmented and incoherent' and based on 'simplistic thinking' (Q4 s.21 cited in Buttigieg 2007a, 162[2]) Common sense is based on an implicit set of assumptions which are themselves already ideological, rather than 'scientific' in the Gramscian sense of being the 'absorption of past knowledge' as a prerequisite for 'the further development of knowledge' (Q6 s.180 cited in Buttigieg 2007b, 131). Common sense cannot give us the necessary 'ideological demystification' of the social totality of class society because this requires 'making visible the incoherence of what common sense takes at face value' (Watkins 1999, 87). However, in the spirit of dialectical enquiry we must understand that common sense is not just false consciousness, it is a 'contradictory thought process' that seems to provide an accurate picture of 'immediate reality' (Patnaik 1988, 7). On an everyday basis, common sense appears to provide a meaningful map with which to navigate the world, even while leading us astray (Watkins 1999). The dialectical nature of common sense is well illustrated by Evan Watkins in his formulation of 'capitalist common sense' derived from the application of Gramscian thinking to popular views of how the market economy functions; the problem we identified in relation to commodity fetishism and the marketplace of ideas in Chapter 15. This is also a good illustration of how the problem of commonsense thinking is manifest in journalists. We would argue that most of them—like most people in capitalist societies—tend to hold an ideological view in which 'the economy' appears to be a 'massive, stable, determinate and omnipresent Force' (Watkins 1999, 84) that cannot—and does not need to—be improved upon. In the commonsense view, capitalism seems not just inevitable and permanent, it is presented to us as the only 'ideologically desirable alternative to communism' (ibid. 85) and it exists outside of any historical sense of time or change (Patterson 2016). In reality, this commonsense idealism 'somehow always manages to legitimize even the most brutal forms of economic exploitation' as 'natural, normal, even desirable' (Watkins 1999, 87). This commonsense view permeates the journalistic profession and has done so for well over 100 years as Victor S. Yarros, noted in the *International Journal of Ethics* in 1922:

> That our newspapers are 'capitalistic,' in the sense that they represent and reflect the opinions and sentiments of the present social and economic order, is of course true...The men who control and direct the Press are perfectly sincere in their policies, though many of them are doubtless

ignorant. Most of them cannot imagine any social order different from the present one, and cannot take any radical 'ism' seriously.

(Yarros 1922, 410–11 ff.)

However, Yarros (1922, 412) plays his hand well and has written quite a biting critique of the newspapers of his day that makes visible the contradiction at the heart of the commercial news media both then and now. He writes that a reliance on advertising revenue distorts editorial values in a direction favourable to the advertisers with the 'inevitable result' that they have 'too much influence…and the readers too little'. This is a critical view and one that we share, but it doesn't help us to shift from a populist understanding—Gramscian 'common sense'—to a higher level of thinking, or what Gramsci called a *philosophy of praxis* (Gramsci Q21 s.1 cited in Green and Ives 2009, 409). There is a bridge between the two as would be expected in a dialectical relationship, and it can move commonsense thinking towards something more systematic and coherent that resembles a philosophy (Meadows et al. 2009, 166). As we shall see, it is a bridge we must cross in order to rebuild public trust in the institutions of journalism.

Which way forward to rebuild trust?

The distinction between traditionalist and engagement-oriented journalists is the centrepiece of a research paper published in the *Journalism and Mass Communication Quarterly* in September 2020 (Zahay et al. 2020). The authors have identified differing approaches to rebuilding trust adopted by the two types of journalist: one is based on 'reinforcing their professional identity' (traditionalists), the other on breaking down perceived boundaries between journalists and audiences (engagement-oriented). This latter approach is characterised as a 'dramatic change' in journalists' self-perception but realistically it has been happening for some time. In our view, despite the good intentions of the authors, the Zahay et al. paper suffers from being within the normative academic tradition which means it descends into jargon—'deliberative public', 'agentic public' and 'enterprise of expertise'—that replaces any meaningful theoretical and holistic analysis. It also relies on a small sample of only 42 interviews with reporters and writers that the research team placed into the traditionalist or engagement-oriented categories prior to the study. Engagement is a problematic concept that must be understood dialectically. Fox News prides itself on engagement, but it sells its audience appealing and well-packaged disinformation. Alex Jones' 'Infowars', the One America News Channel, and Breitbart are all experts at this type of engagement. Populism is built on this model of engagement, but it cannot be valorised as a positive contribution to the public sphere when it propagates deliberate lies in the service of authoritarian conservative politics. When the authors note 'many of those who expressed a traditionally oriented perspective worked in traditional or legacy media outlets, while those who expressed an engagement-oriented perspective worked in media trust initiative organisations' (Zahay et al. 2020, 7) it really doesn't tell us much. We should add that much of the academic literature in journalism studies is of this normative type, it's not just this one paper.

However, the Zahay et al. paper does usefully point to a new series of dialectical contradictions opening up within the field, and an emerging paradox between those who view journalism as a profession built on standards of objectivity, and those who see benefit in breaking down that hierarchy. We agree with Megan Zahay (2020) and her co-authors that a form of journalism 'codified by norms'—objectivity, balance, fairness, and accuracy, for example— is being superseded by new forms that are relational and 'prone to complexity and messiness' (14). There is a stark difference emerging between the traditionalists and the relationship builders.

Our concern is that resolving these differences will not automatically lead to the necessary changes needed to restore public trust in the news institutions and in professional journalism. As we've been suggesting throughout the earlier chapters, we think that the reconceptualisation of journalism needs to begin as a new intellectual project that rests on a fundamentally different ethical paradigm supported by a new epistemology and a refreshed ontology. It is a paradigm that embraces a materialist, dialectical, and historical understanding of the news industry and its interconnected ideological forms. One further criticism we would make of the Zahay et al. paper is its total reliance on normative assumptions about what constitutes a valid and active form of democracy. The authors make no attempt to unpack the idea of democracy, instead relying on terms such as 'deliberative' and 'pluralistic' to describe current arrangements. This is the sort of idealist approach that we criticised in our discussion of Merrill. These descriptive terms are far too abstract and tell us very little about how power is exercised; they effectively divorce the political process from centres of economic power and control. This includes the very market structures of the news industry that generate, reproduce, and perpetuate an ideology that claims some form of democratic legitimacy but which, in fact, masks structural inequalities based on class, and the intersectional categories of ethnicity, gender, and sexual orientation. Unless journalists are prepared to acknowledge these structural deficits in pluralistic market-oriented democratic societies it is hard to have much optimism that real change can take place. To make this change requires that the whole intellectual project of journalism be open to criticism and rebuilding on the basis of a well thought-out response to such a critique. This requires that journalism itself be reimagined, beginning with the foundational principles of objectivity.

Between objectivity and subjectivity

> A major, unresolved and troublesome dilemma in journalistic ethics centres around the predicament of journalism as both an objective observer and subjective participant.
>
> (Burd 1978, 3)

No amount of linguistic acrobatics or philosophical sophistry can overcome the problem that the ideal of objectivity espoused by journalists is no more than a construct of their own subjective consciousness. It is traditional and axiomatic that a text about journalism ethics should address the issue of objectivity, and we are certainly doing that as we have in all previous iterations of our books (Hirst and Patching 2005, 2007; Patching and Hirst 2014). However, in this section we want to address objectivity in another context: the tension between subjectivity and objectivity inherent in the internal relations of the concept and practice of *objectivity*. Our view here is in direct opposition to that of Steven Maras (2013) who outlines why he does not discuss subjectivity in his book *Objectivity in Journalism*: '[I]t can restrict discussion by placing objectivity and subjectivity in too neat and static an opposition, leading to the seemingly inevitable conclusion that objectivity is impossible because we are all subjective and biased' (18). This type of static formulation is only possible if the issue of subjectivity and objectivity is approached undialectically. From the perspective of dialectical thinking, subjectivity and objectivity are two sides of the same coin; they represent a unity of opposites within the internal relations of news production. There can be no objectivity without subjectivity and vice versa. Journalists cannot see this clearly for two reasons: 1. the fetishism of commodities distorts their view; and 2. the epistemological and ontological problems we've outlined. As Michael Schudson (2013, 159) has written, the 'philosophy of journalism' is 'riddled with self-deception'.

Within materialist and dialectical epistemology, it is our actions and relationships—with other people and with social structures and relations—that determine how we think. In other words, the 'objective external world exists independently of the human mind' and in turn 'structures and, indeed, determines the very ideas and concepts which we have of that world' (Kieve 1983, 53). However, there is a paradox in journalism that exists precisely because it does not operate according to this materialist viewpoint. Merrill provides an insight into this paradox by exposing the mental gymnastics through which the journalist appears to create objectivity out of subjectivity, 'he [sic] strains the objectivity of portions of the story through his mental, emotional, and psychological strainer and thereby presents the audience members with a subjective account of "what happened"' (Dennis and Merrill 1984, 108). In dialectical materialism, the objective world of material reality determines the subjective, but in journalism this polarity is reversed—the subjective view of the journalist appears to be an objective view of the world: 'the reporter's subjectivity—values, biases, interpretations and news judgments—always enter into the production of the story' (Dennis and Merrill 1984, 105). Journalistic claims to objectivity are in fact representations of a subjective view of the world. In other words, rather than taking objective reality as it exists, journalists *construct* a belief in objectivity out of their own subjective view of how the world is, or how they think it should be. Thus, the version of objectivity constructed by a journalist can be no more than the sum of their own prejudices, 'a kind of linguistic aura of objectivity' is how John Merrill puts it, adding that 'behind this aura is the reporter's subjectivity; there is *never* any real objectivity in reporting' (Dennis and Merrill 1984, 107, emphasis in original). Merrill's 'linguistic aura' is very much evident in the evasive, equivocal language that supporters use to justify their continued belief in objectivity and the ways in which they surrender critical ground and then try to make it up later: 'No one would argue that journalists can achieve perfection,' writes Everette Dennis in response to Merrill's challenges but then adds, 'I believe that journalistic objectivity is possible if we adopt methods that lead to systematic decisions' (Dennis and Merrill 1984, 114). Dennis' argument is full of such equivocations and resorts to the sort of evaluative language that should not be necessary to support claims to journalistic objectivity. If a reporter considers some types of information of more importance than others, partiality is already entering the newsgathering process: What are (and who decides) the 'reasonable standards by which trained reporters know' what is and isn't news? Who chooses the 'appropriate sources' to be used in a story? Of course, such decisions 'ought to be rational' but by whose standard is rationality judged? If writing 'adds tone and complexity of perception', who decides this is appropriate, and by what criteria? Who decides which of 'the writer's impressions, legitimately expressed' are accurate or meaningful? Dennis concedes that objectivity will still deliver 'a somewhat subjective portrait'. He admits 'values always play an important role,' and concedes that reporters will always 'bring an interpretive or sense-making perspective to the story'. In the end, Dennis reluctantly acknowledges that presuming things 'is the social function of journalism' (examples cited from Dennis and Merrill 1984, 114–118). Once you muddy the water with so many qualifications it is hard to see how a belief in objectivity survives, but it does. In our view this is because journalism has not faced down its own epistemological demons.

This persistent belief in journalistic objectivity is very much an ideological mode of thinking that reflects the constraints of capitalist class society because, by and large, the values of journalists—out of which they subjectively construct the shibboleth of objectivity—are those of bourgeois ideology. Real objectivity is not what the journalist wants to see, or thinks they see, it is what is actually there in its materiality and in its dialectical relations with the full reality of existence. A materialist epistemology is founded on an understanding that concepts and categories of thought derive from the 'objective world'. Materialism does not reject subjectivity and does not dismiss the notion that ideas can help to shape the world. However, it does place a determinate emphasis on the materiality of the objective reality in which we exist as Marx enumerated in a passage from another of his works: 'Men [sic] make their own history, but they do not make it as they please; they do not make it under self-selected circumstances, but under circumstances existing already, given and transmitted from the past' (Marx 1852). In a sense, the journalistic adherence to objectivity as an ethical tenet turns this materialist view on its head, while seeming to adhere to it. The objectivity doctrine in journalism is an abstraction that substitutes a subjective reading of *appearance* for real knowledge of the *essence* of the actual world being looked at through the journalistic lens. Journalistic objectivity begins with abstraction and is therefore an idealist construct and not anchored in materiality. The ideology of objectivity is 'derived from the most abstract, contentless, and indeterminate categories...constructed on idealist premises' (Kieve 1983, 160). In the materialist method, it is the other way around, abstractions can only be derived from an analysis of the 'concrete relations of the material world' (ibid.). The idealist notion of objectivity—that it is a timeless principle of good journalism—is also a value that underpins the ideology of press freedom, at least within the constructed 'marketplace of ideas'. In this regard, the idea of objectivity has become a 'strategic ritual' for journalists who wish to also claim for themselves freedom of the press (Lee 2007, 439). At this point—standing in the ethical crossroads—we must revisit the question of objectivity and subjectivity using the ideological 'vantage point' (Ollman 2003a, 101–112) of the oppressed. Without going into a long digression into economics we can distil the importance of this observation for journalists into one single phrase: objectivity—if it is to be useful—must be understood as 'the manifestations in thought of actual social and historical conditions' (Kieve 1983, 55). On this basis we can cross the bridge and begin to reimagine a new ontology and epistemology for journalism.

Reimagining journalism

> In the struggle my sympathies were not neutral. But in telling the story of those great days I have tried to see events with the eye of a conscientious reporter, interested in setting down the truth.
>
> (Reed 1919, 16)

John Reed was a young American reporter who found himself in Russia on the eve of revolution in October 1917. His passionate account of the Bolshevik rise to power was published as *Ten Days That Shook the World*. On his return from Petrograd and Moscow, Reed became a founding member of the Communist movement in the United States. Reed was unconventional—his own government prosecuted him several times for his anti-war politics and union organising—but he understood something important that set him apart from other journalists of his time: he challenged the dominant journalistic conventions and always situated his writing 'within a larger story of economic and political struggle' (Lehman 2002, 1). However, Reed was also careful to undertake diligent reporting premised on 'careful observation', 'research and analysis' which separated his work out from propaganda. What set him apart, says biographer Daniel Lehman (2002, 2), is that he understood and sided with his largely working class audience in ways that 'cut against the political and social grain'. Reed's career was cut short. He returned to Soviet Russia to cover the civil war in which the American, British, Australian, and French militaries played a role against the Bolsheviks. Reed contracted typhoid and could not return to the United States because Russia's ports were blockaded by imperialist forces. He died in Moscow on 17 October 1920.[3]

John Reed was four days short of his 33rd birthday when he died. His accounts of the Russian revolution and the uprising in Mexico in 1914, shortly before the outbreak of World War One, are now considered classics of war reporting. Reed died too young; we can only imagine what masterpieces of reportage he would have produced in a full life. Reed stands today as a model of what a reimagined journalist might be.

In Chapter 6 we mentioned the story of Desmond Cole, the *Toronto Star* columnist who resigned from the paper rather than give up his social justice activism. The incident was divisive at the masthead and across the city of Toronto. It's time to explore the issue a little more deeply and lay out some further relevant facts.

1   Desmond Cole is Black, a strong advocate for the Black Lives Matter movement in Canada and well known in Toronto for his opposition to the police practice of stopping Black people without probable cause. He is a community activist and the author of the 2020 book *The Skin We're In* chronicling anti-Black racism and police misconduct in Canada.
2   In July 2017—two months after disrupting the Police Board meeting—Cole staged another disruption and was arrested and taken out of the meeting in handcuffs.
3   Cole was a contract freelance columnist at the *Star* and not on staff at the time of the first incident in April. He had resigned before his July arrest.

When Cole very publicly announced his resignation from his part-time role at the *Toronto Star*, fellow columnist Shree Paradkar defended him in a column headlined 'It was wrong to rein in Desmond Cole' in which she wrote that the incident and its aftermath were not an 'academic discussion' but an issue that exploded 'in the messy and viscerally emotional context of race and racism' (Paradkar 2017). Cole provides another potential model for our reimagined journalist.

Integral journalism: Journalist as activist

Throughout this book we have tried to build a picture of journalism as both historically determined and grounded in the material social conditions of society. We have sought to describe how contemporary journalism is a product of historical development based on the political economy of the news business and the dialectical interplay of social forces manifest in various fault lines—the prominent contradictions that generate movement and change within the profession and the industry. As we bring our arguments to a close it is time to turn our attention—and our imagination—to considering what journalism might be. In particular, we want to discuss what we will refer to as dialectical journalism, or perhaps something close to what Antonio Gramsci described as 'integral journalism' in his *Prison Notebooks*. It is unfortunate that Gramsci died before he could complete the work he started in jail and it is not possible to fully create a working model of his ideas from the few pages of notes he left in his 24th Notebook where he tried to systematise his thoughts on what 'integral journalism' might become. However, we think there is enough in Gramsci's fragmented notes to outline an approach that would assist journalism to regain some of the revolutionary zeal it had at its birth in the 19th century. In the period that historian Eric Hobsbawm (1996) called 'the age of revolution', journalists were in the intellectual vanguard of a social class that was struggling to free itself from the oppressive yoke of subservience to a ruling class that had outlived its usefulness on the world stage. In the 20th century, during the revolutionary decades between 1905 and the mid 1920s, we find a period in which debates about the revolutionary potential of journalism were active once more. Like Antonio Gramsci, the Hungarian socialist and journalist Alabert Fogarasi was also interested in how the socialist press could combat bourgeois ideology and the propaganda of the daily press. To do this successfully, Fogarasi (1921, 151) argued, the socialist press must be committed to 'absolutely uncompromising and untrammelled truthfulness' if it is to transform how the working class thinks—overcoming reification—and 'awaken' class consciousness. Fogarasi and Gramsci were fighting the rise of fascism in Europe when they wrote about the socialist press. We don't have to imagine too hard to see the potential for similar authoritarian corporatist politics to rise again a century later when capitalism is in decay. Which means that, once again, we must consider the political role that journalists might play. Any media system—including journalism—that does not expose the corruption at the heart of capitalism is essentially complicit in extending the life of a system that is destroying the planet and the life it supports. Journalism and journalists should be part of the solution, not willing participants in covering up the problems. The old paradigm of objectivity and belief in an ideal market for news cannot address these issues in any meaningful way.

Impartiality or activism?

At this point we are confronted with the central contradiction that defines our ethical crossroads: Should journalists attempt to preserve some form of impartiality, or should they embrace activism when they have knowledge of the inherently problematic nature of contemporary society? Let's put this in stark terms:

- When covering authoritarian leaders who want to jail (or murder) their opponents and trash democratic norms, should journalists attempt to get their side of the story or align themselves with the opposition?
- When confronted with evidence of systematic racism and prejudice, should the journalistic response be to seek both sides of the argument or to vocally denounce racism?
- When confronted with the bloody reality of imperialist war, genocide, and the systematic subjugation of subaltern populations, should the journalist remain neutral or take the side of the oppressed?

- When confronted with overwhelming evidence that capitalism is the cause of global warming, should the journalistic response be to air denialism and excuses or to campaign for solutions?
- When the world is crying out for change, should the journalist side with the status quo or be part of the change?

We know these are confronting and difficult questions but shying away from them and not attempting to provide answers is one of the reasons journalism finds itself in the crisis of legitimacy we outlined in Chapter 6. Clinging to outdated notions of objectivity and impartiality is no longer an effective strategy for journalists. In fact, ethics must be about more than debates about 'dubious' methods—though that's still important—ethics has to be global and committed to something bigger than itself (Eagleton 2009). When the world is confronted by unethical inequalities in economic opportunity and the unequal distribution of political power, it is beholden on the ethical journalist to speak up. Refusing to consciously make such a choice is effectively choosing the side of inequality and injustice. If journalists really want to live up to the virtues of the Fourth Estate—to hold power to account and to represent the public interest—then the whole project of journalism needs to be reimagined, starting with rebuilding from the ground up on new philosophical principles. For example, we were pleased to see a call for the news media to make the idea of racial justice a core value of its journalism (Usher 2020) in the wake of the Black Lives Matter movement. After reviewing how it was covered throughout 2020. Nikki Usher's plea for racial justice to become an ethical principle for journalists is echoed by an inspiring member of the emerging generation of mid-career reporters and editors, Lewis Raven Wallace, a 33-year-old transgender radio journalist whose pronouns are 'he', 'ze' and 'they' (Wallace 2020). Lewis Raven Wallace is another well-credentialled role model for our integral and dialectical journalist.

Wallace became briefly notorious when ze was unceremoniously sacked from their job at the business news site Marketplace in January 2017 just days after Donald Trump's inauguration. Wallace was fired because of a blog post in which ze questioned the value of objectivity:

> When I posted the blog, I knew it might be controversial. What I didn't know was how dramatically it would change the trajectory of my life, as my own story became part of a tense national conversation over truth and journalism.
>
> (Wallace 2019, 3)

Wallace wrote a book, *The View From Somewhere*, with the subtitle, 'Undoing the myth of journalistic objectivity' in which ze traces the history of objectivity in American journalism and quotes one of their producer colleagues, Ramona Martinez, who told them, 'Objectivity is the ideology of the status quo' (cited in Wallace 2019, 9). If you've read the previous chapters, you will know by now that we fundamentally agree with this observation. In writing about recent coverage of the Black Lives Matter movement, Wallace also makes the point that objectivity tries to present available information—often from official sources and literally White-washed—'without any attempt to overcome pre-existing power dynamics...getting the police version was easy, while getting the rest was hard' (Wallace 2019, 26).

This takes us to the sort of journalism we're talking about that would, in Gramsci's words, seek to 'satisfy all the needs (of a certain category) of its public...to create and develop these needs and therefore to rouse its public in order to progressively expand it' (Q24 s.1, cited in Forgacs and Nowell-Smith 1985, 408). The way that Lewis Wallace talks about it highlights what this methodology might look like in practice. In relation to overcoming the official narrative of loyal police reluctantly using force on dangerous Black criminals, doing 'integral journalism' involves exposing the institutionally racist power structures of the police and justice system by, 'filling in the gaping holes in the picture, by helping to answer burning questions: Why had these tragedies happened? Why did they keep happening? Why were police so often protected when they killed innocent or unarmed people, especially Black people?' (Wallace 2019, 27). Wallace notes that the coverage of the issue began to change as the internal relations—the hidden inner dialectics of the conditions under which Black Americans had lived since segregation—were teased out into the open:

> [T]the story became about the structures that led to the protests: the racism, the institutional abuse, the forced segregation and disinvestment... decades of torn-down housing projects, neighbourhoods split by highways, White flight and the collapse of industry, a massive loss of Black wealth in the housing crash and endemic police violence against Black communities...a legacy of White supremacy and anti-Blackness... Bit by bit, that larger story began to be told...
>
> (Wallace 2019, 28)

If, as a reporter, you simply focus on the police press releases and coverage of the rioting and the burning buildings—often set alight in an angry and confused reaction to further police violence—then the story is about the criminal actions of looters. The hidden but *essential* history of racism, alienation, neglect, and justified resistance to oppression disappears and the truth does not get told. Despite the lack of 'truth' in your reporting, you would still be doing 'objective' journalism that attempts to find a 'balance' between the actions of the victim, the police, and the angry response from Black communities. You would end up being part of the problem when the world is crying out for solutions. In a prediction piece for Nieman Journalism Lab, John Ketchum (2020) wrote that more 'journalists of color' are likely to 'harness the power of their experience, audience, and knowledge' to strike out on their own, 'emboldened to start from scratch and build the kind of media ecosystem they want to see'. We'd certainly like to see this happen, but it won't be easy for the reasons we've discussed in previous chapters. We hope that the media ecosystem is ready to accept new styles of journalism, but style itself is not enough. Embracing a Gramscian or Fogarasian view of journalism means a reorientation towards class analysis and class politics because, in its broadest sense, Gramsci's 'certain category' means the working class in general, the most numerous fraction of 'the public' on the planet.

Of course, we cannot just apply Gramsci's formulas unamended. He was writing about a particular type of journalism, one that was explicitly linked to the project of building a mass socialist political party (Forgacs and Nowell-Smith 1985, 386). What we want to do is extrapolate from Gramsci's work to suggest a model for journalistic practice today that can move public opinion from an acceptance of the rule of capital and towards a greater understanding of class, by developing in the public 'concrete thinking' that shifts its worldview from 'simple common sense to coherent and systematic thought' (Q24 s.3, cited in Forgacs and Nowell-Smith 1985, 413). In this note, Gramsci writes about a type of journalism that can move the ordinary reader towards adopting a more 'scientific' way of thinking. This has to be critical and dialectical thinking and the best way for journalists to encourage audiences to be more dialectical in their thinking is to be more dialectical in their own thinking about journalism and the news. Alabert Fogarasi (1921, 152) suggests that journalists work closely with workers in shaping news coverage; perhaps this might be done through the trade union movement, or providing better coverage of strikes and protest movements. In fact, Fogarasi makes the astonishing claim that the type of coverage required to meet the task at hand cannot be written by journalists at all; 'the journalist as specialist corresponds…to the capitalist social order…[and] thereby adopts a piece of capitalist ideology'. This is true, but only in a partial sense. As we've argued all along, we have to view the world through the lens of dialectical thinking and analysis. Therefore, it is wrong to argue that journalists are always fixed in their ideological view. If they are 'grey collar' intellectuals with a contradictory consciousness (Hirst 2003), then they can be pulled in the direction of a materialist ontology and a more critical epistemology—if they're open to it and if the conditions are right.

A period of crisis like we are presently experiencing is precisely the right time to shake people—including journalists—out of an ideological stupor. Unfortunately, Gramsci is relatively silent on how journalists might accomplish the task of freeing themselves from ideology and go about raising class consciousness in the audience, but more contemporary theorists in the dialectical tradition provide some useful clues as to how we might proceed. Our starting point is a solid understanding of how capitalism both develops and disguises its class nature; therefore we can suggest that integral journalism should involve critical, dialectical thinking 'organically intertwined with a specific social-moral stance' that recognises the centrality of human emancipation as a guiding principle (Pavlidis 2010, 85). This means that journalists need to develop their understanding of the totality of relationships, especially 'those that are not immediately obvious' and of the historic relations between past, present, and future, what Bertell Ollman (2003b, 2) describes as relationships between 'what is, what could be, what shouldn't be, and what can be done about it all'. The purpose of such journalism is to help people overcome the 'fragmentation of existence' and to 'recognise the patterns' that emerge from the exploitative and unequal relations of production that define the Capitalist Mode of Production. This will help make the system 'whose effect on people's lives is constantly growing' to become visible so that those people can choose to do something about it (Ollman 2003b, 3). In order to see the world from this materialist and dialectical point of view, journalists need—as part of their new epistemology— to adopt a particular 'vantage point', a 'place from which to view' that provides 'a perspective that colours everything that falls into it, establishing order, hierarchy, and priorities, distributing values, meanings and degrees of relevance and asserting a distinctive coherence between the parts [internal relations]' (Ollman 2003c, 100). Following closely the path set out by Marx, Bertell Ollman discusses two distinct vantage points from which to survey the social system we know as capitalism: the first is from the point of view of the capitalist class as owners and controllers of the means of production who are therefore able to control, direct and profit from the labour of workers; the second is the vantage point of the working class. Unfortunately, most journalism takes the view of the ruling class either directly or by default. It is the prevailing commonsense view of ideology, adopted out of pragmatism or ignorance. David-Hillel Ruben (1979, 109) makes the point that the differences between idealism and materialism—our preferred philosophical stance—is not just about epistemological variations, it is a choice 'between two competing ideologies' and ultimately, a political choice based on the worldview mediated by class relations. It is this second, openly partisan point of view—the vantage point of the oppressed, exploited, and alienated worker—that we are suggesting that journalism should adopt in order to fully appreciate the inner relations and dialectical contradictions that energise capitalism and animate the conditions of inequality that are its essence. This is not some random idea on our part; it is a development of the tradition known as 'standpoint ethics' (Harding 1993).

Standpoint ethics

> The point of good journalism is to achieve social benefit.
>
> (McDonald and Avieson 2020, 34)

Standpoint ethics requires journalists to be on the right side of history. If journalism can recognise that some things achieve a 'social benefit', it must be able to broadly distinguish between right and wrong. Standpoint ethics developed as a response to critiques of a male-centric epistemology in scientific disciplines that claimed to be value neutral (Doucet 2018). This fits nicely with our own approach because of its roots in Hegel and Marx (ibid., 76). Willa McDonald and Bunty Avieson have pioneered bringing knowledge of standpoint ethics into journalism studies to argue that the 'social location' of the reporter colours their worldview (Avieson and McDonald 2017, 138). Meenakshi Durham (1998, 122) calls the discussion of standpoint ethics in journalism a 'necessary step' in resolving the current impasse at the crossroads marked out by 'the contradictions and oppositions inherent in the current news paradigm'. We think she's right. However, the really radical element of standpoint ethics is that it also recognises and challenges the structural inequalities and unequal power differentials of class, gender, and ethnicity that define capitalist society. Avieson and McDonald confine their discussion of standpoint ethics to a defence of undercover reporting used to expose injustice and to shine a light on events, relationships, and struggles that remain largely invisible to elite journalism: '[R]eporting can be seen as an ethical approach to uncover the lived realities of the disadvantaged, as well as a method to gain different insights into the power structures of society' (Avieson and McDonald 2017, 140). This is a good start, but we think it can—and should be—taken a few steps further across the bridge to integral journalism.

Standpoint ethics provides a strong moral, political, and ethical grounding for our advocacy of Gramsci's integral journalism with its focus on reporting from an explicit working class 'vantage point'. The objection might be raised to our argument that journalists already occupy a vantage point—speaking truth to power, holding power to account, the Fourth Estate, etc.—and this is true. Our reply is simply that the epistemology and ontology of these viewpoints is flawed, as we've discussed in previous chapters. This bourgeois point of view is somewhat taken for granted by journalists who are not generally aware that the abstractions they are using to arrive at their position are those of a particular culture and class. Ollman's comment is apt in this context; the journalist's ability to view the world from a different vantage point has become 'atrophied', and the 'one-sided views that result are treated as not only correct but as natural, indeed *as the only possible view*' (Ollman 2003c, 102, emphasis added). It seems to the journalist to be a commonsense view based purely on observation of an objective reality, but—for the reasons we've explained—it is mistaken to think that it reflects the world as it actually is with all its contradictions and hidden inner relations. The reporter is trapped in an ideological vortex in which the 'relations and movements that pertain to the particular problem' are invisible, 'all the while being unaware of the limits on what can be learned from this side alone' (ibid.). In this sense, ideology is not false consciousness, it is an 'overly narrow, partial, out of focus and/or one-sided' perspective created out of a faulty epistemology that misapplies concepts (abstractions, generalisations, and theories) that disrupt the reporter's ability to see clearly 'the essential features of capitalism'. Ollman (2003c, 103) sets out a useful list of the distortions that arise from not adopting the appropriate (class-bound) vantage point: 'the vantage point of the isolated individual, the subjective side of any situation [belief, etc.]…anything connected with the market, and all of what falls on level five of generality, particularly human nature'.

You might be thinking that we are out of bounds with these suggestions and that it is not the role of journalism to agitate for the overthrow of capitalism and for revolution. Our answer is that this is precisely the role that journalism took at the height of the last great period of revolution from the middle of the 17th century until the closing years of the 19th century. Committed, class-based and highly polemical journalism was central to the successful outcomes of the bourgeois revolutions that rocked Europe and America throughout this period, and which actually brought modern capitalism into existence as a global system (Hobsbawm 1996; Pavlidis 2010, 83). The point is that during this period journalists were articulate and active proponents of social upheaval in the service of a revolutionary social class. In our view it is time for them to reclaim this history, to celebrate it, and to recreate it in the service of the oppressed, alienated, and exploited majority today. We are talking here in terms of a new form for journalism, one that will take some time to develop organically, and that can only arise from engaging with current conditions.

A revolutionary break with the epistemology of objectivity

As our historical and contemporary examples show, there is a space opening up for journalism to break with the paradigm of objectivity and *faux* impartiality. We are at the decision point, our ethical crossroads, which it seems is now also the location of a useful bridge! If the news media is to play a positive role in rebuilding democratic institutions, overcoming the challenges of capitalism-induced climate change, and confronting authoritarian anti-democratic politics, then journalists must begin to embrace a new philosophical outlook of engagement and participation in struggle and work alongside community activists. This is the new public interest test for journalists. This is also the beginning of a new discussion that we must have about the value of journalism and the values that journalists hold. Revolutions do not happen overnight, and they are not generated out of thin air. Change takes time, particularly in a tradition-bound field like journalism. It is the crisis itself which dictates the necessity of change, but it is the people involved who must carry it through.

Revolutions also require imagination and a philosophical underpinning. The future arrives first in the imaginary; revolutions begin with ideas and values. This is why we have tried to introduce philosophy into this debate and why we think that ethical values must be at the centre of any discussion about why and how journalism might change. Change is necessary and can no longer be put off. If trust in journalism is not restored soon then the world will continue down its current path towards climate disaster, greater economic inequality, more authoritarianism, and less humanism without any form of informational corrective. The days of journalists just standing on the outskirts of conflict and only reporting are over. Journalists must be part of the solution—their status as information brokers demands it—and this means they must re-evaluate what they do and how they do it. In this book we have set out the problem, but we don't claim to have all the answers. All we know for sure is that the old, traditional ways no longer work, and current experiments that tinker with the business model, but don't address the underlying value propositions, are failing around us. In the 1920s—another period of crisis for democracy—radicals like Gramsci and Fogarasi were arguing for a specifically socialist press, but we think that some of their better ideas can be adapted in a modest and slightly modified way by journalists today who are groping towards a better future.

The idea of 'worker correspondents' might seem too strange, or too radical *today*, but the technical means to make this idea workable *tomorrow* already exist. Social media is a great leveller, and many working people are already creating their own news. With some training and encouragement (Hirst 2018) these amateurs could be a real asset for journalists and newsrooms that really want to shift the debate and make a difference by framing news 'from the workers' point of view' (Workers' Life 1928, 153). There is also an ethical point in this history lesson: the ethical standpoint of the 'worker correspondent' can provide material that helps readers to understand the 'political moral' of the incidents they write about while resisting the urge to 'break out into a sermon' (ibid., 156). The purpose of this kind of class-oriented journalism must be to overcome reification and break the ideological spell of commodity fetishism. This means refocusing journalism on 'the more stubborn contradictions and derangements of our consumer culture' and subjecting the totality of capitalist social relations to 'sustained political criticism' (Lehmann 2015, 38). As we've been implicitly reminding you all along, from crisis comes opportunity. This is journalism's opportunity to play a real and effective role in positive global change. The question is: Will journalism reinvent itself in time to save the world?

That's enough from us. It is up to current and future generations of journalists to seize the opportunity, to work on these problems, and to road-test more thorough-going solutions. This is something they must do in collaboration with their audience, particularly those who are outside the small ruling elites and who will be the driving force of real social change. This is the real strength of Gramsci's 'integral journalism'. Throughout this book we have frequently referred to the work of the late journalism scholar John C. Merrill and we have sought to rescue his legacy from obscurity while critically assessing his ideas about journalism, philosophy, and ethics. Like us, Merrill was an advocate for placing a study of dialectic thinking at the core of journalism theory and practice. We'd like to dedicate this book to his memory and to encourage further engagement with his thinking about how to secure the future of journalism. Merrill was flawed in many ways and quite conservative, but over a period of 30 years his thinking developed and became more nuanced. Importantly, as a student of the dialectic, he believed that change is inevitable and he sought to ensure that journalists are mentally equipped to understand and lead the process of change. It is appropriate that we leave you with his words:

> Journalists, at least those concerned with lasting value, are going to have to recognize the great importance of their own values, not only when they are interpreting the news, but also when they are deciding what it is and

how they will play it. If, and when, this happens, we will witness a real revolution in journalism, for values are at the very foundation of journalism. As values change, journalism changes.

(Merrill 1983, 110)

Questions for discussion

1   Discuss standpoint ethics.
2   Activism or objectivity?
3   Take a stand or stay neutral?
4   Do you see crisis or opportunity?
5   You're at the crossroads; which way do you go?
6   Will you build a bridge and get over it?

Notes

1   *Common sense* is the noun form, *commonsense* is the adjectival form.
2   We are following the convention in Gramscian scholarship of identifying the *Prison Notebooks* source by folio [Q] and entry [s.]
3   Coincidentally, I am writing this on the 100th anniversary of Reed's death. (MH)

Bibliography

Not all online references have a URL or a specific source of publication. In these instances it is because the text (which sometimes appears in more than one source) is easy to find using the headline as a search term. Where there is no given author for an article, the newspaper, online source or TV programme it has come from is used instead.

2GB. 2019. Ben Fordham faces AFP raids after source reveals confidential information. Radio 2GB. 4 June. Accessed 18 July.

@janehansen2000. 2018. Daily Mail lifts story. 16 September.

Abbruzzese, Jason. 2014. In wake of James Foley beheading video, journalists rush to self-censor. Mashable. 20 August. Accessed 20 August.

ABC. 2009. Freed Australian describes hostage ordeal. ABC News. 26 November. Accessed 26 November.

ABC. 2011. Reporter sexually assaulted by mob in Egypt. ABC News. 16 February Accessed 16 February.

ABC. 2013. Guidelines for personal use of social media. Accessed 11 April.

ABC. 2016a. Bill Leak cartoon in The Australian an attack on Aboriginal people, Indigenous leader says. ABC News. 4 August. Accessed 3 November.

ABC. 2016b. Operating official ABC social media accounts ABC editorial policies. ABC News. 29 July. Accessed 22 July 2020.

ABC. 2017. Anthony Weiner jailed for 21 months in teen sexting case. ABC News. 26 September. Accessed 9 January 2021.

ABC. 2018. Serena Williams: Cartoonist Mark Knight defends depiction of US Open tantrum amid accusations of racism. ABC News. 10 September. Accessed 11 September.

ABC. 2019a. Julian Assange's treatment in prison putting his life at risk, UN rights expert warns. 2019. ABC News. 2 November. Accessed 4 November.

ABC. 2019b. Meghan Markle and Prince Harry release photo of Royal baby Archie after private christening. ABC News. 7 July. Accessed 7 July.

ABC. 2020a. ABC journalist Dan Oakes will not be prosecuted over Afghan Files leak. ABC News. 15 October. Accessed 27 November.

ABC. 2020b. Donald Trump accuses Twitter of 'stifling free speech' with fact-check warning, says platform in interfering in US election. 2020. ABC News. 27 May. Accessed 29 May.

ABC. 2020c. Donald Trump threatens Twitter after fact-check on claims about mail-in ballots. 2020. ABC News. 27 May. Accessed 29 May.

ABC. 2020d. Independent broadcaster ABS-CBN shut down by Philippines Government in 'crushing blow' to press freedom. ABC News. 6 May. Accessed 20 May. www.abc.net.au/news/2020-05-06/philippines-news-outlet-closure-abs-cbn-duterte/12218416.

Abdenour, Jesse. 2017. Digital gumshoes: Investigative journalists use of social media in television news reporting. *Digital Journalism* 5 (4): 472–492. https://doi.org/10.1080/21670811.2016.1175312.

Abrams et al. v. United States. 1919. *In 250 U.S.* 616: US Supreme Court.

Addley, Esther, and Beatrice Woolf. 2012. Julian Assange seeking asylum in Ecuadorean embassy in London. *The Guardian*. 20 June. Accessed 29 July 2019.

Adorno, Theodor W. 2017. (1958). *An Introduction to Dialectics*. Translated by Nicholas Walker, edited by Christoph Ziermann. Cambridge, UK: Polity. Reprint, 2020.

Ahmed, Kaamil. 2020. Covid-19 could trigger 'media extinction event' in developing countries. *The Guardian*. 6 May. Accessed 7 May.

Akerman, Tessa. 2019. Age payout to traumatised ex-crime reporter 'under review'. *The Australian*. 19 December. Accessed 23 December.

Alexander, Larry, and Michael Moore. 2016. Deontological ethics. In *Stanford Encyclopedia of Philosophy*, edited by Edward N.Zalta. Stanford, CA: Metaphysics Research Lab, Stanford.

Ali, Yashar. 2019. In San Francisco, an attack on press freedoms and echoes of autocracy. CNN. 18 May. Accessed 20 May.

Alizadeh, Ali. 2019. Marx and art. *In Solubilia: New Work in Contemporary Philosophy*, edited by A.J. Bartlett, Justin Clemens, and Jon Roffe. London and New York: Rowan and Littlefield International.

Allsop, Jon. 2019. A mosque massacre is livestreamed. *Columbia Journalism Review*. 15 March. Accessed 16 March.

Almiron, Nuria. 2010. *Journalism in Crisis: Corporate Media and Financialization (IAMCR series)*. Translated by William McGrath. Cresskill, NJ: Hampton Press.

Alonson, Martin Oller, Carolos Arcila Calderon, and Dasniel Olivera Perez. 2019. Pre-professional journalistic culture of Cuba, Ecuador and Venezuela: Motivation, expectations and professional experience of students of journalism and social communication. *Revista Latina de Comunicacion Social* (74): 477–498.

ALRC. 2014. *Serious Invasions of Privacy in the Digital Era*. Australian Law Reform Commission. 3 September. Accessed 31 March 2019.

Ananian-Welsh, Rebecca. 2020. Security Committee recommends bare minimum of reform to protect press freedom. The Conversation. 27 August. Accessed 28 August.

Anderson, C.W., and Juliette De Maeyer. 2015. Objects of journalism and the news. *Journalism* 16 (1): 3–9. https://doi.org/10.1177/1464884914545728.

Andrejevic, Mark. 2007. *iSpy: Surveillance and Power in the Interactive Era*. Lawrence, KS: University Press of Kansas.

Anthony, Kelvin. 2020. Fijian military leader defends government's right to 'stifle' press during Covid crisis. *The Guardian*. 27 April. Accessed 1 May.

APC. 2019. *Adjudication 1758: Complainant/Herald Sun (February 2019)*. www.press council.org.au/document-search/adj-1758/.

APC. 2020. *Adjudication 1773: Complainant/Woman's Day 17 February)*. www.press council.org.au/document-search/adj-1773/.

Araújo, Bruno, and Hélder Prior. 2020. Framing political populism: The role of media in framing the election of Jair Bolsonaro. *Journalism Practice* 15 (2). https://doi.org/10.1080/17512786.2019.1709881.

Archer, Allison M.N., and Joshua D. Clinton. 2017. Changing owners, changing content: Does who owns the news matter for the news?*Jepson School of Leadership Studies, articles, book chapters and other publications.* Accessed 8October 2019.

Artz, Lee. 2006. On the material and the dialectic: Toward a class analysis of communication. In *Marxism and Communication Studies: The Point Is to Change It* (*Marxism and Media Studies* series), pp. 5–51. New York: Peter Lang.

ASJMC & AEJMC. 2020. Joint statement on arrests and violence towards journalists covering protests across the country. *AEJMC.* 9 June. Accessed 11 June.

Associated Press. 2013. Social media guidelines for AP employees. 7 May. Accessed 11 April 2019. www.ap.org/assets/documents/social-media-guidelines_tcm28-9832.pdf.

Atkinson, Claire. 2019. Sports Illustrated to cut staff as new owner takes over. NBC News. 4 October. Accessed 7 October 2019.

Attia, Gullaume A.W. 2017. How philosophy can make journalism better. Medium. com. Accessed 16 November 2020.

Audi, Robert. 2011. Epistemology: A contemporary introduction to the theory of knowledge. In *Routledge Contemporary Introductions to Philosophy* (third edn), edited by Paul K. Moser. New York and London: Routledge.

Avieson, Bunty, and Willa McDonald. 2017. Dangerous liaisons: Undercover journalism, standpoint theory and social revelation. *Media International Australia* 163 (1): 137–150. https://doi.org/o0r.g1/107.171/1737/2193829787X8X161668866205.

Bacon, Wendy. 2019. Journalism is not a crime—why I support Wikileaks and Julian Assange. wendybacon.com. 5 July. Accessed 12 July.

Bailey, Issac J. 2020. Bob Woodward and the ethics of the presidential scoop. NiemanReports. 10 September. Accessed 18 September.

Baker, Anne, Robert G. Boatright, Anthony J. Corrado, Diana Dwyre, John Green, and Clyde Wilcox. 2020. How super PACs have transformed the federal campaign finance system: A political scientists' Amicus brief to the Supreme Court. https://ssrn.com/abstract=3659999.

Ball, James. 2017. *Post-Truth: How Bullshit Conquered the World.* London: Biteback Publishing.

Bants, Kees, Claes H. de Vreese, Judith Möller, and Philip van Praag. 2010. The real spiral of cynicism? Symbiosis and mistrust between politicians and journalists. *International Journal of Press/Politics* 15 (1): 25–40. https://doi.org/10.1177/1940161209351005.

Barker, Anne. 2018. Dissident journalist Arkady Babchenko's staged assassination delivers propaganda bonanza to Moscow. ABC News. 11 May. Accessed 1 June.

Barns, Greg. 2019. Greg Barns: Australian media need to accept Julian Assange is one of them. *The Daily Telegraph.* 23 June. Accessed 25 June.

Barry, Dan, et al. 2003. Correcting the record: Times reporter who resigned leaves a long trail of deception. 2003. *The New York Times,* 11 May, p. 1.

Barry, Paul. 2018a. Cliff Richard v The BBC. Media Watch, ABC (Episode 24, 2018). 23 July. Accessed 24 July.

Barry, Paul. 2018b. Fury at the Mail. Media Watch, ABC (Episode 39). 5 November. Accessed 5 November.

Barry, Paul. 2019a. Al Jazerra's undercover sting into One Nation and the American gun lobby divides journalists over the covert methods used. Media Watch, ABC (Episode 9). 1 April. Accessed 7 April.

Barry, Paul. 2019b. Assange: Hero or villain? Media Watch, ABC *(Episode 17)*. 3 June. Accessed 5 June.

Barry, Paul. 2020. July 27. Online abuse. Media Watch, ABC *(Episode 25)*. 27 July. Accessed 28 July.

Barthel, Michael. 2017. Despite subscription surges for largest U.S. newspapers, circulation and revenue fall for industry overall. FactTank. 1 June. Accessed 5 July 2018.

Bartzen Culver, Kathleen. 2014. From battlefield to newsroom: Ethical implications of drone technology in journalism. *Journal of Mass Media Ethics* 29 (1): 52–64. https://doi.org/10.1080/08900523.2013.829679.

Baumane-Vitolina, IlonaIgo Cals, and Erika Sumilo. 2016. Is ethics rational? Teleological, deontological and virtue ethics theories reconciled in the context of traditional economic decision-making. *Procedia Economics and Finance* (39): 108–114. https://doi.org/10.1016/S2212–5671(16)30249–0.

Baumbach, Nico, Damon R. Young, and Genevieve Yue. 2016. Revisiting postmodernism: An interview with Fredric Jameson. *Social Text* 34 (2): 143–160. https://doi.org/10.1215/01642472-3468026.

Bayer, Kurt, and Anna Leask. 2020. Life without parole: Wicked, cruel, pitiless mass murderer jailed indefinitely. *NZ Herald*. 28 August. Accessed 28 August.

Baynes, Chris. 2019. 'Police state': Media and MPs decry Met Police threats to prosecute journalists who publish leaked Kim Darroch cables. *Independent* (UK). 14 July. Accessed 20 July.

BBC. 2007. Biography: Alan Johnston. BBC. September. Accessed 16 November.

BBC. 2019a. ABC raid: Outcry as Australian police search public broadcaster. BBC News. 6 June. Accessed 18 July.

BBC. 2019b. Guidance: Social media. Editorial guidelines. BBC. Accessed 18 July. www.bbc.com/editorialguidelines/guidance/social-media.

BBC. 2020a. Buzzfeed closing UK and Australian news operations. BBC News. 13 May. Accessed 20 October.

BBC. 2020b. Why is Trump calling Black Lives Matter a symbol of hate? BBC News. 2 July. Accessed 21 October.

BBC. 2021. Julian Assange: UK judge blocks extradition of Wikileaks founder to US. 2021. BBC News. 4 July. Accessed 5 January.

Beckett, Charlie, and Robin Mansell. 2008. Crossing boundaries: New media and networked journalism. *Communication, Culture & Critique* (1): 92–104. https://doi.org/doi:10.1111/j.1753-9137.2007.00010.x.

Bedo, Stephanie. 2021. Meghan Markle and Prince Harry 'quit social media' after 'almost unsurvivable' experience of online trolling. News.com.au. 10 January. Accessed 11 January.

Beiser, Elana. 2019. China, Turkey, Saudi Arabia, Egypt are world's worst jailers of journalists. CPJ Special Report. 11 December. Accessed 18May 2020.

Beiser, Elana. 2020. Record number of journalists jailed worldwide. Committee to Protect Journalists. 15 December. Accessed 18 December.

Belair-Gagnon, Valerie, Taylor Owen, and Avery E.Holton. 2017. Unmanned aerial vehicles and journalistic disruption. *Digital Journalism* 5 (10): 1226–1239. https://doi.org/10.1080/21670811.2017.1279019.

Bell, Emily. 2019. What 2,000 job cuts tell us: The free market kills digital journalism. *The Observer*. 3 February. Accessed 6 February.

Bell, Emily. 2020. Donald Trump needs the media he despises to fight coronavirus. *The Guardian*. 9 March. Accessed 10 March.

Bellamy Foster, John. 2019. Captialism has failed—what next? *Monthly Review* 70 (9). https://monthlyreview.org/2019/02/01/capitalism-has-failed-what-next/.

Ben-Ghiat, Ruth. 2020. How journalists became objects of hate. CNN. 11 June. Accessed 15 June.

Bender, Stuart. 2019. Social media creates a spectacle society that makes it easier for terrorists to achieve notoriety. The Conversation. 18 March. Accessed 19 March.

Beniac-Brooks, Samantha. 2018. Ending impunity for crimes against journalists. Special Broadcasting Service. 3 November. Accessed 4 November.

Bennett, Catherine. 2019. Tormenting Meghan Markle has become a national sport that shames us. *The Guardian*. 17 February. Accessed 17 February.

Benson, Simon, and Rosie Lewis. 2019. Christchurch shooting: Morrison's call to G20 leaders to bring order to 'ungoverned' internet. *The Australian*. 19 March. Accessed 19 March.

Berkovic, Nicola. 2019. Al Jazeera gun sting beyond spy laws' scope. *The Australian*. 27 March. Accessed 27 March.

Berkowitz, Dan. 1993. Work roles and news selection in local TV: Examining the business-journalism dialectic. *Journal of Broadcasting & Electronic Media* 37 (1): 67–81. https://doi.org/doi.org/10.1080/08838159309364204.

Berkowitz, Dan, and Yehiel Limor. 2003. Professional confidence and situational ethics: Assessing the social-professional dialectic in journalistic ethics decisions *Journalism and Mass Communication Quarterly* 80 (4): 793–801.

Berlatsky, Noah. 2020. The truth behind Bari Weiss's resignation from the 'NYT'. *Observer*. 15 July. Accessed 8 January 2021.

Bernard, Diane. 2019. She went undercover to expose an insane asylum's horrors. Now Nellie Bly is getting her due. *The Washington Post*. 28 July. Accessed 10 January 2021.

Bertuzzi, Robert. 2017. Journalism's prime sources create bias: Can columnists be activists, too? *The Toronto Star*, 15 May. Accessed 9 October 2020. www.pressreader.com/canada/toronto-star/20170515/281655370000014.

Better Programming. 2020. Understanding racial bias in machine learning algorithms. *Medium*, 12 June, Accessed 15 October.

Bezanson, Randall P. 2001. Profits and press freedom: The new business of news. *Human Rights* 28 (4): 20–23. www.jstor.org/stable/27880286.

Bezos, Jeff. 2019. No thank you, Mr. Pecker. Medium.com. 8 February. Accessed 9 February.

Bhaskar, Roy. 1993. *Dialectic: The Pulse of Freedom*. London & New York: Verso.

Bimber, Bruce. 1990. Karl Marx and the three faces of technological determinism. *Social Studies of Science* 20: 333–351.

Binns, Peter. 1973. The Marxist theory of truth. *Radical Philosophy* 1 (4). www.radicalphilosophy.com/article/the-marxist-theory-of-truth.

Birtles, Bill. 2020. In the midst of the coronavirus pandemic, China forces out foreign reporters. ABC News. 9 May. Accessed 12 May.

Bissonette, Devan. 2020. 'Modern day presidential': Donald Trump and American politics in the age of Twitter. *Journal of Social Media in Society* 9 (1): 180–206. www.thejsms.org/tsmri/index.php/TSMRI/article/view/472.

Blackburn, Piper Hudspeth, and Dylan Lovan. 2020. Kentucky grand jury declines to file homicide charges against police officers in death of Breonna Taylor. *Boston Globe*. 23 September. Accessed 2 October.

Blair, Jayson. 2004. *Burning Down My Masters' House*. Beverly Hills, CA: New Millenium Entertainment.

Blasi, Vincent. 2004. Holmes and the marketplace of ideas. *The Supreme Court Review*2004: 1–46. www.jstor.org/stable/3536967.

Blow, Charles M. 2019. Defending the free press. *The New York Times*. 5 May. Accessed 6 May.

Boger, George. 1991. On the materialist appropriation of Hegel's dialectical method. *Science and Society* 55 (1): 26–59. www.jstor.org/stable/40403116.

Borchers, Callum. 2016. On Melania Trump's plagiarism, a laid-off journalist watching in an L.A. Starbucks scooped everyone. *The Washington Post*. 19 July. Accessed 21 July.

Borger, Julian. 2013. NSA files: Why the Guardian in London destroyed hard drives of leaked files. *The Guardian*. 31 August. Accessed 10 January 2021.

Boudana, Sandrine. 2011. A definition of journalistic objectivity as a performance. *Media, Culture & Society* 33 (3): 385–398. https://doi.org/10.1177/0163443710394899.

Bourdieu, Pierre. 1998. *On Television and Journalism*. London: Pluto Press.

Bourke, Latika. 2015. SBS sports reporter Scott McIntyre sacked after Malcolm Turnbull intervention, court to hear. *The Sydney Morning Herald*. 13 October. Accessed 13 October.

Bowcott, Owen. 2019. US court finds Assad regime liable for Marie Colvin's death in Syria. *The Guardian*. 1 February. Accessed 6 February.

Bowcott, Owen, and Daniel Boffey. 2020. Amal Clooney quits UK envoy role over 'lamentable' Brexit bill. *The Guardian*. 19 September. Accessed 19 September.

Bradley, Michael. 2019. The law shouldn't care about the government's hurt feelings. Crikey.com.au. 25 June. Accessed 19 July.

Brenan, Megan, and Gallup Polls. 2019. American's trust in mass media edges down to 41%. 26 September. https://news.gallup.com/poll/267047/americans-trust-mass-media-edges-down.aspx.

Brennan, Nigel, Nicole Bonney, and Kellie Brennan. 2011. *The Price of Life: A True Story of Kidnap & Ransom*. Melbourne: Penguin Books.

Brissenden, Michael. 2019a. *Four Corners*. Hero or Villain: Part 1. ABC. 22 July. Accessed 24 July.

Brissenden, Michael. 2019b. *Four Corners*. Hero or Villain: Part 2. ABC. 29 July. Accessed August 5.

Broersma, Marcel, and Jane B. Singer. 2020. Caught between innovation and tradition: Young journalists as normative change agents in the journalistic field. *Journalism Practice*. https://doi.org/10.1080/17512786.2020.1824125.

Brooks, David. 2020. America is having a moral convulsion. *The Atlantic*. 5 October. Accessed 9 October 2020.

Brown, Brendan. 2019. Trump Twitter archive. 15 December. Accessed 16 December. www.trumptwitterarchive.com/.

Brown, Karina. 2020. Ninth Circuit rules federal agents can't target journalists at Portland protests. *Courthouse News*. October 9. Accessed 12 October.

Browne, Harry. 2010. Foundation-funded journalism: Reasons to be wary of charitable support. *Journalism Studies* 11 (6): 889–903. https://doi.org/10.1080/1461670X.2010.501147.

Bruns, Axel. 2010. Technological determinism and the future of news. Snurblog. 4 October. Accessed 15 October 2020.

Bryant, Heather. 2018. The universe of people trying to deceive journalists keeps expanding, and newsrooms aren't ready. NiemanLab. 19 July. Accessed 23 July.

Bump, Phillip. 2020a. Over and over, Trump has focused on Black Lives Matter as a target of derision or violence. *The Washington Post*. 2 September. Accessed 21 October.

Bump, Phillip. 2020b. A death every 33 seconds. *The Washington Post*. 19 December. Accessed 20 December.

Burd, Gene. 1978. Newspapers as civic participants and observers: Dilemmas in journalistic objectivity/subjectivity. Association for Education in Journalism, Seattle, 13–16 August.

Burris, Val. 1988. Reification: A Marxist perspective. *California Sociologist* 10 (1): 22–43.

Burton, Nylah. 2020. Kanye West's 2020 apology, Kim Kardashian's plea and a harsh truth about mental health. Think. 1 August. Accessed 9 January 2021.

Buttigieg, Joseph A. 2002. On Gramsci. *Daedalus* 131 (3): 67–70. www.jstor.org/stable/20027789.

Buttigieg, Joseph A., ed. 2007a. *Antonio Gramsci Prison Notebooks, Volume II*. New York: Columbia University Press.

Buttigieg, Joseph A., ed. 2007b. *Antonio Gramsci Prison Notebooks, Volume III*. New York: Columbia University Press.

Carlson, Matt. 2015. The robotic reporter: Automated journalism and the redefinition of labor, compositional forms, and journalistic authority. *Digital Journalism: Journalism in an Era of Big Data: Cases, Concepts, and Critiques* 3 (3): 416–431. https://doi.org/10.1080/21670811.2014.976412.

Carlyle, Thomas. 1841. *Heroes, Hero-Worship and the Heroic in History. Thomas Carlyle's Collected Works*. London: Chapman and Hall.

Carson, Andrea, and Kate Farhall. 2019. The real news on 'fake news': politicians use it to discredit media, and journalists need to fight back. The Conversation. 2 October. Accessed 2 October.

Cave, Damien. 2019. Australia may well be the world's most secretive democracy. *The New York Times*. 5 June. Accessed 6 June.

CBS News. 2018. Lesley Stahl: Trump admitted mission to "discredit" press. CBS News. 23 May. Accessed 12 January 2020.

Çetinkaya, Hasret. 2020. Black Lives Matter, COVID-19 and the scene of politics. The New Pretender. 7 June. Accessed 14 January 2021. http://new-pretender.com/2020/06/07/black-lives-matter-covid-19-and-the-scene-of-politics/.

Chadwick, Paul. 2017a. Five categories of fame. *The Guardian*. 18 December. Accessed 18 December.

Chadwick, Paul. 2017b. Prince George, a small boy yet also a symbol in the public conversation. *The Guardian*. 11 December. Accessed 18 December.

Chadwick, Paul, and Jennifer Mullaly. 1997. *Privacy and the Media*. Melbourne: Communications Law Centre.

Chain, Brittany. 2018. 'There is still a story to be told': 60 Minutes journalist Tara Brown opens up about her arrest during the botched Beirut child recovery missing for the first time. *The Daily Mail*. 3 December. Accessed 10 January 2021.

Chalmers, Max. 2015. Media union challenges fairness of social media policies after Scott McIntyre dismissal. *New Matilda*. 27 April. Accessed 27 April.

Champagne, Patrick. 2005. The 'double dependency': The journalistic field between politics and markets. In *Bourdieu and the Journalistic Field*, edited by Rodney Benson, and Erik Neveu, pp. 48–63. Cambridge, UK: Polity Press. Original edition, 1995, Champ politique, champ des sciences sociales, champ journalistique, lecture delivered in Lyons, France.

Chand, Bool. 1944. Dialectical materialism. *The Indian Journal of Political Science,* 5, 205–21.

Chavez, Nicole. 2018. CNN's New York offices given all-clear after bomb threat. CNN.com. 7 December. Accessed 8 December.

Chen, Xiyuan. 2020. Democratic progress, American politics and Donald Trump: An analysis of social media's role in defending freedom of expression. *Politicus* (2020–2021):19–28. www.queenspoliticus.com/s/Special-Issue-December-Final.pdf#page=6.

Chopra, Pran. 1980. Economics of press freedom. *Economic and Political Weekly* 15 (40): 1655–1656. www.jstor.com/stable/4369144.

Christians, Clifford G., John P.Ferré, and Mark Fackler. 1993. *Good News: Social Ethics and the Press.* New York: Oxford University Press.

Chulov, Martin. 2007. Nightmare is over for BBC hostage. *The Australian.* 5 July 2007, p. 11.

Cloud, Dana. 2006. Change happens: Materialist dialectics and communication studies. In *Marxism and Communication Studies: The Point Is to Change It* (*Marxism and Media Studies* series), by Lee Artz, Steve Macek and Dana Cloud*MarxismandMediaStudies*, pp. 53–70. New York: Peter Lang.

Clure, Elias. 2020. ABC journalist Elias Clure on racism and the importance of a black reporter covering a Black Lives Matter protest. ABC News. 12 June. Accessed 12 June.

Cockburn, Patrick. 2020. The Assange extradition case is an unprecedented attack on press freedom – so why's the media largely ignoring it? *Independent* (UK). 2 October. Accessed 4 October.

Coddington, Mark, and Seth C. Lewis. 2020. Journalism faces a crisis in trust. Journalists fall into two very different camps for how to fix it. NiemanLab. 8 October. Accessed 9 October 2020.

Coe, Kevin, and Rachel Alicia Griffin. 2020. Marginalized identity invocation online: The case of President Donald Trump on Twitter. *Social Media and Society*: 1–12. https://doi.org/10157673/20051623059123097139979.

Cole, Desmond. 2017. I choose activism for Black liberation. Coles's Notes. Accessed 2 November 2020.

Coleman, Renita. 1997. The intellectual antecedents of public journalism. *Journal of Communication Inquiry* 21: 60–76. https://doi.org/10.1177/019685999702100103.

Coleman, Renita, Joon Yea Lee, Carolyn Yaschur, Aime Pavia Meader, and Kathleen McElroy. 2018. Why be a journalist? US students' motivations and role conceptions in the new age of journalism. *Journalism* 19 (6): 800–819. https://doi.org/10.1177/1464884916683554.

Colvin, Marie. 2010. Truth at all costs. mariecolvin.org. 10 November. Accessed 7 November 2012.

Conlan, Tara. 2014. BBC Staff told 'don't do anything stupid' on social media. *The Guardian.* 23 May. Accessed 14 July 2020.

Constante, Soraya. 2020. Journalists in Ecuador fight the pandemic and limits on official information. NiemanReports. 23 April. Accessed 9 July.

Conte, Andrew, and Darryl Ford-Williams. 2019. The Pittsburgh Synagogue Shootings: Avoid 'Anniversary' and 'Tragedy' and don't name the shooter. NiemanReports. 15 October. Accessed 28 October.

Cook, John. 2011. *Pay Up. Columbia Journalism Review.* May/June. Accessed 27 June.

Corcoran, Kieran. 2019. Prince Harry won a legal battle with the paparazzi using Europe's GDPR privacy law—and it gives the royals a powerful new weapon against the media. *Business Insider.* 18 May. Accessed 21 May.

Costa e Sliva, Elsa. 2014. Crisis, financialization and regulation: The case of media industries in Portugal. *The Political Economy of Communication* 2 (2). www.polecom. org/index.php/polecom/article/view/38/236.

Costello, Paul. 1979. Ideology: Ideological practice and cultural criticism. *Theoretical Review* 10: 1–13.

Cottle, Michelle. 2020. Drop the curtain on the Trump follies. *The New York Times*. 7 April. Accessed 9 April.

Coy, Maddy, and Meagan Tyler. 2020. Pornographication and heterosexualisation in public space. In *Contentious Cities: Design and the Gendered Production of Space*, edited by Jess Berry, Timothy Moore, Nicole Kalms, and Gene Bawden, pp. 49–59. New York and London: Routledge.

CPJ. 2019a. Journalists injured, fired upon while covering clashes in northern Syria. Committee to Protect Journalists. 29 May. Accessed 14 June.

CPJ. 2019b. US must be global leader in defending press freedom, CPJ tells Congress. Committee to Protect Journalists. 16 May. Accessed 21 May.

CPJ. 2019c. Psychological safety: Online harassment and how to protect your mental health. Committee to Protect Journalists. 4 September. Accessed 24 July 2020.

CPJ. 2020a. Editors' checklist: Preparing for U.S. protest assignments. Committee to Protect Journalists. 6 June. Accessed 9 June.

CPJ. 2020b. Islamic State militants extradited to US to face charges for murders of journalists Foley and Sotloff. Committee to Protect Journalists. 8 October. Accessed 10 October.

CPJ. 2020c. Local prosecutor subpoenas Cleveland newsroom for protest material. Committee to Protect Journalists. 15 June. Accessed 16 June.

Crawley, William. 2008. A prime minister, a party and a ban. BBC News. October 17. Accessed 16 November.

Crystal, Tom. 2020. Christchurch massacre: Brenton Tarrant pleads guilty to killing 51 people, wounding 49. *The Australian*. 26 March. Accessed 26 March.

Cullen, Holly. 2019. Explainer: What charges does Julian Assange face, and what's likely to happen next? The Conversation. 12 April. Accessed 14 April.

Cuneo, Clementine. 2010. Death on Facebook first – teen twins find out online brother killed in triple-fatal crash. *The Daily Telegraph*. Accessed 8 February.

Dalton, R. 2003. NY Times comes clean on reporter who made up the news. *The Australian*. 15 May 2003, p. 10.

Davidson, Helen. 2016. Former SBS reporter Scott McIntyre repeats Anzac Day accusations on Twitter. *The Guardian*. 25 April. Accessed 14 October 2019.

Davie, Tim. 2020. *Tim Davie's introductory speech as BBC Director-General*. 3 September. Accessed 7 September.

Davies, Caroline. 2016. Mazher Mahmood: 'Fake Sheikh' jailed for 15 months. *The Guardian*. 21 October. Accessed 22 October.

Davies, Caroline. 2019a. Meghan: I was warned British tabloids would destroy my life. *The Guardian*. 12 October. Accessed 22 October.

Davies, Caroline. 2019b. Prince William: I'd be absolutely fine if my children were gay. *The Guardian*. 27 June. Accessed 27 June.

Davies, Caroline. 2020. Prince Harry and Meghan to restrict media access in snub to tabloids. *The Guardian*. 9 January. Accessed 9 January.

Davies, Caroline, and agency. 2018. French magazine loses appeal over Duchess of Cambridge topless photos. *The Guardian*. 20 September. Accessed 20 September.

Davies, William. 2019. Why can't we agree on what's true any more? *The Guardian*. 19 September. Accessed 22 October 2020.

Davis, Aeron. 2011. Mediation, financialization, and the global financial crisis: An inverted political economy perspective. In *The Political Economics of Media*, edited by Dwayne Winseck, and Dia Yong Jin, pp. 241–254. London: Bloomsbury Academic.

De Carteret, Daniel. 2019. Police raids on Aussie media fuel calls for journalist protections. *Agence France-Presse* (published by Yahoo.com). 7 June. Accessed 8 June.

Demenchonok, Edward. 2019. Learning from Kant. *Revista Portugesa de Filosofia* 75 (1): 191–230. www.jstor.org/stable/10.2307/26625467.

Denning, Stephanie. 2018. Why Jeff Bezos bought The Washington Post. Forbes. 19 September. Accessed 17 December 2019.

Dennis, Everette E., and John C. Merrill. 1984. Journalistic objectivity. In *Basic Issues in Mass Communication: A Debate*, pp. 103–119. New York: Macmillan.

Di Stefano, Mark. 2019. The Daily Mail let readers download the New Zealand mosque attacker's manifesto directly from its website. Buzzfeed News. 15 March. Accessed 17 March.

Dickey, Christopher. 2018. How Trump's 'fake news' obsession started a global plague of censorship. The Daily Beast. 2 May. Accessed 3 May.

DiManno, Rosie. 2017. You can't make news and cover the news: DiManno. *The Toronto Star*. Accessed 2 November 2020.

Dictionary.com. n.d. 'Misinformation' vs. 'Disinformation': Get informed on the difference. Accessed 29 July 2020.

Doctor, Ken. 2016. Newsonomics: The financialization of news is dimming the lights of the local press. NiemanLab. 19 February. Accessed 20 October 2020.

Dodd, Andrew. 2019. Did Al Jazeera's undercover investigation into One Nation overstep the mark? The Conversation. 26 March. Accessed 26 March.

Domingo, Rafael. 2015. Restoring freedom of conscience. *Journal of Law and Religion* 30 (2): 176–193. www.jstor.org/stable/24739203.

Doran, Matthew. 2019. Media unites to rally for press freedom, taking campaign to front pages and airwaves. ABC News. 21 October. Accessed 21 October.

Doran, Matthew. 2020. Parliamentary committee recommends press freedom changes in the wake of ABC, News Corp raids. ABC News. 26 August. Accessed 27 August.

Doubek, James. 2018. Hundreds of newspapers denounce Trump's attacks on media in coordinated editorials. National Public Radio (NPR). 16 August. Accessed 11 June 2019.

Doucet, Andrea. 2018. Feminist epistemologies and ethics: Ecologoical thinking, stiuated knowledges, epistemic responsibilities. In *The Sage Handbook of Qualitative Research Ethics*, edited by Ron Iphofen, and Martin Tolich, pp. 73–86. London: Sage.

Douglas, Courtney. 2020. Amid Black Lives Matter protests, a crushing moment for journalists facing record attacks, arrests at the hands of law enforcement. Reporters Committee for Freedom of the Press. 4 September. Accessed 10 September.

Duncan, Megan, and Kathleen Bartzen Culver. 2020. Technologies, ethics and journalism's relationship with the public. *Media and Communication (Lisboa)* 8 (3): 101–111. https://doi.org/10.17645/mac.v8i3.3039.

Dunham, Jennifer. 2020. Murders of journalists more than double worldwide. Committee for the Protection of Journalists. 22 December. Accessed 29 December.

Durham, Meenakshi Gigi. 1998. On the relevance of standpoint epistemology to the practice of journalism: the case for 'strong objectivity'. *Communication Theory* 8 (2): 117–140.

Durkin, Erin, and Agencies. 2018. Trump lashes out against US news outlets defending press freedom. *The Guardian*. 17 August. Accessed 18 August.

Dwyre, Diana. 2020. The origin and evolution of Super PACs: A Darwinian examination of the campaign finance species. *Society* (57): 511–519. https://doi.org/10.1007/s12115-020-00523-1.

Eagleton, Terry. 2007. *Ideology: An Introduction*. London and New York: Verso.

Eagleton, Terry. 2009. *Trouble With Strangers: A Study of Ethics*. Oxford: Wiley-Blackwell.

Edelman, Adam. 2016. Hillary Clinton warns Americans about the 'epidemic of fake news' in rare public appearance. *New York Daily News*. 8 December. Accessed 13 December.

Edginton, Steven. 2019. Why I helped expose ambassador's embarrassing cables: Journalist, 19, behind Trump scoop comes forward to reveal his motivation and fears he's being targeted by security forces. *The Mail on Sunday*. 21 July. Accessed 22 July.

Elder, John, and Mike Bruce. 2019. Here's a theory why a tawdry tabloid set out to smear Amazon's Jeff Bezos. The New Daily. 9 February. Accessed 11 February.

Elfrink, Tim. 2019. 'A bad, sad and dangerous day': Australian police raid public broadcaster, seize emails and documents. *The Washington Post*. June 5. Accessed 6 June.

Elliott, Francis. 2012. Teen icon targeted by Taliban. *The Australian*. 10 October. Accessed 17 November.

Elliott, Tim. 2011. Hostage for 462 days…tale of survival out of Africa. *The Sydney Morning Herald*. 25 June. Accessed 16 November.

Ellison, Sarah. 2021. Laura Poitras says she's been fired by First Look Media over Reality Winner controversy. Now she's questioning the company's integrity. *The Washington Post*. 15 January. Accessed 18 January.

Engelke, Katherine M., Valerie Hase, and Florian Wintterlin. 2019. On measuring trust and distrust in journalism: Reflection of the status quo and suggestions for the road ahead. *Journal of Trust Research* 9 (1): 66–86. https://doi.org/10.1080/21515581.2019.1588741.

Engels, Frederick. 1883. *Dialectics of Nature* (unfinished work).

Erlanger, Steven. 2017. 'Fake news,' Trump's obsession is now a cudgel for strongmen. *The New York Times*. 12 December. Accessed 19 December.

Ewart, Jackie, and Kate O'Donnell. 2018. *Reporting Islam: International Best Practice for Journalists*. London and New York: Routledge.

Fahy, Declan. 2018. Objectivity as trained judgment: How environmental reporters pioneered journalism for a 'post-truth' Era. *Environmental Communication* 12 (7): 855–861. https://doi.org/https://doi.org/10.1080/17524032.2018.1495093.

Fargo, Anthony L. 2018. A federal shield law that works: Protecting sources, fighting fake news, and confronting modern challenges to effective journalism. *Journal of International Media and Entertainment Law* 8: 35–69.

Farnsworth, Sarah. 2012. Former Age photographer sues over Bali trauma. ABC News. 19 November. Accessed 19 November.

Farr, Arnold. 2008. The task of dialectical thinking in the age of one-dimensionality. *Human Studies* 31 (2): 233–239. https://doi.org/10.1007/sl0746-008-9087-8. www.jstor.org/stable/40270653.

Farr, Malcolm. 2018. The Barnaby Joyce interview is a new low for Australian politics. News.com.au. 28 May. Accessed 28 May.

Faruqi, Osman. 2017. These Anzac Day 'controversies' reveal the huge hypocrisy of Australian Conservatives. Junkee.com. 26 April. Accessed 27 April.

Fenton, Tim. 2020. Mark Di Stefano—A modern media morality tale. Zelo-Street. 2 May. Accessed 5 May.

Ferguson, Adele. 2019. ATO whistleblower faces six life sentences, roughly the same as Ivan Milat. *The Sydney Morning Herald*. 27 February. Accessed 27 February.

Fernandez-Garcia, Norberto, and Luis Sanchez-Fernandez. 2004. Building an ontology for NEWS applications. http://citeseerx.ist.psu.edu/viewdoc/download?doi=10.1.1. 176.5086&rep=rep1&type=pdf

Ferrucci, Patrick, and Jacob L. Nelson. 2019. The new advertisers: How foundation funding impacts journalism. *Media and Communication (Lisboa)* 7 (4): 45–55. https://doi.org/10.17645/mac.v7i4.2251.

Fine, Duncan. 2017. We should celebrate Yassmin Abdel-Magied, not attack her. *The Sydney Morning Herald*. 26 April. Accessed 26 April.

Finkelstein, Sidney. 1967. Review: Marxism and existentialism. *Science and Society* 31 (1): 58–66. www.jstor.com/stable/4040125.

Fisher, Caroline, Terry Flew, Sora Park, Jee Young Lee, and Uwe Dulleck. 2020. Improving trust in news: Audience solutions. *Journalism Practice*. https://doi.org/10.1080/17512786.2020.1787859.

Fletcher, Richard. 2020. How and why people are paying for online news. Reuters Institute Digital News Report 2020. Accessed 20 October 2020.

Flynn, Kerry. 2020. Hundreds of journalists are being laid off, right when the public needs them the most. CNN. 27 March. Accessed 6 April.

Fogarasi, Alabert. 1921. The tasks of the communist press. In *Communication and Class Struggle: 2. Liberation, socialism*, edited by Armand Mattelart, and Seth Siegelaub, pp. 149–153. New York, Bagnolet, France: IG/IMMRC.

Forgacs, David, and Geoffrey Nowell-Smith, eds. 1985. *Antonio Gramsci: Selections From Cultural Writings*. Cambridge, MA: Harvard University Press.

Fossum, Sam, David Shortell, and Caroline Kelly. 2019. Chelsea Manning sent back to jail after refusing to testify before a grand jury again. CNN. 17 May. Accessed 29 July.

Fracchia, Joseph. 1999. Dialectical itineraries. *History and Theory* 38 (2): 169–197.

Franklin, Roger. 2017. Yassmin Abdel-Magied: How to make enemies and enrage people. The New Daily. Accessed 26 April.

Fray, Peter, and Elaine McKewon. 2018. If love isn't an option, how about trust?*Public Trust in Journalism—An Annotated Bibliography*. 1 June. Accessed 22 October 2020.

Fremlin, Celia. 1938. Dialectical grammar. *Analysis* 6 (1): 10–15. www.jstor.org/stable/3326808.

Friedersdorf, Conor. 2017. Why can't the left win. *The Atlantic*. 4 May.

Fuchs, Christian. 2009. A contribution to the political economy of transnational information capital. *Rethinking Marxism: A Journal of Economics, Culture & Society* 21 (3): 387–402. https://doi.org/10.1080/08935690902955104.

Fuchs, Christian. 2019. Appropriation of digital machines and appropriation of fixed capital as the real appropriation of social being: Reflections on Toni Negri's chapter. In *Digital Objects, Digital Subjects: Interdisciplinary Perspectives on Capitalism, Labour and Politics in the Age of Big Data*, pp. 215–222. London: University of Westminster Press.

Funke, Daniel. 2019. Study: Journalists need help covering misinformation. Poynter.org. 25 April. Accessed 30 July 2020.

Gabbatt, Adam. 2020. US newspapers face 'extinction-level' crisis as Covid-19 hits hard. *The Guardian*. 9 April. Accessed 10 April.

Gade, Peter J. 2011. Postmodernism, uncertainty and journalism. In *Changing the News: The Forces Shaping Journalism in Uncertain Times*, edited by Wilson Lowrey, and Peter J. Gade, pp. 63–82. New York and London: Routledge.

Gallagher, Ian. 2018. Are these the morons who ruined Christmas? *The (UK) Mail on Sunday*, 23 December 2018, p. 1.

Galloway, Anthony. 2021. Morrison needs to counter Australian and American disinformation too. *The Sydney Morning Herald*. 7 January. Accessed 7 January 2021.

Gallup Polls, and Knight Foundation. 2020. American views 2020: Trust, media and democracy. Knight Foundation. 20 August.

Garcia-Liendo, Javier. 2016. Networking: Jose Carlos Mariategui's socialist communication strategy. *Discourse* 38 (1): 46–68. www.jstor.org/stable/10.13110/discourse.38.1. 0046.

Garcia-Orosa, Berta, Xose Lopez-Garcia, and Jorge Vazquez-Herrero. 2020. Journalism in digital native media: Beyond technological determinism. *Media and Communication* 8 (2): 5–15. https://doi.org/10.17645/mac.v8i2.2702.

Gardner, Amy. 2021. 'I just want to find 11,780 votes': In extraordinary hour-long call, Trump pressures Georgia secretary of state to recalculate the vote in his favor. *The Washington Post*. 4 January. Accessed 10 January 2021.

Garnham, Nicholas. 2006. Contribution to a political economy of mass communication. In *Media and Cultural Studies: KeyWorks*, edited by Meeakshi Gigi Durham, and Douglas Kellner, pp. 201–229. Malden, Oxford, Carlton: Blackwell Publishing.

Garside, Juliette. 2020. Justice on trial: Three years after the murder of Daphne Caruana Galizia. *The Guardian*. 15 October. Accessed 19 October 2020.

Gartman, David. 1986. Reification of consumer products: A general history illustrated by the case of the American automobile. *Sociological Theory* 4 (2): 167–185. www. jstor.org/stable/201886.

Garvey, Paul. 2020. Facebook stays with Thai mall gunman Jakrapanth Thomma hours into deadly rampage. *The Australian*. Accessed 10 February.

Gessen, Masha. 2020. Why are some journalists afraid of 'moral clarity'? *The New Yorker*. Accessed 31 October 2020.

Gold Coast Bulletin. 2004. US Marine filmed shooting prisoner. Gold Coast Bulletin. 17 November, p. 11.

Goldstein, Tom. 1985. *The News At Any Cost: How Journalists Compromise Their Ethics to Shape the News*. New York: Simon and Schuster.

Goodman, Amy, and Denis Moynihan. 2019. The U.S. goverment's crusade against Julian Assange and Chelsea Manning. Democracynow.org. 13 June. Accessed 14 June.

Goodman, Kenneth. 1989. Journalism and philosophy. *Proceedings and Addresses of the American Philosophical Association* 63 (1): 35–40. www.jstor.org/stable/3130332.

Gordon, Jill. 1997. John Stuart Mill and the 'Marketplace of Ideas'. *Social Theory and Practice* 23 (2): 235–249. www.jstor.org/stable/23559183.

Gottfried, Paul. 1980. On the social implications and context of the Hegelian dialectic. *Journal of the History of Ideas* 14 (e): 421–432. www.jstor.org/stable/2709402.

Graber, Doris A. 1986. Press freedom and the general welfare. *Political Science Quarterly* 101 (2): 257–275. www.jstor.org/stable/2151391.

Gramenz, Jack. 2021. Vision emerges of police moving barricades to allow rioters into US Capitol, taking selfies. Accessed 7 January 2021.

Grant, Stan. 2020. I can't breathe. *Four Corners*. ABC-TV. 13 July. Accessed 14 July.

Green, Marcus E, and Peter Ives. 2009. Subalternity and language: Overcoming the fragmentation of common sense. *Historical Materialism* (17): 3–30. https://doi.org/10.1163/156920609X399191. https://brill.com/view/journals/hima/17/1/article-p3_1.xml.

Greenslade, Roy. 2008. 25 years ago today…the Sunday Times published Hitler's diaries. *The Guardian*. 24 April. Accessed 10 June 2019.

Greenslade, Roy. 2014. News Corp faces uphill battle to win copyright action against Mail Online. *The Guardian*. 17 June. Accessed 17 June.

Greenslade, Roy. 2018. Fake death is gift to Russia. *The Guardian*. 3 June. Accessed 4 June.

Greenslade, Roy. 2020. Why our newspapers might not survive the contagion of coronavirus. *The Guardian*. 12 April. Accessed 14 April.

Greensmith, Glynn, and Alexandra Wake. 2019. Why Christchurch shooter should (with a few exceptions) not be named. *The Age*. 22 March. Accessed 24 March.

Greenwald, Glenn. 2014. *No Place to Hide: Edward Snowden, the NSA and the Surveillance State*. London: Hamish Hamilton.

Greenwald, Glenn. 2020. My resignation from The Intercept. 30 October Accessed 18 January 2021.

Greste, Peter. 2019. Julian Assange is no journalist: Don't confuse his arrest with press freedom. *The Sydney Morning Herald*. 12 April. Accessed 2 May.

Greve, Joan E. 2020. Social media backlash forces Trump to find new ways to spread his message. *The Guardian*. 5 July. Accessed 8 January 2021.

Griffin, Andrew. 2016. Corona founder didn't actually leave all his money to us, village residents confirm. *Independent* (UK). 25 November. Accessed 7 June 2019.

Grossman, Gary. 2020. Why we're failing to regulate the most powerful tech we've ever faced. VentureBeat. 1 February. Accessed 15 October.

Gruynbaum, Michael M. 2019. Trump discusses claims of 'fake news,' and their impact with New York Times publisher. *The New York Times*. 1 February. Accessed 16 December.

Grynbaum, Michael M., and Sydney Ember. 2016. If Trump tweets it, is it news? A quandary for the news media. *The New York Times*. 29 November. Accessed 1 December.

Guardian Editorial. 2018. The Guardian view on a journalist's return: The death was fake, the damage was not. *The Guardian(editorial)*. 1 June. Accessed 13 June.

Haag, Matthew, and Maya Salam. 2017. Gunman in 'Pizzagate' shooting is sentenced to 4 years in prison. *The New York Times*. 22 June. Accessed 7 June 2018.

Hacked off. 2019. Gatwick drones and Cliff's Law debate: Privacy invasion without public interest justification. Hackinginquiry.org. 11 January. Accessed 13 January.

Hall, Ellie. 2020. Here are 20 headlines comparing Meghan Markle to Kate Middleton that may show why she and Prince Harry are cutting off royal reporters. Buzzfeed. 13 January. Accessed 16 January.

Hallin, Daniel C. 1989. *The 'Uncensored War': The Media and Vietnam*. Berkeley, CA: University of California Press.

Hamada, Basyouni. 2018. Social media: A turning point into global journalism identity and ethics. In *Social Media and Journalism: Trends, Connections, Implications*, edited by Jan Visnovsky, and Jana Radosinska, p. 144. London: IntechOpen.

Hameleers, Michael, Linda Bos, and Claes H. de Vreese. 2019. Shoot the messenger? The media's role in framing populist attributions of blame. *Journalism* 20 (9): 1145–1164. https://doi.org/10.1177/1464884917698170.

Hamilton, Lawrence. 2013. Real modern freedom. *Theoria: A Journal of Social and Political Theory* 60 (137): 1–28. https://doi.org/10.3167/th.2013.6013701. www.jstor.org/stable/42705270.

Hanusch, Folker, Claudia Mellado, Priscilla Boshoff, Maria Luisa Humanes, Salvador de Leon, Fabio Pereira, Mireya Marquez Ramirez, Sergio Roses, Federico Subervi, Vinzenz Wyss, and Lyuba Yez. 2015. Journalism students' motivations and expectations of their work in comparative perspective. *Journalism and Mass Communication Educator* 70 (2): 1141–1160. https://doi.org/10.1177/1077695814554295.

Harding, Sandra. 1993. Rethinking standpoint epistemology: What is 'strong objectivity'? In *Feminist Epistemologies*, edited by Linda Alcoff, and Elizabeth Potter, pp. 49–82. London: Routledge.

Hare, Kristen. 2020. More than 500 journalists and media workers have died from Covid-19. Poynter.org. 28 December. Accessed 30 December.

Harper, Tom, and Michael Bilton. 2019. Flight records allege Prince Andrew flow on Jeffrey Epstein's jet with jailed beauty queen. *The Australian* (originally published in *The Times*). 25 August. Accessed 25 August.

Harris, David A. June 1999. Driving while Black: Racial profiling on our nation's highways. American Civil Liberties Union. www.aclu.org/report/driving-while-black-racial-profiling-our-nations-highways.

Harris, Rob. 2019. 'High price to pay': Australia urges nations to refuse to pay ransoms to terrorists. *The Age*. 7 November. Accessed 8 November.

Hartle, Johan F. 2017. Reification as structural depoliticization: The political ontology of Lukásc and Debord. In *The Spell of Capital: Reification and Spectacle*, edited by Samir Gandesha, and Johan F. Hartle, pp. 21–36. Amsterdam: Amsterdam University Press.

Hartley, John. 1996. *Popular Reality: Journalism, Modernity, Popular Culture*. London: Arnold.

Harvard, Jonas. 2020. Post-hype uses of drones in news reporting: Revealing the site and presenting scope. *Media and Communication (Lisboa)* 8 (3): 85–92. https://doi.org/10.17645/mac.v8i3.3199.

Harvard, Jonas, Mats Hyvönen, and Ingela Wadbring. 2020. Journalism from above: Drones and the media in critical perspective. *Media and Communication (Lisboa)* 8 (3): 60–63. https://doi.org/10.17645/mac.v8i3.3442.

Harvey, Claire. 2008. But are the games really worth the cost. *The Sunday Telegraph*, 24 August 2008, 90–91.

Harvey, Claire. 2019. Annika Smethurst raid was more than an invasion of privacy. *The Daily Telegraph*. June 5. Accessed 5 June.

Hassan, Robert, and Thomas Sutherland. 2017. *Philosophy of Media: A Short History of Ideas and Innovations from Socrates to Social Media*. London: Routledge.

Hayman-Reber, Madeline. 2020. Remaking our newsrooms. *The Saturday Paper*. 20 July. Accessed 20 July.

Hayne, Jordan. 2020a. AFP will not lay charges against Annika Smethurst over publishing of classified intelligence documents. ABC News. 28 May. Accessed 29 May.

Hayne, Jordan. 2020b. Investigation into Afghan Files that sparked ABC raids enters next phase with brief of evidence sent to prosecutors. ABC News. 2 July. Accessed 3 July.

Hazard Owen, Laura. 2020. More Americans are paying for online news—those who do pay say they're unlikely to stop. NiemanLab. 16 June. Accessed 20 October 2020.

Hearns-Branaman, Jesse Owen. 2016a. Dialectic of realism and pragmatism. In *Journalism and the Philosophy of Truth: Beyond Objectivity and Balance*, edited by Jesse Owen Hearns-Branaman. Milton Park: Routledge.

Hearns-Branaman, Jesse Owen. 2016b. *Journalism and the Philosophy of Truth. Routledge Research in Journalism.* New York and London: Routledge.

Heeren, Jörg, and Andeas Zick. 2014. Misleading images: Results from interviews with media producers, journalists and consumers on Muslims and Islam in German media. *Middle East Journal of Culture and Communication* 7 (1): 46–63.

Helmore, Edward. 2021. NSW whistleblower Reality winner released from prison. *The Guardian.* Accessed 2 July 2021.

Henderson, Andrea. 2002. The wanderer and early-nineteenth-century commodity fetishism. *Nineteenth-Century Literature* 57 (1): 1–30. www.jstor.org/stable/10.1525/ncl.2002.57.1.1.

Henke, Jakob, Laura Leissner, and Wiebke Möhring. 2020. How can journalists promote news credibility? Effects of evidences on trust and credibility. *Journalism Practice* 14 (3): 299–318. https://doi.org/10.1080/17512786.2019.1605839.

Henry, Scott. 2019. Prince Harry and Meghan launch legal action against London tabloid. *The Australian.* 2 October. Accessed 2 October.

Herman, Edward S., and Noam Chomsky. 1988. *Manufacturing Consent: The Political Economy of the Mass Media.* New York: Pantheon.

Hermida, Alfred. 2010. From TV to twitter: How ambient news became ambient journalism. *M/C Journal* 13 (2). http://journal.media-culture.org.au/index.php/mcjournal/article/viewArticle/220.

Hess, Kristy, and Robert E. Gutsche. 2019. Power, place, and the spatial dialectic of digital journalism. In *Geographies of Journalism: The Imaginative Power of Place in Making Digital News*, edited by Robert E.Gutsche, and Kristy Hess. Milton Park: Routledge.

Hillstrom, Laurie Collier. 2019. *The #MeToo Movement.* Santa Barbara, CA: ABC-CLIO.

Hilsum, Lindsey. 2019. Marie Colvin verdict gives meaning to her death. *The Observer.* 3 February. Accessed 6 February.

Himelboim, Itai, and Yehiel Limor. 2008. Media perception of freedom of the press. *Journalism* 9 (3): 235–265. https://doi.org/10.1177/1464884907089007.

Hirst, Martin. 1998a. From Gonzo to Pomo: Hunting new journalism down under. In *Journalism Theory and Practice*, edited by Myles Breen. Sydney: McLeay Press.

Hirst, Martin. 1998b. Looking out from Terra Nullius: Journalism, Modernity and the 'Vacant Lot'. *Asia Pacific Media Educator* (4).

Hirst, Martin. 2003. *Grey Collar Journalism: The Social Relations of News Production.* School of Social Sciences and Liberal Studies, Charles Sturt University.

Hirst, Martin. 2011. *News 2.0: Can Journalism Survive the Internet?* Sydney: Allen & Unwin.

Hirst, Martin. 2012a. The cultural politics of journalism: Quotidian intellectuals and the power of media capital. In *Scooped: The Politics and Power Of Journalism in Aotearoa New Zealand*, edited by Martin Hirst, Sean Phelan, and Verica Rupar. Auckland, NZ: AUT University Media.

Hirst, Martin. 2012b. *One tweet does not a revolution make: Technological determinism, media and social change.* The Arab Spring: A Symposium on Social Media and the Politics of Reportage Swinburne University, Melbourne, 8 June.

Hirst, Martin. 2018. *Navigating Social Journalism: A Handbook for Media Literacy and Citizen Journalism.* New York: Routledge.

Hirst, Martin. 2019a. The Twitter wars: Mainstream media v fifth estate. *Independent Australia.* 26 April. Accessed 26 November 2020.

Hirst, Martin. 2019b. Why I'm not signing up to demand the Government legislate press freedom laws. *Independent Australia.* 18 July. Accessed 19 July.

Hirst, Martin, John Harrison, and Patricia Maazepa. 2014. *Communication and New Media: Broadcast to Narrowcast*. Ontario: Oxford University Press.

Hirst, Martin, and Roger Patching. 2005. *Journalism Ethics: Arguments and Cases*. Melbourne: Oxford University Press.

Hirst, Martin, and Roger Patching. 2007. *Journalism Ethics: Arguments & Cases*, second edn. Melbourne: Oxford University Press.

Hobsbawm, Eric. 1996. *The Age of Revolution*. New York: Vintage Books.

Hofweber, Thomas. 2020. Logic and ontology. In *Stanford Encyclopedia of Philosophy*, edited by Edward N.Zalta. Stanford, CA: Metaphysics Research Lab, Stanford.

Hollingsworth, Heather, and Marion Renault. 2020. One-day US deaths top 3,000, more than D-Day or 9/11. *The Associated Press*. 11 December. Accessed 18 December.

Holmes, Jonathon. 2020. ABC loses AFP raid challenge. ABC Alumni. 17 February. Accessed 20 February.

Holpuch, Amanda. 2020. Washington Post says suspended reporter's Kobe Bryant tweet did not violate policy. *The Guardian*. 29 January. Accessed 1 February.

Hopmann, David Nicolas, Christian Elmelund-Praestekaer, and Klaus Levinson. 2010. Journalism students: Left-wing and politically motivated? *Journalism* 11 (6): 661–674. https://doi.org/10.1177/1464884910379706.

Hornery, Andrew. 2013. Women's Day spend up to $150,000 on pregnant Kate. *The Age*. 13 February. Accessed 14 February.

Hoyt, Clark. 2009. Journalistic ideals, human values. *The New York Times*. 5 July. Accessed 7 July.

Hubbard, Sally. 2017. Fake news is a real antitrust problem. Washington Bytes. 19 December. Accessed 7 October 2019.

Huntington, Samuel P. 1993. The clash of civilizations? *Foreign Affairs*, Summer. www.foreignaffairs.com/articles/united-states/1993-06-01/clash-civilizations.

Hurst, John, and Sally White. 1994. *Ethics in Australian News Media*. Melbourne: Macmillan Education.

IFJ/IFEX. 2018. 2018 reverses downward trend in killings of journalists and media staff with 94 victims of violence. International Federation of Journalists. 31 December. Accessed 21 May 2019.

IFJ/IFEX. 2019. Singapore passes 'Orwellian' law on 'fake news'. International Federation of Journalists. 16 May. Accessed 21 May.

IFJ/IFEX 2020a. Covid-19: Pandemic threatens press freedom. International Federation of Journalists. 20 August. Accessed 21 August.

IFJ/IFEX. 2020b. *Exposed: The crisis facing journalism in the face of Covid-19*. International Federation of Journalists. 30 April. Accessed 1 May.

Ingber, Hanna. 2019. The New Zealand attack posed new challenges for journalists. Here are the decisions the Times made. *The New York Times*. 19 March. Accessed 20 March.

International Center for Journalists. 2020. Journalism and the Pandemic Survey. 13 October. Accessed 20 October.

IPSO. 2018. Editors'Code of Practice. Independent Press Standards Organisation (UK). No date. Accessed 21 August 2019.

IPSO. 2019. *Reporting major incidents*. Independent Press Standards Organisation (UK). Accessed 26 June.

IWMF. 2018. Attacks on female journalists are career-altering, survey says. International Women's Media Foundation. 13 September. Accessed 15 September.

Jackson, Daniel, Einar Thorsen, and Sally Reardon. 2019. Fantasy, pragmatism and journalistic socialistion: UK journalism students' aspirations and motivations. *Journalism Practice* 14 (1): 104–124. https://doi.org/10.1080/17512786.2019.1591929.

Jackson, Will, and Alex Easton. 2020. Australian journalists assaulted as police clear George Floyd protesters outside White House. ABC News. 2 June. Accessed 2 October.

Jacob, Mark. 2020a. Chicago journalism Town Hall tackles tough finances, elusive diversity. Local News Initiative. 24 February. Accessed 25 February.

Jacob, Mark. 2020b. Digital Start-ups: Great local news hope or disappointment? Local News Initiative. 27 July. Accessed 20 October 2020.

Jameson, Fredric. 1990. *Late Marxism: Adorno, or, the Persistence of the Dialectic*. London: Verso.

Jay, Martin. 2020. Fake news from the Middle East shifts gear: Meet Raphael and Salma. *Inside Arabia*. 20 July. Accessed 29 July.

Jefferson, Cord. 2011. Why all the Gaddafi death porn? Good.is. 22 October. Accessed 22 October.

Jeffery, Yasmin. 2019. Meghan Markle and Kate Middleon 'feud' has a familiar script for royal watchers. ABC News. 4 February. Accessed 4 February.

Jericho, Greg. 2019. The trouble with journalism. Meanjin.com.au. Summer. Accessed 8 August 2020.

Johnson, Charles D. 1928. Journanology, the new science. *Social Forces* 6 (3): 382–385. www.jstor.org/stable/3004857.

Johnson, Lissa. 2019. Western elites Spruik Media freedom while torturing Julian Assange in Belmarshe supermax. But what's Stanley Milgram got to do with it? New Matilda. 15 July. Accessed 17 July.

Johnson, Stephen. 2019. How wide-ranging police powers designed to stop terrorist attacks and safeguard national security are now being used to crack down on ANYONE who embarrasses the government. *Daily Mail Australia*. 7 June. Accessed 8 June.

Johnston, Alan. 2007. Alan Johnston: My kidnap ordeal. BBC. 25 October. Accessed 16 November.

Johnston, Alan. 2011. *Kidnapped: And Other Dispatches*. London: BBC.

Jones, Tom. 2019. The troubling case of Jill Abramson. Poynter.org. 9 February. Accessed 11 February.

Jones, Tom. 2020a. Attacks on media covering the protests are simply following the president's rhetoric. Poynter.org. 1 June. Accessed 3 June.

Jones, Tom. 2020b. Bob Woodward's decision to sit on Trump quotes for months and other observations from his new book. Poynter.org. 10 September. Accessed 14 September.

Jones, Tom. 2020c. How do we fix the daily White House coronavirus task force conferences? Poynter.org. 15 April. Accessed 16 April.

Jones, Tom. 2020d. President Trump's press conference calls out two enemies: ccoronavirus and the media. Poynter.org. 20 March. Accessed 2 September.

Jones, Tom. 2020e. Protesters who harass the media are simply following President Trump's lead. Poynter.org. 18 May. Accessed 20 May.

Jones, Tom. 2020f. Still making sense of what happened at The New York Times and The Philadelphia Inquirer. Poynter.org. 9 June. Accessed 11 June.

Jordović, Ivan. 2011. Aristotle on extreme tyranny and extreme democracy. *Historia: Zeitschrift für Alte Geschichte* 60 (1): 36–64. www.jstor.org/stable/29777247.

Kang, Cecilia. 2016. Fake news onslaught targets pizzeria as nest of child-trafficking. *The New York Times*. 21 November. Accessed 24 November.

Karp, Paul. 2019a. Afghan Files whistleblower David McBride's trial delayed to protect state secrets. *The Guardian*. 13 June. Accessed 13 June.

Karp, Paul. 2019b. Government 'leaks like a sieve' when it suits it, critics of ABC raid say. *The Guardian*. 6 June. Accessed 6 June.

Karp, Paul. 2020. High Court rules AFP warrant for raid on News Corp journalist's home was invalid. *The Guardian*. 15 April. Accessed 24 April.

Kaye, Byron. 2019. Journalists in jail? Australia weighs implications of police raids on media. Reuters. 6 June. Accessed 8 June.

Keane, Bernard. 2019. Will journalists soon need to get government approval for reporting leaks? Crikey.com.au. 15 August. Accessed 15 August.

Keane, John. 2018. The unfinished robots revolution: Ten tips for humans. In *Digitizing Democracy*, edited by Aljosha Karim Schapals, Axel Bruns, and Brian McNair, pp. 214–224. Milton: Taylor & Francis Group.

Kessler, Glenn. 2018. Fact-checking President Trump's USA Today op-ed on 'Medicare-for-All'. 11 October. Accessed 24 July 2020.

Kessler, Glenn, Salvador Rizzo, and Meg Kelly. 2020a. President Trump has made more than 20,000 false or misleading claims. *The Washington Post*. 13 July. Accessed 3 August.

Kessler, Glenn, Salvador Rizzo, and Meg Kelly. 2020b. Trump is averaging more than 50 false or misleading claims a day. *The Washington Post*. 22 October. Accessed 24 October.

Kessler, Glenn, Salvador Rizzo, and Meg Kelly. 2021. Trump's false or misleading claims total 30,573 over 4 years. *The Washington Post*. 4 January. Accessed 2 February.

Ketchum, John. 2020. More journalists of color become newsroom founders. NiemanLab Predictions for Journalism 2021. n.d. Accessed 12 December.

Khadem, Nassim. 2020. Commonwealth dumps 42 charges against ATO whistleblower Richard Boyle but threat of prison looms. ABC News. 3 July. Accessed 21 September.

Kidder, Rushworth. 2008. *A journalist's kidnapping, an editors' dilemma*. Global Ethics Newsline. 17 November. Accessed 18 November.

Kieve, Ronald A. 1983. The Hegelian inversion: On the possibility of a Marxist dialectic. *Science and Society* 47 (1): 37–65. www.jstor.org/stable/40402441.

Kilgo, Danielle. 2020. Riot or resistance? The way the media frames unrest in Minneapolis will shape the public's view of protest. The Conversation. 30 May. Accessed 3 June.

King, Madonna. 2017. If Yassmin Abdel-Magied was out of line, her attackers were worse. *The Brisbane Times*. 27 April. Accessed 27 April.

Knaus, Christopher. 2019a. Former judge says delays in Witness K case an 'abandonment' of open and fair justice. *The Guardian*. 27 March. Accessed 27 March.

Knaus, Christopher. 2019b. Police investigating national security leak grilled whistleblower about journalists. *The Guardian*. 16 July. Accessed 17 July.

Knaus, Christopher. 2020a. Australian government spends almost $3m waging 'war' on whistleblowers in court. *The Guardian*. 13 August. Accessed 13 August.

Knaus, Christopher. 2020b. Australian special forces involved in murder of 39 Afghan civilians, war crimes report alleges. *The Guardian*. 19 November. Accessed 10 January 2021.

Knaus, Christopher. 2021. Jose Ramos-Horta calls on Timor-Leste to award Australia's Witness K top honour. *The Guardian.* Accessed 2 Juy 2021.

Knight Commission on Trust, Media and Democracy. 2019. *Crisis in Democracy: Renewing Trust in America.* The Aspen Institute; The Knight Foundation.

Knightley, Phillip. 2003. *The First Casualty.* London: André Deutsch.

Knott, Matthew. 2020. Networks flee Trump briefing as he wheels out 'propaganda' video. *The Sydney Morning Herald.* 14 April. Accessed 21 April.

Knowles, Lorna. 2019. AFP officers who raided ABC looking for evidence reporter committed criminal offences, documents show. ABC News. June 23. Accessed 25 June.

Knowles, Lorna, Elise Worthington, and Clare Blumer. 2019. ABC raid: AFP leave Ultimo building with files after hours-long raid over Afghan Files stories. ABC News. June 5. Accessed 6 June.

Knowles, Sophie. 2018. Financial journalists, the financial crisis and the 'crisis' in journalism. In *The Media and Austerity: Comparative Perspectives,* edited by Laura Basu, Steve Schifferes, and Sophie Knowles. New York and London: Routledge.

Kobayashi-Solomon, Erik. 2020. Capitalism is failing us just when we need it most. Forbes. 28 May. Accessed 2 November 2020.

Konieczna, Magda. 2020. Entrepreneurship versus philanthropy: Can the market fund innovation in the news sector? *Journal of Media Business Studies* 17 (2): 1–16. https://doi.org/10.1080/16522354.2020.1719458.

Koob, Simone Fox. 2017. London is calling Yassmin Abdel-Magied. *The Australian.* 3 July. Accessed 4 July.

Korkonosenko, Sergey G. 2013. Professional deontology of journalism: Moral interpretation. *Journal of Mass Communication* 3 (8): 477–485.

Kovel, Joel. 1998. Dialectic as praxis. *Science and Society* 62 (3): 474–482. www.jstor.org/stable/40403738.

Koziol, Michael. 2017. 'One down, many to go'; Peter Dutton calls for ABC purge after Abdel-Magied axing. *The Age.* 26 May. Accessed 29 May.

Kraemer, Benjamin. 2014. Media populism: A conceptual clarification and some theses on its effects. *Communication Theory* 24 (1): 42–60. https://doi.org/10.1111/comt.12029.

Kumar, Deepa. 2004. Media, class and power: Debunking the myth of a classless soceity. In *Class and News,* edited by Don Heider, pp. 6–21. New York & Oxford: Rowman and Littlefield.

Kumar, Deepa. 2006. Media, culture, and society: The relevance of Marx's dialectical method. In *Marxism and Communication Studies: The Point Is to Change It (Marxism and Media Studies* series), edited by 2, Steve Macek, and Dana Cloud, pp. 71–86. New York: Peter Lang.

Kwai, Isabella. 2019. Deception for investigative journalism: Right or wrong? *The New York Times.* 28 March. Accessed 29 March.

Landy, Marcia. 1986. Culture and politics in the work of Antonio Gramsci. *boundary 2* 14 (3): 49–70. www.jstor.org/stable/303233.

Lawrence III, Charles R. 1990. If he hollers let him go: Regulating racist speech on campus. *Duke Law Journal 1990* (3): 431–483. www.jstor.org/stable/1372554.

Lee, Amy. 2011. Myspace collapse: How the social network fell apart. The Huffington Post. 30 June. Accessed 7 October 2019.

Lee, Francis L.F. 2007. Hong Kong citizens' beliefs in media neutrality and perceptions of press freedom: Objectivity as self-censorship. *Asian Survey* 47 (3): 434–454. www.jstor.org/stable/10.1525/as.2007.47.3.434.

Lehman, Daniel Wayne. 2002. *John Reed and the Writing of Revolution.* Athens, OH: Ohio University Press.

Lehmann, Chris. 2015. Marxism and consumer culture. *New Labor Forum* 24 (3): 35–42. https://doi.org/10.1177/1095796015597009; www.jstor.org/stable/24718620.

Levin, Bess. 2020. Trump: Bob Woodward could've saved countless lives if he'd reported my lies sooner. *Vanity Fair.* 10 September. Accessed 14 September.

Lewis, Charlie. 2019. Don't call him by his name: Australian media and the Christchurch shooter. Crikey.com.au. 15 October. Accessed 15 October.

Lewis, David. 2009. International development and the 'perpetual present': Anthropological approaches to the re-historization of policy. *European Journal of Development Research* 21 (1): 32–46.

Lieberman, Mark. 2020. A growing group of journalists has cut back on Twitter, or abandoned it entirely. Poynter.org. 28 July. Accessed 30 July.

Lim, Merlyna. 2018. Challenging technological utopianism. *Canadian Journal of Communication* 43 (3): 375–379. https://doi.org/10.22230/cjc.2018v43n3a3393.

Lindhout, Amanda, and Sara Corbett. 2014. *A House in the Sky: A Memoir of a Kidnapping that Changed Everything.* London: Penguin.

Liptak, Adam. 2005. Reporter jailed after refusing to name source. NYT Online. 7 July. Accessed 8 July.

Lishka, Juliane A. 2019. A badge of honor? How *The New York Times* discredits President Trump's fake news accusations. *Journalism Studies* 20 (2): 287–304. https://doi.org/10.1080/1461670X.2017.1375385.

Littau, Jeremy. 2019. The crisis facing American journalism did not start with the Internet. *Slate.* 26 January. Accessed 6 February.

Liu, Ruqing, and 36Kr. 2020. Dear reporters, leave everything to AI, says Alibaba-Xinhua venture. *NIKKEI Asia.* 28 December. Accessed 2 January 2021.

Livingstone, Tom. 2019. Fire victim's heartbreaking last Facebook post. 9news. 14 November. Accessed 15 November.

Lloyd, Peter. 2010. *Inside Story.* Crows Nest, Sydney: Allen & Unwin.

Loong, Paul. 2008. Blackout on Canadian reporter's kidnapping posed dilemma for media. *The (Canadian) Globe and Mail.* 8 November. Accessed 18 November.

Lorenz, Taylor, Kellen Browning, and Sheera Frankel. 2020. Tik Tok and K-Pop Stans say they sank Trump rally. *The New York Times.* 11 July. Accessed 20 July.

Lowery, Wesley. 2020. A reckoning over objectivity, led by Black journalists. *The New York Times.* 23 June. Accessed 26 June.

Lukács, Georg. 1923. Reification and the consciousnesss of the proletariat. In *History and Class Consciousness*, pp. 65–174. Indo-European Publishing (no place). Original edition.

Luscombe, Richard. 2020. *New York Times* senior editor resigns amid backlash over controversial op-ed. *The Guardian.* 7 June. Accessed 9 June.

Lyons, John. 2019. AFP raid on ABC reveals investigative journalism being put in same category as criminality. ABC News. 15 July. Accessed 16 July.

MacKenzie, Donald, and Judy Wajcman. 1999. Introductory essay: The social shaping of technology. In *The Social Shaping of Technology*, edited by Donald MacKenzie, and Judy Wajcman, pp. 1–50. Buckingham, UK: Open University Press.

Macleod, Christopher. 2020. John Stuart Mill. In *Stanford Encylopedia of Philosophy*, edited by Edward N.Zalta. Stanford, CA: Metaphysics Research Lab, Stanford.

Magnay, Jacquelin. 2018. Gatwick drone: Heads may roll over bungled investigation. *The Australian*. 27 December. Accessed 13 January 2019.

Magnay, Jacquelin. 2019a. Ben Stokes slams London tabloid The Sun for reporting on family tragedy. *The Australian*. 18 September. Accessed 19 September.

Magnay, Jacquelin. 2019b. Royals: Prince Andrew 'sacked after Prince Charles stepped in' over Jeffrey Epstein controversy. *The Australian*. 25 November. Accessed 25 November.

Malan, Mia. 2018. Quid pro 1uo: How donor-funded journalism redefines job descriptions. *African Journalism Studies* 39 (2): 121–129. https://doi.org/10.1080/23743670.2018.1468347.

Maley, Jacqueline. 2018. Sins of the father: Why not publish Barnaby's Joyce's baby news? *The Age*. 8 February. Accessed 8 February.

Maley, Paul. 2020. Christchurch terrorist wrote farewell note to his mother. *The Weekend Australian*, 7–8 September 2020, 1 & 6, 15–16.

Mandel, Ernest. 1990. Introduction. In *Capital*, pp. 11–86. London: Penguin/NLB. Original edition, 1976, Pelican Books in association with New Left Review.

Mann, Tanveer. 2018. Journalist opens up about being raped in 15-month hostage ordeal in Somalia. *Metro*. 8 August. Accessed 12 January 2021.

Marans, Daniel. 2016. Melania Trump speechwriter takes blame for plagiarizing Michelle Obama's speech. The Huffington Post. 21 July. Accessed 21 July.

Maras, Steven. 2013. *Objectivity in Journalism. Key Concepts in Journalism*. Cambridge: Polity Press.

Marcus, Jon. 2019. Is it time for 'strategic silence' in news coverage of mass shootings? NiemanLab. 30 July. Accessed 30 July.

Markson, Sharri. 2014. News warns Mail: stop lifting or we'll sue. *The Australian*. 9 June. Accessed 9 June.

Markson, Sharri. 2018. Bundle of Joyce. *The Daily Telegraph*, 7 February 2018. p. 1.

Marsh, Moira. 2018. Believe me, I'm joking: The dialectics of the legend and the dialectics of humour. *Journal of American Folklore* 131 (522): 444–450. www.jstor.org/stable/10.5406/jamerfolk.131.522.0444.

Marsh, Peter. 2020. US politics updates: Joe Biden secures 270 votes at electoral college as Donald Trump announces William Barr's departure. ABC News. 15 December. Accessed 18 December.

Marszalek, Jessica. 2020. Enemies of the State. *The Courier Mail*, 30 July 2020, p. 1.

Martin, Lisa, Daniel McCulloch, and AAP. 2018. Gay rights campaigner slams 'hypocrite' Barnaby Joyce as his ex wife speaks out on 'devastating' affair. *The West Australian*. 7 February. Accessed 9 January 2021.

Marx, Karl. 1842. Freedom in general. *Rheinische Zeitung*. Accessed 9 September 2020.

Marx, Karl, ed. 1850. *The Class Struggles in France, 1848–1850*. Edited by Frederick Engels: Marxist Internet Archive. Original edition, *Selected Works*, Volume 1.

Marx, Karl. 1852. *The Eighteenth Brumaire of Louis Bonaparte*. www.marxists.org/archive/marx/works/1852/18th-brumaire/ch01.htm.

Marx, Karl. 1867. *Capital*. Translated by Ben Fowkes. Penguin Classics ed. 3 vols. Vol. 1. London: Penguin/NLB. Reprint, 1990. 1976, Pelican Books in association with New Left Review.

Marx, Karl. 1873. Afterword to the second German edition. In*Capital*. *Capital*. Translated by Ben Fowkes. Penguin Classics ed. 3 vols

Mason, Max. 2020. The number of Australians paying for news doubles. *Australian Financial Review*. 16 June. Accessed 20 October 2020.

Massaquoi, Isaac. 2016. *Ditch objectivity to save journalism. Sierra Leone State of the Media Report*. Ed. Ritchard M'Bayo, 19-26. University of Sierra Leone.

Masterton, M., and Roger Patching. 1986. *Now the News in Detail: A Guide to Broadcast Journalism in Australia*. Geelong: Deakin University Press.

Masullo, Gina M., and Carolyn McGourty Supple. 2020. News leaders and tech platforms must safeguard journalists from digital harassment to ensure press freedom. Poynter.org. 8 July. Accessed 9 July.

Matthews, Julian, and Kelechi Onyemaobi. 2020. Precarious professionalism: Journalism and the fragility of professional practice in the global South. *Journalism Studies* 21 (13): 1836–1851. https://doi.org/.o0r.g1/107.171/1774/61486488489419818800099283.

Maybee, Julie E. 2016. *Hegel's Dialectic*. Accessed 15 September 2020.

Mayhew, Freddy. 2018a. Amal Clooney warns press 'under attack like never before' and singles out Trump for giving 'green light' to autocratic regimes. *Press Gazette*. 7 December. 7 December. Accessed 8 December.

Mayhew, Freddy. 2018b. BBC News director says Sir Cliff ruling marks 'dramatic shift against press freedom' as Society of Editors calls High Court judgement 'worrying'. *Press Gazette*. 18 July. Accessed 23 July.

Mayhew, Freddy. 2018c. BBC will not appeal Sir Cliff Richard privacy ruling but asks for government review into law on reporting criminal probes. *Press Gazette*. 15 August. Accessed 16 August.

Mayhew, Freddy. 2019a. Britain's top anti-terror cop attacks newspapers over 'publishing uncensored' extremist propaganda. *Press Gazette*. 20 March. Accessed 21 March.

Mayhew, Freddy. 2019b. Clooney blames Trump rhetoric for hastening global freedom decline. *Press Gazette*. 11 July. Accessed 29 July.

Mayhew, Freddy. 2019c. Daily Mirror changes splash headline describing mosque killer as 'angelic boy'. *Press Gazette*. 18 March. Accessed 19 March.

Mayhew, Freddy. 2019d. Jailed Reuters pair freed by presidential pardon after 500 days behind bars in Myanmar. *Press Gazette*. 7 May. Accessed 9 May.

Mayhew, Freddy. 2019e. Lowest death toll for journalists in 16 years as 49 killed in 2019, says Reporters Without Borders. *Press Gazette*. 17 December. Accessed 31 December.

Mayhew, Freddy. 2019f. Sky News journalists 'deliberately targeted and attacked' while reporting from Syria. *Press Gazette*. 24 May. Accessed 25 May.

Mayhew, Freddy. 2019g. Welsh rugby star Gareth Thomas says journalist revealed his HIV status to his parents. *Press Gazette*. 18 September. Accessed 19 September.

Mayhew, Freddy. 2020a. Covid-19 prompts record digital audience for UK national press with 6.6m extra daily readers. *Press Gazette*. 17 June. Accessed 19 June.

Mayhew, Freddy. 2020b. Ex-Guardian editor Alan Rusbridger: 'Surprising more can't see Assange case is worrying for all journalists'. *Press Gazette*. 21 August. Accessed 24 August.

Mayhew, Freddy. 2020c. Newsrooms eye permanent change to working practices after Covid-19 lockdown. *Press Gazette*. 4 August. Accessed 4 August.

Mayhew, Freddy. 2020d. Report predicts five years of steep global decline for newspaper industry revenue (print and online). *Press Gazette*. 14 September. Accessed 20 October.

Mayhew, Freddy. 2020e. State-funded Press Recognition Panel backs calls for new anti-press privacy law. *Press Gazette*. 18 March. Accessed 20 March.

Mayhew, Freddy, and Charlotte Tobitt. 2020. Covid-19 crisis leads to more than 2,000 job cuts acrosss UK news organisations. *Press Gazette*. 14 August. Accessed 15 August.

McArdle, Megan. 2019. Is journalism's 'pivot to dust' arriving. *The Washington Post*. 26 January. Accessed 6 February.

McBride, Kelly. 2009. Journalists can't uphold standard set by news blackout of Rhode kidnapping. Poynter.org. 24 June. Accessed 30 June.

McBride, Kelly. 2019. Not naming mass shooters (much) is now the norm. Poynter.org. 7 June. Accessed 12 June.

McCallum, Zoe. 2019. Did The Guardian misuse Boris Johnson's private information, and could he sue? – Zoe McCallum. *Informm.org (originally on Matrix Media and Information law website)*. 26 June. Accessed 27 June.

McCarney, Joseph. 2005. *Ideology and false consciousness*. In *Marx, Myths and Legends*. www.marxists.org/archive/mccarney/2005/false-consciousness.htm.

McCarthy, Tom, and Miranda Bryant. 2020. Breonna Taylor: Louisville officials agree to pay family $12m. *The Guardian*. 16 September. Accessed 16 September.

McCauley, Dana. 2017. Exposing sources a 'slippery slope'. *The Australian*. 30 October. Accessed 30 October.

McChesney, Robert W. 2000. *Rich Media, Poor Democracy: Communication Politics in Dubious Times*. New York: The New Press.

McChesney, Robert W. 2008. *The Political Economy of Media: Enduring Issues, Emerging Dilemmas*. New York: Monthly Review Press.

McClelland, Calum. 2020. The impact of artificial intelligence—widespread job losses. *IoT for all*. 1 July. Accessed 16 October.

McDevitt, Michael, Perry Parks, Jordan Stalker, Kevin Lerner, Jesse Benn, and Taisik Hwang. 2018. Anti-intellectualism among US students in journalism and mass communication: A cultural perspective. *Journalism* 19 (6): 782–799. https://doi.org/.o0r.g1/107.171/1774/61486488489411971771100395.

McDonald, Willa, and Bunty Avieson. 2020. Journalism in disguise: Standpoint theory and the ethics of Günter Wallraff's udercover immersion. *Journalism Practice* 14 (1): 34–47. https://doi.org/10.1080/17512786.2019.1596752.

McGowan, Michael. 2019. BuzzFeed apologises to Emma Husar for distress caused by 'slut-shaming' article. *The Guardian*. 30 July. Accessed 10 January 2020.

McGregor, Shannon. 2018. More bogus embedded tweets in our stories. NiemanLab. n.d. Accessed 6 February 2019.

McIntyre, Niamh, Laith al-Khalaf, JessicaMurray, and Pamela Duncan. 2020. Caroline Flack: scale of negative media coverage before death revealed. *The Guardian*. 21 February. Accessed 23 February.

McKewon, Elaine. 2018. *Public Trust in Journalism: An Annotated Bibliography*. Centre for Media Transition, UTS, Sydney.

McKnight, David, and Penny O'Donnell. 2017. Journalism and the intellectual life: The exemplary case of Donald Horne. *Australian Journalism Review* 39 (1): 37–46.

McLaughlin, Greg. 2016. *The War Correspondent*. London: Pluto Press.

McMurtrie, Craig. 2019. Christchurch shooting coverage and why the ABC chose not to share the gunman's 'manifesto'. ABC News. 16 March. Accessed 17 March.

MEAA. 2018. *MEAA Journalist Code of Ethics*. Media, Entertainment and Arts Alliance. Accessed 16 April.

MEAA. 2020. Australia's slump in press freedom standing shows need for reforms. *MEAA News Release*. 23 April. Accessed 27 April.

Meade, Amanda. 2014. News Corp accuses Daily Mail Australia of plagiarism. *The Guardian*. 9 June. Accessed 9 June.

Meade, Amanda. 2015. SBS sports reporter Scott McIntyre sacked over 'despicable' Anzac tweets. *The Guardian*. 26 April. Accessed 27 April.

Meade, Amanda. 2016. Bill Leak defends 'racist' cartoon amid widespread criticism. *The Guardian*. 5 August. Accessed 3 November 2020.

Meade, Amanda. 2017. Source whisperers: press gallery divided over revealing raid leaker. *The Guardian*. 27 October. Accessed 28 October.

Meade, Amanda. 2019. Australian media broadcast footage from Christchurch shootings despite police pleas *The Guardian*. 15 March. Accessed 16 March.

Meade, Amanda. 2020a. Johannes Leak cartoon of Joe Biden and Kamala Harris denounced as racist. *The Guardian*. 14 August. Accessed 14 August.

Meade, Amanda. 2020b. Sparking joy: Alan Kohler's walk on the wild side rocks ABC. *The Guardian*. 28 August. Accessed 28 August.

Meade, Amanda. 2021. Press freedom report recommends stronger laws to protect public interest journalism. *The Guardian*. Accessed 2 July 2021.

Meadows, Michael, Susan Forde, Jackie Ewart, and Kerrie Foxwell. 2009. Making good sense: Transformative processes in community journalism. *Journalism* 10 (2): 155–170. https://doi.org/10.1177/1464884908100599.

Meese, James, and Edward Hurcombe. 2020. Facebook and Google used to be the future of news. But now media companies need more strings to their bow. The Conversation. 28 August. Accessed 20 October.

Mekelburg, Madlin. 2019. Did Trump open a 'major Apple manufacturing plant' in Austin? No. *Politifact*. 21 November. Accessed 16 December 2019.

Merrefield, Clark. 2020. Race and the newsroom: What seven research studies say. NiemanLab. 22 July. Accessed 23 July.

Merrill, John Calhoun. 1983. Axiology: Journalism and values. In *Philosophy and Journalism*, edited by John C, Merrill, and S. Jack Odell, pp. 108–127. New York: Longman.

Merrill, John Calhoun. 1989. *The Dialectic in Journalism: Toward a Responsible Use of Press Freedom*. Baton Rouge, LA: Lousiana State University Press.

Merrill, John Calhoun. 1990. *The Imperative of Freedom*. *Focus on Issues*. New York: Freedom House. Reprint, 1990. 1974.

Merrill, John Calhoun. 1996. *Existential Journalism*. Ames, IA: Iowa State University Press.

Merrill, John Calhoun, and S. Jack Odell. 1983. *Philosophy and Journalism*. New York: Longman.

Merritt, Chris. 2014. *Brandis rejects privacy tort call*. *The Australian*. April 4. Accessed 4 April.

Merritt, Chris. 2019. Actions expose risk to journalism, democracy. *The Australian*. 5 June. Accessed 5 June.

Meyer, Philip. 2004. *The Vanishing Newspaper: Saving Journalism in the Information Age*. Columbia, MO: University of Missouri Press.

Mibba. 2012. Faustian bargain and the Devil's crossroad. *Mibba*. n.d. Accessed 19 January 2021.

Miller, Nick. 2019. Australia leads the Western world on media restrictions: UN rapporteur. *The Sydney Morning Herald*. 12 July. Accessed 15 July.

MIR Chile. 1971. On journalism and objectivity. In *Communication and Class Struggle: 1. Capitalism, Imperialism*, edited by Armand Mattelart, and Seth Siegelaub, pp. 130–135. New York, Bagnolet, France: IG/IMMRC.

Mirkinson, Jack. 2011. *Sexual assault of journalists: Committee to protect journalists' New Report.* The Huffington Post. 8 June. Accessed 27 June.

Mitchell, Chris. 2019. Whistleblowers benefiting the community deserve reward, not punishment. *The Australian.* 17 June. Accessed 17 June.

Mitchell, Georgina. 2020. Khawaja suffered 'debililitating' mental illness when he wrote fake terror notebook, court told. *The Sydney Morning Herald.* 2 October. Accessed 3 October.

Molloy, Shannon. 2020. 7.30 host Leigh Sales shares sickening abuse sent to her after Scott Morrison interview. News.com.au. 23 July. Accessed 28 July.

Moran, Rachel E, and Nikki Usher. 2020. Objects of journalism, revised: Rethinking materiality in journalism studies through emotion, culture and 'unexpected objects'. *Journalism:* 1–18. https://doi.org/.o0r.g1/107.171/1774/6148648848942902909855730.

Morell, Ricki. 2020. Reporting and resilience: How journalists are managing their mental health. NiemanReports. 15 July. Accessed 18 July.

Mosco, Vincent. 1996. *The Political Economy of Communication: Rethinking and Renewal (The Media, Culture & Society series).* London: Sage.

Mosco, Vincent. 2004. *The Digital Sublime: Myth, Power and Cyberspace.* Boston, MA: MIT Press.

Muhlmann, Geraldine. 2010. *Journalism for Democracy.* Translated by Jean Birrell. Cambridge, UK: Polity. 2004.

Mujezinovic, Damir. 2019. Donald Trump gets crowd to booFox News. Inquisitr.com. 21 May. Accessed 23 May.

Mulhern, Francis. 2007. Critical considerations on the fetishism of commodities. *English Literary History* 74 (2): 479–492. www.jstor.org/stable/30029565.

Muller, Denis. 2010. Muller: What Wikileaks means for media ethics. Crikey.com.au. 21 December. Accessed 21 December.

Muller, Denis. 2019. Parliamentary press freedom inquiry: Letting the fox guard the henhouse. The Conversation. 4 July. Accessed 4 July.

Muller, Denis. 2020. Whether a ratings chase or ideological war, News Corp's coronavirus coverage is dangerous. The Conversation. 22 July. Accessed 4 September.

Muller, Rodger. 2019. I went undercover to expose the US, Australia gun lobby. *Al Jazeera.* 25 March. Accessed 26 March.

Munno, Greg, and Munro Craig. 2020. Can journalism be both impartial and empathetic? NiemanLab. 6 August. Accessed 8 August.

Munro, Colin. 1991. Press freedom: How the beast was tamed. *The Modern Law Review* 54 (1): 104–111. www.jstor.com/stable/1096685.

Murdock, Graham, and Janet Wasko, eds. 2007. Media in the age of marketization. Edited by John A.Lent, *The Hampton Press Communication Series: Popular Culture.* Cresskill, NJ: Hampton Press.

Murrell, Colleen. 2017. Manchester and the media: What coverage of the terrorist attack tells us about ourselves. The Conversation. 29 May. Accessed 29 May.

Murtha, Jack. 2016. How fake news sites frequently trick big-time journalists. *Columbia Journalism Review.* 26 May. Accessed 29 May.

Mussachia, M. Mark. 1977. On contradiction in dialectical materialism. *Science and Society* 41 (3): 257–280. www.jstor.org/stable/40402030.

Nadler, Anthony M. 2016. *Making the News Popular: Mobilizing US News Audiences.* Urbana, IL: University of Illinois Press.

Nafissi, Mohammad R. 2000. On the foundations of Athenian democracy: Marx's paradox and Weber's solution. *Max Weber Studies* 1 (1): 56–83. www.jstor.org/stable/24579713.

Nagy, Tony, and Greg Barns. 2020. If Assange is sent to the US, it will endanger journalists everywhere. *The Canberra Times.* 10 September. Accessed 10 September.

Napoli, Philip M., and Robyn Caplan. 2017. Why media companies insist they're not media companies, why they're wrong, and why it matters. *First Monday* 22 (5). https://doi.org/10.5210/fm.v22i5.7051

Natale, Simone, Paolo Bory, and Gabriele Balbi. 2019. The rise of corporational determinism: Digital media corporations and narratives of media change. *Critical Studies in Media Communication* 36 (4): 323–338. https://doi.org/10.1080/15295036.2019.1632469.

National Inquirer. 2019. Bezos' divorce! The cheating photos that ended his marriage. *National Inquirer*, 28 January. p. 1.

Nelson, Jacob L., and Su Jung Kim. 2020. Improve trust, increase loyalty? Analyzing the relationship between news credibility and consumption. *Journalism Practice* 15 (3): 1–18. https://doi.org/10.1080/17512786.2020.1719874.

Newman, Nic. 2020. Executive summary and Key Findings of the 2020 Report. Reuters Institute Digital News Report. 22 May. Accessed 22 June.

News.com.au. 2018. The comments coming back to haunt Barnaby Joyce. News.com.au. 8 February. Accessed 9 January 2021.

News Laundry. 2021. 'Murder the media': Journalists threatened, equipment smashed as pro-Trump mob storms Capitol Hill. News Laundry. 6 January. Accessed 12 January.

New York Post. 2012. Watch: Taliban thugs execute woman for 'adultery' near Kabul. *New York Post.* 8 July. Accessed 9 July.

New York Post. 2014. Savages: ISIS beheads American journalist on YouTube. *New York Post*, 20 August, p. 1.

Nixon, Brice. 2012. Dialectical method and the critical political economy of culture. *Triple C* 10 (2): 439–456.

Nohrstedt, S.A., S. Kaitatzi-Whitlock, Ottosen, and K. Riegert. 2000. From the Persian Gulf to Kosovo—War journalism and propaganda. *European Journal of Communication* 15 (3): 383–404.

Noor, Poppy. 2020a. Has Trump finally met his match? The female reporters setting him straight. *The Guardian.* 15 April. Accessed 21 April.

Noor, Poppy. 2020b. Teargassed, beaten up, arrested: what freedom of the press looks like in the US right now. *The Guardian.* 6 June. Accessed 9 June.

NORCAL, SPJ. 2019. SPJ NORCAL Committee condemns search of freelancer Bryan Carmody as attack on First Amendment. *SPJ Northern California.* 12 May. Accessed 13 May.

Novack, George. 1980. Marxism versus existentialism. In *Understanding History.* New York: Pathfinder Press.

Nover, Scott. 2021. Facebook locks out Trump for the rest of his presidency. *AdWeek.* 7 January. Accessed 8 January 2021.

NUJ. 2011. Code of Conduct. National Union of Journalists. Accessed 20 February.

Nyst, Carly. 2017. Patriotic trolling: How governments endorse hate campaigns against critics. *The Guardian.* 13 July. Accessed 13 July.

O'Brien, Natalie. 2008. ABC correspondent in Singapore drug arrest. *The Weekend Australian.* 19–20 July 2008, p. 9.

O'Carroll, Lisa. 2016. News Corp faces lawsuits from 20 'Fake Sheikh' targets in wake on conviction. *The Guardian*. 6 October. Accessed 7 October.

O'Neill, Timothy. 2009. Abrams v. United States (1919). In *The First Amendment Encyclopedia*, edited by John R.Vile, David L.Hudson Jr, and David Schultz. Murfreesboro, TN: Middle Tennessee State University.

Oakes, Dan. 2020. Dan Oakes explains why being cleared of prosecution over Afghan Files alleged war crimes reporting isn't end of battle. ABC News. 16 October. Accessed 25 October.

Oborne, Peter. 2020. Peter Oborne on Julian Assange: Future generations of journalists will not forgive us if we do not fight extradition. *Press Gazette*. 4 September. Accessed 7 September.

Ochs, George W. 1906. Journalism. *The Annals of the American Academy of Political and Social Science* 38: 38–57. www.jstor.org/stable/1010662.

Okulicz-Kozaryn, Adam. 2014. 'Freedom from' and 'freedom to' across countries. *Social Indicators Research* 118 (3). www.jstor.org/stable/24721049.

Ollman, Bertell. 2003a. *Dance of the Dialectic: Steps in Marx's Method*. Urbana, Chicago and Springfield, IL: University of Illiionois Press.

Ollman, Bertell. 2003b. Introduction. In *Dance of the Dialectic: Steps in Marx's Method*, edited by Bertell Ollman. Urbana, Chicago and Springfield, IL: University of Illinois Press.

Ollman, Bertell. 2003c. Putting dialectics to work. In *Dance of the Dialectic: Steps in Marx's Method*, edited by Bertell Ollman, pp. 59–172. Urbana, Chicago and Springfield, IL: University of Illinois Press.

Ornebring, Henrik. 2010. Technology and journalism-as-labour: Historical perspectives. *Journalism* 11 (1): 57–74. https://doi.org/10.1177/1464884909350644.

Orwell, George. 1988. *Nineteen Eighty-four*. London: Penguin.

Otte, Jedidajah. 2019. Ben Stokes attacks 'despicable' Sun story about family tragedy. *The Guardian*. 18 September. Accessed 19 September.

Overington, Caroline. 2018. Why did it take this long for Barnaby Joyce news to come out? *The Australian*. 7 February. Accessed 7 February.

Palmer, Tim. 2020. Media Diversity Australia verdict on minority representation flawed. *The Australian*. 30 August. Accessed 3 September.

Pannekoek, Anton. 1942. Materialism and historical materialism. *New Essays* VI (2). www.marxists.org/archive/pannekoe/1942/materialism.htm.

Paradkar, Shree. 2017. It was wrong to rein in Desmond Cole: Paradkar. *The Toronto Star*. 12 May. Accessed 2 November 2020.

Park, Sora, Caroline Fisher, Terry Flew, and Uwe Dulleck. 2020. Global mistrust in news: The impact of social media on trust. *International Journal on Media Management* 22 (2): 83–96. https://doi.org/10.1080/14241277.2020.1799794.

Parks, Perry. 2019. Covering Trump's 'carnival': A rhetorical alternative to 'objective' reporting. *Journalism Practice* 13 (10): 1164–1184. https://doi.org/10.1080/17512786.2019.1577696.

Parsons, Jeff. 2020. Artificial intelligence wrote a news article, should I start looking for a new job? *Metro*. 11 September. Accessed 15 October.

Parsons, Michael J. 2019. Fighting for attention: Democracy, free speech and the marketplace of ideas. *Minnesota Law Review* 104: 2157–2256.

Patching, Roger, and Martin Hirst. 2014. *Journalism Ethics: Arguments and Cases for the Twenty-first Century*. London: Routledge.

Patnaik, Arun K. 1988. Gramsci's concept of common sense: Towards a theory of subaltern consciousness in hegemony processes. *Economic and Political Weekly* 23 (5): PE2–PE10. www.jstor.org/stable/4378042.

Patterson, P., and L. Wilkins. 1994. *Media Ethics: Issues and Cases*, second edn. Dubuque, IA: Brown & Benchmark.

Patterson, Thomas C. 2016. Too much common sense, not enough critical thinking. *Dialectical Anthropology* 40: 251–258. https://doi.org/10.1007/s10624-016-9434-5.

Paul, Kari. 2021. Twitter and Facebook lock Donald Trump's account after video address. *The Guardian*. 6 January. Accessed 8 January.

Pavlidis, Periklis. 2010. Critical thinking as dialectics: a Hegelian Marxist approach. *Journal for Critical Education Policy Issues* 8 (2): 75–102.

Pearson, Mark, and Mark Polden. 2019. *The Journalist's Guide to Media Law*, sixth edn. Crows Nest, Sydney: Allen and Unwin.

Peiser, Jaclyn. 2019. The rise of the robot reporter. *The New York Times*. 5 February. Accessed 16 October 2020.

Pengelly, Martin. 2020. Judge orders Chelsea Manning's release from jail in Virginia. *The Guardian*. 13 March. Accessed 20 March.

Perez, Andrew, and David Sirota. 2020. *Bob Woodward Aided Trump's Crime Against Humanity*. 10 September. Accessed 14 September.

Philp, Catherine. 2019. ISIS-held journalist John Cantlie may still be alive. *The Times* (re-published in *The Australian*). 7 February. Accessed 7 February.

Pickard, John. 2006. Basic points of dialectical materialism. Accessed 15 July 2018.

Pierre-Louis, Kendra. 2020. It's time to change the way the media reports on protests. Here are some ideas. NiemanLab. 24 June. Accessed 25 June.

PIJI. 2020. Number of public interest news contractions in Australia tops 200. Public Interest Journalism Initiative press release. 28 May. Accessed 28 April 2021.

Pilkington, Ed, and Adam Gabbatt. 2020. Media leaders agonize over amplifying Trump lies as 2020 election year begins. *The Guardian*. 6 January. Accessed 9 January.

Pingree, Raymond J., Brian Watson, Mingxiao Sui, Kathleen Searles, Nathan P. Kalmoe, Joshua P. Darr, Martina Santia, and Kirill Bryanov. 2018. Checking facts and fighting back: Why journalists should defend their profession. *PLoS ONE* 13 (12). https://doi.org/10.1371/journal.pone.0208600.

Pitluck, Aaron Z., Fabio Mattioli, and Daniel Souleles. 2018. Finance beyond function: Three causal explanations for financialization. *Economic Anthropology* ('Financialization') 5 (2): 1–15. https://doi.org/DOI:10.1002/sea2.12114.

Plekhanov, Georgi Valentinovich. 1899. Historical materialism and art. In *Art and Social Life*, pp. 19–60. Delhi: Aakar Books.

Poitras, Laura. 2021. *Open Letter*. 14 January. Accessed 18 January 2021.

Pompeo, Joe. 2019. Here he is using the term 'treason'; Why A.G. Sulzberger took on Trump in The Wall Street Journal. *Vanity Fair*. 20 June, Accessed 23 June.

Ponsford, Dominic. 2020. Twitter is on fire and journalists should try not to fan the flames. *Press Gazette*. 12 June. Accessed 15 June.

Posetti, Julie. 2009. Top 20 take away tips for tweeting journos. J-scribe.com. 21 June. Accessed 23 June.

Posetti, Julie. 2017. *Protecting Journalism Sources in the Digital Age*. United National Educational, Scientific and Cultural Organisation. Paris: UNESCO.

Posetti, Julie. 2020. *Online violence: The new front line for women journalists*. International Center for Journalists (ICFJ). 24 September. Accessed 4 January 2021.

Posetti, Julie, Emily Bell, and Pete Brown. 2020. *Journalism & the pandemic: A global snapshot of impacts*. International Center for Journalists (ICFJ), 13 October. Accessed 20 October.

Posetti, Julie, Suelette Dreyfus, and Naomi Colvin. 2019. The Perugia principles for journalists working with whistleblowers in the digital age. www.blueprintforfreesp eech.net/en/news/blueprint-launches-perugia-principles-for-journalists-working-with-whistleblowers-in-the-digital-age.

Posetti, Julie, and Alice Matthews. 2018. A short guide to the history of 'fake news' and disinformation. International Center for Journalists. 23 July. Accessed 24 July. www. icfj.org/news/short-guide-history-fake-news-and-disinformation-new-icfj-learning-module.

Posner, Richard A. 1979. Privacy, secrecy, and reputation. James McCormick Mitchell Lecture, University of Chicago Law School.

Post, Jeroen, and Vincent Crone. 2015. Reporting revolution: Technological determinism in journalistic reports on social media and movements. *Digital Journalism* 3 (6): 871–887. https://doi.org/10.1080/21670811.2014.990253.

Post, Senja. 2014. Scientific objectivity in journalism? How journalists and academics define objectivity, assess its attainability, and rate its desirability. *Journalism* 16 (6): 730–749. https://doi.org/https://doi.org/10.1177/2F1464884914541067.

Press Association. 2020. Judge sets January date for decision on Julian Assange US extradition. *Press Gazette*. 1 October. Accessed 3 October.

Press Freedom Tracker. 2020a. Trump, in crisis mode, tweets his 2000th attack on the press. Press Freedom Tracker. 13 April. Accessed 21 April.

Press Freedom Tracker. 2020b. Press freedom in crisis. Press Freedom Tracker. 20 October. Accessed 20 October.

Press Gazette. 2018. Government 'not persuaded' by plans for anonymous arrests in wake of Sir Cliff Richard reports. *Press Gazette*. 4 March. Accessed 5 March.

Press Gazette. 2019. Prince Harry accepts damages from Splash news agency over Cotswolds home helicopter shots. *Press Gazette*. 16 May. Accessed 20 May.

Press Gazette. 2020. Journalism in Egypt now 'effectively a crime', Amnesty International says. *Press Gazette*. 4 May. Accessed 28 April 2021.

Priest, Dana. 2016. War reporter Marie Colvin was tracked, targeted and killed by Assad's forces, family says. *The Washington Post*. 9 July. Accessed 17 July.

Primo, Alex, and Gabriela Zago. 2015. Who and what do journalism. *Digital Journalism* 3 (1): 38–52. https://doi.org/10.1080/21670811.2014.927987.

Prosser, William. 1960. Privacy. *California Law Review* 48 (3): 383–423.

Pullman, Laura. 2019. Doyenne of American journalism admits plagiarism. *The Australian*. 11 February. Accessed 11 February.

Quinn, Aaron. 2007. Moral virtues for journalists. *Journal of Mass Media Ethics* 22 (2–3): 168–186. https://doi.org/10.1080/08900520701315764.

Quinn, Karl. 2015. Scott McIntyre being sacked by SBS is a dreadful move for freedom of speech. *The Sydney Morning Herald*. 27 April. Accessed 27 April.

Raban, Ofer. 2019. Assange's new indictment: Espionage and the First Amendment— Ofer Raban. Inforrm.org (re-published from The Conversation). 30 May. Accessed 30 May.

Radcliffe, Damian. 2020. Covid-19 has ravaged American newsrooms. Here's why that matters. NiemanLab. 20 July. Accessed 21 July.

Radcliffe, Damian. 2021. The impact of COVIC-19 on journalism in emerging economies and the global South. January. Accessed 15 January.

Rahman, Khairiah A. 2016. Dialogue and persuasion in the Islamic tradition: Implications for journalism. *Global Media Journal* 9 (2): 9–26. https://openrepository.aut.ac.nz/handle/10292/10928.

Ramos Jr., Valeriano. 1982. The concepts of ideology, hegemony and organic intellectuals in Gramsci's Marxism. *Theoretical Review* 27: 1–25. www.marxists.org/history/erol/periodicals/theoretical-review/1982301.htm.

Ratcliffe, Rebecca. 2020. Maria Ressa: Rappler editor found guilty of cyber libel charges in Philippines. *The Guardian*. 15 June. Accessed 15 June.

Ravens, Tara. 2012. Will and Kate furious at topless photos. *The Sydney Morning Herald*. 14 September. Accessed 20 June 2018.

Ravi, Narasimhan. 2005. Looking beyond flawed journalism: How national interests, patriotism and cultural values shaped the coverage of the Iraq War. *The Harvard International Journal of Press/Politics* 10 (1): 45–62.

Ravlic, Tom. 2020. 18 months on, Christchurch footage is still available online. Crikey.com.au. 1 October. Accessed 1 October.

Rawlinson, Kevin. 2016. How newsroom pressure is letting fake stories on to the web. *The Guardian*. 18 April. Accessed 19 April.

Rawnsley, Adam. 2020. Right-wing outlets duped by a Middle East propaganda campaign: Does not exist. The Daily Beast. 7 July. Accessed 29 July.

Reed, John. 1919. *Ten Days That Shook the World*. New York: Liveright. Accessed 29 October 2020. www.marxists.org/archive/reed/.

Rees, John. 1998. *The Algebra of Revolution: The Dialectic and the Classical Marxist Tradition*. London and New York: Routledge.

Reeves, Richard V. 2019. Capitalism is failing. People want a job with a decent wage—why is this so hard? Brookings. 29 April. Accessed 2 November 2020.

Reidy, Padraig. 2019. Opinion: Julian Assange did a lot of bad things. Publishing leaks isn't one of them. Buzzfeed. 12 April. Accessed 14 April.

Reporters' Committee. 2019. *Journalists jailed or fined for refusing to identify confidential sources, as of 2019*. Reporters Committee for Freedom of the Press. n.d. Accessed 10 January.

Ressa, Maria. 2020. We can't let the virus infect democracy. *Time magazine*. 14 April. Accessed 20 May.

Richards, Ian. 2005. *Quagmires and Quandries: Exploring Journalism Ethics*. Sydney: UNSW Press.

Richards, Jared. 2020. People are accusing News Corp of hypocrisy after naming Queensland COVID teens. Junkee.com. 30 July. Accessed 6 January 2021.

Ricketson, Matthew, and Alexandra Wake. 2019. Media companies on notice over traumatised journalists after landmark court decision. The Conversation. 6 March. Accessed 6 March.

Ritchie, Annabelle, and Siegfried Clarke. 2019. *The Ethics of Artificial Intelligence: Laws from Around the World*. Oxford: Oxford University Press.

Ritter, Zacc, and Gallup Polls. 2019. How much does the world trust journalists? *Gallup*. 27 December. Accessed 18 May 2021.

Robertson, Geoffrey. 2019. Exposed: A second-rate country unwilling to defend press freedom. *The Sydney Morning Herald*. June 8. Accessed 11 June.

Robie, David. 2020. Pacific governments accused of using coronavirus crisis as cover for media craskdown. The Conversation. 5 May. Accessed 20 May.

Robin, Myriam. 2014. Mail responds to News: stop taking our exclusives. Crikey.com.au. 16 June. Accessed 16 June.

Robin, Myriam. 2016. SBS settles Anzac tweets case, but 'vigilante' Turnbull's role an open question. Crikey.com.au. 11 April. Accessed 11 April.

Robinson, Andrew. 2005. Towards an intellectual reformation: The critique of common sense and the forgotten revolutionary project of Grramscian theory. *Critical Review of International Social and Political Philosophy* 8 (4): 469–481. https://doi.org/10.1080/13698230500205045.

Rodgers, Scott. 2015. Foreign objects? Web content management systems, journalistic cultures and the ontology of software. *Journalism* 16 (1): 10–26. https://doi.org/10.1177/1464884914545729.

Rodrigues, Usha M. 2020. Whitewash on the box: How a lack of diversity on Australian television damages us all. The Conversation. 17 August. Accessed 17 August.

Rogers, Janak. 2020. Australia's media has been too white for too long. This is how to bring more diversity to newsrooms. The Conversation. 7 July. Accessed 9 July.

Romano, Carlin. 2009. We need 'Philosophy of Journalism'. *The Chronicle of Higher Education*. Accessed 16November 2020.

Rosen, Jay. 2008. A most useful definition of citizen journalism. PressThink. 14 July. Accessed 12 March 2010.

Rosen, Jill. 2003. All about the retrospect. *American Journalism Review*. June. Accessed 19 September.

Rosenberg, Eli. 2019. A reporter declined to reveal his source. Then police showed up at his front door with guns. *The Washington Post*. 11 May. Accessed 14 May.

Rourke, Alison. 2019. 'Outcast': How the newspapers covered Prince Andrew's suspension of duties. *The Guardian*. 21 November. Accessed 21 November.

Roy, Eleanor Ainge. 2019a. Christchurch trial: New Zealand media agree to curb white supremacy coverage. *The Guardian*. 1 May. Accessed 1 May.

Roy, Eleanor Ainge. 2019b. Sky NZ fined for broadcasting clips of Christchurch massacre live stream. *The Guardian*. 20 August. Accessed 21 August.

RSF. 2020. RSF's 2020 Round-up: 50 journalists killed, two-thirds in countries 'at peace'. RSF. 28 December. Accessed 29 December.

Ruben, David-Hillel. 1979. Marxism and materialism: A study in Marxist theory of knowledge. *Marxist Theory and Contemporary Capitalism* 10. Atlantic Highlands, NJ: The Harvester Press, Brighton & Humanities Press.

Rundle, Guy. 2019. Assange is in the dock, but it's investigative journalism on trial. Crikey.com.au. 12 April. Accessed 12 April.

Rusbridger, Alan. 2019. Partnering with Assange was unpleasant. But work like his is crucial. *The Washington Post*. 12 April. Accessed 14 April.

Rusbridger, Alan. 2020a. *News and How to Use It*. Edinburgh: Cannongate Books.

Rusbridger, Alan. 2020b. This is a key moment in the public's view of mainstream news. *The Guardian*. 3 May. Accessed 5 May.

Rushe, Dominic, and Kari Paul. 2020. US justice department sues Google over accusation of illegal monopoly . *The Guardian*. 20 October. Accessed 20 October.

Rutenberg, Jim. 2018. Trump's attacks on the news media are working. *The New York Times*. 28 October. Accessed 6 February 2019.

Ryfe, David. 2019. The ontology of journalism. *Journalism* 20 (1): 206–209. https://doi.org/0r.g10/107.171/877/58670568078971981880099246.

Salge, Christopher. 2017. Asimov's laws won't stop robots from harming humans, so we've developed a better solution. The Conversation. 11 July. Accessed 15 October 2020.

Samios, Zoe. 2017. HuffPost: Where did it go wrong? *Mumbrella*. 30 November. Accessed 20 October 2020.

Samios, Zoe, and Richard Ferguson. 2019. Dutton blasted for 'invasion' on free press. *The Australian*. 13 July. Accessed 15 July.

Samios, Zoe, and Lilly Vitorovich. 2019. Democratic freedoms at risk, media bosses warn. *The Australian*. 14 August. Accessed 16 August.

Sanders , Huub. 2009. *Prussian censorship and Karl Marx's brief career as an editor for Rheinische Zeitung*. Institute of Social History. Accessed 9 September 2020.

Sanders, Karen. 2003. *Ethics & Journalism*. London: Sage.

Sanders, Karen, Mark Hanna, Maria Rosa Berganza, and Jose Javier, Sanchez Aranda. 2008. Becoming journalists: A comparison of professional attitudes and values of British and Spanish journalism students. *European Journal of Communication* 23 (2): 133–152. https://doi.org/10.1177/0267323108089219.

Santa-Wood, B. 2020. Christiane Amanpour 'deeply troubled' by US press freedom developments, she tells Helsinki Commission. *Committee to Protect Journalists*. 23 July. Accessed 23 July.

Satariano, Adam. 2020. Coronavirus doctors battle another scourge: Misinformation. *The New York Times*. 17 August. Accessed 19 August.

Sayers, Sean. 1984. Marxism and the Dialectical Method: A critique of G.A. Cohen. In *Radical Philosophy* 36 (36), 4–13.

Scaffidi, Sarah. 2020. Journalism under fire: UNESCO raises alarm over surge of attacks on media workers covering protests. *UN News*. 14 September. Accessed 16 September.

Schaff, Adam. 1960. Marxist dialectics and the principle of contradiction. *The Journal of Philosophy* 57 (7): 241–250. https://doi.org/10.2307/2021865www.jstor.org/stable/2021865.

Schapiro, J. Salwyn. 1943. John Stuart Mill, Pioneer of democratic liberalism in England. *Journal of the History of Ideas* 4 (2): 127–160. www.jstor.org/stable/2707321.

Schleifer, Theodore. 2018. Google CEO Sundar Pichai says AI is more profound than electricity and fire. *Recode*. 19 January. Accessed 15 October 2020.

Schlesinger, David. 2010. *Our need to be in the midst of danger*. blogs.reuters.com. 10 November. Accessed 10 November.

Schmitt, Richard. 1988. The materialist dialectic. *Science and Society* 52 (4): 441–456. www.jstor.org/stable/40402911.

Schudson, Michael. 2001. The objectivity norm in American journalism. *Journalism* 2 (2): 149–170. http://jou.sagepub.com/cgi/content/abstract/2/2/149.

Schudson, Michael. 2013. Reluctant stewards: Journalism in a democratic society. *Daedalus* 142 (2): 159–176. www.jstor.org/stable/43297240.

Schudson, Michael. 2015. What sorts of things are thingy? And what sorts of thinginess are there? Notes on stuff and social construction. *Journalism* 16 (1): 61–64. https://doi.org/10.1177/1464884914545733.

Schudson, Michael. 2019. The fall, rise and fall of media trust. *Columbia Journalism Review* (Winter). Accessed 22 October 2020.

Schultz, Brad, and Mary Lou Sheffer. 2017. Newspaper trust and credibility in the age of robot reporters. *Journal of Applied Journalism & Media Studies* 6 (2): 339–355. https://doi.org/10.1386/ajms.6.2.339_1.

Scire, Sarah. 2020. Journalists are struggling with mental health, financial hardship, and disinformation, according to a 'startling and disturbing' survey. NiemanLab. 13 October. Accessed 20 October.

Scott, Martin, Mel Bunce, and Kate Wright. 2017. Donor power and the news: The influence of foundation funding on international public service journalism. *The International Journal of Press/Politics* 22 (2): 163–184. https://doi.org/10.1177/1940161217693394.

Seely, Natalee. 2019. Journalists and mental health: The psychological toll of covering everyday trauma. *Newspaper Research Journal* 40 (2): 239–259. https://doi.org/10.1177/0739532919835612.

Selva, Meera, and Anthony Feinstein. 2020. COVID-19 is hurting journalists' mental health. News outlets should help them now. Reuters Institute. 17 July. Accessed 28 August.

Sernoffsky, Evan. 2019. San Francisco police chief concedes raid on journalist was wrong –'I'm sorry'. *San Francisco Chronicle*. 24 May. Accessed 25 May.

Seymour, Richard. 2020. Caroline Flack's death shows how social media has democratised cruelty. *The Guardian*. Accessed 24 February.

Shafer, Jack. 2010. Who said it first? Slate. 30 August. Accessed 29 May 2012.

Shaffer, Cory. 2020. Cuyahoga County prosecutor subpoenas cleveland.com and Plain Dealer reporters' photographs, videos of downtown riots and interviews with witnesses. Cleveland.com. 10 June. Accessed 25 June.

Shanahan, Leo. 2019a. News Corp Australia takes AFP raid to the High Court. *The Australian*. 25 June. Accessed 25 June.

Shanahan, Leo. 2019b. Rivals unite on law reform. *The Australian*. 24 June. Accessed 24 June.

Shapiro, Bruce. 2019. Trump's charges against Julian Assange would effectively criminalize investigative journalism. The Nation. 31 May. Accessed 3 June.

Shapiro, Sarah, and Catherine Brown. 2018. The state of civics education. Center for American Progress. 21 February. Accessed 14 January 2021.

Sheaff, Mike. 2019. *Secrecy, Privacy and Accountability: Challenges for Social Research*. University of Plymouth, UK. Accessed 9 January 2021.

Sheth, Sonam. 2020. Trump says that 'if we stop testing right now, we'd have very few cases' of the coronavirus. Business Insider. 15 June. Accessed 6 January 2021.

Shields, Bevan. 2019. Dutton orders AFP to lift the bar on investigating journalists. *The Sydney Moring Herald*. 9 August. Accessed 15 August.

Siddique, Haroon. 2019. Suspected leaker of Kim Darroch cables on Trump 'identified'. *The Guardian*. 14 July. Accessed 16 July.

Simanovych, Olga. 2020. How journalists can deal with trauma while reporting on COVID-19. *Global Investigative Journalism Network*. 24 March. Accessed 6 April.

Simon, Joel. 2020. COVID-19 is spawning a global press-freedom crackdown. *Columbia Journalism Review*. 25 March. Accessed 25 August.

Singer, Jane B. 2008. The journalist network: A shifting rationale for the gatekeeping role and the objectivity norm. *Tripedos* 23: 61–76.

Singh, Maanvi. 2020. *New York Times* says senator Tom Cotton's op-ed did not meet editorial standards. *The Guardian*. 5 June. Accessed 9 June.

Sinnott-Armstrong, Walter. 2019. Consequentialism. In *Stanford Encyclopedia of Philosophy*, edited by Edward N.Zalta. Stanford, CA: Metaphysics Research Lab, Stanford.

Slaček Brlek, Sašo, Jurij Smrke, and Igor Vobič. 2017. Engineering technologies for journalism in the digital age: A case study. *Digital Journalism: Churnalism: Revised and Revisited*. Guest-edited by Jane Johnston, and Susan Forde5 (8): 1025–1043. https://doi.org/10.1080/21670811.2017.1338526.

Slot, Mijke. 2018. About introvert incumbents and extravert start-ups: An exploration of the dialectics of collaborative innovation in the Dutch journalism field. *Journalism.* https://doi.org/10.1177/1464884918794303.

Smee, Ben, and Amanda Meade. 2020. Naming Brisbane women risks 'a second wave of Covid-related racial hostility': Commission. *The Guardian.* 30 July. Accessed 4 August.

Smith, Ben. 2020a. How the media could get the election story wrong. *The New York Times.* Accessed 5 August.

Smith, Ben. 2020b. Inside the revolts erupting in America's big newsrooms. *The New York Times.* Accessed 9 June 2020.

Smith, David. 2019. The lies have it: Republicans abandon truth in Trump impeachment defence. *The Observer.* Accessed 16 December 2019.

Smith, Gerry. 2020. The biggest news story in the world costs journalists their jobs. *Bloomberg Law.* 15 April. Accessed 24 April 2020.

Smith, Joan. 2020. Caroline Flack's tragic death has rightly put the tabloids back in the dock. *The Guardian.* 17 February. Accessed 20 February.

Smith, Sydney. 2014. How media covered James Foley beheading: NYPost's front page like death porn (Commentary). *imediaethics.org.* 20 August. Accessed 22 August.

Smyth, Frank. 2013. *Do news blackouts help journalists held captive?* Committee to Protect Journalists. 26 February. Accessed 1 March.

Snow, Jon. 2012. *Poised for journalism's golden age.* Hugh Cudlipp Lecture. 23 January.

Solove, Daniel J. 2008. *Understanding Privacy.* Boston, MA: Harvard University Press.

Sommer, Will. 2019. Arson Suspected at Comet Ping Pong, the D.C. Restaurant Made Famous by Pizzagate. The Daily Beast. 25 January. Accessed 7 June.

Sorabjee, Soli J. 1986. Freedom of the press: Its contents and facets. *India International Centre Quarterly* 13, no. The Right to be Human (3/4): 173–184. https://doi.org/10.2307/23001444;www.jstor.org/stable/23001444.

Specia, Megan. 2020. In turnabout, global leaders urge U.S. to protect reporters amid unrest. *The New York Times.* 4 June. Accessed 6 June.

Speed, Ewen, and Russell Mannion. 2017. The rise of post-truth populism in pluralist liberal democracies: Challenges for health policy. *International Journal of Health Policy Management* 6 (6): 249–251. https://doi.org/https://dx.doi.org/10.15171%2Fijhpm.2017.19.

Spirkin, Alexander. 1983. The theory of knowledge and creativity. In *Dialectical Materialism.* Moscow: Progress Publishers.

SPJ. 2014. Code of Ethics. Society of Professional Journalists. www.spj.org/pdf/spj-code-of-ethics.pdf

Spocchia, Gino. 2020. Trump mocks journalist shot by rubber bullets during George Floyd protests, said it was a 'beautiful sight'. *Independent* (UK). 20 September. Accessed 29 September.

Srnicek, Nick. 2017. The challenges of platform capitalism: Understanding the logic of a new business model. *Juncture* 23 (4): 254–257.

statista. 2020. *Share of adults who trust news media most of the time in selected countries worldwide as of February 2020.* Statista. 16 July.

Statt, Nick. 2017. The news industry is worried Facebook and Google have far too much power. *The Verge.* 10 July. Accessed 20 October 2020.

Steel, John. 2012. *Journalism and Free Speech.* London & New York: Routledge.

Stelter, Brian. 2020. In newsrooms, 'a raging debate' over the role of journalists should be playing. CNN. 8 June. Accessed 11 June.

Stephens, Mitchell. 2007. *A History of News*, third edn. New York & Oxford: Oxford University Press.

Steup, Matthias, and Ram Neta. 2020. Epistemology. In *The Stanford Encyclopedia of Philosophy*, edited by Edward N.Zalta. Stanford, CA: Metaphysics Research Lab, Stanford.

Stiglitz, Joseph E. 1999. *On liberty, the right to know, and public discourse: The role of transparency in public life*. Oxford Amnesty Lecture, Oxford, UK, 27 January.

Stolberg, Sheryl Gay, and Noah Weiland. 2020. Study finds 'single largest driver' of coronavirus misinformation: Trump. *The New York Times*. 30 September. Accessed 2 October.

Stott, Rob. 2020. We need to talk about Stan culture, anonymously. Junkee.com. 29 July. Accessed 1 August.

Suarez Villegas, J.C. 2015. Ethical and deontological aspects of online journalism. Their perception by journalists. *Revista Latina de Comunicación Social* 70: 91–109. https://doi.org/10.4185/RLCS-2015-1036en.

Sugars, Stephanie. 2019. From fake news to enemy of the people: An anatomy of Trump's tweets. Committee to Protect Journalists. 30 January. Accessed 3 February.

Sullivan, Margaret. 2019a. How the new Assange indictment 'crosses a bright red line for journalists'. *The Washington Post*. 24 May. Accessed 26 May.

Sullivan, Margaret. 2019b. Traditional journalists may abandon Wikileaks' Assange at their own peril. *The Washington Post*. 11 April. Accessed 14 April.

Sullivan, Margaret. 2019c. The Twitter-fed disaster over Epstein's death demands a solution: Slow news. *The Washington Post*. 13 August. Accessed 15 August.

Sullivan, Margaret. 2020a. Should Bob Woodward have reported Trump's virus revelations sooner? Here's how he defends his decision. *The Washington Post*. 10 September. Accessed 19 September.

Sullivan, Margaret. 2020b. What it really means when Trump calls a story 'fake news'. *The Washington Post*. 14 April. Accessed 24 April.

Sulzberger, A.G. 2019. Accusing the New York Times of 'treason', Trump crosses a line. *The Wall Street Journal*. 19 June. Accessed 23 June.

Swaine, Jon. 2018. National Enquirer owner admits to 'catch and kill' payment to ex-Playmate. *The Guardian*. 13 December. Accessed 10 January 2021.

Sweney, Mark. 2020. FT suspends journalist accused of listening to rival outlets' Zoom calls. *The Guardian*. 28 April. Accessed 30 April.

Swift, Art, and Gallup Polls. 2017. *In U.S., confidence in newspapers is still low but rising*. Gallup, 28 June.

Taylor, Lenore. 2020. The coronavirus story is unfathomably large. We must get the reporting right. *The Guardian*. 22 March. Accessed 22 March.

Taylor, Rebecca. 2019. Police tell source of Trump memos leak 'turn yourself in' as Osborne criticises inquiry. *Sky News*. 13 July. Accessed 13 July.

Thatcher, Ian, D. 1991. Trotsky's dialectic. *Studies in Soviet Thought* 41 (2): 127–144. www.jstor.com/stable/20100579.

The Australian. 2010. Cash for comment. *The Australian*. 26 April, p. 28.

The Australian. 2004. Don't shoot (cartoon). *The Australian*. 18 November, p. 22.

The Australian. 2012. The Sun defies royals to publish naked Prince Harry pictures. *The Australian*. 24 August. Accessed 24 August.

The Australian. 2013. Woman's Day editor defends decision to publish Catherine baby bump pictures. *The Australian*. 14 February. Accessed 14 February.

The Australian. 2018. Star reporter admits to making up stories (republished from The Wall Street Journal). *The Australian*. 22 December. Accessed 24 December.

Thebault, Reis, and Teo Armus. 2020. Duelling narratives fuel opposing views of Kenosha protest shooting. *The Washington Post*. 31 August. Accessed 1 September.

The Courier Mail. 2018. Barnaby Joyce breaks new ground in absurdity with $150K interview deal on relationship with Vikki Campion. 2018. *The Courier Mail*. 28 May. Accessed 21 August 2019.

The Daily Mail. 2012. Violence erupts as protesters burn cars and throw rocks at US military base in Afghan capital over anti-Islam video. The Daily Mail. 17 September. Accessed 17 November.

The Daily Telegraph. 2014. Pure evil: Barbarians behead US journalist in grotesque propaganda clip. *The Daily Telegraph*, 21 August 2014. p. 1.

The Economist. 2017. Most Republicans trust the president more than they trust the media. *The Economist*. 3 August. Accessed 22 October 2020.

The Guardian. 2016. Duchess of Cambridge has privacy breach complaints upheld. *The Guardian*. 16 September. Accessed 16 September.

The Guardian. 2019. Singapore invokes 'fake news' law for first time over Facebook post. *The Guardian*. 25 November. Accessed 2 December.

The Information. 2021. Mark Di Stefano [bio]. The Information. Accessed 10 January.

The New Fascism Syllabus. 2020. How to keep the lights on in democracies: An open letter of concern by scholars of authoritarianism. Accessed 2 November.

The New York Times. 2004. TV report says marine shot prisoner. *The New York Times*. 16 November. Accessed 20 November.

The New York Times. 2017. The Times issues social media guidelines for the Newsroom (updated 2020). *The New York Times*. 13 October. Accessed 4 November 2019.

The New York Times. 2019. Editorial: Why are the Australian police rummaging through journalists' files? *The New York Times*. 6 June. Accessed 18 July.

The New York Times. 2020. Editorial: Some Republicans aren't in denial about the virus. Trump still is. *The New York Times*. 23 June. Accessed 26 June.

The Sun. 2012a. Harry grabs the family jewels. *The Sun*. 23 August, p. 1.

The Sun. 2012b. Heir it is! Pic of naked Harry you've already seen on the internet. *The Sun*. 24 August, p. 1.

The Sun. 2019. Hero Ben's brother and sister were shot dead. *The Sun*. 19 September. Accessed 18 May 2021.

The Sydney Morning Herald. 2012. Flash Harry: Prince's 'strip billiards' photos spark a right royal row. *The Sydney Morning Herald*. 23 August. Accessed 24 August.

The Times. 2012. The price of truth. *The Times*. 23 February 2012, p. 1.

The Torch. 2019. 25 journalists were killed this year for their work. The Torch. 20 December. Accessed 20 December.

The Washington Post. 2019. Editorial: The global reach of Trump's 'fake news' outrage. 20 November. *The Washington Post*. Accessed 21 November.

The Washington Post. 2021. Fatal force. *The Washington Post*. 4 January. Accessed 7 January.

The Weekend Australian. 2019. Editorial: No, minister, you're not a defender of press freedom. *The Weekend Australian*. 13 July. Accessed 15 July.

Thomas, Ryan J. 2014. A dialectical approach to journalism ethics: Fascinating yet unfulfilled. *Journal of Mass Media Ethics* 29 (3): 200–202. https://doi.org/10.1080/08900523.2014.922009.

Thorpe, Nakari. 2017. Cartoonist Bill Leak dies, aged 61. SBS News. 10 March. Accessed 3 November 2020.

Tobitt, Charlotte. 2018a. Award-winning German reporter caught after fabricating stories for years could face fraud charges over reader donations. *Press Gazette*. 24 December. Accessed 26 December.

Tobitt, Charlotte. 2018b. Kerslake Report: Press Watchdog should create new guidelines for media operating in aftermath of terror attacks. *Press Gazette*. 27 March. Accessed 24 June 2019.

Tobitt, Charlotte. 2018c. MPs repeat call for 'Cliff's law' to stop suspects being named before charge after Gatwick drone front pages. *Press Gazette*. 24 December. Accessed 26 December.

Tobitt, Charlotte. 2018d. Newspapers back BBC over Sir Cliff privacy ruling creating 'new right to anonymity' for police suspects in 'dark day for journalism'. *Press Gazette*. 19 July. Accessed 23 July.

Tobitt, Charlotte. 2019a. Global freedom of expression 'at ten-year low', report says. *Press Gazette*. 3 December. Accessed 10 December.

Tobitt, Charlotte. 2019b. Stop 'gratuitously' publishing 'titillating' detail about terrorist incidents, commission tells media. *Press Gazette*. 7 October. Accessed 8 October.

Tobitt, Charlotte. 2020a. Amal Clooney media freedom report urges sanctions to 'punish and deter' attacks on journalists. *Press Gazette*. 13 February. Accessed 17 February.

Tobitt, Charlotte. 2020b. 'Culture of fear and cliquiness' in UK newsrooms must end to move diversity conversation forward. *Press Gazette*. 9 July. Accessed 10 July.

Tobitt, Charlotte. 2020c. Young journalists of colour speak out about being 'disenfranchised' and 'alienated' in industry which still lacks diversity. *Press Gazette*. 12 August. Accessed 23 August.

Toews, Rob. 2020. The next generation of artificial intelligence. Forbes. 12 October. Accessed 15 October 2020.

Tompkins, Al. 2020. 23 guidelines for journalists to safely cover protests. Poynter.org. 1 June. Accessed 4 June.

Tonkin, Leigh, Casey Briggs, and Jonathan Hepburn. 2020. Coronavirus death toll hits 1 million. These 10 charts begin to tell the story of loss. ABC News. 29 September. Accessed 29 September.

Torro, Berny. 2018. Revealed: Gatwick drone suspects. *Sunday Express*, 23 December 2018. p. 1.

Tracy, Marc, and Rachel Abrams. 2020. Police target journalists as Trump blames 'Lamestream Media' for protests. *The New York Times*. 1 June. Accessed 2 June.

Tracy, Marc, Rachel Abrams, and Edmund Lee. 2020. New York Times says Senator's op-ed did not meet standards. *The New York Times*. 4 June. Accessed 9 June.

Troll Patrol Findings. 2018. Amnesty International. 12 December. Accessed 1 August 2020.

Trump, Donald J. (@realDonaldTrump). 2019. Today I opened a major Apple manufacturing plant in Texas that will bring high paying jobs back to America. Today Nancy Pelosi closed Congress because she doesn't care about American workers! Trump Twitter Archive V2. 21 November. Accessed 8 January. www.thetrumpa rchive.com/.

Trump Twitter Archive V2. (2021). Retrieved from https://www.thetrumparchive. com/

Truu, Maani. 2019. Former Al Jazeera journalist Peter Greste calls One Nation investigation 'unethical'. SBS TV. 27 June. Accessed 27 June.

Tsay-Vogel, Mina, James Shanahan, and Nancy Signorilli. 2020. Social media cultivating perceptions of privacy: A 5-year analysis of privacy attitudes and self-disclosure behaviors among Facebook users. *New Media & Society* 20 (1): 141–161. https://doi.org/o0r.g1/107.171/1774/611446144484186166600731.

Turley, Jonathon. 2019. Viewpoint: What Assange charges could mean for press freedom. BBC News. 24 May. Accessed 26 May.

Turvill, William. 2020. Covid-19 crisis drives more than a million new digital subs for leading news providers. *Press Gazette*. 2 June. Accessed 3 June.

Ubayasiri, Kasuon. 2017. Journalism in the crosshairs: The Islamic State's exploitation of Western media practices. *Fusion Journal* 11: 1–13.

Umney, Charles. 2018. Technology. In *Class Matters: Inequality and Exploitation in 21st Century Britain*, pp. 136–147. London: Pluto Press.

Underwood, Doug. 1993. *When MBAs Rule the Newsroom: How the Marketers and the Managers are Reshaping Today's Media*. New York: Columbia University Press.

Usher, Nikki. 2018. Re-thinking trust in the news. *Journalism Studies* 19 (4): 564–578. https://doi.org/10.1080/1461670X.2017.1375391.

Usher, Nikki. 2020. 2020 shows the need for institutional news media to make racial justice a core value of journalism. Editors: Daniel Jackson, Danielle Sarver Coombs, Filippo Trevisan, Darren Lilleker and Einar Thorsen. IPSA/AISP & Centre for Comparative Politics and Media Research. Accessed 18 November 2020.

Varga, Remy. 2019. Age challenges trauma payout to crime reporter. *The Age*. 13 June. Accessed 13 June.

Varis, Piia. 2020. Trump tweets the truth: Metric populism and media conspiracy. *Trabalhos em Linguística Aplicada* 59 (1): 429–444. https://doi.org/10.1590/0103181368341162020406.

Vick, Karl. 2018. The Guardians and the war on truth. *Time magazine*. 11 December. Accessed 21 May 2019.

Visser, Nick. 2020. Trump celebrates recent violence against journalists, says it's 'actually a beautiful sight'. The Huffington Post. 23 September. Accessed 29 September.

Voltmer, Katrin. 2014. Making sense of press freedom: A comparison of journalists' perceptions of press freedom in Eastern Europe and East Asia. In *Comparing Political Communication Across Time and Space*, edited by M.J. Canel, and K. Volkmer. London: Palgrave Macmillan.

Von Nordheim, Gerret. 2018. Journalists quote social media content ever more frequently. *European Journalism Observatory*. Accessed 11 December.

von Sikorski, Christian, Jörg Matthes, and Desirée Schmuck. 2018. The Islamic State in the news: Journalistic differentiation of Islamist terrorism from Islam, terror news, proximity and Islamophobic attitudes. *Communication Research*: 1–30. https://doi.org/1.o0r.g1/107.171/0770/9030963560520128188003276.

Wagener, Albin. 2019. Hypernarrativity, storytelling, and the relativity of truth: Digital semiotics of communication and interaction. *Postdigital Science and Education*: 1–23. https://doi.org/10.1007/s42438-019-00066-7.

Waisbord, Silvio. 2019. The vulnerabilities of journalism. *Journalism* 20 (1): 210–213. https://doi.org/.o0r.g1/107.171/1774/614864848941981880099283.

Walden, Max. 2019. Singapore's anti-fake news law criticised as 'Orwellian' threat to freedom of speech. ABC News. 14 May. Accessed 14 May.

Walford, Charles, and Nabila Ramdani. 2012. 'She wanted one more story': Mother of veteran war reporter Marie Colvin said her daughter was due to leave Syria on

SAME DAY she was killed in rocket attack . *Daily Mail* (UK). 23 February. Accessed 7 November.

Walker, James, and Freddy Mayhew. 2019. Mosque massacre: Social media battles to remove terror attack videos as press face criticism over coverage. *Press Gazette*. 15 March. Accessed 17 March.

Walker, Jamie, and Michael McKenna. 2019. Al Jazeera TV sting makes chumps of Hanson pair. *The Australian*. 27 March. Accessed 27 March.

Walker, Shaun. 2020. Hungarian journalists fear coronavirus law may be used to jail them. *The Guardian*. 3 April. Accessed 5 April.

Wallace, Lewis Raven. 2017. Objectivity is dead, and I'm okay with it. Medium.com. 28 January. Accessed 8 January 2021.

Wallace, Lewis Raven. 2019. *The View From Somewhere: Undoing the Myth of Journalistic Objectivity*. Chicago, IL: University of Chicago Press.

Wallace, Lewis Raven. 2020. The view from somewhere. Accessed 24 November.

Ward, Stephen J.A. 2004. *The Invention of Journalism Ethics: The Path to Objectivity and Beyond(McGill-Queen's Studies in the History of Ideas)* Volume 38. Montreal, Canada: McGill-Queen's University Press.

Ward, Stephen J.A. 2020. Truth and objectvity. In *The Routledge Handbook of Mass Media Ethics*, edited by Lee Wilklins, and Clifford G.Christians. New York: Routledge.

Warren, Christopher. 2020a. Australian media refuses to confront racism. Again. Crikey. com.au. 17 August. Accessed 17 August.

Warren, Christopher. 2020b. Here's the news about the mainstream news—the boom might be over. Crikey.com.au. 29 April. Accessed 29 April.

Warren, Christopher. 2020c. The moral clarity of journalism is lost if the news really is from nowhere. Crikey.com.au. 11 June. Accessed 11 June.

Waterson, Jim. 2019a. As HuffPost and BuzzFeed shed staff, has the digital content bubble burst? *The Guardian*. 25 January. Accessed 6 February 2019.

Waterson, Jim. 2019b. *New York Times* editor says Trump has put his reporters' lives at risk. *The Guardian*. 18 November. Accessed 2 December.

Waterson, Jim. 2019c. Police called to loud row at Boris Johnson's home. *The Guardian*. 22 June. Accessed 22 June.

Waterson, Jim. 2020a. Harry and Meghan tell UK tabloids they will no longer deal with them. *The Guardian*. 20 April. Accessed 26 April.

Waterson, Jim. 2020b. Kobe Bryant: *Washington Post* reporter suspended after sexual assault case tweet. *The Guardian*. 28 January. Accessed 1 February.

Watkins, Emily. 2018a. Media roundtable: Was it ethical of the Tele to publish its Barnaby Joyce story? Crikey.com.au. 7 February. Accessed 7 February.

Watkins, Emily. 2018b. Two journalists reportedly killed in a deadly week for press freedom. Crikey.com.au. 9 October. Accessed 9 October.

Watkins, Emily. 2019. 'Psychologically scarred': Age crime reporter wins $180,000 for workplace trauma. Crikey.com.au. 27 February. Accessed 27 February.

Watkins, Evan. 1999. Gramascian politics and capitalist common sense. *Rethinking Marxism: A Journal of Economics, Culture & Society* 11 (3): 83–90. https://doi.org/10. 1080/08935699908685596.

Wayne, Mike. 2003. Marxism and media studies: Key concepts and contemporary trends. In *Marxism and Culture*, edited by Mike Wayne, and Esther Leslie. London: Pluto Press.

Wehner, Peter. 2020. Donald Trump is a broken man. *The Atlantic*. 21 July. Accessed 23 July.

Weir, Richard. 2014. Beheading coverage varies widely from graphic to subdued. *The Boston Herald*. 21 August. Accessed 22 August.

Weiss, Bari. 2020. Resignation letter. 14 July. Accessed 20 July.

Wemple, Erik. 2020. The Post's misguided suspension of Felicia Sonmez over Kobe Bryant tweets. *The Washington Post*. 28 January. Accessed 14 July.

WHO. 2020. From the 'new normal' to a 'new future': A sustainable response to COVID-19. World Health Organization. 13 October. Accessed 6 January 2021.

Wikileaks. 2010. Collateral murder. 5 July Accessed 15 February 2015. www.collatera lmurder.com/.

Wilde, Oscar. 1891. The soul of man under socialism. Essay. Accessed 17 February 2009.

Williams, Philip. 2019. Julian Assange warned of this very scenario for years, and now it's coming to pass. ABC News. 12 April. Accessed 16 April.

Wilson, William. 1990. Confidence and press freedom: A study in judicial activism. *The Modern Law Review* 53 (1): 43–56. www.jstor.org/stable/1096039.

Windschuttle, Keith. 1988. *The Media: A New Analysis of the Press, Television, Radio and Advertising in Australia*. Ringwood, Australia: Penguin.

Winkler, Ira. 2017. Snowden wasn't a Russian agent, but a traitor just the same. The Hill. 5 April. Accessed 7 February 2019.

WNIP. 2018. AI in the newsroom: Robots are now helping drive up subscriptions. *What's New in Publishing*. n.d. Accessed 16 October 2020.

Wolfe, Lauren. 2011. The silencing crime: Sexual violence and journalists. Committee to Protect Journalists. 7 June. Accessed 9 June.

Workers' Life. 1928. The worker correspondent. In *Communication and Class Struggle: 2. Liberation, Socialism*, edited by Armand Mattelart, and Seth Siegelaub, pp. 153–157. New York; Bagnolet, France: IG/IMMRC.

Workman, Alice. 2017. Michaelia Cash's office tipped-off media about AFP raids, and a staffer has now resigned. Buzzfeed. 25 October. Accessed 28 October.

Worthington, Brett. 2019. Attorney-General orders prosecutors seek his approval before charging ABC, News Corp journalists. ABC News. 30 September. Accessed 30 September.

Wu, Yuntao, Wenzhe Ho, Yaowei Huang, Dong-Yan Jin, Shiyue Li, Shan-Lu Liu, Xeu-feng Liu, Jainming Qui, Yongming Sang, Qiuhong Wang, Kwok-Yung Yuen, and Zhi-Ming Zheng. 2020. SSARS-CoV-2 is an appropriate name for the new coronavirus. *The Lancet* 395 (10228): 949–950. https://doi.org/10.1016/S0140-6736(20)30557–30552; www.thelancet.com/journals/lancet/article/PIIS0140-6736(20)30557–30552/fulltext.

Yarros, Victor S. 1922. Journalism, ethics and common sense. *International Journal of Ethics*: 410–419. www.journals.uchicago.edu/doi/pdfplus/10.1086/intejethi.32.4.2377555.

Yates, Dean. 2020. Inside story: How The Age dragged a traumatised reporter through the courts. Crikey.com.au. 4 September. Accessed 4 September.

YouGov Poll. 2018. Public backs Court's decision in Cliff Richard case, 86% favour investigation anonymity. Inform. 24 July. Accessed 26 December.

Young, Mary Lynn, and Alfred Hermida. 2020. The Conversation Canada. In *Citizenship in Connected Canada: A Research and Policy Agenda*, edited by E. Dubois, and F. Martin-Bariteau. Manitoba: University of Ottawa Press.

Younge, Gary. 2018. The Serena Cartoon debate: calling out racism is not 'censorship'. *The Guardian*. 14 September. Accessed 18 September.

Zahay, Megan L., Kelly Jensen, Yiping Xia, and Sue Robinson. 2020. The labor of building trust: Traditional and engagement discourses for practicing journalism in a digital age. *Journalism & Mass Communication Quarterly.* https://doi.org/10.1177/1077699020954854. https://journals.sagepub.com/doi/abs/10.1177/1077699020954854.

Zelizer, Barbie. 2004a. *Taking Journalism Seriously: News and the Academy.* Thousand Oaks, CA: Sage.

Zelizer, Barbie. 2004b. When facts, truth and reality are God-terms: On journalism's uneasy place in cultural studies. *Annenberg School of Communication Departmental Papers*, no. 3–2004.

Zhou, Naaman. 2020. 'It dampens the conversation': No more excuses for Australian media's lack of diversity. *The Guardian.* 28 June. Accessed 29 June.

Zirin, Dave. 2019. The 'Sports Illustrated' layoffs are what happens when we're ruled by vampires. *The Nation.* 4 October. Accessed 8 October.

Index

Page numbers in *italics* refer to figures, *n* indicates notes.

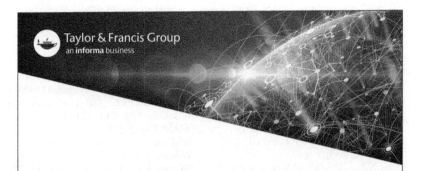